ARISTOTLE

Politics

ARISTOTLE

Politics

Translated,
with Introduction and Notes,
by
C.D.C. Reeve

Hackett Publishing Company
Indianapolis / Cambridge

Aristotle: 384–322 B.C.

Copyright © 1998 by Hackett Publishing Company, Inc.

Printed in the United States of America

09 08 07 06   4 5 6 7 8 9

Cover and interior design by Dan Kirklin

Library of Congress Cataloging-in-Publication Data

Aristotle
   [Politics. English]
   Politics/Aristotle; translated, with introduction and notes, by
C.D.C. Reeve.
       p.   cm.
   Includes bibliographical references and indexes.
   ISBN 0-87220-389-1 (cloth).   ISBN 0-87220-388-3 (pbk.)
   1. Political science—Early works to 1800.   I. Reeve, C.D.C.,
1948–   . II. Title.
   JC71.A41R44   1998   97-46398
   320'.01'1—dc21   CIP

ISBN-13: 978-0-87220-389-1 (cloth)
ISBN-13: 978-0-87220-388-4 (pbk.)

For

Jay and Deborah

Contents

ACKNOWLEDGMENTS

Traduttori traditori, translators are traitors. They are also thieves. I have shamelessly plundered other translations of the *Politics*, borrowing where I could not improve. I hope others will find my own translation worthy of similar treatment.

Anyone who has worked with John Cooper knows what a rare privilege it is to benefit from his vast knowledge, extraordinary editorial skills, and sound judgment. I am greatly in his debt for guiding the crucial early stages of this translation, and for characteristically trenchant and detailed comments on parts of Books I and III. His ideals of translation, "correct as humanly possible" and "ordinary English—where necessary, ordinary philosophical English," I have tried to make my own. Anyone who has translated Aristotle (or any other Greek writer, for that matter) will know that, though easy to state, they are enormously difficult to achieve.

I owe an even larger debt, truly unrepayable, to Trevor Saunders (Books I and II) and Christopher Rowe (III and IV), who late in the game, and by dint of their wonderfully thorough comments, inspired me to a complete revision of the entire translation. It is now much closer to Aristotle than I, who learned Greek regrettably late in life, could ever have made it unaided.

I am also very grateful to David Keyt (Books V and VI) and Richard Kraut (VII and VIII) for allowing me to see their own forthcoming editions of these books, and for allowing me to benefit from their enviable knowledge of them. Keyt also commented perceptively on the Introduction.

Paul Bullen not only arranged to have his Internet discussion list discuss parts of my work, but he himself sent me hundreds of suggestions for improvement, many of which I accepted gladly.

What is of value here belongs to all these generous Aristotelians. The mistakes alone, of which there must surely still be many, are wholly mine.

Finally and wholeheartedly, I thank Hackett Publishing Company for its extraordinary support, and Jay Hullett and Deborah Wilkes, in particular, for their friendship, encouragement, and faith.

NOTE TO THE READER

References to Aristotle's works are made to Immanuel Bekker's edition (1831) and are cited by abbreviated title, page, and line number (e.g., *Metaph.* 980ᵃ1). Most English translations have Bekker page numbers in the margins; however, the line numbers in citations are those of the Greek text, and correspond only approximately to lines in translations. This also applies to the references in the indexes. The abbreviations used are as follows:

APo.	*Posterior Analytics*
APr.	*Prior Analytics*
Cael.	*De Caelo*
Cat.	*Categories*
DA	*De Anima*
EE	*Eudemian Ethics*
Fr.	*Fragments* (Ross)
GA	*Generation of Animals*
HA	*History of Animals*
MM	*Magna Moralia*
Metaph.	*Metaphysics*
Mete.	*Meteorology*
NE	*Nicomachean Ethics*
Oec.	*Economics*
PA	*Parts of Animals*
Ph.	*Physics*
Pol.	*Politics*
Po.	*Poetics*
Pr.	*Problems*
Prt.	*Protrepticus*
Rh.	*Rhetoric*
SE	*Sophistical Refutations*
Top.	*Topics*

(The authenticity of *Magna Moralia*, *Economics*, and *Problems* has been questioned.)

References to Plato are made to the edition of his works produced by Henri Estienne (known as Stephanus) in A.D. 1578, and are cited by author, title, and page number (e.g., Plato, *Republic* 471a). Translations of Plato's works usually have Stephanus numbers in the margins.

Other Greek authors are cited from the following standard collections:

Diehl, E. *Anthologia Lyrica Graeca.* v. I–II. Leipzig: Teubner, 1925.

Diels, H., and Kranz, W. *Die Fragmente der Vorsokratiker.* 6th ed., v. I–III. Berlin: Weidmann, 1951.

Kock, T. *Comicorum Atticorum Fragmenta.* v. I–III. Leipzig: Teubner, 1880.

Nauck, A. *Tragicorum Graecorum Fragmenta.* 2nd. ed., Leipzig: Teubner, 1889.

Translations or editions of the *Politics* referred to by author in the notes are fully identified in the Bibliography. Ross is the basis for this translation, because of its ready availability. Dreizehnter is in some respects preferable, and I have kept in constant contact with it. Significant deviations from Ross's text are recorded in the notes.

The Glossary is fairly wide-ranging. Explicit reference to it is signaled by small capitals (e.g. LAW).

Less well known historical figures are identified in the footnotes when they are first referred to in the text (a glance at the Index of Names will reveal where this is). Places referred to may be located on the Map. All dates in the footnotes and Glossary are B.C.

I have preserved the traditional ordering of the eight books of the *Politics*. But many editors propose a reordering in which IV–VI trade places with VII–VIII, giving us I, II, III, VII, VIII, IV, V, VI as the order of the books. There is perhaps some merit in this proposal (see IV footnote 1), but ease of citation and reference decisively favors tradition, in my view, and does not, of course, prevent the reader from following the alternative order.

Material in square brackets in the translation is my addition.

INTRODUCTION

Aristotle has been intensively studied by a large number of first-rate thinkers beginning over two millennia ago with the Greek commentators. It is difficult to say anything uncontroversial about him. This introduction does not try to avoid controversy, therefore, or to reconstruct scholarly consensus, but to provide a suggestive, sometimes critical way to think about the central argument of the *Politics* that situates it within Aristotle's philosophy as a whole. By exploring the works listed in the Bibliography, and by deeper study of Aristotle, Greek philosophy, and philosophy generally, readers will soon find alternative views, and powerful reasons to disagree with the ones I defend. In trying to determine just where the truth lies, moreover, they will be doing something closely akin to what Aristotle himself is doing in the *Politics*—critically building on the thought of predecessors by weighing conflicting views against one another. It is a reader willing to undertake this task that Aristotle requires and most rewards.

§1 Aristotle the Man

Aristotle was born in 384 B.C. into a well-off family living in Stagira, in northern Greece. His father, Nicomachus, who died while Aristotle was still quite young, was doctor to King Amyntas of Macedon; his mother, Phaestis, was wealthy in her own right. When Aristotle was seventeen, his uncle, Proxenus, sent him to study at Plato's Academy in Athens. He remained there for twenty years, initially as a student, eventually as a researcher and teacher.

Plato died in 347, leaving the Academy in the hands of his nephew, Speusippus. Aristotle then left Athens for Assos in Asia Minor, where the ruler, Hermeias, was a patron of philosophy. He married Hermeias' niece, Pythias, and had a daughter by her, also named Pythias. Three years later, in 345, Aristotle moved to Mytilene, on the island of Lesbos, where he met Theophrastus, who was to become his best student and closest colleague.

In 343 he was invited to be tutor to Philip of Macedon's thirteen-year-old son Alexander, later called the Great. In 335 he returned to Athens and founded his own school, the Lyceum. While he was there his wife died, and he established a relationship with Herpyllis, also a native of Stagira. Their son, Nicomachus, was named for Aristotle's father. In 323 Alexander the Great died, with the result that anti-Macedonian feeling in Athens grew in strength. Aristotle left for Chalcis in Euboea, where he died in 322 at the age of sixty-two.

Legend has it that Aristotle had slender calves and small eyes, spoke with a lisp, and was "conspicuous by his attire, his rings, and the cut of his hair." His will reveals that he had a sizable estate, a domestic partner, two children, a considerable library (he is said to have been the first collector of books), and a large circle of friends. In the will he asks his executors to take particular care of Herpyllis. He directs that his slaves be freed "when they come of age," and that the bones of his wife, Pythias, be mixed with his "as she instructed." He left his library to Theophrastus.

Perhaps as little as a quarter of Aristotle's writings survive, yet in English they occupy almost twenty-five hundred tightly printed pages. Most of these are not works polished for publication, but sometimes incomplete lecture notes and working papers (the *Politics* itself is incomplete). This accounts for some, though not all, of their legendary difficulty. It is unfair to complain, as a Platonist opponent did, that Aristotle "escapes refutation by clothing a perplexing subject in obscure language—using darkness like a squid to make himself hard to catch"; but there is darkness and obscurity enough for anyone, even if none of it is intentional. There is also a staggering breadth and depth of intellect. Aristotle made fundamental contributions to a vast range of disciplines, including logic, metaphysics, epistemology, psychology, ethics, politics, rhetoric, aesthetics, zoology, biology, physics, and philosophical and political history. With other members of the Lyceum, he collected the constitutions of one hundred and fifty-eight Greek city-states; the knowledge and insights he gained from them are manifest throughout the *Politics*. When Dante called Aristotle "the master of those who know," he wasn't exaggerating.

§2 The Methods and Aims of Philosophy

It is often and rightly said that Aristotle's philosophical method is *dialectical*. Here is his own description of it:

As in all other cases, we must set out the phenomena and first of all go through the problems. In this way we must prove the *endoxa* . . . ideally all the *endoxa*, but if not all, then most of them and the most compelling. For if the problems are solved and the *endoxa* are left, it will be an adequate proof. (*NE* 1145ᵇ2–7)

We must set out the phenomena, go through the problems, and prove the *endoxa*. But what are these things? And why is proving the most compelling of the *endoxa* an adequate proof of anything?

Phenomena are things that appear to someone to be the case, whether veridically or nonveridically.[1] They include, in the first instance, empirical observations or perceptual evidence (*APr.* 46ª17–27, *Cael.* 297ª2–6, 297ᵇ23–25). But they also include items that we might not comfortably call observations at all, such as propositions that strike people as true or that are commonly said or believed. For example, the following is a phenomenon: "The weak-willed person knows that his actions are base, but does them because of his feelings, while the self-controlled person knows that his appetites are base, but because of reason does not follow them" (*NE* 1145ᵇ12–14).[2] Phenomena are usually neither proved nor supported by something else. Indeed, they are usually contrasted with things that are supported by proof or evidence (*EE* 1216ᵇ26–28). But there is no *a priori* limit to the degree of conceptualization or theory-ladenness manifest in them. They need not be, and in Aristotle seem rarely if ever to be, devoid of interpretive content; they are not Baconian observations, raw feels, sense data, or the like.

The *endoxa*, or putative *endoxa*, are defined in the *Topics* as "those opinions accepted by everyone or by the majority or by the wise— either by all of them or by most or by the most notable and reputable (*endoxois*)" (100ᵇ21–23). But to count as *endoxa* these opinions cannot be *paradoxical* (104ª10–11); that is to say, the many cannot disagree with the wise about them, nor can "one or the other of these two classes disagree among themselves" (104ᵇ31–36). If there is such disagreement, what we have is a problem. Indeed, if just one notable philosopher rejects a proposition that everyone else accepts, that is sufficient to

---

1. Sometimes the phenomena and the facts do not seem to be distinguished from one another (*PA.* 750ª21–23, 759ª11, *Metaph.* 1090ᵇ19–20). Sometimes the two are contrasted (*Top.* 146ᵇ36, *Metaph.* 1009ª38–1010ª3, *Rh.* 1402ª26–27).
2. We shall meet the weak-willed and the self-controlled again in §5.

create a problem (104ᵇ19–28). It follows that *endoxa* are *deeply* unproblematic beliefs—beliefs based on experience or perception to which
there is simply no worthwhile opposition of any sort (*Top*. 104ᵇ22–24,
170ᵇ6–9).

We now need to discuss what it is to go through problems and why
doing so amounts to an adequate proof. Dialectic is useful to philosophy,
Aristotle says, "because the ability to go through the problems on both
sides of a subject makes it easier to see what is true and what is false"
(*Top*. 101ᵃ24–26). Later, he provides another important clue to what he
has in mind: "Where knowledge and philosophical wisdom are concerned, the ability to discern and hold in one view the consequences of
either hypothesis is no insignificant tool, since then it only remains to
make a correct choice of one of them" (163ᵇ9–12). The picture that
emerges from these passages is something like this. The problem a
philosopher faces is, let's say, to determine whether rule by one person
is better than rule by many (*Pol*. III.16). If he is a competent dialecti-
cian, he will be able to follow out the consequences of supposing that it
is, as well as those of supposing that it is not. He will be able to see what
problems these consequences in turn face, and he will be able to go
through these and determine which can be solved and which cannot.

In the end, he will have concluded, we may suppose, that one person
rule is better, provided that the person himself is outstandingly virtuous
(1288ᵃ15–29). But in the process of reaching that conclusion some of
the *endoxa* on both sides will almost certainly have been modified or
clarified, partly accepted and partly rejected (*Top*. 164ᵇ6–7). Others will
have been decisively rejected as false. But these the philosopher will
need to explain away: "For when we have a clear and good account of
why a false view appears true, that makes us more confident of the true
view" (*NE* 1154ᵃ24–25). In other words, some beliefs that seemed to be
endoxa, that seemed to be deeply unproblematic, will have fallen from
grace. If most of them and the most compelling are still in place, however, that will be an adequate proof of the philosopher's conclusion,
since there will be every reason to accept it and no reason not to.

It is because Aristotle employs this method that he almost always begins by looking at what his predecessors have thought about a topic: the
views of wise people are likely to contain some truth. It also explains
why he often seems to adopt a position in between those of a pair of conflicting parties: if both contain some truth, the best position *should* contain elements of each. There is a joke to the effect that Aristotle died of

an excess of moderation, an excessive love of the middle ground. We can now see why he thought this love was just the love of wisdom.

Aristotle's method is dialectical, but his goal is scientific; it is to develop a science, to acquire scientific knowledge (*epistēmē*). An Aristotelian science is a structure of demonstrations from first principles (*archai*); where propositions are first principles if and only if there are demonstrations of all the other propositions of the science from them but no demonstrations of them from anything else. (The axioms of geometry or formal logic are familiar analogues.)

Aristotle thinks of first principles in a variety of ways. There are ontological first principles, basic entities or fundamental explanatory causal factors out there in the world, and there are epistemic first principles, principles of our knowledge of the world. But if our theories about the world are true, their structure will, on Aristotle's view, reflect or mirror the structure of the world, so that the truth of epistemic first principles depends on ontological ones (*Cat.* 14^{b}14–22, *Metaph.* 993^{b}30–31, 1011^{b}26–28). Aristotle's is therefore a realist conception of truth.

An epistemic first principle could either be a concept or it could be a proposition. The ontological version of this distinction is between universals, conceived of as the nonparticular aspects of the world that concepts pick out, and facts (or ways the world is), conceived of as what makes propositions either true or false. Aristotle sometimes seems to mark this distinction, but just as often he ignores it. For, on his view, a first principle is paradigmatically a definition (*horismos*), which is a type of proposition or fact, one that captures a nature or essence, which is a concept or universal.[3] Thus happiness, or again its definition, is a first principle of ethics (*NE* 1095^{b}6–7, 1102^{a}3, 1139^{b}1–4).

So much for Aristotelian science. A person has scientific knowledge of such a science if and only if he knows its first principles, knows that they are its first principles, and knows the demonstration of all the other propositions of the science from them.

We now have a picture, albeit in somewhat abstract terms, of Aristotle's conception of science and scientific knowledge. An example may help to bring things down to earth. Let us suppose that we want to explain why oak trees lose their leaves in the fall. What we are looking for is some feature of oak trees that causally explains this phenomenon. Such

---

3. See *APo.* 90^{b}24–27, *Top.* 158^{b}1–4, *DA* 402^{b}25–403^{a}2, *Metaph.* 1031^{a}12.

a feature might be, Aristotle thinks, the fact that the sap at the joint between leaf and stem solidifies in colder temperatures. If he is right, the appropriate explanatory demonstration would look something like this (see *APo*. 98^{b}36–38):

(1) All plants in which sap solidifies at the joint between leaf and stem in colder temperatures lose their leaves in the fall.

(2) All oak trees have sap that solidifies at the joint between leaf and stem in colder temperatures.

(3) Therefore, all oak trees lose their leaves in the fall.

But there are important conditions that (1) and (2) must satisfy if this demonstration is to yield a genuine scientific explanation: for example, (1) and (2) must be necessary and more fundamental than (3). Why does Aristotle impose these austere conditions? It is sometimes thought that he does so because he mistakenly assimilates all the sciences to mathematics. There may be some truth in this, but the real reason surely has to do with the ideals of knowledge and explanation. If (1) and (2) are not necessary, they will not adequately explain (3). For given that plants with sap of the kind in question do not have to lose their leaves or that oak trees do not have to have sap of that kind, why do oak trees none the less still inevitably lose their leaves? On the other hand, if (1) and (2) are not biologically more fundamental than (3), they cannot be an adequate explanation of it either. For in the true and complete biological theory the more fundamental (3) will be used to explain (1) and (2). Hence in using them to explain (3) we would be implicitly engaging in circular explanation, and circular explanation is not explanation at all (*APo*. 72^{b}25–73^{a}20).

The nature of our scientific knowledge of derived principles is perhaps clear enough. But what sort of knowledge do we have of first principles, since we cannot possibly demonstrate them (*NE* 1140^{b}33–1141^{a}1)? Aristotle tells two apparently different stories by way of an answer. The first, in *Posterior Analytics* II.19, runs as follows. Cognitive access to first principles begins with (1) perception of particulars (99^{b}34–35). In some animals, perception of particulars gives rise to (2) retention of the perceptual content in the soul (99^{b}39–100^{a}1). When many such perceptual contents have been retained, some animals (3) "come to have an account from the perception of such things" (100^{a}1–3). The retention of perceptual contents is memory; and a collection of remembered or retained perceptual contents, or the account generated from them, is an experience (100ª3–6). (4) From such experiences we reach the universals that are the first principles we are seeking (100ª6–9). In the brief concluding section, Aristotle explains that it is because we human beings have understanding (*nous*), as other animals do not, that the four-step process just described leads in our case to universals and first principles. Without understanding, scientific knowledge of first principles would be impossible (*DA* 430ª25).[4]

There are two ways to take this story. The first is as a normative account of our knowledge of first principles, an explanation of how our claims to know them are *justified*. The second is to take it as a nonnormative account which simply describes the psychological resources involved in acquiring knowledge of first principles, without explaining how our claims to know them are justified. It is commonly believed that Aristotle's story is normative, that he is claiming that understanding is a form of intuitive reason that enables us to detect first principles in a way that justifies us in believing them to be intrinsically necessary. But given the existence of the second story, it seems more plausible to plump for the first option: understanding is just the psychological resource that makes it possible for us to know first principles.

The second story is told in the *Topics*:

> Dialectic is useful with regard to the first principles in each science. For it is impossible to discuss them at all from the principles proper to the science proposed for discussion, since the principles are primary among all [the truths contained in the science]; instead, they must be discussed through the *endoxa* about them. This is distinctive of dialectic, or more appropriate to it than to anything else; for since it examines, it provides a way toward the principles of all lines of inquiry. (*Top.* 101ª26–ᵇ4)

The problem with this story is to explain what dialectic's way, the philosopher's way, toward first principles actually is.

The philosopher knows that the first principles in question are true and their negations false. He has this on authority from the scientist, whose own knowledge is based on experience. Yet when the philosopher uses his dialectical skill to draw out the consequences of these princi-

---

4. *NE* gives a parallel account of our knowledge of happiness (1143ª35–ᵇ5, 1139ᵇ28–29). Understanding is further discussed in §§4, 5, 6.

ples, and of their negations, he sees problems and supporting arguments, based on *endoxa*, on both sides. Since he knows that the principles are empirically true, his goal will be to solve the problems they face, while undoing the arguments that seem to support their negations. If he is successful, the principle will have been shown to be in accord with most of the most compelling *endoxa*, with the preponderance of deeply unproblematic beliefs.

But so what? The principles were already true, already known to the scientist. How are we epistemically any better off now that they have also been shown to be in accord with the most compelling *endoxa*. Presumably, the answer is just this: we are no longer pulled asunder by our epistemic commitments; we see how all the things we believe can be true simultaneously, how each science can be knit into the larger fabric of our deeply unproblematic beliefs. In many texts, indeed, Aristotle characterizes problems as knots in our understanding which dialectical philosophy enables us to untie.[5] In others, he characterizes dialectic as enabling us to make beliefs, including first principles, clear.[6] What dialectical philosophy offers us in regard to the first principles of the sciences, then, is simply clarity of understanding: no knots.[7]

Aristotle categorizes the various sciences as follows:

I   Theoretical sciences: theology or first philosophy, mathematics, natural sciences

II   Practical sciences: ethics, household management, statesmanship. Statesmanship is divided into legislative science and routine politics (which deals with day-to-day political matters). Routine politics is further divided into deliberative science and judicial science (*NE* 1141^{b}29–32). These sciences are concerned with ACTION, in Aristotle's strict sense of the term.

III   Productive sciences (crafts): medicine, housebuilding, etc.

Theoretical sciences are paradigm Aristotelian sciences, with theology (first philosophy, metaphysics) and mathematics being especially exem-

---

5. *Ph.* 253^{a}31–33, 263^{a}15–18, *Metaph.* 995^{a}27–33, 1032^{a}6–11, *NE* 1146^{a}24–27.
6. *APr.* 46^{a}17–30, *DA* 413^{a}11–13, *NE* 1097^{b}22–24, *EE* 1216^{b}26–36.
7. This account of dialectic and its relation to science is further developed and defended in my "Dialectic and Philosophy in Aristotle," in Jyl Gentzler, ed., *Method in Ancient Philosophy* (Oxford: Clarendon Press, 1997). Aristotle's science is well discussed in J. Barnes, ed., *The Cambridge Companion to Aristotle*, Chs. 4 and 5.

plary cases (*Metaph.* 1025ᵇ34–1026ᵃ32). The extent to which ethics or statesmanship fits the demonstrative paradigm, however, is a good deal less clear. One reason for this is that a huge part of ethics and statesmanship has to do, not with the universals theoretical science focuses on, but with particular cases, whose nearly infinite variety cannot be "easily summed up in a formula" (*NE* 1109ᵇ21).[8] The knowledge of what justice is may well be scientific knowledge, but to know what justice requires in a particular case is not; it requires both knowledge of what justice is and DECENCY (*epieikeia*) (*NE* V.10), which is a combination of virtue and a trained eye. Perhaps, then, we should think of practical sciences as having something like a demonstrative core, but as not being reducible to that core. We shall return to this topic in §5.

§3 Perfectionism

We distinguish politics from the intellectual study of it, which we call political science or political philosophy. The former is a hard-headed, practical matter engaged in by politicians; the latter is often a rather speculative and abstract one engaged in by professors and intellectuals. This distinction is alien to Aristotle. On his view, statesmanship or political science (*politikē epistēmē*) is the practical science that genuine statesmen use in ruling, in much the way that medicine is the science genuine doctors use in treating the sick.

We also distinguish (not always very sharply, to be sure) between political philosophy and ethics or moral philosophy.[9] The former deals with the nature of the just or good society; the latter deals with individual rights and duties, personal good and evil, virtue and vice. This distinction too is foreign to Aristotle. On his view, ethics pretty much just is statesmanship: ethics aims to define the human good, which is happiness or *eudaimonia*, so that armed with a dialectically clarified conception of our end in life we can do a better job of achieving it (*NE* 1094ᵃ22–24); statesmanship aims at achieving that same good not just for an individual but for an entire COMMUNITY (1323ᵃ14–23, *NE* 1094ᵇ7–11). But because we are by nature social or political animals (§7), we can achieve our ends as individuals only in the context of a political

---

8. See *NE* 1094ᵃ14–22, 1103ᵇ34–1104ᵃ10, *Rh.* 1374ᵃ18–ᵇ23.
9. This was no doubt more true thirty years ago than it is today. See Will Kymlicka, *Contemporary Political Philosophy* (Oxford: Clarendon Press, 1990): 5–7.

community or CITY-STATE (*polis*), only in the context of a life with others. Hence ethics and statesmanship coincide, and the practical wisdom that enables an individual to achieve happiness is more or less the same thing as the statesmanship that enables a ruler to achieve happiness for a community (*NE* 1141^{b}23–24). A certain conception of ethics, then, together with a certain conception of human nature, leads to a certain conception of statesmanship.

Aristotle's ethics is a type of *perfectionism*. He starts with a conception of human nature or the human essence, arguing that certain properties are constitutive of it. The ethically best life, he then argues, is the one that realizes these properties to the highest degree. On the assumption, which Aristotle makes, that these properties can be realized to the highest degree in a political community, rather than in isolation from others or in a community of some other sort, the ideal political community will be the one in which they are most fully realized.

Aristotle's theory is perfectionist, but it is also *eudaimonistic*: it argues that *eudaimonia* or happiness consists in realizing to a high degree the properties that are definitive of humanity. In one way, then, it is like some contemporary utilitarian theories in taking happiness or welfare as the central concept of ethics. But it is unlike many of them in taking a perfectionist view of happiness rather than (say) identifying it with the satisfaction of our actual desires. It is true, none the less, that Aristotle thinks that a good or happy life must satisfy the desires of the person living it, and that desire satisfaction, with its attendant pleasures, is one important measure of a life's goodness (*NE* 1099^{a}7–31).

Finally, because perfectionist theories identify ethical goodness with the realization to a high degree of properties constitutive or definitive of human nature, they are often naturalistic. Aristotle's theory too is naturalistic. But because it allows as constituents of human nature some properties that *we* might balk at describing as naturalistic, the precise degree of its naturalism is somewhat difficult to gauge (§3).

This conception of ethics is controversial, to be sure, and many contemporary ethicists, especially those influenced by Immanuel Kant, would reject it.[10] Ethics, in their view, is primarily about justice, rights, and duties—not about happiness, or flourishing. It is not so controver-

10. Stephen Engstrom and Jennifer Whiting, eds., *Aristotle, Kant, and the Stoics: Rethinking Duty and Happiness* (Cambridge: Cambridge University Press, 1996) includes some useful comparative studies of Aristotle's ethics with Kant's.

sial, however, as to be wholly implausible. Indeed, many other recent ethicists have defended a return to Aristotle's ethics, or to so-called virtue ethics more generally, as offering us a more promising approach than either Kant-inspired deontological theories or Mill-inspired utilitarian or consequentialist ones.[11] Thickening the controversy is yet a third group of thinkers, those who defend a so-called natural law approach to ethics and politics. For them, Aristotle, especially as interpreted by Saint Thomas Aquinas, has never ceased to be anything but *the* crucial philosopher.[12] Aristotle is an active player in a controversy, therefore, not a casualty on the wayside of advancing philosophical knowledge.

§4 Human Nature

Of the various things that exist, "some exist by nature, some from other causes" (*Ph.* 192^{b}8–9). Those that exist (or come into existence) by nature have a nature of their own, i.e., an internal source of "change and staying unchanged, whether in respect of place, growth and decay, or alteration" (192^{b}13–15). Thus, for example, a feline embryo has within it a source that explains why it grows into a cat, why that cat moves and alters in the ways it does, and why it eventually decays and dies. A house or any other artifact, by contrast, has no such source within it; instead "the source is in something else and external," namely, in the soul of the craftsman who manufactures it (192^{b}30–31, *Metáph.* 1032^{a}32–^{b}10).

A natural being's nature, essence, function (*ergon*), and end (*telos*), or that for the sake of which it exists (*hou heneka*), are intimately related. For its end just is to actualize its nature by performing its function (*Cael.* 286^{a}8–9, *EN* 1168^{a}6–9, *EE* 1219^{a}13–17), and something that cannot perform its function ceases to be what it is except in name (*Mete.* 390^{a}10–13, *PA* 640^{b}33–641^{a}6, *Pol.* 1253^{a}23–25). Aristotle's view of natural beings is therefore "teleological": it sees them as defined by an end for which they are striving, and as needing to have their behavior explained by reference to it. It is this end, essence, or function that fixes

---

11. Philippa Foot, *Virtues and Vices* (Los Angeles: University of California Press, 1978), and Alasdair MacIntyre, *After Virtue* (Indiana: University of Notre Dame Press, 1981), are contemporary classics. Roger Crisp and Michael Slote, eds., *Virtue Ethics* (Oxford: Oxford University Press, 1997), contains some of the best recent papers.
12. John Finnis, *Natural Law and Natural Rights* (Oxford: Clarendon Press, 1980), is a lucid modern defense and exposition.

what is best for the being, or what its perfections or virtues consist in (*NE* 1098ᵃ7–20, *Ph.* 195ᵃ23–25).

Many of the things characterized as existing by nature or as products of some craft are hylomorphic compounds, compounds of matter (*hulē*) and form (*morphē*). Statues are examples: their matter is the stone or metal from which they are made; their form is their shape. Human beings are also examples: their matter is (roughly speaking) their body; their soul is their form. Thus (with a possible exception discussed below) a person's soul is not a substance separate from his body, but is more like the structural organization responsible for his body's being alive and functioning appropriately. Even city-states are examples: their matter is their inhabitants and their form is their CONSTITUTION (§7). These compounds have natures that owe something to their matter and something to their form (*Metaph.* 1025ᵇ26–1026ᵃ6). But "form has a better claim than matter to be called nature" (*Ph.* 193ᵇ6–7). A human being, for example, can survive through change in its matter (we are constantly metabolizing), but if his form is changed, he ceases to exist (*Pol.* 1276ᵇ1–13). For these reasons an Aristotelian investigation into human perfection naturally focuses on human souls rather than on human bodies.

According to Aristotle, these souls consist of hierarchically organized constituents (*NE* I.13). The lowest rung in the hierarchy is nutritive soul, which is responsible for nutrition and growth, and which is also found in plants and other animals. At the next rung up, we find perceptive and desiring soul, which is responsible for perception, imagination, and movement, and so is found in other animals but not in plants. This is the nonrational (*alogon*) part of the soul, which, though it lacks reason, can be influenced by it (*Pol.* 1333ᵃ17–18, *NE* 1103ᵃ1–3, 1151ᵃ15–28). The third part of the soul is the rational part, which has reason (1333ᵃ17) and is identified with *nous* or understanding (1254ᵃ8–9, 1334ᵇ20, *NE* 1097ᵇ33–1098ᵃ8). This part is further divided into the scientific part, which enables us to study or engage in theoretical activity or contemplation (*theōria*), and the deliberative part, which enables us to engage in practical, including political, activity (1333ᵃ25, *NE* 1139ᵃ3–ᵇ5).

Because the soul has these different parts, a perfectionist has a lot of places to look for the properties that define the human good. He might think that the good is defined by properties exemplified by all three of the soul's parts; or he might, for one reason or another, focus on properties exemplified by one of the parts. To discover which of these options Aristotle favors, we need to work through the famous function argument from the *Nicomachean Ethics* (a work whose final chapters lead naturally into the *Politics*). By doing so we shall be armed with the kind of understanding of Aristotle's views on human nature and the good that he supposes we will have when we read the *Politics* (see VII.1–3, 1333ᵃ16–30).

The function argument begins as follows:

> [A] Perhaps we shall find the best good if we first find the function or task (*ergon*) of a human being. For just as the good—i.e., [doing] well—for a flute-player, a sculptor, and every craftsman, and, in general, for whatever has a function and action, seems to depend on its function, the same seems to be true for a human being, if a human being has some function.¹³ [B] Then do the carpenter and the leather worker have their functions and actions, while a human being has none and is by nature inactive without any function? Or, just as eye, hand, foot, and in general every [body] part apparently has its functions, may we likewise ascribe to a human being some function over and above all of theirs? (*NE* 1097ᵇ24–33)

(A) is an expression of Aristotle's perfectionism and is readily intelligible given what we have already said about the connections among function, nature, essence, end, and good. (B) is clearly not so much a direct argument that human beings have a function as an indirect one, which relies on the implausibility of the view that they lack a function. When function is understood in terms of essence and end, of course, the assumption that human beings have a function is somewhat controversial: do we really have an essence? is there really a single end or goal to our lives? But it is also bolstered by a lot more of Aristotle's overall philosophy. Like much else in philosophy, then, (B) is controversial, but not controversial enough to be simply dismissed.

(B) says that the function of a human being is "over and above" all of the functions of his body parts. Does this mean that it is over and above each of them, or all of them taken together? It is difficult to be sure, but other texts seem to show Aristotle committed to the stronger view:

> Just as every instrument is for the sake of something, the parts of the body are also for the sake of something, that is to say, for the sake of some action, so the whole body must evidently be for the sake of

13. See *Pol.* 1326ᵃ13–14.

> some complex action. Similarly, the body too must be for the sake of
> the soul, and the parts of the body for the sake of those functions for
> which they are naturally adapted.[14] (*PA* 645ᵇ14–20)

Thus the parts of the body are for the sake of the complex action of the
body as a whole, but the body as whole is for the sake of the soul and its
activities.

Even within the soul itself, moreover, the function of one part seems
to be for the sake of the function of another, for example, that of practical wisdom for the sake of that of theoretical wisdom (*Pol.* 1333ᵃ24–30,
1334ᵇ17–28).[15] Now theoretical wisdom is the virtue of understanding,
and understanding has a somewhat peculiar status. Unlike many other
capacities of the soul, such as memory or perception, its activities are
completely separate from those of the body: "bodily activity is in no way
associated with the activity of understanding" (*GA* 736ᵇ28–29). Could
it be, then, that our function or essence is over and above the functions
of all of our body parts, precisely because it lies exclusively in our understanding and consists exclusively in theoretical activity? If the answer is yes, Aristotle's perfectionism seems to be narrowly intellectual-
ist: the good or happy life for humans will consist largely in theoretical
activity alone. But it is not clear the answer is yes. Aristotle himself occasionally settles for expressing a weaker disjunctive conclusion: the
human function consists in practical rational activity *or* theoretical rational activity (*Pol.* 1333ᵃ24–30, *NE* 1094ᵃ3–7). None the less, the
stronger conclusion often seems to be in view (§6). For the moment,
then, let us simply content ourselves by noticing how close to the function argument the stronger conclusion lies, however controversial or in-
credible we might initially find it.

I said earlier (§3) that it is difficult to gauge the extent of Aristotle's
naturalism, because it is difficult to determine how naturalistic (in our
terms) some parts of his psychology are. Understanding is the major
source of that difficulty.

Human beings have a function, in any case, which is over and above
the functions of their body parts. The next stage of the argument concerns its identification:

> [C] What, then, could this be? For living is apparently shared with
> plants, but what we are looking for is special; hence we should set

---

14. This doctrine is very much alive in the *Politics* (1333ᵃ16–ᵇ5).
15. Also *EE* 1249ᵇ9–21, *MM* 1198ᵇ17–20, *NE* 1145ᵃ6–9; §6.

aside the life of nutrition and growth. The life next in order is some sort of life of sense-perception; but this too is apparently shared, with horse, ox, and every other animal. The remaining possibility, then, is some sort of action of what has reason. Now this [the part that has reason itself has two parts, each of which has reason in a different way], one as obeying reason, the other as itself having it and exercising understanding. Moreover, life is also spoken of in two ways, and we must take life as activity, since this seems to be called life to a fuller extent. We have found, then, that the human function is the activity of the soul that expresses reason or is not without reason. (*NE* 1097ᵇ33–1098ᵃ8; compare *Pol.* 1333ᵃ16–ᵇ5)

Subtleties aside, the doctrine here seems to be simply this: a thing's essence determines its species (*Metaph.* 1030ᵃ11–14); hence, if human beings shared their essence with plants or beasts, they would belong to the same species as those plants or beasts. Notice that, on this account, (C) is not assuming that whatever is special to human beings is their function. The specialness of the human function derives from the specialness of the human essence to which it is identical, but neither function nor essence is determined by what is special. The function argument is not open to the criticism often urged against it, therefore, that any property special to human beings is as good a candidate for human function as rational activity. It may be true, for example, that prostitution is special to humans, but it is false that it is part of our essence or function to prostitute ourselves.

The life or life activity of growth and nutrition, which is the function of plants and vegetables, and the life activity of perception, which is the function of beasts, cannot be the distinctively human function. "The remaining possibility, then, is some sort of action of what has reason." This is so because Aristotle is presupposing what his biological researches have, he thinks, made evident, that there are just three life activities: nutrition and growth, perception, and some sort of action of what has reason (*DA* 413ᵃ20–415ᵃ13). Since the human function is a life activity, it must then be some sort of action of what has reason.[16]

Having identified the human function, Aristotle is ready to bring out its connection to virtue (*aretē*):

---

16. Does this entail that the human function cannot be theoretical activity or study? No. For Aristotle allows that study is itself a kind of ACTION (*Pol.* 1325ᵇ16–21).

> [D] The function of a harpist is the same in kind, so we say, as the
> function of an excellent harpist. And the same is true without quali-
> fication in every case, when we add to the function the superior
> achievement that expresses the virtue. For a harpist's function, for
> example, is to play the harp, and a good harpist's is to do it well. Now
> we take the human function to be a certain kind of life and take this
> life to be the activity and actions of the soul that accord with reason.
> [Hence] the excellent man's function is to do these finely and well.
> [E] Each action or activity is completed well when its completion ex-
> presses the proper virtue. [F] Therefore, the human good turns out
> to be an activity of the soul that expresses virtue. (*NE* 1098ª9–17)

Part of (D) is reasonably uncontroversial given the identification of
function with essence and end: the essence of a harpist (say) is clearly
the same as the essence of an excellent harpist, and an excellent harpist
is clearly one who best achieves the end (playing the harp), which is that
essence activated. But why does virtue ensure that something will best
achieve its end? Why is it that, as (E) puts it, "each action or activity is
completed well when its completion expresses the proper virtue"? The
best answer is that a genuine virtue is *by definition* something that com-
pletes an activity well or guarantees that it will achieve its end.[17]

This makes (E) into a sort of conceptual truth. But that conceptual
truth cloaks a substantive one. If our rational activities express genuine
virtue, they constitute the human good. That is conceptually guaranteed. But it is not guaranteed that the conventionally recognized ethical
virtues—justice, temperance, courage, and the rest—are genuine
virtues. It is not guaranteed that if our rational activities express *them*,
those activities constitute the human good.[18] Thus Aristotle needs to
show that the conventionally recognized virtues are indeed genuine
ones. We shall return to this topic in §5.

(D)–(E) establish that the goodness or excellence of a harpist consists
in playing the harp well, and that a good harpist is one who plays well.
But do they establish that the good for a harpist is playing the harp well?
They do not. But together with (A), the perfectionist premise, they do.

17. See *Ph.* 246ª10–15, *Metaph.* 1021ᵇ20–23, *Rh.* 1366ª36–ᵇ1; Plato, *Republic*
    352ᵈ–354ª.
18. In other words, it isn't a conceptual truth that the specifically moral virtues
    are what perfect our nature. But neither does Aristotle think that it is. Con-
    trast Thomas Hurka, *Perfectionism* (Oxford: Clarendon Press, 1993): 19–20.

After all, (A) explicitly states that if human beings (or anything else) have a function, the good for them depends on their function. And, again, the fact that a human being's function is his end, or his essence activated, makes this an intelligible view. For to say that the good for human being is to best achieve his end is to say something that is at least a serious candidate for truth.

(F), the conclusion of the function argument, is that the human good is an activity of the soul expressing virtue. But to that conclusion Aristotle adds a difficult coda:

> [G] And if there are more virtues than one, the good will express
> the best and most complete virtue. [H] Further, in a complete life.
> For one swallow does not make a spring, nor does one day; nor, sim-
> ilarly, does one day or a short time make us blessed and happy. (*NE*
> 1098ª17–20)

(H) is perhaps clear enough: happiness needs to be spread throughout our lives in the right sort of way in order for us to count as happy (*NE* 1100ᵇ22–1101ª13). But (G) is difficult. Fortunately, there is no need for us to do more than scratch its surface. Aristotle recognizes two broad classes of virtues. The first of these consists of the familiar ethical virtues of character mentioned a moment ago—justice, temperance, courage, and so on. The second consists of the virtues of thought (*NE* 1138ᵇ35–1139ª17), practical wisdom, which is expressed in excellent practical activities, and theoretical wisdom, which is expressed in excellent theorizing or studying (*NE* 1177ª12–19). Thus the antecedent of the conditional in (G) is true: there *are* more virtues than one. The consequent of the conditional thus comes into play. We are to select from the list of practical virtues and virtues of thought the one that is best and most complete. Which one is that? Naturally enough, this is a controversial matter. But if we conclude that theoretical wisdom alone satisfies this description, the coda to the function argument would also lead us, as (B) did earlier, to identify the human function with understanding, and the human good with excellent understanding, with understanding that expresses wisdom. Again, all I suggest we do for the present is notice how close to the function argument this apparently extravagant view lies.

The function argument, in its weaker version, tells us that it is our nature or essence to be practically or theoretically rational, then; and that the good for us consists in excellent rational activity, in rational activity expressing virtue. The stronger version more narrowly identifies our nature or essence with theoretically rational activity, and our good with such activity when it expresses the virtue of wisdom. The trouble (if that is the right word) is that the function argument is an abstract metaphysical or (maybe) biological argument that seems far removed from life experience, and seems to some degree to be in conflict with it. Certainly, few people, if asked, would say that the good, or the good life, consisted exclusively in being active in politics (remember that practical wisdom is pretty much the same thing as statesmanship for Aristotle) or in theorizing (contemplating). They are far more likely to think that the good is pleasure or enjoyment, and that the good life is a pleasant or enjoyable one.

This is a serious problem, if for no other reason than that people are far more likely to be guided by their experience in these matters than by philosophical arguments. Aristotle himself explicitly recognizes this (*NE* 1172^{a}34–^{b}7, 1179^{a}17–22). But he does not believe that the problem is insurmountable. For he thinks he can show that the various views of happiness defended by ordinary people on the basis of their experience and by philosophers on the basis of experience and argument (*NE* 1098^{b}27–29) are all consistent with the conclusion of the function argument. For example, he thinks that the activities expressing virtue are pleasant, and "do not need pleasure to be added as some sort of ornament" (*NE* 1099^{a}15–16), so that the popular view that happiness is pleasure is underwritten rather than contradicted. Moreover, he concedes that were such conflict to occur, it would be the conclusion of the argument that might have to be modified: "We should examine the first principle [i.e., human good or happiness]," he says, "not only from the conclusion and premises of a deductive argument, but from what is said about it; for all the facts harmonize with a true account, whereas the truth soon clashes with a false one" (*NE* 1098^{b}9–11).

It would be misleading, therefore, flatly to describe the function argument as providing the metaphysical or biological foundations of Aristotelian ethics and statesmanship. This suggests too crude an inheritance from metaphysics and biology, too crude a naturalism. The function argument employs concepts such as those of function, essence, and end which, though perhaps biological in origin, belong to Aristotle's metaphysics. By using these concepts and by showing how they are related to the ethical and political notions of virtue and the good life, the function argument establishes the close connections between metaphysics, on the one hand, and ethics and statesmanship, on the other. But the ultimate test of the function argument is not simply the cogency of its biological or metaphysical roots. If the function argument is underwritten by the facts of ethical and political experience, it helps to underwrite them. If it is not underwritten by those facts, it fails altogether.

This aspect of the function argument makes it a nice paradigm of much of Aristotle's philosophy. On the one hand, we have an intense awareness of the importance of the facts, and of experience. On the other, we have a deeply theoretical mind employing a group of carefully examined concepts and explanatory notions that have earned their keep in widely differing areas. Both these sides of Aristotle's mind are manifest in the *Politics*. His interest in the facts of Greek political history is manifested, for example, in Book V in his discussion of actual constitutions and of what causes them to persist or to perish. The more deeply theoretical side of his interest in politics is manifest, for example, in IV.4, where biology and metaphysics guide his discussion of the various kinds of democracy (1290^b25-39). But in the last analysis these are two sides of a single mind seeking to deal with experience in deeply unified and intellectually scrutable ways, while at the same time testing incipient theoretical explanations against experience.[19]

§5 *Practical Agents*

Our nature, essence, or function lies in the rational part of our souls, in any case, and the human good consists in rational activity expressing virtue. This activity, as we have seen, can be either practical or theoretical or some mix of the two. But what more particularly do these types of rational activity themselves consist in? We shall discuss practical activity in this section, theoretical activity in the next.

Canonical practical ACTION or activity is action that is deliberately chosen, that expresses deliberate choice (*proairesis*). Such choice is a desire based on deliberation (*bouleusis*) that requires a state of character and is in accord with wish (*boulēsis*), a desire for the good or the apparent good.[20] Suppose, for example, that we are faced with a lunch menu. We wish for the good or happiness. We deliberate about which of the actions available to us in the circumstances will best promote it. Should we order the fish (low fat, high protein) or the lasagna (high fat, high fiber)?

19. For further discussion of the function argument, see my *Practices of Reason*, 123–38; and J. Whiting, "Aristotle's Function Argument: A Defense," *Ancient Philosophy* 8 (1988): 33–48.
20. *NE* 1113^a9-14 (reading *kata tēn boulēsin*), 1139^a31-^b5, 1113^a3-5.

We choose fish with a salad (low fat, high fiber), on the grounds that this combines low fat, high protein, *and* high fiber. For we believe that this is the kind of food that best promotes health, and that being healthy promotes our happiness. If our appetite is then for fish and salad, we choose it, and our action accords with our wish and our desire. If our appetite is consistently or habitually in accord with our wish, so that it does not overpower wish and wish does not have to overpower it, Aristotle says that (everything else being equal) we have the virtue of temperance (*sōphrosunē*).

Suppose we deliberately choose as before, but our appetite is for the lasagna; there are then two further possibilities. First, our appetite is stronger than our wish and overpowers it, so that we choose and eat the lasagna. In this case, we are weak-willed. We know the good but don't do it. Second, our wish is stronger and overpowers our still very insistent appetite. In this case, we are self-controlled. We do what we think best in the teeth of our insistent and soon-to-be-frustrated appetite. Now these three things, weak will, self-control, and virtue are precisely states of character. And it is in part because our deliberate choices exhibit these that they involve such states.

This is one way character is involved in deliberate choice, but there is another. It is revealed by a fourth possibility. Here appetite is in accord with wish, but wish is only for the apparent and not the genuine human good (*Pol.* 1331^b26–34). This possibility is realized by a vicious person (a person who has vices). He wishes for the good, but he mistakenly believes that the good consists (say) in gratifying his appetites. So if his appetite is for a high-fat diet, such as lasagna with extra cheese followed by a large ice cream sundae, that is what he wishes for and orders.

Some people (virtuous, self-controlled, and weak-willed ones) have true conceptions of the good, then; others (vicious ones) have false conceptions. What explains this fact? Aristotle's answer in a nutshell is habits, especially those habits developed early in life (*NE* 1095^b4–8)—although nature and reason also have a part to play (*Pol.* 1332^a38–^b8). We come to enjoy fatty foods, for example, by being allowed to eat them freely when we are children and developing a taste for them (or perhaps by being forbidden them in a way that makes them irresistibly attractive). If we had acquired "good eating habits" instead, we would have a different conception of that part of the good that involves diet. We would want and would enjoy the fish and salad and not hanker for the lasagna and ice cream at all. Failing that, we would, as weak-willed or self-controlled people, at least not wish for it.

Extending the picture, it is our habits more generally, which together determine the type of life we lead, that do much to fill in the rest of our picture of the good. If we have been brought up to do whatever we feel like doing, so that we cannot postpone gratification, it will usually be difficult for us to experience the goods that require discipline and long study to experience. And without that experience we will usually find it difficult even to understand an argument in favor of those goods: "someone whose life follows his feelings would not listen to an argument turning him away or even understand it" (*NE* 1179^{b}26–28). Our habits, therefore, limit our capacities for new experiences of what is good or valuable, and so lock us to some extent into our old values, which consequently continue to seem to be the only genuine ones. To be sure, we should not overdo the metaphors of locks and chains. Habits can be broken. Bad habits can be replaced by better ones and vice versa. All the same, "it is not easy to alter what has long been absorbed by habit" (*NE* 1179^{b}16–18).

Three broad patterns emerge in lives thus formed, yielding "roughly three most favored types of lives: the lives of gratification, of political activity, and, third, of study" (*NE* 1095^{b}18–20).[21] And it is on the basis of these lives, these patterns of habit, that "people not unreasonably reach their conception of the good, that is to say, of happiness" (*NE* 1095^{b}14–18). What makes a certain conception correct, however, is not that it happens to emerge from some type of life in this way, but that it agrees with the experientially sanctioned conclusion of the function argument. Our nature, function, or essence, and not what we happen to wish for or choose, determines what the good is for us.

None the less, our habits do still largely determine our *conception* of the good. So it is clearly of the greatest importance that we develop good habits of liking and disliking or desiring and rejecting, habits that will lead us both to conceive the good correctly and to choose and do what will most promote it. That is one reason, indeed, why it is crucial to be brought up in a constitution with correct laws:

> It is hard for someone to be trained correctly for virtue from his youth if he has not been brought up under correct laws. . . . Perhaps, however, it is not enough for people to get the correct upbringing when they are young—they must continue the same prac-

---

21. This should remind us of the money lovers, honor lovers, and wisdom lovers of Plato's *Republic*.

tices and be habituated to them when they become men. (*NE* 1179^{b}31–1180^{a}3)

But what more precisely are the good habits that correct laws foster? What is it that is true of our feelings, our desires and emotions, when they are such as good or bad habits make them?

Aristotle's answer is that properly habituated emotions "listen to reason" (*NE* 1102^{b}28–1103^{a}1), and so are in accord with wish, aiming at the same thing it does (*NE* 1119^{b}15–18). When this happens, the feelings are said to be "in a mean" between excess and deficiency: "If, for example, our feeling is too intense or too weak, we are badly off in relation to anger, but if it is in a mean, we are well off; and the same is true in other cases" (*NE* 1105^{b}25–28; also *Ph.* 247^{a}3–4). Some of Aristotle's advice about how we might achieve this mean state helps explain its nature:

> We must also examine what we ourselves drift into easily. For different people have different natural tendencies toward different ends, and we come to know our own tendencies by the pleasure and pain that arise in us. We must drag ourselves off in the contrary direction. For if we pull far away from error, as they do in straightening bent wood, we shall reach the mean. (*NE* 1109^{b}1–7)

By noticing our natural proclivities, we can correct for them. Over time, with habit and practice, our feelings typically change, becoming more responsive or less resistant to wish, more in harmony with it. Provided that wish embodies a correct conception of the good, we are then far more likely to achieve the good and be happy than if our feelings successfully oppose wish or have to be overpowered by it. In the former case, we miss the good altogether; in the latter, we achieve it but only at the cost of the pain and frustration of our unsatisfied feelings. We eat fish and salad but we remain "hungry" and, in some cases, no doubt, obsessed with the forbidden lasagna and ice cream: an uncomfortable and unstable condition, as we know.

In §4 we noticed a problem. It is conceptually guaranteed that if our rational activities express genuine virtue, they constitute the human good. But it is not guaranteed that the conventionally recognized ethical virtues—justice, temperance, courage, and the rest—are genuine ones. The doctrine of the mean is intended to solve this problem. A genuine virtue is a state that is in a mean between excess and deficiency. Hence if the conventionally recognized virtues are such states, they are genuine virtues. Books III–V of the *Nicomachean Ethics* are for the most part intended to show that the antecedent of this conditional is true. We shall not probe their details here, not all of which are entirely persuasive. It is enough for our purposes to see that the doctrine of the mean is intended to fill what would otherwise be a lacuna in Aristotle's argument.[22]

Feelings are concerned with external goods; that is to say, with "goods of competition," which include money, honor, bodily pleasure, and in general goods that people tend to fight over; and with having friends, which "seems to be the greatest external good" (*NE* 1169^b9–10). We would expect, therefore, that the virtues of character would be particularly concerned with external goods. And indeed they are. The vast majority are concerned with the goods of competition. Courage is concerned with painful feelings of fear and pleasant feelings of confidence; temperance, with the pleasures of taste and touch (*NE* 1118^a23–^b8); generosity and magnificence, with wealth; magnanimity, with honor; special justice, with ACQUISITIVENESS (*pleonexia*), with wanting more and more without limit of the external goods of competition (*NE* 1129^b1–4). General justice (*NE* 1129^b25–27) is especially concerned with friendship and community. It is our needs for these goods that lead us to form communities that are characterized as much by mutuality of interest as by competition (I.1–2). But it is these same needs that often bring us into conflict with one another. The single major cause of political instability, indeed, is competition, especially between the rich and the poor, for external goods such as wealth and honor (V.1). The political significance of the virtues is therefore assured; without them no constitution can long be stable. For "the law has no power to secure obedience except habit" (1269^a20–21).

Imagine that all our feelings, all our emotions and desires are in a mean, so that we have all the virtues of character. Our feelings are in accord with our wish, and our wish is for the real and not merely the apparent good. Haven't we got all we need to ensure, as far as any human being can, that we will achieve the good and live happily? Not quite. Until we have engaged in the kind of dialectical clarification of our conception of happiness undertaken in the *Nicomachean Ethics*, until we have seen how to solve the problems to which it gives rise, and how to

---

22. J. O. Urmson, "Aristotle's Doctrine of the Mean," *American Philosophical Quarterly* 10 (1973): 223–30; and Rosalind Hursthouse, "A False Doctrine of the Mean," *Proceedings of the Aristotelian Society* 81 (1980–81): 57–72, are worthwhile discussions.

criticize competing conceptions, we do not have the clear and explicit conception that we need for success in all circumstances (§2). On the one hand, then, Aristotle thinks that we need to have been brought up with good habits and have feelings that are in a mean "if we are to be adequate students of what is noble and just and of political questions generally" (*NE* 1095ᵇ4–6). And, on the other, he thinks that ethics is a practical science whose end or goal is "action not knowledge" (*NE* 1095ᵃ5–6). Its contribution (or one of its contributions) to action is that it makes us "more likely to hit the right mark" (*NE* 1094ᵃ22–24), by providing us with a clear and problem-free conception of it.

When philosophy has done this work of clarification and problem solving, and the clear conception of the good is added to our virtuous soul, at that point we acquire practical wisdom. But it is also true that we simultaneously acquire the full-blown virtues of character: "We cannot be fully good without practical wisdom, or have practical wisdom without virtue of character . . . as soon as someone has practical wisdom, which is a single state, he has all the virtues as well" (*NE* 1144ᵇ30–1145ᵃ2). What we have before that is what Aristotle calls habituated virtue: we are disposed to listen to reason, but we do not yet have the kind of understanding of our goal in life that comes from philosophical inquiry.

But what philosophy tells us, as we discovered in §4, is that our goal is rational activity that expresses virtue. And what we wanted to know was what one type of this activity is, namely, practical rational activity. How much closer are we to getting what we wanted? We are, in fact, pretty much there. The exercise of practical wisdom, which involves and expresses all of the virtues of character, simply is practical activity. Reflect for a moment on what this means. Our feelings, our emotions and desires, are concerned with external goods. When they are in a mean, when they are in accord with wish or listen to reason, practical wisdom ensures, so far as is humanly possible, that they are satisfied in a way that achieves the good or promotes our happiness. We need these goods; we need money, honor, pleasure; we above all need friends, in order to lead happy lives. But the very activity of practical wisdom, which ensures that our desires are satisfied, is more valuable than the satisfactions it (if anything) ensures. Perhaps this will seem less strange when we reflect that practical wisdom, being the same as statesmanship, is best exemplified in a life of political activity. For we might well think—in any case, we can surely find it intelligible to think—that a political life, suitably equipped with external goods, would be a recognizably valuable one.

Given the identity of practical wisdom and statesmanship, we can perhaps also better understand why being able to solve the problems that arise for our own conception of the good, while being able effectively to criticize other competing conceptions, might prove particularly important.

So far we have been focusing primarily on practical wisdom as it is manifested in the life of an individual, in order to understand what practical wisdom and the virtues of character are, and how they guarantee a correct conception of happiness. Armed with that understanding, we are in a position to understand why, when practical wisdom assumes the role of statesmanship, it has the characteristics that Aristotle ascribes to it in IV.1. Its primary task is to study the best constitution: *Pol.* II, VII, and VIII are devoted to this task. To carry it out successfully a STATESMAN must know what happiness is (1323^a14–16). For happiness is the same thing for a city-state or constitution as for an individual (1325^b30–32, *NE* 1094^b7–8), and the ideal constitution is precisely the one in which all the citizens are as happy as possible (1324^a23–25; §10).

Since happiness is rational activity expressing virtue, the laws of the ideal constitution must be designed to inculcate the virtues. Indeed, Aristotle argues that if the legislation in a community is not designed to foster virtue, the community isn't really a city-state at all (1280^a34–$^b15$). The statesman's knowledge of the virtues and his possession of them will obviously help him with this task. In the ideal constitution, the laws that suit the constitution inculcate the unqualified virtues of character. But in other constitutions this is not so. There the laws inculcate virtues that, while suited to the constitution, are not unqualified virtues. We shall see why this is so in §9.

Not every population can attain the ideal constitution; so in addition to studying it, a statesman must also study other things. First, the constitution that is best for a given type of people. Book IV.12–16 deals with this problem. Second, the constitution that is most appropriate for all city-states. This is the so-called MIDDLE CONSTITUTION (1296^a7), a type of POLITY, discussed in IV.11. A substantial portion of the *Politics* deals with the final tasks of statesmanship, which is to study the various ways in which any variety of constitution can be preserved and destroyed. The various subvarieties of the various types of constitutions are discussed in IV.4–10, the ways they are best preserved and destroyed in Books V and VI.

The fact that statesmanship engages in *all* these tasks may seem deeply problematic. Statesmanship is something only an unqualifiedly virtuous person can know or possess. Its exercise is an exercise in virtue, since the psychological state activated in its exercise just is complete virtue (*NE* 1145^{a}1–6). How, then, can a statesman do something so apparently unethical as to provide a tyrant with the type of information Aristotle provides in V.11, information that helps him stay in power? Tyranny is an unjust constitution, aiming not at the common benefit but at that of the tyrant himself (§9). Isn't helping to keep it in existence itself an act of injustice?

A distinction Aristotle uses in discussing rhetoric has important bearing on this matter. "One person," he says, "may be called a rhetorician on the basis of his scientific knowledge and another on the basis of his deliberate choice" (*Rh.* 1355^{b}18–20). The first sort of person is someone who knows all of the various techniques of rhetorical persuasion, including the illegitimate ones. The second is someone who knows what the first person knows but will use even illegitimate persuasive devices when needed. On Aristotle's view, we need to know what the first person knows, so that we can confute anyone who "argues unfairly," but we should not use the illegitimate techniques ourselves (*Rh.* 1355^{a}29–33). Now all Aristotle tells us is that a statesman must "study" (1288^{b}22) the various things we listed. And that is quite compatible, of course, with his making only ethical use of what he finds out as a result of such study. But is that how Aristotle uses his own political knowledge in the *Politics*? Arguably, it is. For the advice that he gives the tyrant—and the oligarchs and democrats, for that matter—seems to have the effect, at least, of making their constitutions more just by making them come closer to promoting the common benefit.[23]

The fact that Aristotle thinks that statesmen (whether as political leaders themselves or as advisors to them) need to study more than just the ideal constitution is a tribute, on the one hand, to his own hard-headedness (see 1288^{b}33–39), and, on the other, to the recalcitrance of reality, which seldom presents us with ideal circumstances. The world is the way it is, resources are what they are, power is distributed as it is; and the statesman has to make the best of it.[24]

In the *Politics* Aristotle focuses on an aspect of practical wisdom which is much less prominent in the *Nicomachean Ethics*. The difference is instructive. In the *Politics* Aristotle focuses on what we might call the *universalist* side of practical wisdom, on its role in designing constitutions

23. See 1309^{a}14–26, 1309^{b}18–35, 1310^{a}2–12, 1315^{a}40–^{b}10.
24. 1324^{b}22–1325^{a}14 is particularly worth reading in this regard.

and developing universal laws appropriate to them or to existing ones. He claims that the laws should be as complete and detailed as possible, and should leave as little as possible to "so unreliable a standard as human wish" (1272ᵇ5–7).[25] In the *Nicomachean Ethics*, on the other hand, the *particularist* side of practical wisdom is more in focus. Here the emphasis is on deciding what it is best to do in a particular case in which laws give at best fairly minimal guidance. We are forcefully reminded, therefore, of the limited utility of laws and principles: "questions about actions and expediency, like questions about health, have no fixed answers. And when our universal account is like that, the account of particular cases is all the more inexact" (1104ᵃ3–7; also 1094ᵇ14–22, *Rh*. 1374ᵃ18–ᵇ23).

The explanation of this difference of focus is plain enough: private individuals within a city-state are given by the constitution itself the laws that must guide their decisions; they do not have to devise them for themselves. The major task they face is therefore the particularist one of determining what to do in these particular circumstances in light of the laws. The statesman, by contrast, is charged with the business of developing laws in the first place, or of modifying existing ones. Hence the universalist side of his wisdom comes to the fore. It goes without saying, however, that even statesmen will often have to be particularists as well in order to deal effectively with problems that outstrip the letter of the law. In any case, if we are to understand practical wisdom or statesmanship correctly, we need to see both its sides; we need to study both the *Ethics* and the *Politics*.[26]

§6 Theorizers

The political life is one of the three most favored types of lives. Another is the life of study or contemplation (*bios theōrētikos*), in which theoretical activity plays a very important role. Our focus now will be on the nature of that activity, the second type of rational activity in which our good consists, and on the relationship between it and the practical activity we discussed in §5.

Study of any of the various sciences Aristotle recognizes is an exercise of understanding (*nous*) and is a theoretical activity of some sort:

25. See 1269ᵃ9–12, 1272ᵇ5–7, 1282ᵇ1–6, 1286ᵃ7–ᵇ40, 1287ᵃ28–32, *NE* 1137ᵇ13–32, *Rh*. 1374ᵃ18–ᵇ23.
26. For further discussion of the topics covered in this section, see my *Practices of Reason*, 69–92, 56–98, 139–97.

Of all beings naturally composed, some are ungenerated and imperishable for the whole of eternity, whereas others are subject to coming-to-be and perishing. The former possess value—indeed divinity—but we can study them less, because both the starting points of the inquiry and the things we want to know about present extremely few appearances to sense perception. We are better equipped to acquire knowledge about the perishable plants and animals because they grow beside us, and much can be learned about each existing kind if one is willing to take sufficient pains. Both studies have their attractions. For although we grasp only a little of the former, yet because of the value of what we grasp, we get more pleasure from it than from all the things around us; just as a small and random glimpse of those we love pleases us more than an exact view of other things, no matter how numerous or large they are. But because our information about the things around us is better and more plentiful, our knowledge of them has the advantage over the other. And because they are closer to us and more akin to our nature, they have their own compensations in comparison with the philosophy concerned with divine things. . . . For even in the study of animals that are unattractive to the senses, the nature that fashioned them likewise offers immeasurable pleasures to those who are naturally philosophical and can learn the causal explanations of things. (*PA* 644^{b}22–645^{a}10)

As we see from this passage, things that are ungenerated and imperishable for the whole of eternity are the best kind to study. Among these, the very best is God himself. Hence the very best theoretical activity consists in the study of God: theology. That is why only the study of theology fully expresses wisdom (*NE* 11412^{a}16–20 with *APo.* 87^{a}31–37).

One reason Aristotle holds this view about theology is this.[27] The Aristotelian cosmos consists of a series of concentric spheres, with the earth at its center. God is the eternal first mover, or first cause of motion in the universe. But he does not act on the universe to cause it to move. He is not its efficient cause. He moves it in the way that an object of love causes motion in the things that love or desire it (*DA* 415^{a}26–^{b}7). He is

27. The other reasons are these: God is the best or most estimable thing there is, so that theology, the science that studies him, is the most estimable science (*Metaph.* 983^{a}5–7, 1074^{b}34, 1075^{a}11–12). He is also the most intelligible or most amenable to study of all things, because he is a pure or matterless form (*Metaph.* 1026^{a}10–32).

its teleological cause, an unmoved mover (*Metaph*. 1072^{a}25–27). Things express their love for God by trying to be as like him as possible, something they accomplish by trying to realize their own natures or forms as completely or perfectly as he realizes his. This is a struggle for life or existence, since the loss of form, as we saw in §4, is the loss of life or existence. Now God realizes his form perfectly and, since he is ungenerated and imperishable, eternally. But most living things are both generated and perishable. Hence they best approximate God's condition by giving birth to offspring with the same form, and so belonging to the same species, as themselves:

> The most natural act for any living thing that has developed normally . . . is to produce another like itself (an animal producing an animal, a plant, a plant), in order to partake as best it can in the eternal and divine. That is what all things strive for, and everything they do naturally is for the sake of that. (*DA* 415^{a}26–^{b}2)

Because all things are in essence trying to be as much like God as possible, we cannot understand them fully unless we see them in that light. And once we do see them in that light we still do not understand them fully until we understand theology, until we understand what God is. Theology is more intelligible, and hence better to study, than the other sciences for just this reason: the other sciences contain an area of darkness that needs to be illuminated by another science; theology can fully illuminate itself.[28]

Human beings participate in the divine in the same way as other animals do by having children. But they can participate in it yet more fully because they have understanding. For God, on Aristotle's view, is a pure understanding who is contemplating or holding in thought the complete science of himself: theology (*Metaph*. 983^{a}6–7).[29] Hence when human beings are actually studying theology they are participating in the very activity that is God himself. They thus become much more like God than they do by having children, or doing anything else. In the process, Aristotle claims, they achieve the greatest happiness possible (*NE* 1177^{b}26–1179^{a}32).

---

28. *APo*. 87^{a}31–37, *Metaph*. 1074^{b}34, 1075^{a}11–12, *NE* 1141^{a}16–20, 1141^{b}2–8.
29. That is what is meant by the famous, and famously opaque, formulation that God is *noēsis noēseōs noēsis*: "thought thinking itself" or "an understanding that is an understanding of understanding" (*Metaph*. 1074^{b}33–35).

If we ask how Aristotle reaches this conclusion, we are returned to his perfectionism and to the function argument. We saw how close that argument comes to identifying our nature or essence with theoretically rational activity. We are, as Aristotle says, "most of all our understanding" (*NE* 1168^b31–33 with 1178^a2–8). Once that is granted, perfectionism straightway identifies happiness with the activity of understanding fully realized (*Pol.* 1334^b15). Aristotle often explicitly says, indeed, that no being can be happy to any degree without understanding (*NE* 1178^b24–32, *EE* 1217^a24–29). What the present argument adds is that understanding is fully realized when it is the study of the most intelligible science: theology.

Since this view of happiness has deep roots in Aristotle's larger theories, it is not something that he could abandon without major surgery on his metaphysics, theory of knowledge, and psychology. Yet Aristotle's commitment to it often seems equivocal or faint-hearted. In the *Politics*, for example, he identifies philosophy as the virtue needed for the best use of leisure (1334^a23), extolling its pleasures as highest of all (1267^a10–12). Similarly, when he is discussing the soul in connection with the goals of legislation in VII.14, he strongly implies that theoretical activity is preferable to practical activity (1333^a27–29). These texts lead us to expect a round defense of the more divine life of study as the best human life. Yet when he turns to an explicit discussion of the best life in VII.2–3, he is cagey, dialectically balancing the claims of the political life against the philosophical, but not giving decisive precedence to either.

What explains this caginess may not be faint-heartedness on Aristotle's part, however, but a confusion on ours. We need to distinguish the question of what *happiness* is from the question of what *the best or happiest life* is. Aristotle himself is quite decisive and consistent on the first question: happiness is activity expressing virtue; the contenders are practical activity and theoretical activity; the palm of victory invariably goes to theoretical activity, although practical activity is often awarded second prize. This is as true in the *Politics* as it is in the *Nicomachean Ethics*. But it does not tell us what the best life is.

Here, as in the case of activities, there are two contenders, the political life and the philosophical or theoretical life (*Pol.* 1324^a29–31). These lives sound like the activities already discussed but must not be confused with them. The political life involves taking part in politics with other people and participating in a city-state (1324^a15–16); the philosophical life is that of "an alien cut off from the political community"

(1324ᵃ16–17) and "released from external concerns" (1324ᵃ27–28). When we raise the question of which of these is best, we can do so in two different ways (1324ᵃ13–23): first, presupposing that life in a city-state is preferable for everyone, because a human being is a political animal (§7); second, without making that presupposition (this way of raising the question is set aside as not an appropriate one for statesmanship).

If we adopt the first approach, the question to be answered is: Which of the two lives should the best constitution provide to its citizens? This is a question statesmanship does try to answer.[30] And what we see from the answer it gives is that the best life must involve *both* unleisured political activity and leisured theoretical activity (1333ᵃ30–ᵇ5), and must be organized so that the former is for the sake of the latter (1334ᵃ4–5). Manifestly, this is not the life of "an alien cut off from the political community." It cannot be the philosophical life, then, and so must be the political one. But it is not a life in which practical political activity is the primary goal; it is one in which theoretical activity occupies that position. In this respect it is like the philosophical life.

On this topic too the *Nicomachean Ethics* seems to tell the same story as the *Politics* (although it may well be telling it *without* presupposing that life in a city-state is best for everyone). Theoretical activity is complete happiness "if it receives a complete span of life" (1177ᵇ24–26). But a life filled with that activity alone, the philosophical life as characterized in the *Politics*, "would be too high for a human being" (1177ᵇ26–27). It is too high, because our "nature is not self-sufficient enough for theoretical activity" (1178ᵇ33–35). We have needs and interests that stem from our emotions, desires, and appetites, from our merely human nature (1178ᵃ9–22), as well as a need to theorize that stems from our understanding, which is "something divine" (1177ᵇ30). Thus a happy human life needs an adequate supply of external goods (*NE* 1101ᵃ14–17) to satisfy those appetites and desires; it must be choiceworthy and lacking in nothing for a political animal whose happiness depends on that of his parents, wife, children, friends, and fellow citizens (*NE* 1097ᵇ8–14; §7); and it must be organized so as to promote and facilitate theoretical activity (1177ᵇ1–24, 1178ᵇ3–7, *EE* 1249ᵇ9–21).

It is the task of practical wisdom (statesmanship) to provide human beings with a life of this sort: practical wisdom is thus "a kind of steward of wisdom, procuring leisure for it and its task" (*MM* 1198ᵇ17–20). This life is "happiest in a secondary way" (*NE* 1178ᵃ9), when compared

30. That seems to be the gist of 1324ᵃ13–29.

to the philosophical life, because it has to contain a substantial amount of political activity, which is second-class happiness (1178ᵃ8–10; §5).

§7 Political Animals

Aristotle famously claims that a human being is by nature a political animal.[31] Less famously, but perhaps more controversially, he also claims that the city-state is itself a natural phenomenon, something that exists by nature (*Pol.* 1252ᵇ30, 1253ᵃ1). These doctrines are closely related—so closely, indeed, that they are based on the very same argument (1252ᵃ24–1253ᵃ19). We shall analyze that argument below, but before we do we should look at the doctrines themselves.

According to Aristotle, political animals are a subclass of herding or gregarious animals that "have as their task (*ergon*) some single thing that they all do together." Thus bees, wasps, ants, and human beings are all political animals in this sense (*HA* 487ᵇ33–488ᵃ10). But human beings are more political than these others (*Pol.* 1253ᵃ7–18), because they are naturally equipped for life in a type of community that is itself more quintessentially political than a beehive or an ant nest, namely, a household or city-state. What equips human beings to live in such communities is the natural capacity for rational speech, which they alone possess. For rational speech "is for making clear what is beneficial or harmful, and hence also what is just or unjust . . . and it is community in these that makes a household and a city-state" (1253ᵃ14–17).

It may well be as uncontroversial to say that human beings have a natural capacity to live in communities with others as it is to make parallel claims about bees and ants. But why should we think that they will best actualize this capacity in a community of a particular sort, such as an Aristotelian household or city-state? Why not think that, unlike bees and ants, human beings might realize their natures equally well either in isolation or in some other kind of political or nonpolitical community?[32] We shall return to these questions in due course.

We now have some idea at least of what Aristotle means by saying that a human being is a political animal. But what does he mean by the far

---

31. See *Pol.* 1253ᵃ7–18, 1278ᵇ15–30, *NE* 1162ᵃ16–19, 1169ᵇ16–22, *EE* 1242ᵃ19–28.
32. In *HA* 487ᵇ33–488ᵃ14, Aristotle says that man "dualizes," that some live in groups, while others live solitary lives. The latter is represented as abnormal. But it might instead be taken to mark simply a difference in values or preferences.

more mysterious claim that the city-state exists by nature? We saw in §4 that Aristotle thinks that things exist by nature only when they have a nature, an inner "source of change and staying unchanged whether in respect of place, growth and decay, or alteration" (*Ph.* 192^{b}13–15). For convenience, I shall say that something that has such a source has a *canonical* nature. Doctrinal continuity alone, then, would suggest that when Aristotle says that the city-state exists by nature, he means that it has a canonical nature. And this suggestion is borne out, indeed, by the way he introduces his argument. "As in other cases," he says, "the best way to study these things is to observe their natural development from the beginning" (1252^{a}24–26). This is strong evidence that he is intending to establish that city-states have a canonical nature, since something that comes into existence by nature has one (*Ph.* 192^{b}8–9).

Not everything that has a canonical nature, however, realizes or perfects its nature *by* nature: craft is sometimes needed "to perfect or complete the task that nature is unable to perfect or complete" (*Ph.* 199^{a}15–16). For example, human beings exist by nature and so have canonical natures (*Ph.* 193^{b}5–6), but to perfect these they must acquire the virtues, and these are acquired in part through habituation and the craft of education (*NE* 1103^{a}17–26, *Pol.* 1332^{a}39–^{b}11, 1336^{b}40–1337^{a}3). To be sure, things that exist by nature are disjoint from things that are the products of a craft (*Ph.* 192^{b}8–33). But things that have their canonical natures perfected by craft are not products of craft. Their forms (or formal natures) do not flow into them from the souls or minds of a craftsman, as happens in the case of genuine craft products (*Metaph.* 1032^{a}32–^{b}10). Instead, potentialities that are parts of their natures are further actualized by craft. Thus the mere fact of a thing's needing to have its nature completed by craft or the like is no obstacle to its nature's being canonical.

So much for the doctrines; now for Aristotle's argument in support of them. We shall first go through the argument much as Aristotle does, commenting on each stage of it as we go. Then we shall step back from the details of the argument to assess its overall strategy.

Like other animals, human beings have a natural desire to reproduce, because in this way they participate to some degree at least in the divine (§6). Since they are sexually dimorphic, this desire leads them to form a couple (a type of community or communal relation) with members of the opposite sex (1252^{a}27–30). So far, so good: our desire to reproduce *is* something we share in common with the other animals, and is surely as much a natural fact about us as it is about them. But it is easy to slide from what is uncontentious into what is controversial. Is Aristotle just claiming that sexual coupling for the purposes of reproduction is natural? Or is he saying more than this?

In the *Nicomachean Ethics*, the human desire for sexual union is further characterized as follows: "The friendship of man and woman also seems to be natural. For human beings naturally tend to form couples more than to be political, to the extent that the household is prior to the city-state, and more necessary, and child-bearing is shared more widely among the animals" (1162ª16–19; also *EE* 1242ª22–26). But this characterization is obviously controversial. We might wonder, for example, whether the empirical evidence actually favors the view that human beings form couples in the way suggested, or whether this is not rather a social norm than a norm of nature.[33] More important, we might wonder whether they do naturally form Aristotelian *households*. Two features of these are bound to give us particular pause in this regard. The first is that the household involves the subordination of WOMEN to men. To be sure, Aristotle believes that this subordination is itself natural: women ought to be ruled by men, because they are "naturally inferior" to them, since the deliberative part of their souls "lacks authority" (1260ª13). Probably what he has in mind is that women lack authority over others, because they lack the spirit (*thumos*) required for command. No doubt the observation of oppressed Greek women, socialized into passivity, provided him with some empirical justification for this view. But a clear-eyed survey of the animal kingdom, or of unoppressed or differently socialized women, would do much to undermine this as a general hypothesis about all females.[34] In any case, the fact that it is built into Aristotle's conception of the household as something natural shows clearly just how controversial that conception actually is.

Yet more controversial is Aristotle's claim that the household essentially contains natural SLAVES (1252ᵇ9–12) or "animate property" (1253ᵇ32), people who benefit from being wholly under the authority of a MASTER because their souls altogether lack a deliberative element (1254ª10, 1260ª12). Are there such people? Probably not. That is one problem. But even if there were natural slaves, it is not clear why they

---

33. 1335ᵇ37–1336ª2 is worth reading in this regard.
34. It is regrettable that Aristotle does not discuss Plato's claims (*Republic* V) that the natural differences between men and women should have no political consequences, that men and women with the same natural abilities and talents should receive the same education and play the same social roles. See my *Philosopher-Kings*, 217–20.

would need masters, or why the latter would need them. Aristotle's own view is that masters and slaves form a union "for the sake of their own survival" (1252ª30–31). But this is very implausible. Animals also lack the capacity to deliberate, on Aristotle's view, yet they seem to survive quite nicely without human masters who can deliberate;[35] freed (supposedly) natural slaves do not simply die like flies. Masters may indeed benefit from having slaves to do the donkey work, while they spend their leisure on philosophy or politics (1255ᵇ36–37), but, since masters have bodies of their own and are capable of working on their own behalf, it is unclear why they need slaves *in order to survive*. We don't have slaves, and we survive.

Not only is Aristotle's conception of the household politically or ethically controversial, then, but it isn't clear that, even if we granted him its controversial elements, he could succeed in showing that it is natural because "naturally constituted to satisfy everyday needs" (1252ᵇ12–14).

Somewhat similar problems beset the next stage in the emergence of the city-state: the village. First, the village is "constituted from several households for the sake of satisfying needs other than everyday ones" (1252ᵇ15–16). To determine whether these nonroutine needs are natural, we have to be told what they are. But all that Aristotle says is that households have to engage in barter with one another when the need arises (1257ª19–25). This does not help very much, because the things they exchange with one another seem to be just the sorts of things that the household itself is supposed to be able to supply, such as wine and wheat (1257ª25–28). Second, to count as a village a community of several households must be governed in a characteristic way, namely, by a king (1252ᵇ20–22). This is natural, Aristotle explains, because villages are offshoots of households, in which the eldest is king (1252ᵇ20–22). The problem is that on Aristotle's own view households involve various kinds of rule, not just kingly rule. For example, a head of household rules his wife with political rule (I.12). We might wonder, therefore, why a village has to be governed with kingly rule rather than with political rule, that is to say, with all the heads of households ruling and being ruled in turn.

The final stage in the emergence of the city-state, and the conclusion of Aristotle's argument that the city-state exists by nature and that a human being is a political animal, is presented in the following terse and convoluted passage:

35. Aristotle also believes, however, that it is better for animals to be ruled by man "since this will keep them safe" (1254ᵇ10–13).

[A] A complete community, constituted out of several villages, once it reaches the limit of total self-sufficiency, practically speaking, is a city-state. [B] It comes to be for the sake of living, but it remains in existence for the sake of living well. [C] That is why every city-state exists by nature, since the first communities do. For the city-state is their end, and nature is an end; for we say that each thing's nature—for example, that of a human being, a horse, or a household—is the character it has when its coming-into-being has been completed. [D] Moreover, that for the sake of which something exists, that is to say, its end, is best, and self-sufficiency is both end and best. [E] It is evident from these considerations, then, that a city-state is among the things that exist by nature, that a human being is by nature a political animal, and that anyone who is without a city-state, not by luck but by nature, is either a poor specimen or else superhuman. (1252^b27–1253^a4)

(A) tells us that the city-state, unlike the village, has reached the goal of pretty much total SELF-SUFFICIENCY. What does this mean? It seems fairly clear that enough basic human needs are satisfied outside of the city-state for human life to be possible there: households and villages that are not parts of city-states do manage to persist for considerable periods of time (1252^b22–24, 1261^a27–29); individuals too can survive even in solitude (1253^a31–33, *HA* 487^b33–488^a14). None the less, more of these needs seem to be better satisfied in the city-state than outside it (see 1278^b17–30). For it is always need that holds any community together as a single unit (*NE* 1133^b6–7).

(B) separates what gives rise to the city-state from what sustains it once it exists. Fairly basic human needs do the former, but what sustains a city-state in existence is that we are able to live well and achieve happiness only in it. Thus the city-state is self-sufficient not simply because our essential needs are satisfied there but because it is the community within which we perfect our natures (1253^a31–37).

(D) and (E) are the crucial clauses. (D) tells us that household, village, and city-state are like embryo, child, and mature adult: a single nature is present at each stage but developed or completed to different degrees. Where is that nature to be located? (E) suggests that it lies within the individuals who constitute the household, village, and city-state: they are political animals because their natural needs lead them to form, first, households, then villages, then city-states. "An impulse toward this sort of community," we are told, "exists by nature in everyone" (1253^a29–30).

The common nature of household, village, and city-state lies in their inhabitants, then. But why assume that there is such a nature? Why not assume that there is just the collective natures of the inhabitants and nothing else? Imagine, for a moment, a newborn baby. He is not born into a presocial state of nature of the sort described in Thomas Hobbes's *Leviathan*; he is born into a family. Hence from the very beginning he is leading a sort of communal life. And because he is leading such a life he is acquiring virtue of a sort (household virtue[36]); for it is "in the household we have the first sources and springs of friendship, constitution, and justice" (*EE* 1242ᵃ40–ᵇ1). Since the human function or nature is rational activity expressing virtue, each member of the household will have a nature of a sort that identifies him as a member of a household, that marks him off as such. This justifies us in speaking of a nature that is not simply constituted by the collective natures that individuals living anywhere would have, but of one that is the nature of household dwellers as such. This common nature, located in the inhabitants of the household, is the nature of the household.

The same line of argument applies in the case of the village and the city-state. Each community educates its inhabitants into a type of virtue that suits them to be members of it. As a result, each indexes their natures to itself. The clearest examples of this sort of indexing are provided by the various types of constitutions that city-states can have: a democracy, Aristotle says, should suit its citizens to it by stamping democratic virtues into their souls by means of public education; an oligarchy should do the same with oligarchic virtues; and so on (1310ᵃ12–36, 1337ᵃ10–18). Hence an individual who is a citizen of a democracy has a nature that marks him as such. When he performs his function or realizes his nature by engaging in rational activity expressing virtue, he shows himself to be, as it were, by nature democratic. But, to pick up the point made in (D), this nature should not be thought of as wholly different from that possessed by citizens of other constitutions or by members of a village or household. Rather it is the same nature realized, developed, or perfected to different degrees.

It is worth expanding briefly on the further significance of this conclusion, even though we shall return to it in greater detail in §9. As we saw, the virtues of character determine one's conception of happiness (§5). If one has them in their unqualified form, one's conception of hap-

---

36. Aristotle distinguishes household justice (*to oikonomikon dikaion*) from city-state or political justice at *NE* 1334ᵇ15–18.

piness will be correct, and one will possess practical wisdom in its un-qualified form (*NE* 1144^b30–1145^b2). But it is only in the best constitu-tion that the virtues inculcated in a citizen through public education are unqualifiedly virtues of character (III.4, 1293^b1–7). It follows that in no other constitution will the virtues that suit citizens to the constitution provide them with a correct conception of their happiness or with un-qualified practical wisdom. Starting with the household, then, what we have is a series of types of virtue and types of practical wisdom suited to different types of communities and constituting a single nature that is realized or developed to different degrees in these different communities.

It is for this reason that Aristotle thinks that human beings are by na-ture political animals, not just in the sense that, like bees, they are natu-rally found in communities, but also in the stronger sense that they per-fect their natures specifically in political communities of a certain sort. The function argument has shown that human nature consists in ratio-nal activity, whether practical (political) or theoretical. Hence to perfect their natures human beings must acquire the unqualified virtues of character. But this they do, Aristotle has argued, only in a city-state; more specifically, in a city-state with the best constitution.

The move from household to village or from village to city-state coin-cides, then, with a development in human virtue and practical wisdom. How should we conceive of this development as occurring? If human beings were nonrational animals, the development would itself be one that occurred through the operation of nonrational natural causes. But because human beings have a rational nature, their natural development (which is always communal, as we have seen) essentially involves a devel-opment in their rational capacities; for example, an increase in the level of the practical wisdom they possess. Imagine, then, that the household already exists. Its adult males possess a level of practical wisdom which they bring to bear in solving practical problems. The household is not self-sufficient: it produces a surplus of some needed items, not enough of others. This presents a practical problem which it is an exercise of practical wisdom to solve. And it might be solved, for example, by notic-ing that other nearby households are in the same boat, and that exchang-ing goods with them would improve life for everyone involved. But ex-change eventually leads to the need for money and with it to the need for new communal roles (that of merchant, for example), new forms of communal control (laws governing commerce), new virtues of character (such as generosity and magnificence which pertain to wealth), and new opportunities for the exercise of (a further developed) practical wisdom.[37] It is by engaging in this bootstrapping process that practical wisdom both causes new forms of communal life to emerge and causes itself to develop from the vestigial forms of it found in the household to the unqualified form of it found in Aristotle's best constitution.

The appearance of the city-state at a stage in this process can now quite naturally be thought of as an exercise of practical wisdom or statesmanship, as the result (say) of a legislator having crafted a constitution for a collection of suitably situated villages which, when appropriately realized by them and their members, will be a city-state, a self-sufficient political community.[38] Notice that Aristotle himself often characterizes the city-state as something crafted by legislators, and often likens statesmanship to a craft.[39] If things possessing a canonical nature had to perfect their natures by nature, this sort of talk would be disturbing, since it would conflict with the characterization of the city-state as existing by nature. But, as we have seen, many canonical natures, including our own, need to be perfected by craft. That the city-state's nature is among them is not only no threat to its being a canonical nature, therefore, but it is just what we would expect given the close ties between our natures and its nature.

The nature of a city-state, understood in the way we have been discussing, is manifestly internal to it. It thus has one of the defining marks of a canonical nature. But does it have the others? Is it a "source of change and staying unchanged whether in respect of place, or growth and decay, or alteration"? A city-state is a hylomorphic compound, a compound of matter and form: its form is its constitution; its inhabitants are its matter (*Pol.* 1276^{b}1–13). Since, as we saw in §4, a thing's

---

37. This account is modeled on the one Aristotle tells at 1257^{a}14–^{b}8.
38. That the legislator in question may not have been brought up in the community for which he is developing a constitution should not blind us to the fact that the practical wisdom he exercises in developing that constitution is itself a communal achievement—an achievement internal to community.
39. See *Pol.* 1253^{a}30–31, 1268^{b}34–38, 1273^{b}32–33, 1274^{b}18–19, 1282^{b}14–16, 1325^{b}40–1326^{a}5. It is important to be clear, however, that the fact that Aristotle speaks of statesmanship (practical wisdom) as crafting (*dēmiourgein*) a city-state or its constitution does not mean that either is a product of craft, like a table, or that statesmanship (practical wisdom) is itself a craft. After all, Aristotle speaks of nature as crafting animals and other things (*PA* 645^{a}7–10, *GA* 731^{a}24), and analogizes nature to a craft (*GA* 730^{b}27–32, 743^{b}20–25, 789^{b}8–12). But nature is not a craft nor are its products craft products. Statesmanship (practical wisdom) is in fact not a craft, but a virtue of thought (*NE* VI.4–8).

form has a better claim to being called its nature than does its matter, what we are really asking is whether Aristotle thinks that a city-state's constitution is a source of its stability and change in the way that a canonical nature is. And surely he does. A city-state can change its matter (population) over time, but cannot sustain change from one kind of constitution to another (1276^a34-^b1), or dissolution of its constitution altogether (1272^b14-15). Thus its identity over time is determined by its constitution. A population constitutes a single city-state if it shares a single constitution (1276^a24-26). Thus its synchronic unity, its identity at a time, is also determined by its constitution. A city-state can grow or shrink in size, but its constitution sets limits to how big or small it can be (VII.4–5). What causes it to decay or to survive is also determined by the type of constitution it has (Book V discusses these constitution-specific causes in considerable detail). Thus a city-state's constitution is indeed a canonical nature, an inner source of stability and change, and the city-state meets all of Aristotle's conditions for existing by nature. It is no surprise, therefore, to find Aristotle claiming that the various kinds of constitutions, the various kinds of natures that city-states possess, are to be defined in the same way as the different natures possessed by animals belonging to different species (1290^b25-39).

So far we have been discussing the individual human beings in a city-state. But the very same process of nature indexing that occurs in them as they become parts of a city-state also occurs in the various subcommunities that make up that city-state. Consider the village, for example. When it is not yet part of a city-state, a village is a kingship. But when it becomes part of a democratic city-state (say), though it may perhaps have a village elder of some sort, it is no longer a kingship plain and simple. For in a democracy authority is in the hands of all the free male citizens. Hence though the village elder may exercise kingly rule over village affairs, he must do so in a way that fits in with the democratic constitution of which his village is a part. And in that constitution he is under the authority of others as a real king is not. The same is true of the household. Various types of rule are present in the household, as we saw, but these are transformed when the household becomes part of a city-state. For the sort of virtue that a head of household possesses and the sort he tries to develop or encourage in its other members must themselves be suited to the larger constitution of which his household is a part (*Pol.* I.12–13). Thus households and villages that are parts of a city-state have natures that are transformed by being indexed to the constitution of that city-state. It is this that makes them into genuine parts of it.

With the details of Aristotle's argument before us, we are in a position to assess its merits. We have seen that Aristotle's precise characterization of the emergence of the city-state is not very compelling: his conceptions of the household and the village are far too contentious to be credible. None the less, he is surely right in thinking that we are (in some sense or other) social animals from the very beginning of our lives, and that more sophisticated forms of communal life emerge from more primitive ones through some sort of rational bootstrapping. We might agree with Aristotle in principle, therefore, while wanting to haggle over the details. But, details aside, has Aristotle really shown that we are indeed *political* animals, that we do perfect our natures in a specifically political community, in a city-state?

To answer this question we need to explore Aristotle's views on political communities or city-states in a little more detail. In *Politics* I, Aristotle characterizes the city-state in rather abstract ways: the city-state is the community with the most authority; it is the most self-sufficient community, one that is ruled in its own characteristic way, different from that in which a master rules his slaves or a head of household rules his wife and children. When he puts meat on these abstract bones, however, we see that an Aristotelian city-state is quite like a modern state in these important respects: it establishes the constitution, designs and enacts the laws, sets foreign and domestic policy, controls the armed forces and police, declares war, enforces the law, and punishes criminals (for example, 1328^b2-23). Our question can then be reformulated as follows: has Aristotle shown that human beings can only perfect their natures in a political community that is in these ways like a state? Or in any other community just in case it is a part of such a community?

Many people believe that leading the good life involves practicing a religion and living according to its dictates as a member of a religious community or church. But there are many different religions with different such dictates, many different religious communities. If the city-state enforced any one religion or exerted more than fairly minimal authority within the religions it allowed, it would have to prevent many of its citizens from leading the good life as they understand it. To ensure that this does not happen the city-state must be largely neutral on matters of religion, church and city-state must be separate, and the good life must be lived somewhat outside the purview of the city-state, in religious communities largely protected from city-state intrusion. People who conceive of the good life in this way, therefore, will not accept Aristotle's argument. They will, perhaps, see the need for a city-state, but they will reject the idea that we perfect our natures or achieve our good only as members of it: it is as members of nonpolitical communities that we do that.

Many people also believe that leading the good life involves following the cultural traditions and speaking the language of their own culture or ethnic group. Aristotle would agree with them, but this is very largely because he assumes that city-states (or at least their citizens) will be ethnically, nationally, and even religiously homogeneous (1127^b22-36, 1328^b11-13): he is no cosmopolitan. Modern states by contrast are increasingly multicultural and polyethnic. If they are to respect the rights of their citizens, and allow them (within limits) to pursue their own conceptions of the good, they need to be supportive of cultural and ethnic diversity. They should not use their coercive powers to promote one culture or one ethnicity at the expense of others. Again, this means that most people will achieve the good or perfect their natures as members of different ethnic communities, and not as members of city-states as such.

Religion, nationality, and ethnicity aside, it is perhaps more natural for us to think of public political life as being like work, something we engage in in order to "be ourselves" in our private lives and leisure time. We are most ourselves, we think, not in any public sphere, but in the private one. Politics, like work, is necessary, but it is valuable primarily for what it makes possible, not in itself.

These styles of objection can of course be generalized. Many people, including probably most of us, believe that, at least as things stand, there are many different, equally defensible conceptions of the human good and the good life. We want to make room in the city-state for many of these conceptions. We want to be left free to undertake what John Stuart Mill calls "experiments in living" in order to discover new conceptions. Consequently, we do not want the city-state to enforce any one conception of the good life but to be largely neutral. We want it to allow different individuals and different communities (religious, ethnic, national) to pursue their own conceptions of the good, provided that they do so in ways that allow other individuals and communities to do the same. If we hold views of this sort, we will not agree with Aristotle that we perfect our natures or achieve our good as members of the city-state. We will claim instead that we do so as members of communities that share our conception of the good, but that lack the various powers, most particularly the coercive powers, definitive of the city-state.

Needless to say, it might be responded on Aristotle's behalf that this criticism of his argument for the naturalness of the city-state simply ignores the function argument, since it implicitly denies (or at least seriously doubts) that the human good just does consist in practical activity or in theorizing. This is a reasonable response so far as it goes. But, as we saw in §4, the function argument is compelling only to the degree that it is underwritten by the facts of ethical and political experience. And what is surely true is that those facts no longer underwrite it completely. What experience has taught *us* is that there are many different human goods, many different good lives, many different ways to perfect ourselves, and much need for further experimentation and discovery in these areas. That is one reason we admire somewhat liberal states which recognize this fact and give their citizens a lot of liberty to explore various conceptions of the good and to live in the way that they find most valuable and worthwhile.[40]

§8 Rulers and Subjects

A human being is by nature a political animal, but there is more than one way for him to encounter the political: he can do so either as a ruler or as a subject. Moreover, just how he *should* encounter it is determined by his nature, and by the natures of the other people in his city-state.

Though all human beings share a nature, they also differ from one another by nature: men are naturally different from women, adults from children, naturally free people from natural slaves. Some of these natural differences, such as differences in physical strength, are ethically and politically inert (1282^{b}23–1283^{a}14). But others, because they are differences in the very properties that Aristotle's perfectionism sees as constitutive of human nature, are not like that; they do have ethical and political significance. Women's souls have a deliberative element but it lacks authority; those of free children have a deliberative element but it is immature; those of natural slaves have no deliberative element at all. Hence none of these people can have unqualified practical wisdom or

---

40. Recent discussions of the topics in this section include D. Keyt, "Three Basic Theorems in Aristotle's *Politics*," W. Kullmann, "Man as a Political Animal in Aristotle," and F. D. Miller, *Nature, Justice, and Rights in Aristotle's Politics*, 3–66. Some recent works on the natural origins of human communities and virtues include J. H. Barkow, L. Cosmides, and J. Tooby (eds.), *The Adapted Mind: Evolutionary Psychology and the Generation of Culture* (New York: Oxford University Press, 1992); M. Ridley, *The Origins of Virtue: Human Instincts and the Evolution of Cooperation* (New York: Viking, 1997); R. Wright, *The Moral Animal* (New York: Vintage, 1994).

ethical virtue (1260ᵃ9–ᵇ20). And because they cannot, Aristotle thinks that they should properly encounter the political only as subjects (1254ᵇ13–14 with 1277ᵇ25–30). In the case of women and slaves, this is their permanent status; in the case of the male children of free people, it is theirs until they are mature adults.

But even adult males, such as the citizens of Aristotle's best constitution, who possess unqualified practical wisdom and virtue, and who may encounter the political as rulers, are not guaranteed always to encounter it in this fashion. If someone of outstanding practical wisdom emerges in their community, they are obliged to become his subjects and accept him as their king (1284ᵇ25–34). Thus a man's status as a ruler, unless he happens to have a degree of unqualified practical wisdom and virtue that is unsurpassable, is a fragile or vulnerable one; it is not absolute.

A person encounters the political as a ruler or a subject, but he also encounters it as a ruler *of a certain kind* or as a subject *of a certain kind*. And here too the determining factors are his own degree of practical wisdom or virtue and that of others. Lacking a deliberative element, natural slaves are properly ruled with a master's rule (which is nonconsultative and only incidentally in the slave's best interests). Possessed of an immature deliberative element, free children are properly ruled with kingly rule (which is nonconsultative but in the subject's best interests). Possessed of a mature deliberative element that lacks authority, free women are properly ruled with something close to political rule (which is consultative and in their best interests). Possessed of a mature and authoritative deliberative element that is none the less imperfect, free adult males should sometimes rule their fellow citizens with political rule and sometimes be ruled by them, turn and turn about. But where some other male has superior practical wisdom and virtue, they should be permanently ruled by him with kingly rule. In other words, they should be as children to their superior in virtue and wisdom.

Aristotle thinks, then, that whether one encounters the political as a ruler or as a subject, as a ruler of a certain sort or as a subject of a certain sort, should depend in part on one's own degree of practical wisdom and virtue and in part on the degree of practical wisdom and virtue possessed by others. This is a normative ethical or political doctrine. But he also thinks that people do naturally differ in their degree of practical wisdom and virtue in the ways we have just described. This is a factual claim, subject to empirical refutation, a fate that some parts of it have actually suffered; for what sensible person now believes in the subordination of women to men or in natural slaves? But even if the factual claim were entirely true, it is not clear that it would support the normative ethical and political doctrines Aristotle rests on it.

Why should our status as rulers or subjects depend on the degree of our practical wisdom or virtue? Aristotle does not directly confront this question. And one reason he doesn't is that, like Plato before him, he sees the city-state as analogous to the individual soul. In *Politics* I.5, for example, he argues as follows: it is best for the body and desire to be ruled by the part of the soul that has reason, that is to say, by practical wisdom acting as the steward of understanding or theoretical reason (§6); the city-state is analogous to the soul; hence it is best for those with unqualified practical wisdom to rule those without it, whether they are women, natural slaves, or wild animals (1254^{b}6–20).

The psychological side of this analogy is relatively uncontroversial: given Aristotle's characterization of practical wisdom as alone possessing knowledge of the human good and of how best to achieve it, it surely *is* best that practical wisdom should have authority over or rule the other parts of the soul, since that maximizes the chances that the whole soul and body, the whole person, will achieve what is best. But the political side of the analogy is vastly more problematic.

We think that individual freedom or autonomy is a very important political value. We think not only that individuals want to achieve what is in fact best, but that they want to be free to evaluate for themselves what is best for them, and to act on their own judgment about it. They want to own their lives and choose their goals and projects for themselves, even if this means that they sometimes make mistakes and regret their choices. We are suspicious of paternalism, especially when it is exercised by the state, and balk at the idea of having others determine what we should do with our lives, even when they might be better qualified to make such determinations than we are. Because autonomy does not reach down below the individual, there is no comparable worry about the parts of the soul. Autonomy is a personal, not a subpersonal, value. Thus in making use of the analogy between the soul and the city-state as a device for justifying rule in the latter, Aristotle conceals from himself what is for us a fundamental political problem.[41]

41. Another aspect of this problem is worth mentioning. It is harmless to claim that practical wisdom should govern our economic activities. But it is very controversial to claim, as Aristotle does (1321^{b}12–18), that politics or the city-state should regulate economic activities. Defenders of a free market would object to the latter, not the former.

It might be replied in Aristotle's defense that he believes that those capable of autonomy should be given it. It's just that he thinks that the only truly free, the only genuinely autonomous people, the only ones who are better off ruling themselves than being ruled by others, are those who possess unqualified practical wisdom, since they alone are capable both of knowing their own good and of best achieving it. This is an initially attractive defense, but it fails to be wholly compelling for an interesting reason. We think that autonomy is intrinsic to a person. We think that our status as autonomous beings depends on our intrinsic features, not on those of other people. But Aristotle does not think analogous thoughts about practical wisdom. For, as we saw, he thinks that even people who have unqualified practical wisdom of a very high degree can lose their status as rulers (as autonomous beings) if someone with a much higher degree of practical wisdom appears in their community. It is clear, therefore, that one's own degree of practical wisdom is not for Aristotle a measure of one's degree of autonomy. One can have more than enough practical wisdom to be autonomous, and still be under the authority of others, when the others possess a higher degree of practical wisdom than one's own.[42]

Because we think that autonomy is very important, we also think that there is a deep problem of political legitimacy, a problem for the state in justifying whatever degree of authority it claims to exercise over the lives and actions of its citizens. The larger the impact this authority has on autonomy, the more difficult the problem becomes. To see how difficult it is for Aristotle, therefore, we need to look at how much impact the kind of authority he advocates has on the autonomy of the citizens subject to it.

Aristotle claims that a constitution should provide public education from early childhood that gives its future citizens the sort of character, the sorts of virtues, that will suit them to be *its* citizens in particular: a democracy should stamp democratic virtues into its citizens' souls; an oligarchy, oligarchic ones; and so on (1310^a12-36, 1337^a10-18). These different types of virtue are quite different, as we see from the discussion of oligarchic and democratic conceptions of justice in III.9. Since

---

42. Notice that this would be a very surprising result if the exercise of statesmanship in ruling others were the human good (happiness) or the most important component of it. For Aristotle thinks that the reason A should rule B is that B is better off or happier being ruled by A than by ruling himself. But B could not be better off being ruled by anyone, if in fact ruling were happiness or its most important component.

the virtues determine a person's conception of happiness or the human good (§§5, 7, 9), it follows that Aristotelian constitutions, through their control of education, largely determine their citizens' conceptions of the good. Hence the impact of such constitutions on autonomy is substantial. For discovering or deciding for oneself what one's good is, what one's goals in life are to be, is surely one of the most important exercises in autonomy.

Aristotle has a substantial problem of political legitimacy, then. Yet, as in the case of the problem of autonomy itself, he largely ignores it. To some degree, this is once again because he accepts the analogy between the city-state and the soul we discussed earlier: we positively and unproblematically want practical wisdom to exercise goal-determining authority within the soul of an individual, since that guarantees his happiness; so we want those who possess practical wisdom to exercise goal-determining authority in the city-state, since that will guarantee its happiness. But to the degree that this analogy provides any solution to the problem of political legitimacy at all, it seems to do so only for constitutions whose rulers do indeed have genuine practical wisdom. In Aristotle's ideal constitution, for example, men possessed of unqualified practical wisdom rule one another by turns. Since they know what human happiness really is, and how best to achieve it, they are able to design a system of public education that will pass on their knowledge to future citizens by inculcating the unqualified virtues of character in them. Since it is arguably in everyone's best interests to have those virtues and the true conception of happiness they guarantee, the goal-determining authority exercised by the rulers in the ideal constitution is arguably in the best interests of the citizens. In democratic or oligarchic constitutions, however, it is a very different story, for the virtues inculcated in citizens to suit them to those constitutions do not coincide with the unqualified virtues of character, and so do not ensure the correct conception of happiness (§9). Since it does not seem to be in anyone's best interests to have such virtues, it does not seem to be in anyone's best interests to consent to the kind of goal-determining rule found in such nonideal constitutions.

Aristotle does not respond directly to this criticism, but one can to some extent see how he would respond. He thinks that people are better off living in a stable constitution of some kind. He thinks that an education that suits the constitution is the best safeguard of stability (1310^a14–18). It is a small step to his confident conclusion that "living in a way that suits the constitution should not be considered slavery but salvation" (1310ª34–36). The problem with this defense is that it seems to confuse stability with rigidity. A rigid, nonideal constitution resists all change, even change for the better, and educates its citizens accordingly. A stable but nonrigid, nonideal constitution, on the other hand, will be supply adaptive; it will allow for its own peaceful and orderly transformation into a constitution that better serves its citizen's interests; and it will educate its citizens to be the engines of such transformation; for example, by arming them with the means of discovering newer and more adequate conceptions of happiness. Plainly, one would be better off living in such a constitution than in a rigid nonideal one. Hence a stable, because rigid, nonideal constitution cannot justify its goal-determining authority over its citizens by arguing that such authority serves their best interests.

If the analogy between city-state and soul justifies goal-determining rule in any constitution, it would have to justify it in the best constitution. But we might well wonder whether this is true. After all, Aristotle's ideal constitution is committed to allowing for its own transformation into an absolute kingship (1284ᵇ25–34). But given the importance of autonomy, it is not clear that it is in one's best interests to live in a community that allows one's autonomy to be vulnerable to that sort of threat. Surely a community that provided greater safeguards for autonomy would be a better option.

Autonomy is an important value, but on Aristotle's perfectionist view it is not the most important one; happiness in the shape of practical political activity or theoretical activity takes that prize. That is the perfectionist message of the function argument (§4). It is not perfectionism *per se* that threatens autonomy, however, but Aristotle's rather narrow brand of it. If our natures could be perfected in many different, even if related ways, as surely they can, or if the exercise of autonomy were itself a perfection, as arguably it is, there would be room for an individual to exercise autonomy in choosing which way in particular to perfect his nature, and a perfectionistically justified constitution would have to safeguard his capacity to make that choice and his capacity to live in the light of it.

The best safeguard might, as liberal theorists of the state argue, be a steadfast neutrality that allows individuals to work out their own life plans unimpeded but also largely unaided by the state.[43] But it is also possible, and perhaps more plausible, that the state might need actively

---

43. G. Sher, *Beyond Neutrality* (Cambridge: Cambridge University Press, 1997), critically reviews liberal arguments.

to safeguard the capacity for autonomy by, among other things, providing the kind of public education, and fostering the kind of public debate, that promotes it, and by preparing its citizens precisely to be citizens who themselves promote and safeguard autonomy.

§9 Constitutions

Human beings encounter the political either as rulers or as subjects. That is one sort of political diversity. But there is another: the diversity exhibited by constitutions themselves. Hence just what a ruler or subject encounters in encountering the political also depends on the type of constitution he encounters it in. Our task in the present section is to understand these different constitutions, and Aristotle's characterization of them as either correct or deviant.

The traditional Greek view is that a constitution can be controlled by "the one, the few, or the many" (1279^a26-28): it can be either a monarchy, an oligarchy, or a democracy. Aristotle accepts this view to some extent, but introduces some important innovations. First, he argues that differences in wealth are of greater theoretical importance than difference in numbers. Oligarchy is really control by the wealthy; democracy is really control by the poor. It just so happens that the wealthy are always few in number, while the poor are always many ($1279^b20-1280^a6$, 1290^b17-20). This allows him to see the importance of the middle classes, those who are neither very rich nor very poor but somewhere in between (1295^b1-3), and to recognize the theoretical significance of a constitution, a so-called POLITY, in which they play a decisive part (1293^a40-^b1). Second, Aristotle departs from tradition in thinking that each of these three traditional types of rule actually comes in two major varieties, one of which is correct and the other deviant (1289^b5-11). Rule by "the one" is either a kingship (correct) or a tyranny (deviant); rule by "the few" is either an aristocracy (correct) or an oligarchy (deviant); rule by "the many" is either a polity (correct) or a democracy (deviant).

One important difference between these constitutions is that they have different aims or goals (1289^a17-28), different conceptions of happiness: "it is by seeking happiness in different ways and by different means that individual groups of people create different ways of life and different constitutions" (1328^a41-^b2).[44] The goal of the ideal constitu-

---

44. Compare *NE* $1095^a17-1096^a10$: people agree that the human good is called happiness, but they disagree about what happiness actually is or consists in.

tion, whether it is a kingship or an aristocracy (1289ª30–32), is unqualified or blessed happiness (1324ª23–25), which is "a complete activation or use of virtue" (1332ª9–10). The goal of a polity is a more modest level of that same sort of happiness, a level that most people and most city-states can hope to attain (1295ª25–40). The goal of oligarchy is multiply characterized: sometimes as wealth or property (1280ª25–28), sometimes as life as opposed to living well (1280ª31–32). But these accounts are related: people pursue wealth or property because they value life, not living well (1257ᵇ40–1258ª14). Similarly, the goal of democracy is also multiply characterized: sometimes as freedom (1310ª29, 1317ª40–41), sometimes as physical gratification (1258ª3–4, *NE* 1095ᵇ14–17); and sometimes it too is said to be life as opposed to living well (1280ª31–32). Here the relationship between the accounts is a little more difficult to see. But perhaps what Aristotle has in mind is this: to value life is to value the freedom to satisfy those physical appetites that must be satisfied if life is to be sustained.

A second important difference between these constitutions, a consequence of the first, is that they have different conceptions of justice (III.9). All of them agree that justice consists in awarding political goods (such as unqualified citizenship, participation in office, or authority over the constitution) on the basis of one's contribution to achieving the goal of the constitution. They all agree that justice is based on merit. But because they disagree about what the goal of a constitution should be, they disagree about what this basis is. Oligarchs think it is wealth. So they think that the wealthiest should have authority over the constitution, and that participation in office should be subject to a property assessment. Democrats think that the basis is freedom: all free citizens bring an equal share into the constitution, so all should get an equal share out, and all should participate equally in office and its prerogatives. Aristocrats, in the ideal constitution, on the other hand, think that the goal is neither wealth nor freedom, but noble or virtuous living. Hence they think that it is just for participation in the constitution to be based on virtue (1283ª24–26).

A third important difference is a consequence of the first two. Because different constitutions embody different conceptions of happiness, they must also embody different conceptions of the virtues. For, as we saw in §4, a genuine virtue is by definition something which guarantees that a thing will achieve its end. Hence if the conception of the end differs, so must the conceptions of the virtues that promote it. By the same token, justice is complete virtue in relation to another (*NE*

1129^{b}25–27). Hence if different constitutions have different conceptions of justice, then, for that reason too, they must have different conceptions of the other virtues that together make up complete virtue (1309^{a}36–39). To be sure, this difference isn't as systematically "thematized" in the *Politics* as are the other two, but it is there all the same, and it is just as important as they are. Thus Aristotle argues that virtues and the education that inculcates them must suit the constitution (1260^{b}8–20, 1337^{a}11–21), and criticizes oligarchic virtue for being based on a misconception of happiness (1271^{a}41–^{b}10, 1333^{b}5–1334^{a}10).

Aristotle distinguishes, however, between what the rulers in a constitution typically think the virtues suited to their constitutions are and what these virtues actually are (1309^{b}20–35, 1310^{a}12–36). The virtues truly suited to a constitution are those that will enable it to survive for a long time (1310^{a}19–22, 1320^{a}2–4), not those that represent the tendency of the constitution at its most extreme. These invariably make the constitution more moderate, more inclusive, and aimed more at the common benefit than exclusively at that of the rulers themselves. But the goal of these more moderate constitutions, the conceptions of happiness they embody, are still different. Thus even the virtues that really do promote the stable, long-term realization of those goals are distinct from one another. The justice that is truly suited to an oligarchy, for example, still distributes political office and benefit on the basis of wealth; though now it is careful to ensure that as a result of the distribution "the multitude of those who want the constitution is stronger than the multitude of those who do not" (1309^{b}17–18).

Of these different conceptions of happiness, justice, and virtue generally, only one is correct: the one that accords with nature, with the conclusion of the function argument. This is the conception embodied in a kingship or aristocracy (and, though to a lesser extent, in a polity). Only in these constitutions do the virtues of a good man coincide with the virtues of a good citizen (1288^{a}37–39, 1293^{b}5–6). None the less, the conceptions embodied in the other constitutions, though deviant, are not simply wrong; they are true to an extent (*NE* 1134^{a}24–30). For example, both democrats and oligarchs "grasp justice of a sort, but they only go to a certain point and do not discuss the whole of what is just in the most authoritative sense" (1280^{a}9–11). The same could no doubt be said about their conceptions of happiness and the other virtues (*NE* I.5).

A final difference between the constitutions is, as we have seen, that some of them are correct, while others are deviations from the correct ones. Aristotle explains this difference as follows: correct constitutions aim at "the common benefit"; deviant ones at the benefit of the rulers (1279^{a}26–31). His explanation is not very helpful, however, because he doesn't specify the group, G, whose benefit is the common one, and he doesn't tell us whether the common benefit is that of the individual members of G, or that of G taken as some kind of whole. When we try to provide the missing information, moreover, we run into difficulties.

A natural first thought about G, for example, is that it is the group of unqualified citizens, those who participate in judicial and deliberative office (III.1–2, 5). But if G is restricted to these citizens, the common benefit and the private one coincide, since only the rulers participate in these offices. Moreover, even the deviant constitutions aim at the benefit of a wider group than that of the unqualified citizens, since they also seem to aim at the benefit of the wives and children of such citizens (1260^{b}8–20 with 1310^{a}34–36).

Perhaps, then, G consists of all the free native inhabitants of the constitution. No, that won't do either, because now even some correct constitutions, such as a polity, will count as deviant. For the common benefit in a correct constitution is a matter of having a share in noble or virtuous living (1278^{b}20–23, *NE* 1142^{b}31–33). Hence a polity will not aim at the benefit of its native-born artisans, tradesmen, or laborers, since there is "no element of virtue" in these occupations (1319^{a}26–28).

These common characterizations of G all fail, but the last failure points in a promising direction. Let us begin with the class, N, of the free native inhabitants of the constitution. There are two ways to construct the class of unqualified citizens from N. The first is to do so on the basis of the type of justice internal to the constitution; the second is to do so on the basis of unqualified justice. If we proceed in the first way, and the constitution is an oligarchy, for example, the unqualified citizens will be the wealthy male members of N. But if we proceed in the second way, the unqualified citizens of our oligarchy will be those who have an unqualifiedly just claim to that status. And Aristotle thinks that the virtuous, the rich, and the poor all have such a claim, one that is proportional to their virtue (1283^{a}14–26, 1280^{b}40–1281^{a}8, 1294^{a}19–20). Thus they ought to be unqualified citizens of any constitution. In fact, however, they are so only in correct constitutions, not in deviant ones.

What I suggest, then, is that we construct G as follows: all the members of N, who have an unqualifiedly just claim to be unqualified citizens of the constitution, are members of G; all the wives and children of members of G are members of G; no one else is a member of G. If a constitution aims at the benefit of G, it aims at the common benefit and is correct; if it aims at the benefit of the subset of G consisting of the rulers who have authority over the constitution (and their families), it is deviant. This is what Aristotle has in mind when he writes: "the political good is justice,[45] and justice is the common benefit" ($1282^b16–18$).

A correct constitution *aims* only at the benefit of G, but Aristotle probably thinks that it will be incidentally beneficial to all its subjects, whether they are members of G or not. In any case, he certainly thinks that it is (incidentally) beneficial for household slaves to be ruled by virtuous masters (1252^a34, $1278^b32–37$).[46] Presumably, then, he ought to think the same things about the public slaves or non-Greek serfs who do all the work in his ideal constitution.

Aristotle assumes that G, as a matter of unqualified justice, ought to be constructed from N, that the group to be benefited by a constitution ought to be restricted to native inhabitants of it. This sort of assumption is broadly shared, but is it really justified? If one's level of virtue qualifies one to be a citizen of the ideal constitution, for example, why should the fact that one has been born outside its borders (or born to people born outside its borders) always preclude one from being its citizen? Why, in other words, should nationality be relevant to citizenship ethically conceived? (Imagine if Kant had argued that one could not be a member of the kingdom of ends unless one had been born in Prussia.)

So much for the membership of G. We turn now to the second problem I mentioned. Is the common benefit that of each of the members of G? or is it that of G taken as some kind of whole? Is the common benefit to be understood individualistically or holistically? Some views espoused in the *Politics* suggest that Aristotle had fairly significant holistic or organicist leanings. His argument in I.2 that individuals are parts of city-states in the way that hands are parts of individuals ($1253^a18–29$), for example, suggests that it might be as uncontroversial (or almost as uncontroversial) to sacrifice an individual for the good of the city-state as it would be to sacrifice a hand for the good of the individual whose hand it is. His views on the use of ostracism seem to show him endorsing precisely such a sacrifice. It surely isn't beneficial to the superior person to be ostracized from his city-state, yet even correct constitutions may ostracize him, Aristotle argues, when doing so serves the common benefit ($1284^b4–20$). True enough, the ideal constitution and other

45. $1279^a17–19$ makes it clear that unqualified justice is meant.
46. The advantage of slaves is not a matter of their sharing in genuine happiness, however, since they are incapable of that ($1280^a30–34$).

well-constructed, correct constitutions will not need such a remedy, because of the foresight of their legislators. But the point remains that correctness in a constitution is no guarantee that the benefit of each individual in G will be safeguarded there. Even in such constitutions, moreover, ostracism seems not to be needed only because the legislator has ensured that no superior person will emerge in the constitution (1302^b19-21), not because he has recognized that no individual, however superior, should have his benefit justly sacrificed to the common benefit.

Aristotle also uses the doctrine that individuals are parts of the city-state to justify fairly massive intrusion of the political into what we would consider to be the private sphere. "One should not consider," he writes, "that any citizen belongs to himself alone, but that each of them belongs to the city-state, since he is a part of it. And it is natural for the supervision of each part to look to the supervision of the whole" (1337^a27-30).[47] Hence the ideal constitution should have laws that regulate or constrain the freedom of association of many of its inhabitants (1327^a37-40), their freedom to marry, reproduce, and rear their offspring ($1335^a4-{}^b19$, 1335^b22-25), their freedom to have extramarital affairs (1336^a1-2), their religious freedom (1330^a8-9), their freedom of expression and artistic freedom (1336^b3-23), and even their freedom to dine as they choose (1330^a3-8). These views sound a good deal worse than just holistic.

Many other texts in the *Politics* suggest, however, that Aristotle means to be espousing some sort of individualism. The following is a small sample: "it is impossible for the whole to be happy unless some, most, or all of its parts are happy" (1264^b17-19); "even when they do not need one another's help, they no less desire to live together. Although it is also true that the common benefit brings them together, to the extent that it contributes some share of living well to each" (1278^b20-23); aristocrats "rule with a view to what is best for the city-state and those who share in it" (1279^a35-37); "it is evident that the best constitution must be the organization in which anyone might do best and live a blessedly happy life" (1324^a23-25); "the best life, whether for a whole city-state collectively or for an individual, would be a life of action" (1325^b15-16); "a city-state is excellent because the citizens who participate in the constitution are excellent. And in our city-state all the citizens participate in the constitution." (1332^a32-35). These texts show that Aristotle is an

---

47. In I.13, a similar claim is made about virtue: "the virtue of a part must be determined by looking to the virtue of the whole" (1260^b14-16).

individualist in at least this important sense: he believes that the ideal constitution, and the very intrusive laws that are part of it, promote the virtue and so the happiness of the individuals in G.

The question is how can he believe this and also treat ostracism in the way he does? How is his apparent holism to be combined with his apparent individualism? Aristotle's treatment of ostracism makes it clear that he thinks that a just constitution may require members of G to do things that do not promote their individual benefit. At the same time, he thinks that such a constitution must promote the benefit of the individual members of G. These views are compatible provided that promoting the benefit of the individual members of G need be no more than *generally congruent* with their actually being benefited. Thus, for example, a correct constitution that has no need of ostracism is better, Aristotle thinks, than one that does need it, presumably because the former constitution better promotes the benefit of each of the individuals in G than the latter. At the same time, if an individual in G actually threatens the stability of the correct constitution, and the justice it embodies, the constitution may have to sacrifice his benefit to that of the other members of G. What it does, in other words, is to sacrifice the benefit of an individual in G in a case in which failing to do so would risk destroying a constitution that promotes the benefit of each of the other members of G. In these circumstances, that is the closest the constitution can come to preserving the congruence I mentioned. In times of war or scarcity, this congruence is likely to be quite hard to preserve; in times of peace and plenty, much easier. But the general point remains: no constitution short of an omnipotent and omniscient one can absolutely guarantee that this congruence will always be absolute.

Aristotle is not an extreme individualist, then, who thinks that the happiness of the city-state simply consists in the happiness of each of the individual members of G, so that to achieve the happiness of the former is necessarily to achieve the happiness of the latter. By the same token, he is not an extreme holist who thinks of the happiness of the whole of G as something distinct from the happiness of each of the individuals in it, so that it is possible to achieve the happiness of the former without achieving the happiness of the latter. What he is is a moderate individualist, someone who thinks that the happiness of a city-state must be generally congruent with the happiness of the individual members of its G class. But whether we should call this position moderate individualism (as I have opted to do) or moderate holism is perhaps more a matter of taste than of substance.

The fact that there need be no more than this sort of general congruence between a city-state's happiness and the happiness of the individuals in its G class also explains why Aristotle's doctrine that individuals are parts of a city-state is no threat to his moderate individualism. A hand can perform its task only as part of a body; there is general congruence between the health of a body and the health of all its parts; but in some circumstances, the closest we can come to preserving this congruence involves sacrificing a part. In this respect, Aristotle thinks, we are like hands. One will find this insufficiently reassuring only if one thinks that general congruence between the aim of a just city-state and that of an individual in G is not enough, that more is required, that congruence must be guaranteed in all circumstances. Aristotle certainly fails to provide such reassurance, but this is almost certainly a strength rather than a weakness of his view.

Properly or at least plausibly interpreted, then, Aristotle's treatment of ostracism and his view that individuals are parts of city-states seem to be compatible with the sort of moderate individualism he espouses.[48]

§10 The Ideal Constitution

Aristotle believes that the ideal constitution aims at the individual benefit of each of the members of G, then, because it aims to promote the virtue and happiness of each. At the same time, he believes that the ideal constitution is unqualifiedly just, because it distributes political offices and other political or social benefits on the basis of virtue. He believes, in other words, that his ideal constitution succeeds where others fail: it is more unqualifiedly just than they are and happier than they are. Is he right to believe this?

Aristotle divides the original adult inhabitants of the ideal constitution into two groups: the citizens (who are equally virtuous men of practical wisdom) and their wives, on the one hand, and the noncitizens, who are either natural slaves or non-Greek serfs (1329ª25–26), on the other. We may suppose, for the sake of argument, that this division is made justly. But he then seems simply to assume that it is just to treat the children of citizens and noncitizens in the same way as their respective parents. Thus, for example, he believes that it is just to distribute

---

48. Some of the topics in this section are further discussed in J. Barnes, "Aristotle on Political Liberty," and F. D. Miller, *Nature, Justice and Rights in Aristotle's Politics*, 143–308.

public education to the children of citizens and not to those of the noncitizens. But this seems arbitrary and unjust: one's life chances should not depend so crucially on the accident of one's birth. Indeed, it is arbitrary and unjust even in Aristotle's own terms, because it cannot be based on virtue. For virtue is not something that young children actually possess.

What may have caused Aristotle not to notice this defect in his conception of the best city-state is probably this. He believes that free people, natural slaves, and non-Greek serfs form natural classes (or natural kinds), and that natural classes breed true to type (1254^{b}27–34, 1255^{b}1–4, 1283^{a}36, 1327^{b}19–38). Hence he believes that the children of the free citizens will have the natural potential for virtue, while those of noncitizens will lack it. Hence he believes that to distribute political benefits on the basis of membership of a natural class is as uncontroversially just as distributing it on the basis of already developed virtue. The weakness is this line of thought, however, as Aristotle himself usually recognizes, is that these natural laws or regularities are far from being exceptionless: natural classes for the most part breed true to type, but there are exceptions (1254^{b}32). There are bound, then, to be cases in which a citizen child lacks the potential for virtue, while a noncitizen child possesses it.[49] It follows that citizen children who lack the potential to develop virtue will receive benefits to which they are not justly entitled, while noncitizen children who have that potential will fail to receive them.

No just person would want to be born into such an unjust constitution. And, if we accept Aristotle's view of happiness as rational activity expressing virtue, no rationally prudent one would either. For any such person would want to be born into a society that helps him develop his virtue to the fullest extent his nature allows. But if he is unlucky enough to be born to the wrong parents, Aristotle's constitution will not do that. Indeed, it will assign him a life and a type of work that will make it very likely that he will *fail* to develop the virtues no matter how capable he is of developing them. Since all subsequent benefits are distributed on the basis of virtue, we can see what a catastrophe that would be. A pruden-

---

49. No doubt Aristotle, like Plato, believes that city-state–sponsored regulation of reproduction (the ancient equivalent of genetic counseling) can reduce the number of these cases. But since such regulation is itself a political advantage, distributing it to citizens alone would be unjust. Moreover, the number of cases cannot be reduced to zero, as Plato recognizes. Hence he, unlike Aristotle, allows qualified offspring from one class to enter another.

tial catastrophe, obviously, but also an ethical one, since injustice in the distribution of what constitutes the basis for all other distributions infects all those other distributions with injustice as well.

Aristotle's ideal constitution thus fails to be just in its own terms; it fails to meet its own standards of justice. This is a major problem. But it points the way to a yet more serious one and then to a possible solution. Aristotle believes that unqualified justice must be based on virtue. He also believes that virtue is not something children possess at birth. More than that, he believes that virtue is a social or political output, a consequence of receiving benefits, such as public education, that a constitution itself bestows. But no constitution can distribute *all* benefits on the basis of a property, such as virtue, which is itself the result of the distribution of benefits. If justice is going to be based on some feature of individuals, it must be one that individuals do not acquire through a process which may itself be either just or unjust. Aristotle's theory fails to meet this groundedness requirement, and so is strictly unsatisfiable.

Yet the fact that Aristotle's theory of justice is unsatisfiable for this sort of reason suggests a way forward. His theory of justice needs to be modified, so that the means of acquiring virtue are distributed on the basis, not of virtue, but of a feature, such as being human, that is unproblematically possessed to an equal degree by all the children born in the constitution, whether male or female, whether born to citizens or to noncitizens. The ideal constitution would have to provide equal opportunities to *all* the children possessing this feature. Then, at the appropriate stage, it would have to cull out as its future citizens those who had indeed acquired virtue in this way. If this process were fairly carried out, it would ensure that people acquired their virtue in a just way. Subsequent virtue-based distributions of benefits would then not be unjustly based. If Aristotle's ideal constitution were constructed in this way, it would, of course, have to be very different from the constitution he describes, but at least it wouldn't fail to meet its own standards of justice.

That problem, perhaps now to some extent solved, has to do with the basis on which benefits are distributed in the ideal constitution. The next problem concerns what gets distributed. If someone is a natural slave or a non-Greek of one sort or another, Aristotle thinks that he has pretty well no natural potential for virtue. Provided that his lack of such potential is determined by a fair process, it will then be unqualifiedly just, on Aristotle's view, for the ideal constitution to assign him no share or a very small share in political benefits or in true happiness. But it does not follow that it will be just to assign him a share of political *harms*. For example, there are some occupations that Aristotle thinks it would be harmful for a citizen of the ideal constitution to have. Thus citizens can't be farmers because happiness cannot exist without virtue, leisure is needed to develop virtue ($1329^a1–2$), and farmers do not have leisure ($1318^b11–12$). For a similar reason they cannot be VULGAR CRAFTSMEN or tradesmen, "since lives of these sorts are ignoble and inimical to virtue" ($1328^b40–41$). But he thinks it is perfectly all right to require (I intentionally use a fairly weak verb) natural slaves to work as farmers. True, farming won't be harmful to a natural slave in the way that it would be to a citizen; it won't have a negative effect on his capacity for virtue, but that doesn't mean that it won't be harmful to him in other ways. Being required by a constitution to be a farmer, when one hates farming, might well be considered just such a harm.

If Aristotle is right about farming, trading, and artisanship, the appropriate conclusion to draw is that they are ethically reprehensible occupations, because inimical to virtue, and that no one in the ideal constitution should pursue them in a way that threatens his virtue (1277^b 3–7, $1333^a6–16$). Perhaps, like political office itself, the citizens themselves should undertake them turn and turn about for short enough periods to leave their virtue and leisure sufficiently unscathed.

If the ideal constitution is to be unqualifiedly just, to repeat, distribution of political benefits must be proportional to virtue, it must be equal for the unqualified citizens, since Aristotle stipulates that they are equal in virtue. But how are we to tell whether or not the ideal constitution— or any other constitution, for that matter—meets this requirement? Aristotle claims that when political benefits are justly distributed, people who are equal in virtue receive "reciprocally equal" amounts of them. This, he says, is what preserves the constitution (*Pol.* $1261^a30–31$, *NE* 1132^b33, *MM* $1194^a16–18$). But reciprocal equality is by no means easy to understand. In the *Nicomachean Ethics*, where it is called "proportional reciprocity," it is initially introduced in connection with the exchange of property of different sorts: if n shoes are an equal exchange for one house, n shoes are reciprocally equal to one house. This is the sort of equality that applies to political benefits, Aristotle thinks, because, like exchangeable property, they aren't all of one sort ($1261^a32–^b6$, $1300^b10–12$). Political offices themselves, for example, are very different in nature, scope, and authority. If A holds political office x, then, and B holds a very different office y, how are we to ensure that A's share in ruling is equal to B's, that A's share of political benefits is the same size as B's? When we know the answer to this question, Aristotle thinks, we will have established a reciprocal equality between x and y, and will be on our way to understanding what proportional equality applied to political benefits actually amounts to.

In the case of exchangeable goods, money provides the units of measurement, "since it measures everything" (*NE* 1133ª20–21). So one house is equal to n pairs of shoes because one house equals n units of money (n dollars, say), while a pair of shoes equals one unit (one dollar). But that does not tell us how to establish that one house equals n units of money or that one pair of shoes equals only one such unit. Indeed, this is just the original problem all over again, since it is no easier to establish equalities between shoes and money than it is to establish them between shoes and houses. There is some suggestion that Aristotle may have thought that need (*chreia*) offers us some assistance with this problem: "Everything, then, must be measured by a single standard. In reality, this standard is need. . . . But need has come to be conventionally represented by money" (*NE* 1133ª25–30). This suggestion is itself problematic, however, since it is not easy to determine the conditions under which otherwise similar needs for different things are equal. What, for example, could explain the fact that a need for shoes is equal to a need for houses just in case the one is a need for n pairs of shoes, while the other is a need for one house? Aristotle himself may have been aware of this problem, since he says that things so different as shoes and houses "cannot become commensurate in reality," but that "they can become sufficiently (*hikanōs*) so in relation to our needs" (1133ᵇ19–20; also *Pol.* 1283ª4–10). But it is difficult to see how we could establish a type of commensurability between houses and shoes that was adequate for Aristotle's purposes on the basis of need.

When we turn from exchangeable goods to virtue, political benefits, and the like, our problems multiply. Here we do not even have a credible unit of measurement like money to rely on, and it is even less clear how need might come into the picture. But if we are not able to tell some sort of reasonable story, the claim that the ideal constitution is unqualifiedly just will be bound to seem like stipulation rather than fact. Indeed, the more fundamental claim that Aristotelian justice is true and unqualified justice because it alone is based *on nature* will itself come to have that same appearance: it will seem like magic rather than naturalistic metaphysics.

The ideal constitution fails to be just in its own terms, then, and would require substantial restructuring not to fail quite so badly. But even such restructuring would not solve the problems presented by the terms themselves, which are far too vague to do the work required of them. Let us suppose for the sake of argument, however, that this defect, like the others, could be remedied, so that the ideal constitution was just in its own terms. Would it, then, be the ideal constitution to live in from the point of view of happiness, once again granting that happiness is, as Aristotle thinks, activity expressing virtue?

There are many ways to look at this question. We shall consider just one very important one, private property, which together with proportional equality is the sole guarantee of stability in a constitution ($1307^{a}26-27$). Property is a necessary component of the happy life: "Why should we not say that someone is happy when his activities express complete virtue and he has an adequate supply of external GOODS, not for some chance period but throughout a complete life?" (*NE* $1101^{a}14-16$). But that does not tell us how the ideal constitution should handle property ownership. Aristotle firmly rejects the idea, defended by Plato, that private property should be abolished and that the citizens of the ideal constitution should possess their property in common. He does so for three reasons. First, communally owned property is neglected. Second, "it is very pleasant to help one's friends, guests, or companions, and do them favors, as one can if one has property of one's own" ($1263^{b}5-7$). And, third, without private property one cannot practice the virtue of generosity ($1263^{b}11-14$). To avoid these defects in Plato's proposals, as well as those generated by strictly private property, Aristotle designs an intermediate position: some property should be communally owned and some should be privately owned, but the use of even the privately owned property should be communal ($1329^{b}36-$ $1330^{a}31$). Is this proposal an improvement on Plato's? Is it one that should attract us to a constitution that embodies it?

To own property, according to the *Rhetoric*, is to have the power to alienate or dispose of it through either gift or sale ($1361^{a}21-22$). But Aristotle stipulates that each of the unqualified citizens in the ideal constitution (each male head of household) should be given an equal allotment of land, one part of which is near the town, the other near the frontier ($1330^{a}14-18$). Moreover, he seems to favor making these allotments inalienable ($1266^{b}14-31$, $1270^{a}15-34$).[50] But if they are inalienable, so that one cannot sell them or give them away, what does owning them actually consist in? The natural thought is that it must consist in

---

50. If they were not inalienable, they could hardly continue to serve the purpose they are introduced to serve at $1330^{a}14-25$.

having private or exclusive use of them. But that thought is derailed, because the use of private property is communal. It seems, then, that a major portion of what is called the private property of a citizen of the ideal constitution is not something that he really and truly owns.

Another passage from the *Rhetoric* tells us that ownership of property is secure if the use of it is in the owner's power (1361ª19–21). Privately owned but communally used property would therefore seem to be insecurely owned at best. To be sure, this isn't what Aristotle intends to be true in the ideal constitution. He thinks that the use of private property remains in the owner's power but that he will grant it to his fellow citizens out of virtue and friendship and not because the law requires him to do it (*Pol.* 1263ª21–40). None the less, the expectation on the part of one citizen that another will do what virtue requires of him is pretty well bound to make the owner's power seem notional rather than real.

So what we have in the ideal constitution is a somewhat notional ownership of not very much (nonlanded) property. This will hardly recommend the constitution to those who think that private property is a good thing. Indeed, it seems to be not much more than a notational variant on a system of communal ownership. It is scarcely surprising, therefore, that it does not help much with the problems Aristotle raises for Plato. If communally owned property tends to be neglected, why will privately owned but communally used property fare any better? If I can use even what I don't own, and so don't particularly have to take care of and maintain, ownership seems more like a curse than a blessing. By the same token, to give someone something of which he already has the use and you continue to retain the use is a wishy-washy sort of generosity at best, a pale pleasure compared to that of using what one actually owns to do favors for one's friends. The system of property adopted in the ideal constitution, then, does not seem to be best from the point of view of maximizing the citizen's happiness. Many other systems seem much more preferable; for example, fair taxation on private property and income, with the proceeds used to maintain public property and provide public services.[51]

51. Topics treated in this section are discussed in T. H. Irwin, *Aristotle's First Principles*, 399–469; S. Meikle, *Aristotle's Economic Thought*; F. D. Miller, *Nature, Justice, and Rights in Aristotle's Politics*, 191–251; and M. Nussbaum, "Nature, Function, and Capability: Aristotle on Political Distribution," with a reply by David Charles.

§11 Conclusion

We have been looking at the central argument of the *Politics*, and at the way Aristotle's perfectionism plays out there. We have seen the enormous price he pays in terms of political credibility for having too narrow a conception of what human perfection consists in (§§7–10): the political and philosophical lives are worthwhile but they are not the only ones that are; virtue is worthwhile but it provides a poor basis for distributive justice. We have seen the even larger price he pays for making false factual claims that are accretions to his perfectionism: without natural slaves or women whose nature makes them incapable of ruling, Aristotle's ideal constitution would have to look very different than it does. None the less, if we strip away those accretions and broaden the perfectionism, we have a theory with considerable attractions and possibilities.[52] Arguably it is Aristotle's most important political legacy, both historically speaking and in fact.

The central argument is just that, however: a major highway connecting the *Politics* to the rest of Aristotle's philosophy. But the *Politics* isn't reducible to its central argument; much fascinating material is to be found on the side roads. The discussion in Books V and VI, for example, of how different constitutions are preserved and destroyed is full of astute observations about people and their motives.

In some ways, indeed, the *Politics* is best thought of not simply as an argument, but rather as an opportunity to think about some of the most important human questions in unparalleled intellectual company. Engaged in the dialectical process of doing politics with Aristotle, one experiences the great seductive power of the philosophical life full force, but one also experiences the rather different power of the political life. To some degree, indeed, one senses that the two are, Aristotelian theory to the contrary, not all that different, that the give and take of dialectic is very like the give and take of politics, and that life's problems are no easier to solve in theory than in practice. This is not quite what the *Politics* tells us, to be sure, but it is, in a way that is mildly subversive of its message, what it dramatizes.

---

52. Thomas Hurka, *Perfectionism*, is one of the best general accounts of this sort of modified Aristotelian theory. Parts of it discuss Aristotle explicitly; all of it is relevant to understanding his thought.

ADRIATIC

SEA

ILLYRIA

•Epidamnus

•Apollonia

MACEDONIA

ITALY   *IAPYGIA*   Elimeia

TYRRHENIAN   •Tarentum   THESSALY

SEA   Sybaris/Thurii   •Larissa

Malea•
Ambracia•
Phocis•Opus
IONIAN   Leucas ○   Delphi   •Th

SEA   Sicyon•
Elis•   •Corinth
•Locri   Olympia•   ARCADI
Zancle•   Argos•
SICILY   Rhegium   •Heraea
•Mantine
Catana•   Sparta•
Leontini•
Gela•   •Syracuse   PELOPONNESE

Carthage•

MEDITERRANEAN

SEA

LIBYA

0   100   200   300 Miles
0   100   200   300 Kilometers

The World of the *Politics*

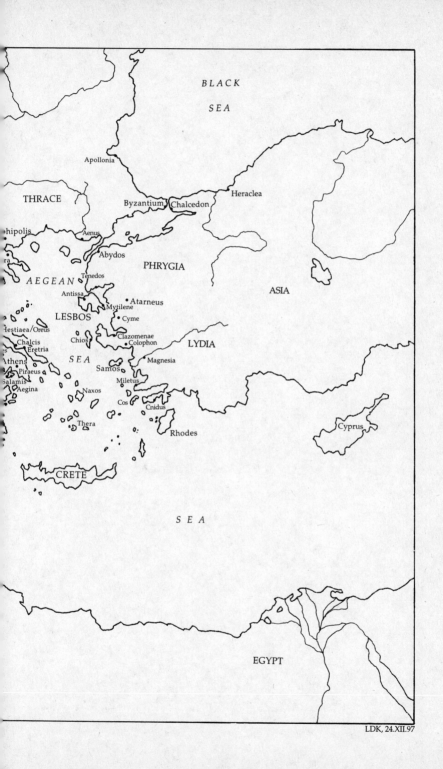

BOOK I

Chapter 1

We see that every CITY-STATE is a COMMUNITY of some sort, and that 1252ᵃ every community is established for the sake of some GOOD (for everyone performs every ACTION for the sake of what he takes to be good). Clearly, then, while every community aims at some good, the community that has the most AUTHORITY of all and encompasses all the others aims 5 highest, that is to say, at the good that has the most authority of all. This community is the one called a city-state, the community that is political.[1]

Those,[2] then, who think that the positions of STATESMAN, KING, HOUSEHOLD MANAGER, and MASTER of slaves are the same, are not correct. For they hold that each of these differs not in kind, but only in whether the subjects ruled are few or many: that if, for example, someone rules few people, he is a master; if more, a household manager; if still more, he has the position of statesman or king—the assumption 10 being that there is no difference between a large household and a small city-state. As for the positions of statesman and king, they say that someone who is in charge by himself has the position of king, whereas someone who follows the principles of the appropriate SCIENCE, ruling 15 and being ruled in turn, has the position of statesman. But these claims are not true. What I am saying will be clear, if we examine the matter ac-

---

1. *kuriōtatē koinonia*: the most sovereign community, the one with the most authority, is the city-state, because all the other communities are encompassed (*periechein*) by it or are its parts, so that the goods for whose sake they are formed are pursued in part for the sake of the good for which it is formed (see I.2). These subcommunities include households, villages, religious societies, etc. The good with the most authority is HAPPINESS, since everything else is pursued in part for its sake, while it is pursued solely for its own sake. The science with the most authority, STATESMANSHIP, directs the entire city-state toward happiness. A more detailed version of this opening argument is given in *NE* I.1–2. Here it is being adapted to define what a city-state is.
2. Plato, *Statesman* 258e–261a. Compare Xenophon, *Memorabilia* III.iv.12, III.vi.14.

cording to the method of investigation that has guided us elsewhere. For as in other cases, a composite has to be analyzed until we reach things that are incomposite, since these are the smallest parts of the whole, so if

20 we also examine the parts that make up a city-state, we shall see better both how these differ from each other, and whether or not it is possible to gain some expertise in connection with each of the things we have mentioned.[3]

Chapter 2

If one were to see how these things develop naturally from the begin-
25 ning, one would, in this case as in others, get the best view of them. First, then, those who cannot exist without each other necessarily form a couple, as [1] female and male do for the sake of procreation (they do not do so from DELIBERATE CHOICE, but, like other animals and plants, because the urge to leave behind something of the same kind as them-
30 selves is natural), and [2] as a natural ruler and what is naturally ruled do for the sake of survival. For if something is capable of rational foresight, it is a natural ruler and master, whereas whatever can use its body to labor is ruled and is a natural SLAVE. That is why the same thing is ben-eficial for both master and slave.[4]

There is a natural distinction, of course, between what is female and
1252ᵇ what is servile. For, unlike the blacksmiths who make the Delphian knife, nature produces nothing skimpily, but instead makes a single thing for a single TASK, because every tool will be made best if it serves to perform one task rather than many.[5] Among non-Greeks, however, a
5 WOMAN and a slave occupy the same position. The reason is that they do not have anything that naturally rules; rather their community consists of a male and a female slave. That is why our poets say "it is proper for Greeks to rule non-Greeks,"[6] implying that non-Greek and slave are in nature the same.

The first thing to emerge from these two communities[7] is a house-

---

3. That is to say, do household managers, masters, statesmen, and kings each employ a different type of technical expertise in ruling? Expertise (*technikon*) is technical knowledge of the sort embodied in a CRAFT or SCIENCE.
4. This claim is qualified at 1278ᵇ32–37 and elaborated upon in I.5–7.
5. A Delphian knife seems to have been a multipurpose and cheaply made tool of some sort. See 1299ᵇ10 and note.
6. See Euripides, *Iphigenia in Aulis* 1266, 1400.
7. The communities of husband and wife, master and slave.

hold, so that Hesiod is right when he said in his poem, "First and fore-   *10*
most: a house, a wife, and an ox for the plow."[8] For an ox is a poor man's
servant. The community naturally constituted to satisfy everyday needs,
then, is the household; its members are called "meal-sharers" by
Charondas and "manger-sharers" by Epimenides the Cretan.[9] But the
first community constituted out of several households for the sake of   *15*
satisfying needs other than everyday ones is a village.

As a COLONY or offshoot from a household,[10] a village seems to be particularly natural, consisting of what some have called "sharers of the
same milk," sons and the sons of sons.[11] That is why city-states were
originally ruled by kings, as nations still are. For they were constituted
out of people who were under kingships; for in every household the el-   *20*
dest rules as a king. And so the same holds in the offshoots, because the
villagers are blood relatives.[12] This is what Homer is describing when he
says: "Each one lays down the law for his own wives and children."[13] For
they were scattered about, and that is how people dwelt in the distant
past. The reason all people say that the gods too are ruled by a king is
that they themselves were ruled by kings in the distant past, and some
still are. Human beings model the shapes of the gods on their own, and   *25*
do the same to their way of life as well.

A complete community constituted out of several villages, once it
reaches the limit of total SELF-SUFFICIENCY, practically speaking, is a
city-state. It comes to be for the sake of living, but it remains in existence for the sake of living well. That is why every city-state exists by
NATURE,[14] since the first communities do. For the city-state is their end,   *30*
and nature is an end; for we say that each thing's nature—for example,
that of a human being, a horse, or a household—is the character it has
when its coming-into-being has been completed. Moreover, that for the

---

8. *Works and Days* 405.

9. Charondas was a sixth-century legislator from Catana in Chalcidice in the
   southern part of Macedonia. Epimenides was a religious teacher of the late
   sixth and early fifth century. The works from which Aristotle is quoting are
   lost.

10. See Plato, *Laws* 776a–b.

11. Plato, *Laws* 681b.

12. A somewhat different explanation is given at 1286^{b}8–11.

13. *Iliad* X.114–15. To lay down the law (*themisteuein*) is to give judgments in
    particular cases about what is right or fitting (*themis*).

14. This claim and the argument Aristotle is about to give for it are discussed in
    the Introduction xlviii–lix.

sake of which something exists, that is to say, its end, is best, and self-sufficiency is both end and best.

1253ᵃ

It is evident from these considerations, then, that a city-state is among the things that exist by nature, that a human being is by nature a political animal,[15] and that anyone who is without a city-state, not by luck but by nature, is either a poor specimen or else superhuman. Like the one Homer condemns, he too is "clanless, lawless, and homeless."[16]

5   For someone with such a nature is at the same time eager for war, like an isolated piece in a board game.[17]

It is also clear why a human being is more of a political animal than a bee or any other gregarious animal. Nature makes nothing pointlessly,[18]

10   as we say, and no animal has speech except a human being. A voice is a signifier of what is pleasant or painful, which is why it is also possessed by the other animals (for their nature goes this far: they not only perceive what is pleasant or painful but signify it to each other). But speech is for making clear what is beneficial or harmful, and hence also what is

15   just or unjust. For it is peculiar to human beings, in comparison to the other animals, that they alone have perception of what is good or bad, just or unjust, and the rest. And it is community in these that makes a household and a city-state.[19]

The city-state is also PRIOR in nature to the household and to each of

20   us individually, since the whole is necessarily prior to the part. For if the whole body is dead, there will no longer be a foot or a hand, except homonymously,[20] as one might speak of a stone "hand" (for a dead hand will be like that); but everything is defined by its TASK and by its capacity; so that in such condition they should not be said to be the same things but homonymous ones. Hence that the city-state is natural and

25   prior in nature to the individual is clear. For if an individual is not self-sufficient when separated, he will be like all other parts in relation to the

---

15. See Introduction xxvi, xlvii–xlviii, li–lv, lvii–lxv.
16. *Iliad* IX.63–64. Homer is describing a man who "loves fighting with his own people."
17. A piece particularly vulnerable to attack by an opponent's pieces, and so needing constantly to fight them off.
18. The idea is that features are present in a thing's nature in order to promote its end, not that nature is an agent (a kind of god, say) that makes things for a purpose. See Introduction xxvii–xxxv.
19. Explained at 1280ᵇ5–12.
20. That is to say, a foot or a hand that shares no more than a name with a living, functioning foot or hand. See *Cat.* 1ᵃ1–2.

whole. Anyone who cannot form a community with others, or who does not need to because he is self-sufficient, is no part of a city-state—he is either a beast or a god. Hence, though an impulse toward this sort of community exists by nature in everyone, whoever first established one was responsible for the greatest of goods. For as a human being is the best of the animals when perfected, so when separated from LAW and JUSTICE he is worst of all. For injustice is harshest when it has weapons, and a human being grows up with weapons for VIRTUE and PRACTICAL WISDOM to use, which are particularly open to being used for opposite purposes.[21] Hence he is the most unrestrained and most savage of animals when he lacks virtue, as well as the worst where food and sex are concerned. But justice is a political matter; for justice is the organization of a political community, and justice[22] decides what is just.

30

35

Chapter 3

Since it is evident from what parts a city-state is constituted, we must first discuss household management, for every city-state is constituted from households. The parts of household management correspond in turn to the parts from which the household is constituted, and a complete household consists of slaves and FREE. But we must first examine each thing in terms of its smallest parts, and the primary and smallest parts of a household are master and slave, husband and wife, father and children. So we shall have to examine these three things to see what each of them is and what features it should have. The three in question are [1] mastership, [2] "marital" science (for we have no word to describe the union of woman and man), and [3] "procreative" science (this also lacks a name of its own). But there is also a part which some believe to be identical to household management, and others believe to be its largest part. We shall have to study its nature too. I am speaking of what is called WEALTH ACQUISITION.[23]

1253ᵇ

5

10

21. The weapons referred to are presumably various human capacities, such as intelligence, that can be used for good or bad purposes.

22. Reading *dikē* with Dreizehnter and the ms. Here to be understood, perhaps, as the judicial justice administered by the courts. See 1322ᵃ5–8, 1326ᵃ29–30.

23. "Marital" science (*gamikē*) and "procreative" science (*teknopoiētikē*) are shown at work in VII.16. Rule over wives, which is an exercise of the former, and rule over children, of the latter, are discussed in I.12–13. Mastership is discussed in I.4–7 and wealth acquisition in I.2, 8–11.

15   But let us first discuss master and slave, partly to see how they stand
in relation to our need for necessities, but at the same time with an eye to
knowledge about this topic,[24] to see whether we can acquire some better
ideas than those currently entertained. For, as we said at the beginning,
some people believe that mastership is a sort of science, and that mastership, household management, statesmanship, and the science of kingship are all the same. But others[25] believe that it is contrary to nature to
20 be a master (for it is by law that one person is a slave and another free,
whereas by nature there is no difference between them), which is why it
is not just either; for it involves force.

Chapter 4

Since property is part of the household, the science of PROPERTY ACQUI-
SITION is also a part of household management (for we can neither live
nor live well without the necessities). Hence, just as the specialized
25 crafts must have their proper tools if they are going to perform their
tasks, so too does the household manager. Some tools are inanimate,
however, and some are animate. The ship captain's rudder, for example,
is an inanimate tool, but his lookout is an animate one; for where crafts
30 are concerned every assistant is classed as a tool. So a piece of property
is a tool for maintaining life; property in general is the sum of such
tools; a slave is a piece of animate property of a sort; and all assistants are
like tools for using tools. For, if each tool could perform its task on command or by anticipating instructions, and if like the statues of Daedalus
35 or the tripods of Hephaestus—which the poet describes as having "entered the assembly of the gods of their own accord"[26]—shuttles wove
cloth by themselves, and picks played the lyre, a master craftsman would
not need assistants, and masters would not need slaves.

1254ᵃ   What are commonly called tools are tools for production. A piece of
property, on the other hand, is for ACTION. For something comes from a

---

24. The discussion of the theoretical aspects of wealth acquisition occupies
I.4–10 (see 1258ᵇ9–10, which advertises this fact). I.11 is devoted to its
practical aspects.
25. For example, Alcidamas (a pupil of the sophist Gorgias), who says that "nature never made any man a slave."
26. *Iliad* XVIII.376. Daedalus was a legendary craftsman and inventor, who
made the maze for the Minotaur and the thread for Ariadne. His statues
were so life-like that they ran away unless they were tied down (*DA*
406ᵇ18–19; Plato, *Meno* 97d). Hephaestus was blacksmith to the gods.

shuttle beyond the use of it, but from a piece of clothing or a bed we get only the use. Besides, since action and production differ in kind, and both need tools, their tools must differ in the same way as they do. Life consists in action, not production. Therefore, slaves too are assistants in the class of things having to do with action.[27] Pieces of property are spoken of in the same way as parts. A part is not just a part of another thing, but is *entirely* that thing's. The same is also true of a piece of property. That is why a master is just his slave's *master*, not his simply, while a slave is not just his master's *slave*, he is entirely his.

It is clear from these considerations what the nature and capacity of a slave are. For anyone who, despite being human, is by nature not his own but someone else's is a natural slave. And he is someone else's when, despite being human, he is a piece of property; and a piece of property is a tool for action that is separate from its owner.[28]

Chapter 5

But whether anyone is really like that by nature or not, and whether it is better or just for anyone to be a slave or not (all slavery being against nature)—these are the things we must investigate next. And it is not difficult either to determine the answer by argument or to learn it from actual events. For ruling and being ruled are not only necessary, they are also beneficial, and some things are distinguished right from birth, some suited to rule and others to being ruled. There are many kinds of rulers and ruled, and the better the ruled are, the better the rule over them always is;[29] for example, rule over humans is better than rule over beasts. For a task performed by something better is a better task, and where one thing rules and another is ruled, they have a certain task. For whenever a number of constituents, whether continuous with one another or discontinuous, are combined into one common thing, a ruling element and a subject element appear. These are present in living things, because this is how nature as a whole works. (Some rule also exists in lifeless things:

---

27. A hammer is the tool of a producer or craftsman. A slave is a tool of a head of household, a free agent who engages in action, not production.
28. Unlike our bodies, which are tools or instruments of our souls, but not slaves, because not separate from us (*DA* 415[b]18–19, *PA* 642[a]11). See 1255[b]11–12.
29. See 1315[b]4–7, 1325[a]27–30, 1333[b]26–29.

for example, that of a harmony.[30] But an examination of that would perhaps take us too far afield.[31])

Soul and body are the basic constituents of an animal: the soul is the
35   natural ruler; the body the natural subject. But of course one should examine what is natural in things whose condition is natural, not corrupted. One should therefore study the human being too whose soul and
body are in the best possible condition; one in whom this is clear. For in
depraved people, and those in a depraved condition, the body will often
1254ᵇ   seem to rule the soul, because their condition is bad and unnatural.[32]

At any rate, it is, as I say, in an animal that we can first observe both
rule of a master and rule of a statesman. For the soul rules the body with
5   the rule of a master, whereas understanding rules desire with the rule of
a statesman or with the rule of a king.[33] In these cases it is evident that it
is natural and beneficial for the body to be ruled by the soul, and for the
affective part to be ruled by understanding (the part that has reason),
and that it would be harmful to everything if the reverse held, or if these
elements were equal. The same applies in the case of human beings with
10   respect to the other animals. For domestic animals are by nature better
than wild ones, and it is better for all of them to be ruled by human beings, since this will secure their safety.[34] Moreover, the relation of male
to female is that of natural superior to natural inferior, and that of ruler
15   to ruled. But, in fact, the same holds true of all human beings.[35]

Therefore those people who are as different from others as body is
from soul or beast from human, and people whose task, that is to say, the
best thing to come from them, is to use their bodies are in this condi-

30. The reference is to the *mesē* or *hēgemōn* (leader), which is the dominant note
    in a chord (*Pr.* 920ᵃ21–22, *Metaph.* 1018ᵇ26–29).
31. *exōterikōteras*: see 1278ᵇ31 note.
32. The difference between depraved people and those in a depraved condition
    is unclear. The former are perhaps permanently in the condition that the
    latter are in temporarily; the former incorrigibly depraved, the latter corri-
    gibly so. In any case, both make poor models.
33. Both statesmen and kings rule willing subjects; in the virtuous desires obey
    understanding "willingly." See Introduction xxv–xxxviii.
34. Alternatively: "It is better for all of the tame ones to be ruled." But the dis-
    tinction between tame and wild animals is not hard and fast: "All domestic
    (or tame) animals are at first wild rather than domestic, . . . but physically
    weaker"; "under certain conditions of locality and time sooner or later all
    animals can become tame" (*Pr.* 895ᵇ23–896ᵃ11). Presumably, then, it is bet-
    ter even for wild animals to be ruled by man.
35. For example, it is natural for Greeks to rule non-Greeks.

tion—those people are natural slaves. And it is better for them to be subject to this rule, since it is also better for the other things we mentioned. For he who can belong to someone else (and that is why he actually does belong to someone else), and he who shares in reason to the extent of understanding it, but does not have it himself (for the other animals obey not reason but feelings), is a natural slave. The difference in the use made of them is small, since both slaves and domestic animals help provide the necessities with their bodies.

Nature tends, then, to make the bodies of slaves and free people different too, the former strong enough to be used for necessities, the latter useless for that sort of work, but upright in posture and possessing all the other qualities needed for political life—qualities divided into those needed for war and those for peace. But the opposite often happens as well: some have the bodies of free men; others, the souls. This, at any rate, is evident: if people were born whose bodies alone were as excellent as those found in the statues of the gods, everyone would say that those who were substandard deserved to be their slaves. And if this is true of the body, it is even more justifiable to make such a distinction with regard to the soul; but the soul's beauty is not so easy to see as the body's.

It is evident, then, that there are some people, some of whom are naturally free, others naturally slaves, for whom slavery is both just and beneficial.[36]

Chapter 6

But it is not difficult to see that those who make the opposite claim[37] are also right, up to a point. For slaves and slavery are spoken of in two ways: for there are also slaves—that is to say, people who are in a state of slavery—by *law*. The law is a sort of agreement by which what is conquered in war is said to belong to the victors. But many of those conversant with the law challenge the justice of this. They bring a writ of illegality against it, analogous to that brought against a speaker in the assembly.[38] Their

---

36. A more complex conclusion than we might expect. The idea is perhaps this: being a slave might not be just or beneficial for a natural slave who has long been legally free; similarly, being legally free might not be just or beneficial for a naturally free person who has long been a legal slave.
37. That slavery is unjust.
38. A speaker in the Athenian assembly was liable to a writ of illegality or *graphē paranomōn* if he proposed legislation that contravened already existing law; i.e., the "war" rule would not be allowed in a civil context.

supposition is that it is monstrous if someone is going to be the subject
and slave to whatever has superior power and is able to subdue him by
10   force. Some hold the latter view, others the former; and this is true even
among the wise.

The reason for this dispute, and for the overlap in the arguments, is
this: virtue, when it is equipped with resources, is in a way particularly
15   adept in the use of force; and anything that conquers always does so because it is outstanding in *some* good quality.[39] This makes it seem that
force is not without virtue, and that only the justice of the matter is in
dispute. For one side believes that justice is benevolence,[40] whereas the
other believes that it is precisely the rule of the more powerful that is
just. At any event, when these accounts are disentangled, the other argu-
20   ments have neither force nor anything else to persuade us that the one
who is more virtuous should not rule or be master.[41]

Then there are those who cleave exclusively, as they think, to justice
of a sort (for law is justice of a sort), and maintain that enslavement in
war is just. But at the same time they imply that it is not just. For it is
possible for wars to be started unjustly, and no one would say that some-
25   one is a slave if he did not deserve to be one;[42] otherwise, those regarded

39. Virtue together with the necessary external goods or resources are what enable someone to do something well, including use force. If someone is able
to conquer his foes, this at least suggests that he has the virtues needed for
success. See 1324^{b}22–1325^{a}14.
40. Reading *eunoia* with Dreizehnter and the mss.
41. The two parties to the dispute share common ground because they both believe that "force never lacks virtue." But they disagree in their accounts of
justice, and hence about whether the enslavement of conquered populations
is unjust. Those who believe that justice is the rule of the more powerful believe that such enslavement is just, because justice (by definition) is always
on the side of the conqueror, since his victory shows him to have the greater
power. Those who believe that justice is benevolence (i.e., that it is the good
of another) believe that enslavement is unjust because not beneficial for the
slaves. Both accounts are canvassed by Thrasymachus in Book I of Plato's
Republic (338c, 343c). Once their accounts are disentangled it is readily apparent that their contrasting positions do nothing to confute Aristotle's own
view that the one who is more virtuous *should* rule (I.13).
42. Aristotle is assuming that even an unjust war will be undertaken in accordance with the laws governing declarations of war, and so will be "legal."
Thus by admitting that a person enslaved by the victor in an unjust war has
been unjustly but legally enslaved, the proponent of the view here in question denies both that enslaving is always just and that what is legal is always
just.

as the best born would be slaves or the children of slaves, if any of them
were taken captive and sold. That is why indeed they are not willing to
describe *them*, but only non-Greeks, as slaves. Yet, in saying this, they
are seeking precisely the natural slave we talked about in the beginning.　*30*
For they have to say that some people are slaves everywhere, whereas
others are slaves nowhere.

The same holds of noble birth. Nobles regard themselves as well born
wherever they are, not only when they are among their own people, but
they regard non-Greeks as well born only when they are at home. They
imply a distinction between a good birth and freedom that is unqualified
and one that is not unqualified. As Theodectes' Helen says: "Sprung　*35*
from divine roots on both sides, who would think that I deserve to be
called a slave?"[43] But when people say this, they are in fact distinguishing slavery from freedom, well born from low born, in terms of virtue
and vice alone. For they think that good people come from good people　*40*
in just the way that human comes from human, and beast from beast.
But often, though nature does have a tendency to bring this about, it is　*1255ᵇ*
nevertheless unable to do so.[44]

It is clear, then, that the objection with which we began has something to be said for it, and that the one lot are not always natural slaves,
nor the other naturally free. But it is also clear that in some cases there is　*5*
such a distinction—cases where it is beneficial and just[45] for the one to
be master and the other to be slave, and where the one ought to be ruled
and the other ought to exercise the rule that is natural for him (so that he
is in fact a master), and where misrule harms them both. For the same
thing is beneficial for both part and whole, body and soul; and a slave is　*10*
a sort of part of his master—a sort of living but separate part of his body.
Hence, there is a certain mutual benefit and mutual friendship for such
masters and slaves as deserve to be by nature so related.[46] When their relationship is not that way, however, but is based on law, and they have
been subjected to force, the opposite holds.　*15*

---

43. Nauck 802, fr. 3. Theodectes was a mid–fourth-century tragic poet who
    studied with Aristotle. Helen is Helen of Troy.
44. See 1254ᵇ27–33.
45. Reading *kai dikaion*.
46. "Every human being seems to have some relations of justice with everyone
    who is capable of community in law and agreement. Hence there is also
    friendship between master and slave, to the extent that a slave is a human
    being" (*NE* 1161ᵇ1–8).

Chapter 7

It is also evident from the foregoing that the rule of a master is not the same as rule of a statesman and that the other kinds of rule are not all the same as one another, though some people say they are. For rule of a statesman is rule over people who are naturally free, whereas that of a master is rule over slaves; rule by a household manager is a monarchy, since every household has one ruler; rule of a statesman is rule over peo-
20 ple who are free and equal.

A master is so called not because he possesses a SCIENCE but because he is a certain sort of person.[47] The same is true of slave and free. None the less, there could be such a thing as mastership or slave-craft; for ex-ample, the sort that was taught by the man in Syracuse who for a fee
25 used to train slave boys in their routine services. Lessons in such things might well be extended to include cookery and other services of that type. For different slaves have different tasks, some of which are more esteemed, others more concerned with providing the necessities: "slave is superior to slave, master to master,"[48] as the proverb says. All such
30 SCIENCES, then, are the business of slaves.

Mastership, on the other hand, is the science of using slaves; for it is not in acquiring slaves but in using them that someone is a master. But there is nothing grand or impressive about this science. The master needs to know how to command the things that the slave needs to know
35 how to do. Hence for those who have the resources not to bother with such things, a steward takes on this office, while they themselves engage in politics or PHILOSOPHY.[49] As for the science of acquiring slaves (the just variety of it), it is different from both of these,[50] and is a kind of warfare or hunting.

These, then, are the distinctions to be made regarding slave and master.

Chapter 8

Since a slave has turned out to be part of property, let us now study
1256ᵃ property and wealth acquisition generally, in accordance with our guid-

---

47. One with practical wisdom.
48. Kock II.492, fr. 54. A line from the comic poet Philemon.
49. See VII.2–3.
50. Both a master's science and a slave's.

ing method.[51] The first problem one might raise is this: Is wealth acquisition the same as household management, or a part of it, or an assistant
to it? If it is an assistant, is it in the way that shuttle making is assistant   5
to weaving, or in the way that bronze smelting is assistant to statue making? For these do not assist in the same way: the first provides tools,
whereas the second provides the matter. (By the matter I mean the sub-
strate, that out of which the product is made—for example, wool for the
weaver and copper for the bronze smelter.)   10

It is clear that household management is not the same as wealth acquisition, since the former uses resources, while the latter provides
them; for what science besides household management uses what is in
the household? But whether wealth acquisition is a part of household
management or a science of a different kind is a matter of dispute. For if
someone engaged in wealth acquisition has to study the various sources
of wealth and property, and[52] property and wealth have many different   15
parts, we shall first have to investigate whether farming is a part of
household management[53] or some different type of thing, and likewise
the supervision and acquisition of food generally.

But there are many kinds of food too. Hence the lives of both animals
and human beings are also of many kinds. For it is impossible to live   20
without food, so that differences in diet have produced different ways of
life among the animals. For some beasts live in herds and others live
scattered about, whichever is of benefit for getting their food, because
some of them are carnivorous, some herbivorous, and some omnivorous.   25
So, in order to make it easier for them to get hold of these foods, nature
has made their ways of life different. And since the same things are not
naturally pleasant to each, but rather different things to different ones,
among the carnivores and herbivores themselves the ways of life are different.

Similarly, among human beings too; for their ways of life differ a
great deal. The idlest are nomads; for they live a leisurely life, because   30
they get their food effortlessly from their domestic animals. But when
their herds have to change pasture, they too have to move around with
them, as if they were farming a living farm. Others hunt for a living, differing from one another in the sort of hunting they do. Some live by   35

---

51. Described at 1252ª17–20.
52. Reading *hē de* with Dreizehnter.
53. Reading *oikonomikēs* with Dreizehnter. The mss. have *chrēmatistikēs*
("wealth acquisition").

raiding; some—those who live near lakes, marshes, rivers, or a sea con-
taining fish—live from fishing; and some from birds or wild beasts. But
40   the most numerous type lives off the land and off cultivated crops.
Hence the ways of life, at any rate those whose fruits are natural and do
not provide food through EXCHANGE or COMMERCE, are roughly speak-
1256ᵇ   ing these: nomadic, raiding, fishing, hunting, farming. But some people
contrive a pleasant life by combining several of these, supplementing
their way of life where it has proven less than self-sufficient; for example, some live both a nomadic and a raiding life, others, both a farming
5   and a hunting one, and so on, each spending their lives as their needs
jointly compel.

It is evident that nature itself gives such property to all living things,
both right from the beginning, when they are first conceived, and similarly when they have reached complete maturity. Animals that produce
10   larvae or eggs produce their offspring together with enough food to last
them until they can provide for themselves. Animals that give birth to
live offspring carry food for their offspring in their own bodies for a certain period, namely, the natural substance we call milk. Clearly, then, we
15   must suppose in the case of fully developed things too that plants are for
the sake of animals, and that the other animals are for the sake of human
beings, domestic ones both for using and eating, and most but not all
wild ones for food and other kinds of support, so that clothes and the
20   other tools may be got from them. If then nature makes nothing incomplete or pointless, it must have made all of them for the sake of human
beings. That is why even the science of warfare, since hunting is a part of
it, will in a way be a natural part of property acquisition. For this science
ought to be used not only against wild beasts but also against those
25   human beings who are unwilling to be ruled, but naturally suited for it,
as this sort of warfare is naturally just.

One kind of property acquisition is a natural part of household management,⁵⁴ then, in that a store of the goods that are necessary for life
and useful to the community of city-state or household either must be
available to start with, or household management must arrange to make
30   it available. At any rate, true wealth seems to consist in such goods. For
the amount of this sort of property that one needs for the self-sufficiency that promotes the good life is not unlimited, though Solon in his
poetry says it is: "No boundary to wealth has been established for

54. Alternatively: "one form of natural property acquisition is a part of household management."

human beings."[55] But such a limit or boundary has been established, just as in the other crafts. For none has any tool unlimited in size or num- 35 ber,[56] and wealth is a collection of tools belonging to statesmen and household managers.

It is clear, then, that there is a natural kind of property acquisition for household managers and statesmen, and it is also clear why this is so.

Chapter 9

But there is another type of property acquisition which is especially called wealth acquisition, and justifiably so. It is the reason wealth and 40 property are thought to have no limit. For many people believe that 1257ᵃ wealth acquisition is one and the same thing as the kind of property acquisition we have been discussing, because the two are close neighbors. But it is neither the same as the one we discussed nor all that far from it: one of them is natural, whereas the other is not natural, but comes from a sort of experience and craft.[57]

Let us begin our discussion of the latter as follows. Every piece of 5 property has two uses. Both of these are uses of it as such,[58] but they are not the same uses of it as such: one is proper to the thing and the other is not. Take the wearing of a shoe, for example, and its use in exchange. Both are uses to which shoes can be put. For someone who exchanges a shoe, for MONEY or food, with someone else who needs a shoe, is using 10 the shoe as a shoe. But this is not its proper use because it does not come to exist for the sake of exchange. The same is true of other pieces of property as well, since the science of exchange embraces all of them. It first arises out of the natural circumstance of some people having more 15 than enough and others less. This also makes it clear that the part of wealth acquisition which is commerce does not exist by nature: for people needed to engage in exchange only up to the point at which they had enough. It is evident, then, that exchange has no task to perform in the first community (that is to say, the household), but only when the com- 20

55. Diehl I.21, fr. 1.71. Solon (*c.* 640–560) was an Athenian statesman and poet, and first architect of the Athenian constitution. The limit to the amount of property needed for the good or happy life is determined by what happiness is. See 1257ᵇ28, *NE* 1128ᵇ18–25, 1153ᵇ21–25, *EE* 1249ᵃ22–ᵇ25.
56. See 1323ᵇ7–10.
57. See 1257ᵃ41–ᵇ5, 1258ᵃ38–ᵇ8.
58. *kath' hauto*: what something is as such or in itself or in its own right is what it is UNQUALIFIEDLY.

munity has become larger. For the members of the household used to share all the same things, whereas those in separate households shared next many different things, which they had to exchange with one another through barter when the need arose, as many non-Greek peoples
25 still do even to this day. For they exchange useful things for other useful things, but nothing beyond that—for example, wine is exchanged for wheat, and so on with everything else of this kind.

This kind of exchange is not contrary to nature, nor is it any kind of wealth acquisition; for its purpose was to fill a lack in a natural self-suf-
30 ficiency.[59] None the less, wealth acquisition arose out of it, and in an intelligible manner. Through importing what they needed and exporting their surplus, people increasingly got their supplies from more distant foreign sources. Since not all the natural necessities are easily trans-
35 portable, the use of money had of necessity to be devised. So for the purposes of exchange people agreed to give to and take from each other something that was a useful thing in its own right and that was convenient for acquiring the necessities of life: iron or silver or anything else of that sort. At first, its value was determined simply by size and weight,
40 but finally people also put a stamp on it, so as to save themselves the trouble of having to measure it. For the stamp was put on to indicate the amount.

1257^b   After money was devised, necessary exchange gave rise to the second of the two kinds of wealth acquisition, commerce. At first, commerce was probably a simple affair, but then it became more of a craft as experience taught people how and from what sources the greatest profit could be made through exchange. That is why it is held that wealth ac-
5 quisition is concerned primarily with money, and that its task is to be able to find sources from which a pile of wealth will come. For it is productive of wealth and money, and wealth is often assumed to be a pile of money, on the grounds that this is what wealth acquisition and commerce are concerned to provide.
10   On the other hand, it is also held that money itself is nonsense and wholly conventional, not natural at all. For if those who use money alter it, it has no value and is useless for acquiring necessities; and often someone who has lots of money is unable to get the food he needs. Yet it is absurd for something to be wealth if someone who has lots of it will

59. "Eating indiscriminately or drinking until we are too full is exceeding the quantity that suits nature, since the aim of a natural appetite is to fill a lack" (*NE* 1118^b18–19).

die of starvation, like Midas in the fable, when everything set before him 15
turned to gold in answer to his own greedy prayer. That is why people
look for a different kind of wealth and wealth acquisition, and rightly so;
for natural wealth and wealth acquisition *are* different. Natural wealth
acquisition is a part of household management, whereas commerce has 20
to do with the production of goods, not in the full sense, but *through
their exchange*. It is held to be concerned with money, on the grounds
that money is the unit and limit of exchange.[60]

The wealth that derives from this kind of wealth acquisition *is* without limit. For medicine aims at unlimited health, and each of the crafts 25
aims to achieve its end in an unlimited way, since each tries to achieve it
as fully as possible. (But none of the things that promote the end is unlimited, since the end itself constitutes a limit for all crafts.) Similarly,
there is no limit to the end of this kind of wealth acquisition, for its end
is wealth in that form, that is to say, the possession of money. The kind
of wealth acquisition that is a part of household management, on the
other hand, does have a limit, since this is not the task of household 30
management.

In one way, then, it seems that every sort of wealth has to have a limit.
Yet, if we look at what actually happens, the opposite seems true, for all
wealth acquirers go on increasing their money without limit. The explanation of this is that the two are closely connected. Each of the two 35
kinds of wealth acquisition makes use of the same thing, so their uses
overlap, since they are uses of the same property. But they do not use it
in accordance with the same principle. For one aims to increase it,
whereas the other aims at a different end. So some people believe that
this is the task of household management, and go on thinking that they
should maintain their store of money or increase it without limit. 40

The reason they are so disposed, however, is that they are preoccu-
pied with living, not with living well.[61] And since their appetite for life is
unlimited, they also want an unlimited amount of what sustains it. And 1258ᵃ
those who do aim at living well seek what promotes physical gratification. So, since this too seems to depend on having property, they spend
all their time acquiring wealth. And the second kind of wealth acquisi- 5
tion arose because of this. For since their gratification lies in excess, they
seek the craft that produces the excess needed for gratification. If they

60. The unit (*stoicheion*) for obvious reasons; the limit (*peras*) because the price
    of something delimits its exchange value. See Introduction lxxvi.
61. See 1252ᵇ29–30, 1280ᵃ31–32.

cannot get it through wealth acquisition, they try to do so by means of
something else that causes it, using each of their powers in an unnatural
10   way. For the end of courage is not to produce wealth but to produce confidence in the face of danger; nor is it the end of generalship or medicine
to do so, but rather victory and health. None the less, these people make
all of these into forms of wealth acquisition in the belief that acquiring
wealth is the end, and that everything ought to promote the end.

15   We have now said what unnecessary wealth acquisition is and why we
need it. We have also said that the necessary kind is different, that it is a
natural part of household management concerned with the means of
life, and that it is not limitless like this one, but has a limit.

Chapter 10

Clearly, we have also found the solution to our original problem about
whether the craft of wealth acquisition is that of a household manager or
20   a statesman, or not—this having rather to be available. For just as statesmanship does not make human beings, but takes them from nature and
uses them, so too nature must provide land or sea or something else as a
25   source of food, and a household manager must manage what comes from
these sources in the way required. For the task of weaving is not to make
wool but to use it, and to know which sorts are useful and suitable or
worthless and unsuitable. For one might be puzzled as to why wealth acquisition is a part of household management but medicine is not, even
30   though the members of a household need health, just as they need life
and every other necessity. And in fact there is a way in which it is the
task of a household manager or ruler to see to health, but in another way
it is not his task but a doctor's. So too with wealth: there is a way in
which a household manager has to see to it, and another in which he
does not, and an assistant craft does. But above all, as we said, nature
35   must ensure that wealth is there to start with. For it is the task of nature
to provide food for what is born, since the surplus of that from which
they come serves as food for every one of them.[62] That is why the craft of
acquiring wealth from crops and animals is natural for all people.

But, as we said, there are two kinds of wealth acquisition. One has to
do with commerce, the other with household management. The latter is
necessary and commendable, but the kind that has to do with exchange is

62. See 1256b10–12.

justly disparaged, since it is not natural but is from one another.[63] Hence   *1258ᵇ*
usury is very justifiably detested, since it gets wealth from money itself,
rather than from the very thing money was devised to facilitate. For
money was introduced to facilitate exchange, but interest makes money
itself grow bigger. (That is how it gets its name; for offspring resemble   *5*
their parents, and interest is money that comes from money.)[64] Hence of
all the kinds of wealth acquisition this one is the most unnatural.

Chapter 11

Now that we have adequately determined matters bearing on knowledge,
we should go through those bearing on practice.[65] A FREE person has
theoretical knowledge of all of these, but he will gain practical experi-   *10*
ence of them to meet necessary needs.[66] The practical parts of [1] wealth
acquisition are experience of: [1.1] livestock, for example, what sorts of
horses, cattle, sheep, and similarly other animals yield the most profit in
different places and conditions; for one needs practical experience of
which breeds are by comparison with one another the most profitable,   *15*
and which breeds yield the most profit in which places, as different ones
thrive in different places. [1.2] Farming, which is now divided into land
planted with fruit and land planted with cereals.[67] [1.3] Bee keeping and
the rearing of the other creatures, whether fish or fowl, that can be of
some use. These, then, are the parts of the primary and most appropriate kind of wealth acquisition.   *20*

[2] Exchange's most important part, on the other hand, is [2.1] trading, which has three parts: [2.1.1] ship owning, [2.1.2] transport, and
[2.1.3] marketing. These differ from one another in that some are safer,
others more profitable. The second part of exchange is [2.2] money
lending; the third is [2.3] wage earning. As for wage earning, some wage
earners are [2.3.1] vulgar craftsmen, whereas [2.3.2] others are un-   *25*
skilled, useful for manual labor only.

[3] A third kind of wealth acquisition comes between this kind and

63. Because for everyone who makes a profit in a commercial transaction, someone else makes a loss? See *Rh.* 1381ᵃ21–33, *Oec.* 1343ᵃ27–30.
64. *Tokos* means both "offspring" and "interest." See Plato, *Republic* 507a.
65. See 1253ᵇ14–18.
66. Alternatively: "but he cannot avoid practical experience of them."
67. Ancient farming consisted in the cultivation of wheat and other cereals on
flat open plains (*psilē*) and the cultivation of grapes, olives, etc. on more hilly
areas (*pephuteumenē*).

the primary or natural kind, since it contains elements both of the natural kind and of exchange. It deals with inedible but useful things from
30   the earth or extracted from the earth. Logging and mining are examples.
Mining too is of many types, since many kinds of things are mined from
the earth.

A general account has now been given of each of them. A detailed and
precise account might be useful for practical purposes, but it would be
35   VULGAR to spend one's time developing it.[68] (The operations that are
most craftlike depend least on luck; the more they damage the body, the
more vulgar they are; the most slavish are those in which the body is
used the most; the most ignoble are those least in need of virtue.) Besides, some people have written books on these matters which may be
studied by those interested. For example, Chares of Paros and Apol-
1259ᵃ lodorus of Lemnos[69] have written on how to farm both fruit and cereals,
and others have written on similar topics.

Moreover, the scattered stories about how people have succeeded in
acquiring wealth should be collected, since all of them are useful to
5   those who value wealth acquisition. For instance, there is the scheme of
Thales of Miletus.[70] This is a scheme for getting wealthy which, though
credited to him on account of his wisdom, is in fact quite generally applicable. People were reproaching Thales for being poor, claiming that it
10   showed his philosophy was useless. The story goes that he realized
through his knowledge of the stars that a good olive harvest was coming.
So, while it was still winter, he raised a little money and put a deposit on
all the olive presses in Miletus and Chios for future lease. He hired them
at a low rate, because no one was bidding against him. When the olive
season came and many people suddenly sought olive presses at the same
15   time, he hired them out at whatever rate he chose. He collected a lot of
money, showing that philosophers could easily become wealthy if they
wished, but that this is not their concern. Thales is said to have demonstrated his own wisdom in this way. But, as I said, his scheme involves a
20   generally applicable principle of wealth acquisition: to secure a monopoly if one can. Hence some city-states also adopt this scheme when they
are in need of money: they secure a monopoly in goods for sale.

68. See 1337ᵇ15–21.
69. Apollodorus was a contemporary of Aristotle's who wrote on practical farming; Chares is otherwise unknown.
70. Sixth-century philosopher and thinker who regarded water as the fundamental principle of all things.

There was a man in Sicily who used some money that had been lent to him to buy up all the iron from the foundries, and later, when the mer- 25 chants came from their warehouses to buy iron, he was the only seller. He did not increase his prices exorbitantly and yet he turned his fifty silver talents into one hundred and fifty. When Dionysius[71] heard about this, he told the man to take his wealth out, but to remain in Syracuse no longer, as he had discovered ways of making money that were harmful to 30 Dionysius' own affairs. Yet this man's insight was the same as Thales': each contrived to secure a monopoly for himself.

It is also useful for statesmen to know about these things, since many city-states have an even greater need for wealth acquisition and the associated revenues than a private household does. That is why indeed some 35 statesmen restrict their political activities entirely to finance.

Chapter 12

Household management has proved to have three parts: [1] one is mastership (which we discussed earlier), [2] another that of a father, and [3] a third, marital.[72] For a man rules his wife and children both as free people, but not in the same way: instead, he rules his wife the way a states- 40 man does,[73] and his children the way a king does. For a male, unless he 1259ᵇ is somehow constituted contrary to nature, is naturally more fitted to lead than a female, and someone older and completely developed is naturally more fitted to lead than someone younger and incompletely developed.

In most cases of rule of a statesman, it is true, people take turns at ruling and being ruled, because they tend by nature to be on an equal 5 footing and to differ in nothing. Nevertheless, whenever one person is ruling and another being ruled, the one ruling tries to distinguish him-

---

71. Probably Dionysius I, tyrant of Syracuse (406–367).
72. Mastership is discussed in I.7. At 1253ᵇ8–12 (see note) the science used by a father in ruling his children was called procreative science. The next sentence explains why such science needs to be distinguished from marital science. It seems that the natural kind of property acquisition, which is a branch of household management (1256ᵇ26–27), is here being included within slave mastery.
73. Rule of a statesman normally involves ruling and being ruled in turn (1259ᵇ4–6), but a husband always rules his wife and is never ruled by her (1259ᵇ9–10).

self in demeanor, title, or rank from the ruled; witness what Amasis said about his footbath.[74] Male is permanently related to female in this way.

10   The rule of a father over his children, on the other hand, is that of a king, since a parent rules on the basis of both age and affection, and this is a type of kingly rule. Hence Homer did well to address Zeus, who is the king of them all, as "Father of gods and men."[75] For a king should
15   have a natural superiority, but be the same in stock as his subjects; and this is the condition of older in relation to younger and father in relation to child.

Chapter 13

It is evident, then, that household management is more seriously con-
20   cerned with human beings than with inanimate property, with their virtue more than with its (which we call wealth), and with the virtue of free people more than with that of slaves.

The first problem to raise about slaves, then, is this: Has the slave some other virtue more estimable than those he has as a tool or servant, such as temperance, courage, justice, and other such states of character?
25   Or has he none besides those having to do with the physical assistance he provides? Whichever answer one gives, there are problems. If slaves have temperance and the rest, in what respect will they differ from the free? If they do not, absurdity seems to result, since slaves are human and have a share in reason. Roughly the same problem arises about
30   women and children. Do they too have virtues? Should women be temperate, courageous, and just, or a child be temperate or intemperate? Or not?

The problem of natural rulers and natural subjects, and whether their virtue is the same or different, needs to be investigated in general terms. If both of them should share in what is noble-and-good,[76] why should

74. The story of Amasis (596–525) is recounted in Herodotus II.172. When Amasis first became king of the Egyptians, they treated him with contempt because he was of humble origins. So he had a gold footbath made into a statue of a god. The Egyptians treated the statue with great respect. Amatis pointed out that he was like the footbath. He had once been an ordinary person, but he was now a king, worthy of honor and respect.

75. For example, *Iliad* I.544. See *NE* 1160^{b}24–27.

76. *kalokagathia*: if someone is noble-and-good, he must have a share in the virtues of character (*EE* 1248^{b}8–1249^{a}16). A noble-and-good man is, in our parlance, a gentleman.

one of them rule once and for all and the other be ruled once and for all? 35
(It cannot be that the difference between them is one of degree. Ruling
and being ruled differ in kind, but things that differ in degree do not
differ in that way.) On the other hand, if the one shares in what is noble-
and-good, and not the other, that would be astonishing. For if the ruler
is not going to be temperate and just, how will he rule well? And if the
subject is not going to be, how will he be ruled well? For if he is intem- 40
perate and cowardly, he will not perform any of his duties. It is evident, 1260ª
therefore, that both must share in virtue, but that there are differences
in their virtue (as there are among those who are naturally ruled).[77]

Consideration of the soul leads immediately to this view. The soul by
nature contains a part that rules and a part that is ruled, and we say that 5
each of them has a different virtue, that is to say, one belongs to the part
that has reason and one to the nonrational part. It is clear, then, that the
same holds in the other cases as well, so that most instances of ruling
and being ruled are natural. For free rules slaves, male rules female, and
man rules child in different ways, because, while the parts of the soul 10
are present in all these people, they are present in different ways. The
deliberative part of the soul is entirely missing from a SLAVE; a WOMAN
has it but it lacks authority; a child has it but it is incompletely developed. We must suppose, therefore, that the same necessarily holds of the
virtues of character too: all must share in them, but not in the same way; 15
rather, each must have a share sufficient to enable him to perform his
own task. Hence a ruler must have virtue of character complete, since
his task is unqualifiedly that of a master craftsman, and reason is a master craftsman,[78] but each of the others must have as much as pertains to
him. It is evident, then, that all those mentioned have virtue of character, and that temperance, courage, and justice of a man are not the same 20
as those of a woman, as Socrates supposed:[79] the one courage is that of a
ruler, the other that of an assistant, and similarly in the case of the other
virtues too.

If we investigate this matter in greater detail, it will become clear. For
people who talk in generalities, saying that virtue is a good condition of 25
the soul, or correct action, or something of that sort, are deceiving
themselves. It is far better to enumerate the virtues, as Gorgias does,

77. Reading *archomenōn* with Dreizehnter.
78. See 1253ᵇ33–1254ª1.
79. See Plato, *Meno* 73a6–c5.

than to define them in this general way.[80] Consequently, we must take
what the poet says about a woman as our guide in every case: "To a
woman silence is a crowning glory"[81]—whereas this does not apply to a
30   man. Since a child is incompletely developed, it is clear that his virtue
too does not belong to him in relation to himself but in relation to his
end and his leader.[82] The same holds of a slave in relation to his master.
But we said that a slave is useful for providing the necessities, so he
35   clearly needs only a small amount of virtue—just so much as will prevent him from inadequately performing his tasks through intemperance
or cowardice.

If what we have now said is true, one might raise the problem of
whether VULGAR CRAFTSMEN too need to have virtue; for they often fail
to perform their tasks through intemperance. Or are the two cases actually very different? For a slave shares his master's life, whereas a vulgar
40   craftsman is at a greater remove, and virtue pertains to him to just the
extent that slavery does; for a vulgar craftsman has a kind of delimited
1260ᵇ   slavery. Moreover, a slave is among the things that exist by nature,
whereas no shoemaker is, nor any other sort of craftsman. It is evident,
then, that the cause of such virtue in a slave must be the master, not the
one who possesses the science of teaching him his tasks. Hence those
5   who deny reason to slaves, but tell us to give them orders only, are mistaken;[83] for slaves should be admonished more than children.

But we may take these matters to be determined in this way. As for
man and woman, father and children, the virtue relevant to each of
10   them, what is good in their relationship with one another and what is not
good, and how to achieve the good and avoid the bad—it will be necessary to go through all these in connection with the constitutions.[84] For
every household is part of a city-state, these are parts of a household,
and the virtue of a part must be determined by looking to the virtue of
15   the whole.[85] Hence both women and children must be educated with an
eye to the constitution, if indeed it makes any difference to the virtue of

80. See Plato, *Meno* 71d4–72a5, where Meno, following Gorgias, lists the dis-
    tinct virtues of men, women, children, and slaves.
81. Sophocles, *Ajax* 293. See 1277ᵇ22–24, Thucydides II.45.
82. That is to say, the end he will have as a mature adult (happiness), and toward
    which his father is leading him.
83. A reference to Plato, *Laws* 777e.
84. No full discussion of these topics appears in the *Politics* as we have it.
85. See 1253ᵃ18–29, 1337ᵃ27–30.

a city-state that its children be virtuous, and its women too. And it must make a difference, since half the free population are women, and from children come those who participate in the constitution.

So, since we have determined some matters, and must discuss the rest   *20* elsewhere, let us regard the present discussion as complete, and make a new beginning. And let us first investigate those who have expressed views about the best constitution.

BOOK II

Chapter 1

Since we propose to study which political community is best of all for people who are able to live as ideally as possible,[1] we must investigate other constitutions too, both some of those used in city-states that are

30 said to be well governed, and any others described by anyone that are held to be good, in order to see what is correct or useful in them, but also to avoid giving the impression that our search for something different from them results from a desire to be clever. Let it be held, instead, that we have undertaken this inquiry because the currently available consti-

35 tutions are not in good condition.

We must begin, however, at the natural starting point of this investigation. For all citizens must share everything, or nothing, or some things but not others. It is evidently impossible for them to share nothing. For

40 a constitution is a sort of community, and so they must, in the first instance, share their location; for one city-state occupies one location, and

1261ᵃ citizens share that one city-state. But is it better for a city-state that is to be well managed to share everything possible? Or is it better to share some things but not others? For the citizens could share children,

5 women, and property with one another, as in Plato's *Republic*.[2] For Socrates claims there that children, women, and property should be communal. So is what we have now better, or what accords with the law described in the *Republic*?

Chapter 2

10 That women should be common to all raises many difficulties. In particular, it is not evident from Socrates' arguments why he thinks this legis-

---

1. As not many people are; see 1288ᵇ23–24. Ideal conditions are literally those that are answers to our prayers (*kat' euchēn*).
2. See 423e–424a, 449a–466d.

lation is needed. Besides, the end he says his city-state should have is impossible, as in fact described, yet nothing has been settled about how one ought to delimit it. I am talking about the assumption that it is best for a city-state to be as far as possible all one unit; for that is the assumption Socrates adopts.[3] And yet it is evident that the more of a unity   15
a city-state becomes, the less of a city-state it will be. For a city-state naturally consists of a certain multitude; and as it becomes more of a unity, it will turn from a city-state into a household, and from a household into a human being. For we would surely say that a household is more of a unity than a city-state and an individual human being than a   20
household. Hence, even if someone could achieve this, it should not be done, since it will destroy the city-state.

A city-state consists not only of a number of people, but of people of different kinds, since a city-state does not come from people who are alike. For a city-state is different from a military alliance. An alliance is useful because of the weight of numbers, even if they are all of the same   25
kind, since the natural aim of a military alliance is the sort of mutual assistance that a heavier weight provides if placed on a scales. A nation will also differ from a city-state in this sort of way, provided the multitude is not separated into villages, but is like the Arcadians.[4] But things from which a unity must come differ in kind. That is why reciprocal EQUAL-
ITY preserves city-states, as we said earlier in the *Ethics*,[5] since this must   30
exist even among people who are free and equal. For they cannot all rule at the same time, but each can rule for a year or some other period. As a result they all rule, just as all would be shoemakers and carpenters if they changed places, instead of the same people always being shoemak-   35
ers and the others always carpenters. But since it is better to have the latter also where a political community is concerned, it is clearly better, where possible, for the same people always to rule. But among those where it is not possible, because all are naturally equal, and where it is at the same time just for all to share the benefits or burdens of ruling, it is   1261ᵇ
at least possible to approximate to this if those who are equal take turns and are similar when out of office. For they rule and are ruled in turn, just as if they had become other people. It is the same way among those   5
who are ruling; some hold one office, some another.

3. See *Republic* 462a.
4. The Arcadians of Aristotle's day were organized into a confederacy of city-states.
5. See *NE* 1132ᵇ32–1134ᵃ30, 1163ᵇ32–1164ᵃ2, *EE* 1242ᵇ1–21, 1243ᵇ29–36.
   Further discussed at III.9, Introduction lxv–lxvi.

It is evident from these considerations that a city-state is not a natural unity in the way some people say it is, and that what has been alleged to be the greatest good for city-states destroys them, whereas what is good 10 for a thing preserves it.[6] It is also evident on other grounds that to try to make a city-state too much a unity is not a better policy. For a household is more self-sufficient than a single person, and a city-state than a household; and a city-state tends to come about as soon as a community's population is large enough to be fully self-sufficient. So, since what is more self-sufficient is more choiceworthy, what is less a unity is 15 more choiceworthy than what is more so.

Chapter 3

But even if it is best for a community to be as much a unity as possible, this does not seem to have been established by the argument that everyone says "mine" and "not mine" at the same time (for Socrates takes this as an indication that his city-state is completely one).[7] For "all" is am-20 biguous. If it means each individually, perhaps more of what Socrates wants will come about, since each will then call the same woman his wife, the same person his son, the same things his property, and so on for each thing that befalls him. But this is not in fact how those who have 25 women and children in common will speak. They will *all* speak, but not *each*. And the same goes for property: all, not each. It is evident, then, that there is an equivocation involved in "all say." (For "all," "both," "odd," and "even," are ambiguous, and give rise to contentious argu-30 ments even in discussion.)[8] Hence in one sense it would be good if all said the same, but not possible, whereas in the other sense it is in no way conducive to concord.

But the phrase is also harmful in another way, since what is held in common by the largest number of people receives the least care. For people give most attention to their own property, less to what is commu-

6. See *Republic* 608e.
7. See *Republic* 462a–e.
8. "A contentious (*eristikos*) argument is one that appears to reach a conclusion but does not" (*Top.* 162b3–5). "In discussion" perhaps refers to formal philosophical or dialectical discussions, where higher standards of argumentation may be expected. For an example of a different sort, see 1307b36–39.

nal, or only as much as falls to them to give.[9] For apart from anything
else, the thought that someone else is attending to it makes them neglect   *35*
it the more (just as a large number of household servants sometimes give
worse service than a few). Each of the citizens acquires a thousand sons,
but they do not belong to him as an individual: any of them is equally
the son of any citizen, and so will be equally neglected by them all. Be-   *40*
sides, each says "mine" of whoever among the citizens is doing well or   *1262ᵃ*
badly[10] in this sense, that he is whatever fraction he happens to be of a
certain number. What he really means is "mine or so-and-so's," referring in this way to each of the thousand or however many who constitute
the city-state. And even then he is uncertain, since it is not clear who has
had a child born to him, or one who once born survived. Yet is this way   *5*
of calling the same thing "mine" as practiced by each of two or ten thousand people really better than the way they in fact use "mine" in city-
states? For the same person is called "my son" by one person, "my
brother" by another, "my cousin" by a third, or something else in virtue   *10*
of some other connection of kinship or marriage, one's own marriage, in
the first instance, or that of one's relatives. Still others call him "my fellow clansman" or "my fellow tribesman." For it is better to have a cousin
of one's own than a son in the way Socrates describes.

    Moreover, it is impossible to prevent people from having suspicions
about who their own brothers, sons, fathers, and mothers are. For the re-   *15*
semblances that occur between parents and children will inevitably be
taken as evidence of this. And this is what actually happens, according to
the reports of some of those who write accounts of their world travels.
They say that some of the inhabitants of upper Libya have their women
in common, and yet distinguish the children on the basis of their resem-   *20*
blance to their fathers.[11] And there are some women, as well as some females of other species such as mares and cows, that have a strong natural
tendency to produce offspring resembling their sires, like the mare in
Pharsalus called "Just."[12]

---

9. For example, someone might have official responsibility for or a special in-
    terest in some common property.
10. See *Republic* 463e2–5.
11. See Herodotus IV.180. At *Rh.* 1360ᵃ33–35, Aristotle comments on the util-
    ity of such travel writings in drafting laws.
12. She is called "Just" because in producing offspring like the sire, she made a
    just return on his investment, and showed herself to be a virtuous and faith-
    ful wife. See *HA* 586ᵃ12–14. Pharsalus was in Thessaly in northern Greece.

Chapter 4

Moreover, there are other difficulties that it is not easy for the establish-
25 ers of this sort of community to avoid, such as voluntary or involuntary
homicides, assaults, or slanders. None of these is pious when committed
against fathers, mothers, or not too distant relatives (just as none is even
against outsiders).[13] Yet they are bound to occur even more frequently
30 among those who do not know[14] their relatives than among those who
do. And when they do occur, the latter can perform the customary expi-
ation, whereas the former cannot.

It is also strange that while making sons communal, he forbids sexual
intercourse only between lovers,[15] but does not prohibit sexual love itself
or the other practices which, between father and son or a pair of broth-
35 ers, are most indecent, since even the love alone is. It is strange, too, that
Socrates forbids such sexual intercourse solely because the pleasure that
comes from it is so intense, but regards the fact that the lovers are father
40 and son or brother and brother as making no difference.[16]

It would seem more useful to have the farmers rather than the
guardians share their women and children.[17] For there will be less
1262[b] friendship where women and children are held in common.[18] But it is
the *ruled* who should be like that, in order to promote obedience and
prevent rebellion.

In general, the results of such a law are necessarily the opposite of
5 those of a good law, and the opposite of those that Socrates aims to
achieve by organizing the affairs of children and women in this way. For
we regard friendship as the greatest of goods for city-states, since in this
condition people are least likely to factionalize. And Socrates himself

---

13. Reading *hōsper kai pros apōthen* with the mss. The sentence is ambiguous,
even if *kai* is omitted, as it is by Ross and Dreizehnter. But it cannot mean
or imply that homicides, assaults, and slanders *are* pious when committed
against outsiders. The implication is that these acts are *particularly* impious
when committed against relatives, since even against outsiders they are so.
See Plato, *Laws* 868c–873c.
14. Reading *gnōrizontōn* with Dreizehnter and the mss.
15. Homosexual male lovers are meant.
16. See *Republic* 403a–c.
17. The ideal city-state described in the *Republic* has three parts, producers
(farmers), guardians, and philosopher-kings. The latter two share their
women, children, and other property in common. The text is less clear
about whether this is also true of the producers. See 1264[a]11–[b]5.
18. Perhaps for the sort of reason given at 1263[a]8–21.

particularly praises unity in a city-state, something that is held to be, and that he himself says is, the result of friendship. (Similarly, in the 10 erotic dialogues, we know that Aristophanes says that lovers, because of their excessive friendship, want to grow together and become one instead of two.[19] The result in such circumstances, however, is that one or both has necessarily perished.) But in a city-state this sort of community inevitably makes friendship watery, in that father hardly ever says 15 "mine" of son, or son of father. For just as adding a lot of water to a drop of sweet wine makes the mixture undetectable, so it is with the kinship connections expressed in these names, since in a constitution of this sort a father has least reason to cherish his sons as sons, or a son his father as 20 a father, or brothers each other as brothers. For there are two things in particular that cause human beings to love and cherish something: their own and their favorite. And neither can exist among those governed in this way.[20]

But there is also a lot of confusion about the way in which the children, once born, will be transferred from the farmers and craftsmen to 25 the guardians, and vice versa.[21] Those who do the transferring and receiving are sure to know who has been transferred to whom. Besides, in these cases the results we mentioned earlier must of necessity happen even more often—I mean assaults, love affairs, and murders. For those 30 who have been transferred to the other citizens will no longer call the guardians "brothers," "children," "fathers," or "mothers," nor will those who have been transferred to the guardians use these terms of the other citizens, so as to avoid committing, through kinship, any such offenses.

So much for our conclusions about community of women and chil- 35 dren.

---

19. Aristophanes appears as a character in Plato's *Symposium*, where he expresses the view under discussion (192c–193a).
20. Aristotle's discussion of favorite things (*to agapēton*) at *Rh.* 1365^{b}16–20 explains what he has in mind: "A favorite thing, since it is unique, is a greater good than something that is one among others. Hence someone who puts out the eye of a one-eyed man does not do the same harm as someone who does this to a man who has two eyes, since he deprives him of a favorite thing." Hence, in Aristotle's view, there are no favorites in Socrates' ideal city-state because everyone there *is* just "one among others." Plato, of course, wants to draw the opposite conclusion: that *everyone* is a favorite there.
21. See *Republic* 415a–c.

Chapter 5

The next topic to investigate is property, and how those in the best constitution should arrange it. Should it be owned in common, or not? One
could investigate these questions even in isolation from the legislation
dealing with women and children. I mean even if women and children
belong to separate individuals, which is in fact the practice everywhere,
it still might be best for property either to be owned or used communally. For example, [1] the land might be owned separately, while the
crops grown on it are communally stored and consumed (as happens in
some nations). [2] Or it might be the other way around: the land might
be owned and farmed communally, while the crops grown on it are divided up among individuals for their private use (some non-Greeks are
also said to share things in this way). [3] Or both the land and the crops
might be communal.

1263ᵃ

  If the land is worked by others, the constitution is different and easier. But if the citizens do the work for themselves, property arrangements will give rise to a lot of discontent. For if the citizens happen to be
unequal rather than equal in the work they do and the profits they enjoy,
accusations will inevitably be made against those who enjoy or take a lot
but do little work by those who take less but do more. It is generally difficult to live together and to share in any human enterprise, particularly
in enterprises such as these. Travelers away from home who share a journey together show this clearly. For most of them start quarreling because
they annoy one another over humdrum matters and little things. Moreover, we get especially irritated with those servants we employ most regularly for everyday services.

  These, then, and others are the difficulties involved in the common
ownership of property. The present practice, provided it was enhanced
by virtuous character[22] and a system of correct laws, would be much superior. For it would have the good of both—by "of both" I mean of the
common ownership of property and of private ownership. For while
property should be in some way communal, in general it should be private. For when care for property is divided up, it leads not to those
mutual accusations, but rather to greater care being given, as each will
be attending to what is his own. But where use is concerned, virtue will
ensure that it is governed by the proverb "friends share everything in
common."

5

10

15

20

25

30

---

22. Reading *ēthesi* with Dreizehnter and some mss.

Such a practice is already present in outline form in some city-states, which implies that it is not impracticable. In well-managed city-states, in particular, some elements exist, whereas others could come to be. For although each citizen does own private property, he makes part of it available for his friends to use and keeps part for his own use.[23] For example, in Sparta they pretty much have common[24] use of each other's slaves, and dogs and horses also; and when on a journey in the country- 35 side, they may take what provisions they need from the fields. Evidently, then, it is better for property to be private and its use communal. It is the legislator's special task to see that people are so disposed.[25]

Besides, to regard a thing as one's own makes an enormous difference 40 to one's pleasure. For the love each person feels for himself is no acci- dent, but is something natural. Selfishness is rightly criticized. But it is 1263[b] not just loving oneself, it is loving oneself more than one should, just as in the case of the love of money (since practically everyone does love each of these things). Moreover, it is very pleasant to help one's friends, 5 guests, or companions, and do them favors, as one can if one has prop- erty of one's own. But those who make the city-state too much a unity by abolishing private property exclude these pleasures. They also openly take away the tasks of two of the virtues: of temperance in regard to women (for it is a fine thing to stay away from another man's woman out of temperance), and generosity with one's property, since one cannot 10 show oneself to be generous, nor perform any generous action (for it is in the use made of property that generosity's task lies).

Such legislation may seem attractive, and humane. For anyone who 15 hears it accepts it gladly, thinking that all will have an amazing friend- ship for all, particularly when someone blames the evils now existing in constitutions on property's not being communal (I mean lawsuits brought against one another over contracts, perjury trials, and flattery of 20 the rich).[26] Yet none of these evils is caused by property not being com- munal but by vice. For we see that those who own and share communal property have far more disagreements than those whose property is sep- arate. But we consider those disagreeing over what they own in common 25 to be few, because we compare them with the many whose property is private. Furthermore, it would be fair to mention not only how many

23. Reading *idiois* with Richards.
24. Reading *koinois* with Richards.
25. That is to say, disposed to treat property in that way. See 1329[b]36–1330[a]33.
26. See *Republic* 464d–465d.

evils people will lose through sharing, but also how many good things. The life they would lead seems to be totally impossible.

30   One has to think that the reason Socrates goes astray is that his assumption is incorrect. For a household and a city-state must indeed be a unity up to a point, but not totally so. For there is a point at which it will, as it goes on, not be a city-state, and another at which, by being nearly not a city-state, it will be a worse one. It is as if one were to reduce a har-

35 mony to a unison, or a rhythm to a single beat. But a city-state consists of a multitude, as we said before,[27] and should be unified and made into a community by means of education. It is strange, at any rate, that the one who aimed to bring in education, and who believed that through it the city-state would be excellent, should think to set it straight by measures of this sort, and not by habits, philosophy, and laws[28]—as in Sparta and Crete, where the legislator aimed to make property communal by

40 means of the MESSES.

1264ᵃ   And we must not overlook this point, that we should consider the immense period of time and the many years during which it would not have gone unnoticed if these measures were any good. For practically speaking all things have been discovered,[29] although some have not been collected, and others are known about but not used. The matter would

5 become particularly evident, however, if one could see such a constitution actually being instituted. For it is impossible to construct his city-state without separating the parts and dividing it up into common messes or into clans and tribes. Consequently, nothing else will be legislated except that the guardians should not do any farming, which is the

10 very thing the Spartans are trying to enforce even now.

    But the fact is that Socrates has not said, nor is it easy to say, what the arrangement of the constitution as a whole is for those who participate in it. The multitude of the other citizens constitute pretty well the entire multitude of his city-state, yet nothing has been determined about them,

---

27. At 1261ᵃ18.
28. Good habits promote the virtues of character; philosophy, here probably to be understood fairly loosely, promotes the virtues of thought, and the good use of LEISURE; laws sustain both.
29. See also 1329ᵇ25–35. Two of Aristotle's other views explain this otherwise implausible claim: (1) The world and human beings have always existed (*Mete.* 352ᵇ16–17, *GA* 731ᵇ24–732ᵃ3, 742ᵇ17–743ᵃ1, *DA* 415ᵃ25–ᵇ7). (2) Human beings are naturally adapted to form largely reliable beliefs about the world and what conduces to their welfare in it (*Metaph.* 993ᵃ30–ᵇ11, *Rh.* 1355ᵃ15–17).

whether the farmers too should have communal property or each his   *15*
own private property, or whether their women and children should be
private or communal.[30] If all is to be common to all in the same way, how
will they differ from the guardians? And how will they benefit from sub-
mitting to their rule? Or what on earth will prompt them to submit to
it—unless the guardians adopt some clever stratagem like that of the
Cretans? For the Cretans allow their slaves to have the same other things   *20*
as themselves, and forbid them only the gymnasia and the possession of
weapons. On the other hand, if they[31] too are to have such things, as they
do in other city-states, what sort of community will it be? For it will inevitably be two city-states in one, and those opposed to one another.[32]   *25*
For he makes the guardians into a sort of garrison, and the farmers,
craftsmen, and the others into the citizens.[33] Hence the indictments,
lawsuits, and such other bad things as he says exist in other city-states
will all exist among them. And yet Socrates claims that because of their
education they will not need many regulations, such as town or market   *30*
ordinances and others of that sort. Yet he gives this education only to the
guardians.[34] Besides, he gives the farmers authority over their property,
although he requires them to pay a tax.[35] But this is likely to make them
much more difficult and presumptuous than the helots,[36] serfs, and
slaves that some people have today.   *35*

But be that as it may, whether these matters are similarly essential or
not, nothing at any rate has been determined about them; neither are the
related questions of what constitution, education, and laws they will
have. The character of these people is not easy to discover, and the difference it makes to the preservation of the community of the guardians
is not small. But if Socrates is going to make their women communal
and their property private, who will manage the household in the way   *1264ᵇ*

---

30. Aristotle is justified in thinking that Socrates is vague about this. Farmers
     initially seem to have a traditional family life and to possess private prop-
     erty. But casual remarks at 433d and 454d–e suggest that this may not be so,
     that female producers will not necessarily be housewives, but will be trained
     in the craft for which their natural aptitude is highest.
31. The citizens other than the guardians.
32. This is a criticism that Socrates brings against other city-states at *Republic*
     422e–423b.
33. See *Republic* 415a–417b, 419a–421c, 543b–c.
34. See *Republic* 424a–426e.
35. See *Republic* 416d–e.
36. Helots were the serf population of Sparta.

the men manage things in the fields? Who will manage it, indeed, if the farmers' women and property are communal? It is futile to draw a comparison with wild beasts in order to show that women should have the
5   same way of life as men: wild beasts do not go in for household management.[37]

The way Socrates selects his rulers is also risky. He makes the same people rule all the time, which becomes a cause of conflict even among people with no merit, and all the more so among spirited and warlike
10   men.[38] But it is evident that he has to make the same people rulers, since the gold from the god has not been mixed into the souls of one lot of people at one time and another at another, but always into the same ones. He says that the god, immediately at their birth, mixed gold into the souls of some, silver into others, and bronze and iron into those who are
15   going to be craftsmen and farmers.

Moreover, even though Socrates deprives the guardians of their happiness, he says that the legislator should make the whole city-state happy.[39] But it is impossible for the whole to be happy unless all, most, or some of its parts are happy. For happiness is not made up of the same
20   things as evenness, since the latter can be present in the whole without being present in either of the parts,[40] whereas happiness cannot. But if the guardians are not happy, who is? Surely not the skilled craftsmen or the multitude of VULGAR CRAFTSMEN.

These, then, are the problems raised by the constitution Socrates de-
25   scribes, and there are others that are no less great.

Chapter 6

Pretty much the same thing holds in the case of the *Laws*, which was written later, so we had better also briefly examine the constitution

37. See *Republic* 451d–e.
38. The guardians are spirited and warlike. The rulers (philosopher-kings) are selected from among them. Aristotle is claiming that those who are not selected will resent this. Presumably, he has the provisional selection of rulers at *Republic* 412b–417b in mind, since it contains the Myth of the Metals, and not the selection of philosopher-kings that replaces it at 535a–536d.
39. Aristotle is referring to *Republic* 420b–421c, 519e–520d. What Socrates actually says there is that the aim of the legislator is not to make the guardians or any other single group "*outstandingly* happy but to make the whole city-state so, as far as possible." He thinks that the guardians will still be as happy as possible. See, e.g., 465d–e.
40. Two is an even number, but its integral parts are both odd.

there. In fact, Socrates has settled very few topics in the *Republic*: the
way in which women and children should be shared in common; the system of property; and the organization of the constitution. For he divides   30
the multitude of the inhabitants into two parts: the farmers and the defensive soldiers. And from the latter he takes a third, which is the part of
the city-state that deliberates and is in authority.[41] But as to whether the
farmers and skilled craftsmen will participate in ruling to some extent or
not at all, and whether or not they are to own weapons and join in bat-   35
tle—Socrates has settled nothing about these matters.[42] He does think,
though, that guardian women should join in battle and receive the same
education as the other guardians. Otherwise, he has filled out his account with extraneous discussions,[43] including those about the sort of
education the guardians should receive.   40

Most of the *Laws* consist, in fact, of laws, and he has said little about   1265ᵃ
the constitution. He wishes to make it more generally attainable by actual city-states,[44] yet he gradually turns it back toward the other constitution.[45] For, with the exception of the communal possession of women
and property, the other things he puts in both constitutions are the   5
same: the same education,[46] the life of freedom from necessary work,[47]
and, on the same principles, the same messes—except that in this constitution he says that there are to be messes for women too;[48] and
whereas the other one consisted of one thousand weapon owners, this
one is to consist of five thousand.[49] All the Socratic dialogues have some-   10
thing extraordinary, sophisticated, innovative, and probing about them;
but it is perhaps difficult to do everything well. Consider, for example,
the multitude just mentioned. We must not forget that it would need a
territory the size of Babylon or some other unlimitedly large territory to

41. See *Republic* 412b–417b, 428c–d, 535a–536d.
42. Aristotle overlooks *Republic* 434a–c, where Socrates provides explicit guid-
    ance on these topics.
43. Reading *tois exōthen logois* with Dreizehnter and the mss.
44. See *Laws* 739a ff., 745e ff., 805b–d, 853c.
45. The constitution described in the *Republic*.
46. See *Laws* 961a–968b.
47. See *Laws* 741e, 806d–807d, 842d, 846d, 919d ff.
48. In the *Republic*, female guardians share the same messes as the men
    (458c–d). In the *Laws*, all the female citizens have messes of their own, sep-
    arate from the men's (780d ff., 806e–807b, 842b).
49. See *Laws* 737e, 740c. Aristotle probably gets the number one thousand from
    Republic 423a.

15   keep five thousand people in idleness, and a crowd of women and servants along with them, many times as great. We should assume ideal
conditions, to be sure, but nothing that is impossible.

It is stated that a legislator should look to just two things in establish-
20   ing his laws: the territory and the people.[50] But it would also be good to
add the neighboring regions too, if first, the city-state is to live a political life,[51] not a solitary one; for it must then have the weapons that are
useful for waging war not only on its own territory but also against the
25   regions outside it. But if one rejects such a life, both for the individual
and for the city-state in common, the need to be formidable to enemies
is just as great, both when they are invading its territory and when they
are staying away from it.[52]

The amount of property should also be looked at, to see whether it
would not be better to determine it differently and on a clearer basis. He
says that a person should have as much as he needs in order to live tem-
30   perately, which is like saying "as much as he needs to live well." For the
formulation is much too general. Besides, it is possible to live a temperate life but a wretched one. A better definition is "temperately and generously"; for when separated, the one will lead to poverty, the other to
luxury. For these are the only choiceworthy states that bear on the use of
35   property. One cannot use property either mildly or courageously, for example, but one can use it temperately and generously. Hence, too, the
states concerned with its use must be these.

It is also strange to equalize property and not to regulate the number
40   of citizens, leaving the birth rate unrestricted in the belief that the existence of infertility will keep it sufficiently steady no matter how many
births there are, because this seems to be what happens in actual city-
1265ᵇ states.[53] But the same exactness on this matter is not required in actual
city-states as in this one. For in actual city-states no one is left destitute,
because property can be divided among however great a number. But, in
this city-state, property is indivisible,[54] so that excess children will nec-

---

50. This is not said anywhere in our text of the *Laws*, but Aristotle may be in-
ferring it from 704a–709a, 747d, 842c–e. His subsequent criticisms overlook
737d, 758c, 949e ff.
51. City-states typically lead a political life in part by interacting with other
city-states (1327ᵇ3–6), but even isolated city-states can lead such a life provided their parts interact appropriately (1325ᵇ23–27).
52. Reading *apousin* with Bender. The mss. have *apelthousin*: "when they are
leaving it." The political life is discussed in the Introduction xlvi–xlvii.
53. Aristotle apparently overlooks *Laws* 736a, 740b–741a, 923d.
54. See *Laws* 740b, 741b, 742c, 855a–b, 856d–e.

essarily get nothing, no matter whether they are few or many. One might 5
well think instead that it is the birth rate that should be limited, rather
than property, so that no more than a certain number are born. (One
should fix this number by looking to the chances that some of those born
will not survive, and that others will be childless.) To leave the number
unrestricted, as is done in most city-states, inevitably causes poverty 10
among the citizens; and poverty produces faction and crime. In fact,
Pheidon of Corinth,[55] one of the most ancient legislators, thought that
the number of citizens should be kept the same as the number of household estates, even if initially they all had estates of unequal size. But in 15
the *Laws*, it is just the opposite.[56] Our own view as to how these things
might be better arranged, however, will have to be given later.[57]

Another topic omitted from the *Laws* concerns the rulers: how they
will differ from the ruled. He says that just as warp and woof come from
different sorts of wool, so should ruler be related to ruled.[58] Further- 20
more, since he permits a person's total property to increase up to five
times its original value,[59] why should this not also hold of land up to a
certain point? The division of homesteads also needs to be examined, in
case it is disadvantageous to household management. For he assigns two
of the separate homesteads resulting from the division to each individual; but it is difficult to run two households.[60] 25

The overall organization tends to be neither a democracy nor an oligarchy but midway between them; it is called a POLITY, since it is made
up of those with HOPLITE weapons.[61] If, of the various constitutions, he
is establishing this as the one generally most acceptable to actual city-
states, his proposal is perhaps good, but if as next best after the first con- 30

---

55. Otherwise unknown.
56. Plato fixes the number of household estates and makes them of equal size,
    but, in Aristotle's view, he does not effectively limit the number of citizens.
    See 1330^{a}2–23, 1335^{b}19–26.
57. At 1335^{b}19–1336^{a}2.
58. See *Laws* 734e–735a, but also 632c, 818a, 951e ff., 961a ff., *Statesman*
    308d–311c.
59. See *Laws* 744e.
60. See *Laws* 745c–e, 775e–776b. The point of the division seems to be to pro-
    vide a married son with a household of his own (776a). Despite these reser-
    vations, Aristotle himself adopts a similar arrangement in his ideal city-
    state, though for different reasons (1330^{a}14–25).
61. This is a larger class than the class of wealthy citizens, which rules in an oli-
    garchy, but, since hoplite weapons are expensive, a smaller one than the en-
    tire citizen body, which rules in a democracy. Hence a polity is midway (or
    in a mean) between an oligarchy and a democracy.

stitution, it is not good.[62] For one might well commend the Spartan constitution, or some other more aristocratic one. Some people believe, in-
35   deed, that the best constitution is a mixture of all constitutions, which is
why they commend the Spartan constitution. For some say that it is
made up of oligarchy, monarchy, and democracy; they say the kingship
is a monarchy, the office of senators an oligarchy, and that it is governed
democratically in virtue of the office of the overseers (because the overseers are selected from the people as a whole). Others of them say that
40   the overseership is a tyranny, and that it is governed democratically because of the messes and the rest of daily life.[63] But in the *Laws* it is said
1266*ᵃ*   that the best constitution should be composed of democracy and
tyranny, constitutions one might well consider as not being CONSTITU-
TIONS at all, or as being the worst ones of all.[64] Therefore, the proposal
of those who mix together a larger number is better, because a constitu-
5   tion composed of a larger number is better.[65]

Next, the constitution plainly has no monarchical features at all, but
only oligarchic and democratic ones, with a tendency to lean more toward
oligarchy. This is clear from the method of selecting officials. For to select
by lot from a previously elected pool is common to both. But it is oligarchic to require richer people to attend the assembly, to vote for offi-
10   cials, and to perform any other political duties, without requiring these
things of the others.[66] The same is true of the attempt to ensure that the
majority of officials come from among the rich, with the most important
ones coming from among those with the highest PROPERTY ASSESSMENT.[67]

62. Plato seems to have chosen his constitution for both reasons (*Laws* 739a ff.,
     745e ff., 805b–d, 853c).
63. See 1294ᵇ13–40. On senators, kings, and overseers, see II.9 and notes.
64. Plato describes monarchy (not tyranny) and democracy as the "mothers" of
     all constitutions (*Laws* 693d–e). He describes the constitution he is propos-
     ing, which is not the best but the second best, as a mean between monarchy
     and democracy (756e). In the *Republic*, where he sets out the best constitu-
     tion, he agrees with Aristotle that democracy and tyranny are the worst con-
     stitutions possible (580a–c).
65. The conclusion hardly follows. But the point is perhaps this: a constitution
     in which principles drawn from a large number of other constitutions are
     mixed will serve the interests of more citizens (whatever their own political
     leanings) and so will be more stable (1270ᵇ17–28) and more just
     (1294ᵃ15–25).
66. See *Laws* 756b–e, 763d–767d, 951d–e.
67. This is true of the market and city-state managers but it is not so clearly true
     of other important officials. See *Laws* 753b–d, 755b–756b, 766a–c, 946a.

He also makes the election of the council oligarchic.[68] First, everyone is required to elect candidates from the first property-assessment class, then again in the same way[69] from the second, then from members of the third—except that not everyone was required to elect candidates from members of it or of the fourth class, and only members of the first and second classes are required to elect candidates from members of the fourth. Then from these, he says, an equal number must be selected from each assessment class. As a result, those from the highest assessment classes will be more numerous and better, since some of the common people will not vote because they are not required to.

It is evident from this, and from what we shall say later when our investigation reaches this sort of constitution,[70] that such a constitution should not be constituted out of democracy and monarchy. As for the elections of officials, electing from the elected is dangerous. For, if even a relatively small number of people combine, the election will always turn out the way they want.

This, then, is how things stand concerning the constitution of the *Laws*.

Chapter 7

There are other constitutions, too, proposed either by private individuals or by philosophers and statesmen. But all of them are closer to the established constitutions under which people are actually governed than either of Plato's. For no one else has ever suggested the innovations of sharing children and women, or of messes for women.[71] Rather, they begin with the necessities. Some of them hold, indeed, that the most important thing is to have property well organized, for they say that it is over property that everyone creates faction. That is why Phaleas of Chalcedon,[72] the first to propose such a constitution, did so; for he says that the property of the citizens should be equal. He thought this was not difficult to do when city-states were just being founded, but that in those already in operation it would be more difficult. Nonetheless, he thought that a leveling could very quickly be achieved by the rich giving but not

---

68. At *Laws* 756b–e.
69. Reading *isōs* with Dreizehnter and Saunders.
70. See IV.7–9, 1296b34–1297a13.
71. Aristotle gives a longer list of Platonic innovations at 1274b9–15.
72. An older contemporary of Plato.

receiving dowries, and the poor receiving but not giving them. (Plato,
5   when writing the *Laws*, thought that things should be left alone up to a
certain point, but that no citizen should have more than five times the
smallest amount, as we also said earlier.)[73] However, people who make
such laws should not forget, as in fact they do, that while regulating the
quantity of property they should regulate the quantity of children too.
10   For if the number of children exceeds the amount of property, it is certainly necessary to abrogate the law. But abrogation aside, it is a bad
thing for many to become poor after having been rich, since it is a task to
prevent people like that from becoming revolutionaries.

15   That leveling property has some influence on political communities
was evidently understood even by some people long ago; for example,
both by Solon in his laws,[74] and the law in force elsewhere which prohibits anyone from getting as much land as he might wish. Laws likewise
prevent the sale of property, as among the Locrians[75] where the law for-
20   bids it unless an obvious misfortune can be shown to have occurred. In
yet other cases it is required that the original allotments be preserved intact. It was the abrogation of this provision, to cite one example, that
made the constitution of Leucas[76] too democratic, since as a result men
no longer entered office from the designated assessment classes. But
25   equality of property may exist and yet the amount may be too high, so
that it leads to luxurious living, or too low, so that a penny-pinching life
results. It is clear, then, that it is not enough for the legislator to make
property equal, he must also aim at the mean. Yet even if one prescribed
a moderate amount for everyone, it would be of no use. For one should
level desires more than property, and that cannot happen unless people
30   have been adequately educated by the laws.[77]

Phaleas would perhaps reply that this is actually what he means; for
he thinks that city-states should have equality in these two things: property and education. But one also ought to say what the education is
going to be. And it is no use for it be one and the same. For it can be one
35   and the same, but of the sort that will produce people who deliberately
choose to be ACQUISITIVE of money or honor or both. Besides, people re-

73. At 1265ᵇ21–23.
74. Discussed at 1273ᵇ35–1274ᵃ21.
75. A Greek settlement in southern Italy. Their legislator Zaleucus (mentioned
    at 1274ᵃ22–31) was famous for trying to reduce class conflict, and may have
    been the author of the law in question.
76. A Corinthian colony founded in the seventh century.
77. See 1337ᵃ10–32, *NE* 1179ᵃ33–1181ᵇ23.

sort to faction because of inequality not only of property but also of honors, although in opposite ways in each case: the many do so because of *inequality* in property; cultivated people because of honors, if they happen to be *equal*. Hence the saying: "Noble and base are held in a single honor."[78]

Human beings do not commit injustices only to get the necessities, which Phaleas thinks equality of property will cure (in that they will not steal because of cold or hunger); they also commit them to get enjoyment and assuage their desires. For if they have a desire for more than the necessities, they will seek to remedy it by committing injustice. Nor is this remedy the only motive: but even without desires, they will commit injustices in order to enjoy the pleasures that are without pain.[79] What, then, is the cure for these three? For the first, moderate property and an occupation. For the second, temperance. Third, if anyone wants to enjoy things because of themselves,[80] he should not look for a cure beyond PHILOSOPHY, since all other pleasures require human beings.[81] The greatest injustices, in any case, are committed because of excess and not because of the necessities. For example, no one becomes a tyrant to escape the cold. That is why the honors are great when one kills not a thief but a tyrant. So Phaleas' style of constitution would be a help only against minor injustices.

Moreover, he wants to arrange most things to provide a basis on which they will govern well in the case of their relations to one another, whereas their relations with neighbors and outsiders as a whole should also be considered. Therefore it is necessary for the constitution to have been organized with an eye to military power, about which he has said

40

1267ᵃ

5

10

15

20

78. Homer, *Iliad* IX.319. Achilles is complaining that if his war prizes can be taken away by Agamemnon, then noble and base are being honored to the same degree.

79. The pleasure of satisfying one's hunger comes in part from alleviating the pains of hunger, but other pleasures need involve no pain. See *NE* 1173ᵇ13–20; Plato, *Republic* 359c, 373a–d, 583b–588a.

80. Reading *autōn* with some mss. Alternatively (Ross and Dreizehnter): "if anyone should wish to find enjoyment through themselves (*hautōn*)." But this makes Aristotle's proposed cure irrelevant to its target.

81. On Aristotle's view there are two relevant candidate pleasures—the pleasure of practical political activity and the pleasure of philosophical contemplation. The former, however, which involves living a life with other people, involves pain, while the latter, which is compatible with living a solitary life, does not. The contrast is particularly clear at *NE* 1177ᵃ22–ᵇ26.

nothing. The case of property is similar. Enough needs to be available for use within the city-state, but also to meet external dangers. That is why there should not be so much property on hand that more powerful neighbors will covet it, and the owners will be unable to repel the attack-

25 ers, nor so little that they cannot sustain a war even against equal or similar people. Phaleas has not settled how much wealth is beneficial to have, but it must not be overlooked. Perhaps the best limit is such that those who are stronger will not profit if they go to war because of the ex-

30 cess, but as they would if the property were not so great. For example, when Autophradates was about to lay siege to Atarneus, its ruler, Eubulus,[82] told him to consider how long it would take to capture the place, and then to figure what such time would cost, for he said he was willing

35 to abandon Atarneus at once for less. These words caused Autophradates to have second thoughts and to abandon the siege.

So, while equalizing the property of citizens is among the things that helps prevent faction, it is certainly no big thing, so to speak. For cultivated people would get dissatisfied, on the grounds that they do not

40 merit equality. That is why they are often seen to engage in sedition and start faction. Besides, human greed is an insatiable thing. Thus two

1267ᵇ obols is enough at first,[83] but once that has become traditional, they go on always asking for more, until they go beyond all limit. For there is no natural limit to desires, and satisfying them is what the many spend their lives trying to do.[84] The starting point in such matters, therefore, rather

5 than leveling property, is to arrange that naturally decent people are disposed not to want to be acquisitive, and that base ones cannot be (and this is the case if they are weaker and are not treated unjustly). But even what he has said about the equalizing of property is not correct. For he equalizes only land holdings, but wealth also exists in the form of slaves,

10 livestock, and money, and when there is a lot of so-called moveable property. So we should either seek to equalize or moderate all these, or we should leave all of them alone.

82. A wealthy money-changer who united Atarneus and Assos (two strongholds on the coast of Asia Minor) into a single kingdom, which was attacked by the Persian general Autophradates *c*. 350, and where Aristotle lived in the late 340s.

83. An obol is one sixth of a drachma. The two-obol payment (*diōbelia*) was introduced after the fall of the oligarchy of 411/10. It seems to have been, in effect, a form of poor relief. See *Ath.* XXVIII. 3.

84. See 1257ᵇ40–1258ᵃ14.

It is also evident from his legislation that the city-state he is establishing is a small one—at any rate, if all the craftsmen are to be public slaves   *15*
and will not contribute to filling out the membership of the city-state.
But if there have to be public slaves, it should be those engaged in public works (as, for example, in Epidamnus, under the scheme Diophantus
tried to introduce in Athens).[85]

These remarks about Phaleas' constitution should enable one to see
pretty well whether he has actually proposed anything good.   *20*

Chapter 8

Hippodamus of Miletus, the son of Euryphon, invented the division of
city-states and laid out the street plan for Piraeus.[86] His love of honor
caused him also to adopt a rather extraordinary general lifestyle. Some
people thought he carried things too far, indeed, with his long hair, ex-   *25*
pensive ornaments, and the same cheap warm clothing worn winter and
summer. He also aspired to understand nature as a whole, and was the
first person, not actually engaged in politics, to attempt to say something
about the best constitution.

The city-state he designed had a multitude of ten thousand citizens,   *30*
divided into three parts. He made one part the craftsmen, another the
farmers, and a third the defenders who possess the weapons. He also divided the territory into three parts: sacred, public, and private. That
which provided what is customarily rendered to the gods would be sacred; that off which the defenders would live, public; and the land be-   *35*
longing to the farmers, private. He thought that there are just three
kinds of law, since the things lawsuits arise over are three in number: AR-
ROGANT behavior, damage,[87] and death. He also legislated a single court
with supreme authority, consisting of a certain number of selected elders, to which all lawsuits thought to have not been well decided are to
be referred. He thought that verdicts in law courts should not be ren-   *40*

---

85. Epidamnus in the Adriatic was a colony of Corinth and Corcyra founded in
    the seventh century. The identity of Diophantus is uncertain, and his
    scheme otherwise unknown.
86. Hippodamus was a fifth-century legislator and city-state planner. Around
    the middle of the fifth century he went as a colonist to Italy, where he laid
    out the city-state of Thurii. Piraeus is the harbor area near Athens. Aristotle
    comments on city-state planning at 1330^b29–31.
87. *blabēn*: covering both personal injury and damage to property.

1268ª   dered by casting ballots. Rather, each juror should deposit a tablet: if he
convicts unqualifiedly, he should write the penalty on the tablet; if he
acquits unqualifiedly, he should leave it blank; if he convicts to some extent and acquits to some extent, he should specify that. For he thought
5   that present legislation is bad in this regard, because it forces jurors to
violate their judicial oath by deciding one way or the other.[88] Moreover,
he established a law that those who discovered something beneficial to
the city-state should be honored, and one another that children of those
who died in war should receive support from public funds. He assumed
that this had not been legislated elsewhere, whereas in reality such a law
10   existed both in Athens and in some other city-states. All the officials
were to be elected by the people, and the people were to be made up of
the city-state's three parts. Those elected should take care of community, foreign affairs, and orphans. These, then, are most of the features
15   of Hippodamus' organization, and the ones that most merit discussion.
     The first problem is the division of the multitude of citizens. The
craftsmen, farmers, and those who possess weapons all share in the constitution. But the fact that the farmers do not possess weapons, and that
the craftsmen possess neither land nor weapons, makes them both virtu-
20   ally slaves of those who possess weapons. So it is impossible that *every*
office be shared. For the generals, civic guards, and practically speaking
all the officials with the most authority will inevitably be selected from
those who possess weapons. But if the farmers and craftsmen cannot
participate, how can they possibly have any friendly feelings for the con-
25   stitution? "But those who possess weapons will need to be stronger than
both the other parts." Yet that is not easy to arrange unless there are lots
of them. And, in that case, is there any need to have the others participate in the constitution or have authority over the selection of officials?
Besides, what use are the farmers to Hippodamus' city-state? Skilled
30   craftsmen are necessary (every city-state needs them), and they can support themselves by their crafts, as in other city-states. It would be reasonable for the farmers to be a part of the city-state, if they provided

88. In Athenian law juries decided guilt or innocence by casting a ballot. The
    penalty for some crimes was prescribed by law. For others, the jury had to
    choose between a penalty proposed by the prosecutor and a counterpenalty
    proposed by the defendant. In neither case could a juror propose some
    penalty of his own devising. Hippodamus is proposing to give a juror more
    discretion in both sorts of cases. Jurors in Athens took a judicial oath to ren-
    der the most just verdict possible.

food and sustenance for those who possess weapons. But, as things stand, they have private land and farm it privately.

Next, consider the public land, which is to feed the defenders. If they *35* themselves farm it, the fighting part will not be different from the farming one, as the legislator intends. And if there are going to be some others to do so, different from those who farm privately and from the warriors, they will constitute a fourth part in the city-state that participates in nothing and is hostile to the constitution. Yet if one makes those who *40* farm the private land and those who farm the public land the same, the quantity of produce from each one's farming will be inadequate for two households.[89] Why will they not at once feed themselves and the soldiers *1268ᵇ* from the same land and the same allotments? There is a lot of confusion in all this.

The law about verdicts is also bad, namely, the requirement that the juror should become an ARBITRATOR and make distinctions in his decisions, though the charge is written in unqualified terms. This is possible *5* in arbitration, even if there are lots of arbitrators, because they confer together over their verdict. But it is not possible in jury courts; and, indeed, most legislators do the opposite and arrange for the jurors *not* to confer with one another.[90] How, then, will the verdict fail to be confused *10* when a juror thinks the defendant is liable for damages, but not for as much as the plaintiff claims? Suppose the plaintiff claims twenty minas, but the juror awards ten (or the former more, the latter less), another awards five, and another four. It is clear that some will split the award in *15* this way, whereas some will condemn for the whole sum, and others for nothing. How then will the votes be counted? Furthermore, nothing forces the one who just acquits or convicts unqualifiedly to perjure himself, provided that the indictment prescribes an unqualified penalty. A juror who acquits is not deciding that the defendant owes nothing, only that he does not owe the twenty minas. A juror who convicts without be- *20* lieving that he owes the twenty minas, however, violates his oath straightway.

As for his suggestion that those who discover something beneficial to the city-state should receive some honor, such legislation is sweet to lis-

---

89. Presumably, because of the lost efficiency of scale. One can produce less from two farms than from a single farm of the same acreage.
90. Athenian juries of five hundred to one thousand members were not unusual. They gave their verdicts directly without conferring.

ten to, but not safe.[91] For it would encourage "sychophancy,"[92] and
might perhaps lead to change in the constitution. But this is part of another problem and a different inquiry. For some people[93] raise the question of whether it is beneficial or harmful to city-states to change their
traditional laws, if some other is better. Hence if indeed change is not
beneficial, it is not easy to agree right off with Hippodamus' suggestion,
though it is possible someone might propose that the laws or the constitution be dissolved on the grounds of the common good.

Now that we have mentioned this topic, however, we had better ex-
pand on it a little, since, as we said, there is a problem here, and change
may seem better. At any rate, this has certainly proved to be beneficial in
the other sciences. For example, medicine has changed from its traditional ways, as has physical training, and the crafts and sciences generally. So, since statesmanship is held to be one of these, it is clear that
something similar must also hold of it. One might claim, indeed, that
the facts themselves provide evidence of this. For the laws or customs of
the distant past were exceedingly simple and barbaric. For example,
the Greeks used to carry weapons and buy their brides from one another. Moreover, the surviving traces of ancient law are completely
naïve; for example, the homicide law in Cyme says that if the prosecutor
can provide a number of his own relatives as witnesses, the defendant is
guilty of murder. Generally speaking, everyone seeks not what is traditional but what is good. But the earliest people, whether they were
"earth-born" or the survivors of some cataclysm, were probably like ordinary or foolish people today (and this is precisely what is said about
the earth-born indeed).[94] So it would be strange to cling to *their* opinions. Moreover, it is not better to leave even written LAWS unchanged.
For just as it is impossible in the other crafts to write down everything
exactly, the same applies to political organizations. For the universal law
must be put in writing, but actions concern particulars.

91. Though Aristotle does favor such legislation in at least one kind of case, see
    1309ᵃ13–14.
92. By the middle of the fifth century some people in Athens, known as sycho-
    phants, made a profession of bringing suits against others for financial, po-
    litical, or personal reasons. Aristotle worries that Hippodamus' law will en-
    courage sychophancy through giving people an incentive to pose as public
    benefactors by bringing false charges of sedition and the like against others.
93. See Herodotus III.80; Plato, *Laws* 772a–d, *Statesman* 298c ff.; Thucydides
    I.71.
94. The cataclysm view is expressed in Plato, *Laws* 677a ff., *Timaeus* 22c ff. The
    earth-born are described at *Statesman* 272c–d and *Laws* 677b–678b.

So it is evident from these considerations that some laws must sometimes be changed. But to those who look at the matter from a different perspective, great caution will seem to be required. For if the improvement is small and it is a bad thing to accustom people to casual abrogation of the laws, then some of the rulers' or legislators' errors should 15 evidently be left unchanged, since the benefit resulting from the change will not be as great as the harm resulting from being accustomed to disobey the officials. Moreover, the model drawn from the crafts is false, since making a change in a craft is not like changing a law. For the law has no power to secure obedience except habit; but habits can only be 20 developed over a long period of time. Hence casual change from existing laws to new and different ones weakens the power of law itself. Finally, if laws are indeed to be changed, are they all to be changed, and in every constitution? And who is to change them? Anyone at all or certain peo- 25 ple? For these things make a big difference. Let us therefore abandon this investigation for the present: there will be other occasions suitable for it.[95]

Chapter 9

There are two things to investigate about the constitution of Sparta, of Crete, and, in effect, about the other constitutions also. First, is there 30 anything legislated in it that is good or bad as compared with the best organization? Second, is there anything legislated in it that is contrary to the fundamental principle or character of the intended constitution?

It is generally agreed that to be well-governed a constitution should have leisure from necessary tasks. But the way to achieve this is not easy 35 to discover. For the Thessalian serfs often attacked the Thessalians, just as the helots—always lying in wait, as it were, for their masters' misfortunes—attacked the Spartans. Nothing like this has so far happened in the case of the Cretans. Perhaps the reason is that, though they war with 40 one another, the neighboring city-states never ally themselves with the 1269ᵇ rebels: it benefits them to do so, since they also possess SUBJECT PEOPLES themselves. Sparta's neighbors, on the other hand, the Argives, Messenians, and Arcadians, were all hostile. The Thessalians, too, first experi- 5 enced revolts because they were still at war with their neighbors, the Achaeans, Perrhaebeans, and Magnesians. If nothing else, it certainly seems that the management of serfs, the proper way to live together with

---

95. This investigation is not pursued in the *Politics*.

them, is a troublesome matter. For if they are given license, they become
arrogant and claim to merit equality with those in authority, but if they
10   live miserably, they hate and conspire. It is clear, then, that those whose
system of helotry leads to these results still have not found the best way.[96]

Furthermore, the license where their women are concerned is also
detrimental both to the deliberately chosen aims of the constitution and
to the happiness of the city-state as well. For just as a household has a
15   man and a woman as parts, a city-state, too, is clearly to be regarded as
being divided almost equally between men and women. So in all constitutions in which the position of women is bad, half the city-state should
be regarded as having no laws. And this is exactly what has happened in
Sparta. For the legislator, wishing the whole city-state to have en-
20   durance, makes his wish evident where the men are concerned, but has
been negligent in the case of the women. For being free of all constraint,[97] they live in total intemperance and luxury. The inevitable result, in a constitution of this sort, is that wealth is esteemed.[98] This is
particularly so if the citizens are dominated by their women, like most
25   military and warlike races (except for the Celts and some others who
openly esteemed male homosexuality). So it is understandable why the
original author of the myth of Ares and Aphrodite paired the two;[99] for
all warlike men seem obsessed with sexual relations with either men or
30   women. That is why the same happened to the Spartans, and why in the
days of their hegemony, many things were managed by women. And yet
what difference is there between women rulers and rulers ruled by
women? The result is the same. Audacity is not useful in everyday mat-
35   ters, but only, if at all, in war. Yet Spartan women were very harmful
even here. They showed this quite clearly during the Theban invasion;[100]
for they were of no use at all, like women in other city-states,[101] but
caused more confusion than the enemy.

96. The best way to have leisure from necessary tasks.
97. Reading *aneimenōs* with Richards.
98. See Plato, *Republic* 547b–555b.
99. Ares, the god of war, is often portrayed as the partner of Aphrodite, the
goddess of sexual love (e.g., Homer, *Odyssey* 8.266–366). Aristotle thinks
that myths generally contain a core of wisdom, though it may not be easy to
discover at first glance (1341^b2–8, *Metaph.* 1074^a38–$^b14$).
100. In 369 under Epaminondas. See Plato, *Laws* 813e–814c; Xenophon, *Hellenica* VI.5.28.
101. The clause is ambiguous, but probably means that women in other city-
states were useful in wartime. Thucydides II.4.2, III.74.2 attests to the importance of women during sieges.

So it seems that license with regard to women initially occurred in
Sparta for explicable reasons. For Spartan men spent a great deal of time
away from home during their wars with the Argives, and again with the   *40*
Arcadians and Messenians. So when leisure returned, they placed them-   *1270ᵃ*
selves in the hands of their legislator,[102] already prepared thanks to military life, which includes many parts of virtue. But we are told that when   *5*
he attempted to bring the women under his laws, they resisted and he
retreated. These, then, are the causes of what happened, and so, clearly,
of the present error as well. But of course we are not investigating the
question of whom we should excuse and whom not, but what is correct   *10*
and what is not.

The fact that the position of women is not well handled seems not
only to create a certain unseemliness in the constitution, as we said before, but also to contribute something to the love of money. For what one
might criticize next, after the foregoing, is the uneven distribution of
property. For because some of the Spartans came to own too much   *15*
wealth and others very little, the land passed into the hands of a few.
This is poorly organized by the laws as well. For the legislator quite
rightly made it improper to buy or sell an existing land holding, but he   *20*
left owners free to give or bequeath their land if they wished, even
though this inevitably leads to the same results as the other.[103] Indeed,
nearly two-fifths of all the land belongs to the women, both because
many become heiresses and because large dowries are given. It would
have been better if it had been organized so that there was no dowry or   *25*
only a small or moderate one. But, as it is, one may marry an heiress
daughter to whomever one wishes, and if a man dies intestate, the person he leaves as his heir gives her to whom he likes. As a result, in a land
capable of supporting fifteen hundred cavalry and thirty thousand hoplites, there were fewer than a thousand. The very facts have clearly   *30*
shown that the organization of these matters served them badly. For
their city-state did not withstand one single blow,[104] but was ruined because of its shortage of men.

It is said that at the time of their early kings, they used to give a share
in the constitution to others, so that there was no shortage of men, de-   *35*

---

102. Lycurgus, the legendary architect of the Spartan constitution.
103. Allowing estates to be sold in part leads to estates that are too small to sup-
     port their owners adequately. Partial bequests have the same result.
104. Aristotle is referring to the battle of Leuctra in 371, when the Thebans in-
     flicted a shattering defeat on the Spartans.

spite lengthy wars. Indeed, they say that there were once ten thousand Spartiates.[105] Whether this is true or not, a better way to keep high the number of men in a city-state is by leveling property. But the law dealing with the procreation of children militates against this reform. For the

1270ᵇ legislator, intending there to be as many Spartiates as possible, encourages people to have as many children as possible, since there is a law exempting a father of three sons from military service, and a father of four from all taxes. But it is evident that if many children are born, and the

5 land is correspondingly divided, many people will inevitably become poor.

Matters relating to the board of overseers[106] are also badly organized. For this office has sole authority over the most important matters; but the overseers are drawn from among the entire people, so that often very

10 poor men enter it who, because of their poverty, are[107] open to bribery. (This has been shown on many occasions in the past too, and recently among the Andrians; for some, corrupted by bribes, did everything in their power to destroy the entire city-state.[108]) Moreover, because the office is too powerful—in fact, equal in power to a tyranny—even the kings were forced to curry favor with the overseers. And this too has

15 harmed the constitution, for from an aristocracy a democracy was emerging.

Admittedly, the board of overseers does hold the constitution together; for the people remain contented because they participate in the most important office. So, whether it came about because of the legisla-

20 tor or by luck, it benefits Spartan affairs. For if a constitution is to survive, every part of the city-state must want it to exist and to remain as it is.[109] And the kings want this because of the honor given to them; the noble-and-good, because of the senate (since this office is a reward of

25 virtue); and the people, because of the board of overseers (since selec-

105. Adult male Spartan citizens.
106. *ephoreia*: Five ephors or overseers were elected annually by the Spartiates. They supervised the operation of the political and judicial system as a whole, and served as a limit on the powers of the two kings (see below).
107. Reading *eisin* with Richards.
108. Aristotle's reference is otherwise unknown.
109. This principle is repeated in various forms throughout the *Politics*, e.g., 1294ᵇ34–40, 1320ᵃ14–17. It should probably be distinguished from the principle expressed, for example, at 1296ᵇ14–16, 1297ᵇ4–6, 1309ᵇ16–18, 1320ᵇ26–28. Generally speaking, the more extreme versions of deviant constitutions satisfy the latter principle, but not the former.

tions for it are made from all). Still, though the overseers should be chosen from all, it should not be by the present method, which is exceedingly childish.[110]

Furthermore, the overseers have authority over the most important judicial decisions, though they are ordinary people. Hence it would be better if they decided cases not according to their own opinion, but in accordance with what is written, that is to say, laws. Again, the overseers' 30 lifestyle is not in keeping with the aim of the constitution.[111] For it involves too much license, whereas in other respects[112] it is too austere, so that they cannot endure it, but secretly escape from the law and enjoy the pleasures of the body.[113] 35

Matters relating to the senate also do not serve the Spartans well.[114] If the senators were decent people, with an adequate general education in manly virtue, one might well say that this office benefits the city-state. Although, one might dispute about whether they ought to have lifelong authority in important matters,[115] since the mind has its old age as well as the body.[116] But when they are educated in such a way that even the legis- 40 / 1271ᵃ lator himself doubts that they are good men, it is not safe. And in fact in many matters of public concern, those who have participated in this office have been conspicuous in taking bribes and showing favoritism. This is precisely why it is better that the senators not be exempt from INSPECTION, as they are at present. It might seem that the overseers should in- 5 spect every office, but this would give too much to the board of overseers, and is not the way we say inspections should be carried out.

The method of electing senators is also defective. Not only is the selection made in a childish way,[117] but it is wrong for someone worthy of 10

110. The overseers may have been chosen by acclamation, like the senate, but it is also possible that they were chosen by lot. See Plato, *Laws* 692a.

111. Reading *tēs politeias* with Scaliger. Alternatively: "not in keeping with the aim of the city-state (*tēs poleōs*)."

112. *en de tois allois*: or "in the case of other people."

113. See Plato, *Republic* 548b.

114. The senate (*gerousia*) had 28 members in addition to the two kings (discussed below). All were over 60 years old, and were probably selected from aristocratic families. The senate prepared the agenda of the citizen assembly, and had other political and judicial functions.

115. The apparent conflict with the characterization of the overseers at 1270ᵇ28–29 is perhaps removed by 1275ᵇ9–11.

116. See *Rh.* 1389ᵇ13–1390ᵃ24.

117. Members of the senate were chosen by an elaborate process of acclamation. See 1306ᵃ18–19, Plutarch, *Lycurgus* XXVI.

the office to ask for it: a man worthy of the office should hold it whether he wants to or not. But the fact is that the legislator is evidently doing the same thing here as in the rest of the constitution. He makes the citizens love honor and then takes advantage of this fact in the election of
15 the senators; for no one would ask for office who did not love honor. Yet the love of honor and of money are *the* causes of most voluntary wrongdoings among human beings.

The question of whether or not it is better for city-states to have a kingship must be discussed later;[118] but it is better to choose each new
20 king, not as now,[119] but on the basis of his own life. (It is clear that even the Spartan legislator himself did not think it possible to make the kings noble-and-good. At any rate he distrusts them, on the grounds that they are not sufficiently good men. That is precisely why they used to send out a king's opponents as fellow ambassadors, and why they regard fac-
25 tion between the kings as a safeguard for the city-state.)

Nor were matters relating to the messes (or so-called *phiditia*) well legislated by the person who first established them. For they ought to be publicly supported, as they are in Crete.[120] But among the Spartans each individual has to contribute, even though some are extremely poor and
30 unable to afford the expense. The result is thus the opposite of the legislator's deliberately chosen aim. He intended the institution of messes to be democratic, but, legislated as they are now, they are scarcely democratic at all, since the very poor cannot easily participate in them. Yet
35 their traditional way of delimiting the Spartan constitution is to exclude from it those who cannot pay this contribution.

The law dealing with the admirals has been criticized by others, and rightly so, since it becomes a cause of faction.[121] For the office of admiral is established against the kings, who are permanent generals, as pretty
40 much another kingship.

One might also criticize the fundamental principle of the legislator as
1271[b] Plato criticized it in the *Laws*.[122] For the entire system of their laws aims at a part of virtue, military virtue, since this is useful for conquest. So, as

118. At III.14–17.
119. Sparta had two hereditary kings, each descended from a different royal house, both of whom were members of the senate and ruled for life. They had a military as well as a political and religious function.
120. See 1272[a]12–27.
121. For examples, see 1301[b]18–21, 1306[b]31–33.
122. At 625c–638b.

long as they were at war, they remained safe. But once they ruled supreme, they started to decline, because they did not know how to be at leisure, and had never undertaken any kind of training with more 5 AUTHORITY than military training. Another error, no less serious, is that although they think (rightly) that the good things that people compete for are won by virtue rather than by vice, they also suppose (not rightly) that these GOODS are better than virtue itself.[123]

Matters relating to public funds are also badly organized by the Spar- 10 tiates. For they are compelled to fight major wars, yet the public treasury is empty, and taxes are not properly paid; for, as most of the land belongs to the Spartiates, they do not scrutinize one another's tax payments.[124] Thus the result the legislator has produced is the opposite of beneficial: 15 he has made his city-state poor and the private individuals into lovers of money.

So much for the Spartan constitution. For these are the things one might particularly criticize in it.

Chapter 10

The Cretan constitution closely resembles that of the Spartans; in some 20 small respects it is no worse, but most of it is less finished. For it seems, or at any rate it is said,[125] that the constitution of the Spartans is largely modeled on the Cretan; and most older things are less fully elaborated than newer ones. They say that after Lycurgus relinquished the guardianship of King Charillus[126] and went abroad, he spent most of his 25 time in Crete, because of the kinship connection. For the Lyctians were colonists from Sparta, and those who went to the colony adopted the or- ganization of the laws existing among the inhabitants at that time. Hence even now their subject peoples employ these laws, in the belief that 30 Minos[127] first established the organization of the laws.

The island seems naturally adapted and beautifully situated to rule

---

123. This criticism of Sparta and other oligarchies is repeated with various elaborations and emphases at 1334ª2–ᵇ5, 1324ᵇ5–11, 1333ᵇ5–11.
124. Thucydides I.132 tells us that the regular custom of the Spartans was "never to act hastily in the case of a Spartan citizen and never to come to any irrevocable decision without indisputable proof."
125. See Herodotus I.65; Plato, *Minos* 318c–d, 320a, b.
126. The posthumous son of Lycurgus' elder bother King Polydectes.
127. Semimythical Cretan king, husband of Pasiphaë, the mother of the Mino-taur.

the Greek world since it lies across the entire sea on whose shores most
35 of the Greeks are settled. In one direction it is not far from the Peloponnese, and in the other from Asia (the part around Cape Triopium) and
from Rhodes. That is why Minos established his rule over the sea too,
subjugating some islands, establishing settlements on others, and finally
attacking Sicily, where he met his death near Camicus.[128]

40   The Cretan way of organizing things is analogous to the Spartan. The
helots do the farming for the latter, the subject peoples for the former.
1272ª Both places have messes (in ancient times, the Spartans called these *an-
dreia* rather than *phiditia*,[129] like the Cretans—a clear indication that they
came from Crete). Besides, there is the organization of the constitution.
For the overseers have the same powers as the order keepers (as they are
5   called in Crete), except that the overseers are five in number and the
order keepers ten. The senators correspond to the senators, whom the
Cretans call the council. The Cretans at one time had a kingship, but later
they did away with it, and the order keepers took over leadership in war.
10 All Cretans participate in the assembly, but its authority is limited to vot-
ing together for the resolutions of the senators and order keepers.

Communal meals are better handled among the Cretans than among
the Spartans. In Sparta, as we said earlier,[130] each person must contribute a fixed amount per capita; if he does not, a law prevents him from
15 participating in the constitution. In Crete, on the other hand, things are
done more communally. Out of all the public crops and livestock and the
tributes paid by the subject peoples, one part is set aside for the gods
20 and for PUBLIC SERVICES, and another for the messes, so that all—
women and children and men—are fed at public expense.[131] The legislator regarded frugality as beneficial and gave much thought to securing
it, and to the segregation of women, so as to prevent them from having
many children, and to finding a place for sexual relations between men.
There will be another opportunity to examine whether this was badly
25 done or not.[132] It is evident, then, that the messes have been better organized by the Cretans than by the Spartans.

128. See Thucydides I.4, 8, 15.
129. *Sussitia* is the normal Attic term.
130. At 1271ª26–37.
131. Women and children did not participate in communal meals, but presum-
      ably enough was left over to feed them at home. See 1274ᵇ9–11, where
      Aristotle cites communal meals for women as a peculiarity of Plato's con-
      stitution, and Plato, *Laws* 780e–781a.
132. Aristotle never returns to this topic. But see 1262ª32–40, 1269ᵇ23–31,
      1335ᵇ38–1336ª2.

Matters relating to the order keepers, on the other hand, are even less well organized than those relating to the overseers. For the board of order keepers shares the defect of the board of overseers (that it is composed of ordinary people), but the benefit to the constitution there is absent here. For there the people participate in the most important office, and so wish the constitution to continue, because the election is from all.[133] But here the order keepers are elected not from all but from certain families, and the senators are elected from those who have been order keepers. And the same remarks might be made about the senators as about those who become senators in Sparta: their exemption from inspection and their life tenure are greater prerogatives than they merit, and it is dangerous that they rule not in accordance with what is written but according to their own opinion.

The fact that the people remain quiescent even though they do not participate is no indication that it has been well organized. For unlike the overseers, the order keepers have no profit, because they live on an island, far away, at least, from any who might corrupt them. The remedy they use for this offense is also strange, not political but characteristic of a DYNASTY. For the order keepers are frequently expelled by a conspiracy either of their colleagues themselves or of private individuals. Order keepers are also allowed to resign before their term has expired. But surely it is better if all these things should take place according to LAW and not human wish, which is not a safe standard.

Worst of all, however, is the suspension of order keepers,[134] often brought about by the powerful, when they are unwilling to submit to justice. For this makes it clear that whereas the organization has something of a constitution about it, yet it is not a constitution but more of a dynasty. Their habit is to divide the people and their own friends, create anarchy,[135] form factions, and fight one another. Yet how does this sort of thing differ from such a city-state ceasing temporarily to be a city-state, and the political community dissolving? A city-state in this condition is in danger, since those who wish to attack it are also able to so. But, as we said, Crete's location saves it, since its distance has served to keep foreigners out.[136] This is why the institution of subject peoples survives

30

35

40

1272^b

5

10

15

133. See 1270^{b}17–28.
134. *akosmia*: literally, "disorder." Thus *akosmia* (suspending the order keepers) results in *akosmia* (disorder).
135. *anarchia*: alternatively (Dreizehnter and the mss.): "create a monarchy (*monarchia*)."
136. *xenēlasia*: the Spartan practice of expelling foreigners. See Plato, *Laws* 848a.

among the Cretans, whereas the helots frequently revolt. For the Cretans do not rule outside their borders—though a foreign war has recently
20   come to the island, which has made the weakness of its laws evident.[137]
    So much for this constitution.

Chapter 11

The Carthaginians also are thought to be well-governed, and in many
25   respects in an extraordinary way (compared to others), though in some
respects closely resembling the Spartans. For these three constitutions,
the Cretan, Spartan, and, third, the Carthaginian, are all in a way close
to one another and very different from others. Many of their arrangements work well for them, and it is an indication that their constitution
30   is well organized that the people willingly[138] stick with the way the constitution is organized, and that no faction even worth talking about has
arisen among them, and no tyrant.
    Points of similarity to the Spartan constitution are these. The com-
panions' messes are like the *phiditia*; the office of the one-hundred-
35   and-four is like that of the overseers, except that it is not worse (for the
overseers are drawn from ordinary people, whereas they elect to this office on the basis of merit). Their kings and senate are analogous to those
of Sparta; but it is better that the kings are neither from the same family
nor from a chance one; but if any family distinguishes itself, then the
kings are elected from its members, rather than selected on the basis of
40   seniority. For they have authority in important matters, and if they are
insignificant people, they do a lot of harm to the city-state (as they al-
1273[a]   ready have done to the city-state of the Spartans).
    Most of the criticisms one might make because of its deviations from
the best constitution are actually common to all the constitutions we
have discussed. But of those that are deviations from the fundamental
principle of an aristocracy or a POLITY,[139] some deviate more in the di-
5   rection of democracy, others more in the direction of oligarchy. For the
kings and senators have authority over what to bring and what not to

137. Outside dominions involve foreign wars, which are one cause of serf revolts. See 1269[b]5–7.
138. Reading *hekousion* with Dreizehnter.
139. A polity is a mixed constitution (1265[b]26–28). Aristotle usually uses the
term "aristocracy" to refer to a single component of a mixed constitution.
But here—as at 1294[b]10–11—he treats it and "polity" as equivalents.

bring before the people, provided they all agree; but if they do not, the people have authority over these matters also. Moreover, when they make proposals, the people not only are allowed to hear the officials' res-olutions, but have the authority to decide them; and anyone who wishes may speak against the proposals being made. This does not exist in the other constitutions.

On the other hand, it is oligarchic that the boards of five, which have authority over many important matters, elect themselves, and elect to the office of one-hundred,[140] which is the most important office. More-over, it is also oligarchic that they hold office longer than the others (for they rule before taking office and after they have left it). But we must re-gard it as aristocratic that they are neither paid nor chosen by lot, or any-thing else of that sort. And also that all legal cases are decided by the boards of five, and not, as in Sparta, some by some and others by others.[141]

But the major deviation of the organization of the Carthaginians away from aristocracy and toward oligarchy is their sharing a view that is held also by the many: that rulers should be chosen not solely on the basis of their merit but also on the basis of their wealth, since poor people can-not afford the leisure necessary to rule well. Hence, if indeed it is oli-garchic to choose rulers on the basis of their wealth, and aristocratic to choose them on the basis of their merit, then this organization, accord-ing to which the Carthaginians have organized matters relating to the constitution, will be a third sort. For they elect to office with an eye to both qualities, especially in the case of the most important officials, the kings and the generals.

But this deviation from aristocracy should be regarded as an error on the part of their legislator. For one of the most important things is to see to it from the outset that the best people are able to be at leisure and do nothing unseemly, not only when in office but in private life. But even if one must look to wealth too, in order to ensure leisure, still it is bad that

---

140. Referred to as "the one-hundred–and-four" at 1272ᵇ34–35.
141. It is oligarchic to assign different judicial powers to different groups, be-cause the power to execute or exile can then end up in the hands of a very small number (see 1294ᵇ31–34). And, indeed, in Sparta, some cases could be tried by a single overseer (1275ᵇ9–10). It is less clear why it is aristo-cratic to adopt the Carthaginian model. But perhaps Aristotle's idea is that because Carthaginian officials are elected on the basis of merit or virtue, giving them all the same judicial powers comes close to the aristocratic ideal of vesting those powers in the best people.

the most important offices, those of king and general, should be for sale.
For this law gives more esteem to wealth than to virtue, and makes the
entire city-state love money. For whatever those in authority esteem, the
40   opinion of the other citizens too inevitably follows theirs. Hence when
virtue is not esteemed more than everything else, the constitution can-
1273ᵇ   not be securely governed as an aristocracy. It is reasonable to expect too
that those who have bought office will become accustomed to making a
profit from it, when they rule by having spent money. For if a poor but
decent person will want to profit from office, it would certainly be odd if
a worse one, who has already spent money, will not want to. Hence those
5   who are able to rule best should rule.[142] And even if the legislator neglected the wealth of the decent people, he had better look to their
leisure, at least while they are ruling.

It would also seem to be bad to allow the same person to hold several
offices, a thing held in high esteem among the Carthaginians. For one
10   task is best performed by one person. The legislator should see to it that
this happens, and not require the same person to play the flute and make
shoes. So, where the city-state is not small, it is more political,[143] and
more democratic, if more people participate in the offices. For it is more
widely shared, as we said, and each of the offices[144] is better carried out
15   and more quickly. (This is clear in the case of military and naval affairs,
since in both of them ruling and being ruled extend through practically
speaking everyone.)

But though their constitution is oligarchic, they are very good at escaping faction by from time to time sending some part of the people out
to the city-states to get rich.[145] In this way they effect a cure, and give
20   stability to their constitution. But this is the result of luck, whereas they
ought to be free of faction thanks to their legislator. As things stand,
however, if some misfortune occurs and the multitude of those who are
ruled revolt, the laws provide no remedy for restoring peace.

This, then, is the way things stand with the Spartan, Cretan, and
25   Carthaginian constitutions, which are rightly held in high esteem.

---

142. Reading *arist' archein* with Spengel.
143. More like a genuinely political or statesman-like community.
144. Reading *archōn* with Dreizehnter. Alternatively (Ross and the mss.): "and
     each of the same things (*autōn*) is better carried out." Or: "each task, as it
     belongs to the same persons (*autōn*), is better carried out."
145. See 1320ᵇ4–7. The city-states in question are presumably colonies of some
     sort where citizens could make money as government officials or in some
     other way.

Chapter 12

Some of those who have had something to say about a constitution took
no part in political actions, but always lived privately. About them pretty
much everything worth saying has been said. Others became legislators,   *30*
engaging in politics themselves, some in their own city-states, others in
foreign ones as well. Some of these men crafted LAWS only, whereas others, such as Lycurgus and Solon, crafted a CONSTITUTION too, for they
established both laws and constitutions.

We have already discussed that of the Spartans.[146] As for Solon, some   *35*
think he was an excellent legislator because: he abolished an oligarchy
which had become too unmixed; he put an end to the slavery of the common people;[147] and he established the ancestral democracy, by mixing
the constitution well. For they think the council of the Areopagus is oligarchic;[148] the election of officials aristocratic; and the courts democra-   *40*
tic. But it seems that the first two, the council and the election of offi-   *1274ª*
cials, existed already, and Solon did not abolish them. On the other
hand, by making law courts open to all, he did set up the democracy.
That, indeed, is why some people criticize him. They say that when he
gave law courts selected by lot authority over all legal cases, he destroyed
the other things. For when this element became powerful, those who   *5*
flattered the common people like a tyrant changed the constitution into
the democracy we have now: Ephialtes and Pericles[149] curtailed the
power of the Areopagus, and Pericles introduced payment for jurors.[150]
In this way, each popular leader enhanced the power of the people and
led them on to the present democracy.   *10*

It seems that this did not come about through Solon's deliberate
choice, however, but rather more by accident. For the common people
were the cause of Athens's naval supremacy during the Persian wars. As

146. Which was the work of Lycurgus.
147. Many poorer people had become enslaved through a process of debt
     bondage in which they offered their own persons as security on loans.
     Solon canceled all existing debts and put an end to this practice.
148. From earliest times, the council of the Areopagus had jurisdiction over
     homicide cases. Solon made it the special guardian of his constitution.
     Since its members were all rich, it was a powerful oligarchic element in the
     constitution.
149. Ephialtes and Pericles were POPULAR LEADERS in Athens. In 462/1,
     Ephialtes joined Pericles in introducing legislation which stripped the Are-
     opagus of most of its privileges, and was murdered in that same year.
150. Allowing the poorer people to serve on them without financial loss.

a result, they became arrogant, and chose inferior people as their popular leaders when decent people opposed their policies.[151] Solon, at any
15 rate, seems to have given the people only the minimum power necessary,
that of electing and INSPECTING officials (since if they did not even have
authority in these, the people would have been enslaved and hostile).[152]
But he drew all the officials from among the notable and rich: the *pen-*
20 *takosiomedimnoi*, the *zeugitai*, and the third class, the so-called *hippeis*.
But the fourth class, the *thetes*, did not participate in any office.[153]

Zaleucus became a legislator for the Epizephyrian Locrians, and
Charondas of Catana for his own citizens and for the other Chalcidian
city-states in Italy and Sicily. (Some people actually try to establish con-
25 nections by telling the following story: Onomacritus was the first person
to become an expert in legislation. Though a Locrian, he trained in
Crete while on a visit connected with his craft of divination. Thales was
his companion; Lycurgus and Zaleucus were pupils of Thales; and
Charondas was a pupil of Zaleucus. But when they say these things, they
30 speak without regard to chronology.)[154]

There was also Philolaus of Corinth,[155] a member of the Bacchiad
family, who became a legislator for the Thebans. He became the lover of
Diocles, the victor in the Olympic games. Diocles left Corinth in disgust
35 at the lust his mother, Alcyone, had for him, and went off to Thebes,
where they both ended their days. Even now people point out their
tombs, which are in full view of one another, although one is visible

151. See 1304ᵃ17–24; Plato, *Laws* 707a–d.
152. See 1281ᵇ31–2.
153. The first class consisted of men whose property produced the equivalent
     of 500 measures (*medimnoi*) of corn, olive oil, or wine; the second, those
     whose property produced 300 measures, and so were able to maintain a
     team of oxen (*zeugos*); the third, those whose property produced 200 mea-
     sures, and who could keep a horse and fight as cavalrymen (*hippeis*); the
     rest of the citizens made up the fourth class. Since these divisions were
     based solely on wealth or property, not on lineage, they permitted the kind
     of upward mobility that the earlier lineage system effectively excluded. See
     Aristotle, *Ath.* VII.
154. Zaleucus was a seventh-century legislator for the Locrians living in south-
     ern Italy. Charondas was probably sixth century. Ononmacritus may be the
     poet and divine of that name who was active in Athens at the end of the
     sixth century. Thales (Thaletas), who worked in Sparta, was a seventh-cen-
     tury poet from Gortyn in Crete.
155. Otherwise unknown.

from the land of the Corinthians and the other is not. The story goes that they arranged to be buried in just this way, Diocles having the land of Corinth not be visible from his burial mound because of his loathing for what he had experienced there, and Philolaus so that it might be vis- *40* ible from his. It was for this sort of reason, then, that the two of them settled among the Thebans. But Philolaus became legislator both on *1274ᵇ* other matters and about procreation (which they call "the laws of adoption"). This is peculiar to his legislation, its purpose being to keep the number of estates fixed. *5*

There is nothing peculiar to Charondas except lawsuits for perjury; he was the first to introduce denunciations for perjury. But in the precision of his laws, he is more polished than even present-day legislators. The feature peculiar to Phaleas is the leveling of property. And to Plato: the sharing of women, children, and property;[156] messes for women; the law *10* about drinking, that the sober should preside at drinking parties;[157] and the one requiring ambidextrous training for soldiers, on the grounds that one of the hands should not be useful and the other useless.

There are also Draco's laws,[158] but Draco established his laws for an existing constitution. There is nothing peculiar to his laws worth talking *15* about, except the severity of the punishments. Pittacus too crafted laws, but not a constitution. A law peculiar to him requires a drunken person to be punished more severely for an offense than a sober one. For since *20* more drunken people than sober ones commit acts of arrogance, Pittacus paid attention not to the greater indulgence one should show to those who are drunk, but to what is beneficial.[159] Androdamus of Rhe-

---

156. The equalizing of women, children, and property is distinctively Platonic, but not the equalizing of property as such (see 1266ᵃ34–36), which is here attributed to Phaleas. At 1267ᵇ9–10, Aristotle points out that Phaleas equalized only landed property.

157. *symposiarchei*: serve as the symposiarch, who controlled the toasts at a drinking party or symposium (*sumpōsia*), and so the amount of wine consumed (*Laws* 637a–b, 671a–672d).

158. Draco published a code of laws for Athens in 621 notorious for its severity (hence our word "draconian").

159. Pittacus, one of the fabled Seven Sages, was appointed tyrant of Mytilene in 589 to restore order. He is mentioned again at 1285ᵃ35–40. On his treatment of drunken offenders, see *NE* 1113ᵇ30–33, 1110ᵇ24–33, *Rh.* 1402ᵇ8–12. Pittacus seems to have thought that drunkenness was indeed a mitigating circumstance, but that social benefit was more important than equity.

gium[160] became a legislator for the Chalcidians in the region of Thrace: those dealing with homicides and heiresses are his. But there is nothing peculiar to them to report.

So much, then, for our study of the various constitutions, both those that are actually in force and those described by certain people.

25

160. Otherwise unknown.

Book III

Chapter 1

When investigating constitutions, and what each is and is like, pretty well the first subject of investigation concerns a city-state, to see what the city-state is. For as things stand now, there are disputes about this. Some people say, for example, that a city-state performed a certain action, whereas others say that it was not the city-state that performed the action, but rather the oligarchy or the tyrant did. We see, too, that the *35* entire occupation of statesmen and legislators concerns city-states. Moreover, a constitution is itself a certain organization of the inhabitants of a city-state. But since a city-state is a composite, one that is a whole and, like any other whole, constituted out of many parts,[1] it is clear that we must first inquire into citizens. For a city-state is some sort *40* of multitude of citizens. Hence we must investigate who should be called a citizen, and who the citizen is. For there is often dispute about the cit- *1275ª* izen as well, since not everyone agrees that the same person is a citizen. For the sort of person who is a citizen in a democracy is often not one in an oligarchy.

We should leave aside those who acquire the title of citizen in some exceptional way; for example, those who are made citizens.[2] Nor is a cit- *5* izen a citizen through residing in a place, for resident aliens and slaves share the dwelling place with him. Again, those who participate in the justice system, to the extent of prosecuting others in the courts or being judged there themselves, are not citizens: parties to treaties can also do that (though in fact in many places the participation of resident aliens in *10* the justice system is not even complete, but they need a sponsor, so that their participation in this sort of communal relationship is in a way

---

1. Composites are always analyzed into their parts (1252ª17–20). A whole (*holon*) is a composite that is a substance possessing an essence or nature (*Metaph.* 1041ᵇ11–33). See Introduction xxvii–xxxv.
2. Presumably, honorary citizens and the like.

65

incomplete).[3] Like minors who are too young to be enrolled in the citizen lists or old people who have been excused from their civic duties,[4]
15   they must be said to be citizens *of a sort*, but not UNQUALIFIED citizens. Instead, a qualification must be added, such as "incomplete" or "superannuated" or something else like that (it does not matter what, since what we are saying is clear). For we are looking for the unqualified citizen, the one whose claim to citizenship has no defect of this sort that
20   needs to be rectified (for one can raise and solve similar problems about those who have been disenfranchised or exiled).

The unqualified citizen is defined by nothing else so much as by his participation in judgment and office. But some offices are of limited tenure, so they cannot be held twice by the same person at all, or can be
25   held again only after a definite period. Another person, however, holds office indefinitely, such as the juror or assemblyman. Now someone might say that the latter sort are not officials at all, and do not, because of this,[5] participate in any office as such. Yet surely it would be absurd to deprive of office those who have the most authority.[6] But let this make no difference, since the argument is only about a word. For what a juror
30   and an assemblyman have in common lacks a name that one should call them both. For the sake of definition, let it be indefinite office. We take it, then, that those who participate in office in this way are citizens. And this is pretty much the definition that would best fit all those called citizens.

We must not forget, however, that in case of things in which what underlies differs in kind (one coming first, another second, and so on), a
35   common element either is not present at all, insofar as these things are such, or only in some attenuated way.[7] But we see that constitutions dif-

---

3. Resident aliens in Athens had to have a citizen "sponsor" (*prostatēs*), but they could represent themselves in legal proceedings. Elsewhere, it seems, their sponsor had to do this for them.
4. At the age of 18, young Athenians were enrolled in the citizen list kept by the leader of the *deme*. Older men were released from having to serve in the military, and perhaps also from jury duty and attendance at meetings of the assembly.
5. Because of being jurors, assemblymen, and the like.
6. As jurors and members of the assembly do in certain sorts of democracies (1273^{b}41–1274^{a}11).
7. Exercise is healthy, a complexion is healthy, and a certain physical condition is healthy. Each of them underlies the property of being healthy, or is the subject of which that property is predicated. But exercise is healthy because it

fer in kind from one another, and that some are posterior and others prior; for mistaken or deviant constitutions are necessarily posterior to those that are not mistaken.[8] (What we mean by "deviant" will be apparent later.)[9] Consequently, the citizen in each constitution must also be different.

1275[b]

That is precisely why the citizen that we defined is above all a citizen in a democracy, and may possibly be one in other constitutions, but not necessarily. For some constitutions have no "the people" or assemblies they legally recognize, but only specially summoned councils and judicial cases decided by different bodies. In Sparta, for example, some cases concerning contracts are tried by one overseer, others by another, whereas cases of homicide are judged by the senate, and other cases by perhaps some other official. It is the same way in Carthage, since there certain officials decide all cases.[10] None the less, our definition of a citizen admits of correction. For in the other constitutions,[11] it is not the holder of indefinite office who is assemblyman and juror, but someone whose office is definite. For it is either to some or to all of the latter that deliberation and judgment either about some or about all matters is assigned.

5

10

15

It is evident from this who the citizen is. For we can now say that someone who is eligible to participate in deliberative and judicial office is a citizen in this city-state, and that a city-state, simply speaking, is a multitude of such people, adequate for life's self-sufficiency.

20

Chapter 2

But the definition that gets used in practice is that a citizen is someone who comes from citizens on both sides, and not on one only—for exam-

---

causes a certain bodily condition: health; a complexion is healthy because it *signifies* that condition; and a bodily condition (having a temperature of 98.4° etc.) is healthy because it *is* that condition. Here the bodily condition is healthy in the primary way, because it figures in the *different* accounts of why a complexion and exercise are healthy. See *NE* 1096[a]17–23, *EE* 1218[a]1–10.

8. The correct constitution is PRIOR to the deviant because the latter is defined in terms of the former.
9. See III.6–7.
10. See 1273[a]18–20 and note.
11. The nondemocratic ones.

ple, that of father or of mother. Some people look for more here too, going back, for example, two or three or more generations of ancestors. But quick political definitions of this sort lead some people to raise the
25   problem of how these third- or fourth-generation ancestors will be citizens. So Gorgias of Leontini, half perhaps to raise a real problem and half ironically, said that just as mortars are made by mortar makers, so Lariseans too are made by craftsmen, since some of them are Larisean
30   makers.[12] But this is easy: if the ancestors participated in the constitution in the way that accords with the definition just given,[13] they were citizens. For "what comes from a citizen father and mother" cannot be applied to even the first inhabitants or founders.

But perhaps a bigger problem is raised by the next case: those who come to participate in a constitution after a revolution, such as the citi-
35   zens created in Athens by Cleisthenes[14] after the expulsion of the tyrants (for he enrolled many foreigners and alien slaves in the tribes). But the dispute in relation to these people is not which of them is a citizen, but whether they are rightly or wrongly so. And yet a further question might be raised as to whether one who is not rightly a citizen is a citizen at all,
1276ᵃ as "wrong" and "false" seem to have the same force. But since we see that there are also some people holding office wrongly, whom we say *are* holding it though not rightly, and since a citizen is defined as someone who holds a sort of office (for someone who participates in such office is
5   a citizen, as we said), it is clear that these people too must be admitted to be citizens.

Chapter 3

The problem of rightly and not rightly is connected to the dispute we mentioned earlier.[15] For some people raise a problem about how to determine whether a city-state has or has not performed an action, for example, when an oligarchy or a tyranny is replaced by a democracy. At

---

12. Gorgias was a famous orator and sophist (*c.* 483–376) who visited Athens in 427. In Larissa, and other place, the word *dēmiourgos*, which means "craftsman," is also the title of a certain sort of public official. A Larisean is both a citizen of Larissa and a kind of pot made there.

13. At 1275ᵇ17–21.

14. Cleisthenes was a sixth century Athenian statesman whose wide-ranging reform of the Athenian constitution was as significant and abiding as that of Solon.

15. At 1274ᵇ34–36.

these times, some do not want to honor treaties, since it was not the city-state but its tyrant who entered into them, nor to do many other things of the same sort, on the grounds that some constitutions exist by force and not for the common benefit.[16] Accordingly, if indeed some democrats also rule in that way, it must be conceded that the acts of their constitution are the city-state's in just the same way as are those of the oligarchy or the tyranny.

There seems to be a close relation between this argument and the problem of when we ought to say that a city-state is the same, or not the same but a different one.[17] The most superficial way to investigate this problem is by looking to location and people. For a city-state's location and people can be split, and some can live in one place and some in another. Hence the problem must be regarded as a rather tame one. For the fact that a thing is said to be a city-state in many different ways makes the investigation of such problems pretty easy.[18]

Things are similar if one asks when people inhabiting the same location should be considered a single city-state. Certainly not because it is enclosed by walls, since a single wall could be built around the Peloponnese. Perhaps Babylon is like that, or anywhere else that has the dimensions of a nation rather than a city-state. At any rate, they say that when Babylon was captured, a part of the city-state was unaware of it for three days.[19] But it will be useful to investigate this problem in another context. For the size of the city-state, both as regards numbers and as regards whether it is beneficial for it to be one or[20] several, should not be overlooked by the statesman.

But when the same people are inhabiting the same place, is the city-state to be called the same as long as the inhabitants remain of the same stock, even though all the time some are dying and others being born (just as we are accustomed to say that rivers and springs remain the

10

15

20

25

30

35

16. See Introduction, lxvi–lxxii.
17. Because the problem about whether or not a city-state performed a given action hinges exclusively on the identity conditions for city-states.
18. When people say that something is a city-state, they may mean that it is (1) a political community or (2) a place, or something else. If (1) is what is meant, a single city-state can have a split population and location. If (2) is what is meant, a city-state whose population and location splits will be two city-states, not one.
19. Herodotus (I.177–91) describes Babylon as "a vast city-state in the form of a square with sides nearly fourteen miles long."
20. The text is uncertain. Reading *hen ē* with Lord for the conjectural *ethnos hen ē*.

same, even though all the time some water is flowing out and some flowing in)? Or are we to say that human beings can remain the same for this
40   sort of reason, but the city-state is different? For if indeed a city-state is
*1276*ᵇ a sort of community, a community of citizens sharing a constitution,
then, when the constitution changes its form and becomes different, it
would seem that the city-state too cannot remain the same. At any rate, a
chorus that is at one time in a comedy and at another in a tragedy is said
5   to be two different choruses, even though the human beings in it are
often the same. Similarly, with any other community or composite: we
say it is different if the form of the composite is different.[21] For example,
we call a melody composed of the same notes a different melody when it
is played in the Dorian harmony than when it is played in the Phrygian.
10 But if this is so, it is evident that we must look to the constitution above
all when saying that the city-state is the same. But the name to call it
may be different or the same one whether its inhabitants are the same or
completely different people.[22]

But whether it is just to honor or not to honor agreements when a
15 city-state changes to a different constitution requires another argument.

Chapter 4

The next thing to investigate after what we have just discussed is
whether the virtue of a good man and of a good citizen should be regarded as the same, or not the same. But surely if we should indeed investigate this, the virtue of a citizen must first be grasped in some sort of
outline.

Just as a sailor is one of a number of members of a community, so, we
20 say, is a citizen. And though sailors differ in their capacities (for one is
an oarsman, another a captain, another a lookout, and others have other
sorts of titles), it is clear both that the most exact account of the virtue of
each sort of sailor will be peculiar to him, and similarly that there will

21. See Introduction xxvii–xxviii, lvi.
22. Aristotle thinks that the name (*onoma*) of a thing can be replaced by an account (*logos*) or definition (*horismos*) signifying the essence or form of that
thing (*Metaph.* 1012ᵃ22–24, 1045ᵃ26, *Top.* 101ᵇ38). His point here is not,
therefore, that Corinth can continue to be called "Corinth" or have its name
changed to "Argos" whether its population remains the same or not. He is
claiming that the form or constitution of a city-state, and hence the name
that signifies that form, can remain the same whether its inhabitants change
or not.

also be some common account that fits them all. For the safety of the   *25*
voyage is a task of all of them, since this is what each of the sailors strives
for. In the same way, then, the citizens too, even though they are dissimilar, have the safety of the community as their task. But the community
is the constitution. Hence the virtue of a citizen must be suited to his
constitution. Consequently, if indeed there are several kinds of constitu-   *30*
tion, it is clear that there cannot be a single virtue that is the virtue—the
complete virtue—of a good citizen. But the good man, we say, does express a single virtue: the complete one. Evidently, then, it is possible for
someone to be a good citizen without having acquired the virtue expressed by a good man.   *35*

By going through problems in a different way, the same argument can
be made about the best constitution. If it is impossible for a city-state to
consist entirely of good people, and if each must at least perform his
own task well, and this requires virtue, and if it is impossible for all the
citizens to be similar, then the virtue of a citizen and that of a good man   *40*
cannot be a single virtue. For that of the good citizen must be had by all   *1277ᵃ*
(since this is necessary if the city-state is to be best), but the virtue of a
good man cannot be had by all, unless all the citizens of a good city-state
are necessarily good men. Again, since a city-state consists of dissimilar
elements (I mean that just as an animal consists in the first instance of   *5*
soul and body, a soul of reason and desire, a household of man and
woman, and property of master and slave, so a city-state, too, consists of
all these, and of other dissimilar kinds in addition), then the citizens
cannot all have one virtue, any more than can the leader of a chorus and   *10*
one of its ordinary members.²³

It is evident from these things, therefore, that the virtue of a man and
of a citizen cannot be unqualifiedly the same.

But will there, then, be anyone whose virtue is the same both as a
good citizen and as a good man? We say, indeed, that an excellent ruler is
good and possesses practical wisdom, but that a citizen²⁴ need not pos-   *15*
sess practical wisdom. Some say, too, that the education of a ruler is
different right from the beginning, as is evident, indeed, from the sons
of kings being educated in horsemanship and warfare, and from Euripi-

---

23. The examples given are all of natural ruler-subject pairs. Aristotle has al-
    ready shown in I.13 that the virtues of natural rulers and subjects are differ-
    ent.
24. Reading *politēn* with Ross and Dreizehnter. Alternatively (mss.): "but that a
    statesman (*politikon*) need not be practically-wise."

des saying "No subtleties for me . . . but what the city-state needs,"[25] (since this implies that rulers should get a special sort of education). But 20 if the virtue of a good ruler is the same as that of a good man, and if the man who is ruled is also a citizen, then the virtue of a citizen would not be unqualifiedly the same as the virtue of a man (though that of a certain sort of citizen would be), since the virtue of a ruler and that of a citizen would not be the same. Perhaps this is why Jason said that he went hungry except when he was a tyrant.[26] He meant that he did not know how to be a private individual.

25   Yet the capacity to rule and be ruled is at any rate praised, and being able to do both well is held to be the virtue of a citizen.[27] So if we take a good man's virtue to be that of a ruler, but a citizen's to consist in both, then the two virtues would not be equally praiseworthy.

Since, then, both these views are sometimes accepted,[28] that ruler and 30 ruled should learn different things and not the same ones, and that a citizen should know and share in both, we may see what follows from that. For there is rule by a master, by which we mean the kind concerned with the necessities. The ruler does not need to know how to produce these, but rather how to make use of those who do. In fact, the former is 35 servile. (By "the former" I mean actually knowing how to perform the actions of a servant.) But there are several kinds of slaves, we say, since their tasks vary. One part consists of those tasks performed by manual laborers. As their very name implies, these are people who work with 1277ᵇ their hands. VULGAR CRAFTSMEN are included among them. That is why among some peoples in the distant past craftsmen did not participate in office until extreme democracy arose. Accordingly, the tasks performed by people ruled in this way should not be learned by a good person, nor by[29] a statesman, nor by a good citizen, except perhaps to satisfy some 5 personal need of his own (for then it is no longer a case of one person becoming master and the other slave).[30]

But there is also a kind of rule exercised over those who are similar in birth and free. This we call "political" rule. A ruler must learn it by

25. From the lost play *Aeolus* (Nauck 367 fr. 16. 2–3). King Aeolus is apparently speaking about the education his sons are to receive.
26. Jason was tyrant of Pherae in Thessaly (*c*. 380–370).
27. See Plato, *Laws* 643e–644a.
28. Reading *dokei amphō hetera* with Dreizehnter.
29. Reading *oude ton*.
30. See 1341ᵇ10–15.

being ruled, just as one learns to be a cavalry commander by serving under a cavalry commander, or to be a general by serving under a general, or under a major or a company commander to learn to occupy the office. Hence this too is rightly said, that one cannot rule well without having been ruled.[31] And whereas the virtues of these *are* different, a good citizen must have the knowledge and ability both to be ruled and to rule, and this is the virtue of a citizen, to know the rule of free people from both sides.

In fact, a good man too possesses both, even if a ruler does have a different kind of justice and temperance. For if a good person is ruled, but is a free citizen, his virtue (justice, for example) will clearly not be of one kind, but includes one kind for ruling and another for being ruled, just as a man's and a woman's courage and temperance differ. For a man would seem a coward if he had the courage of a woman, and a woman would seem garrulous if she had the temperance of a good man,[32] since even household management differs for the two of them (for his task is to acquire property and hers to preserve it). Practical wisdom is the only virtue peculiar to a ruler; for the others, it would seem, must be common to both rulers and ruled. At any rate, practical wisdom is not the virtue of one who is ruled, but true opinion is. For those ruled are like makers of flutes, whereas rulers are like the flute players who use them.[33]

So then, whether the virtue of a good man is the same as that of an excellent citizen or different, and how they are the same and how different, is evident from the preceding.

Chapter 5

But one of the problems about the citizen still remains. For is the citizen really someone who is permitted to participate in office, or should vulgar craftsmen also be regarded as citizens? If, indeed, those who do not share in office should be regarded as citizens, then this sort of virtue[34] cannot belong to every citizen (for these will then be citizens). On the

---

31. A saying to this effect, "Learn to obey before you command," is attributed to Solon. See Diogenes Laertius I.60.
32. See 1260[a]28–31. Greek women were expected to say very little, whereas being a good speaker was a male virtue.
33. See 1282[a]17–23; Plato, *Republic* 429b–430c, 433c–d, 473c–480a, 601d–602b.
34. The virtue that enables one to rule and be ruled well.

other hand, if none of this sort is a citizen, in what category should they each be put?—for they are neither resident aliens nor foreigners.

Or shall we say that from *this* argument, at least, nothing absurd follows, since neither slaves nor freed slaves are in the aforementioned classes either? For the truth is that not everyone without whom there would not be a city-state is to be regarded as a citizen. For children are not citizens in the way men are. The latter are unqualified citizens, whereas the former are only citizens given certain assumptions: they are citizens, but incomplete ones. Vulgar craftsmen were slaves or foreigners in some places long ago, which is why most of them still are even today. The best city-state will not confer citizenship on vulgar craftsmen, however; but if they too are citizens, then what we have characterized as a citizen's virtue cannot be ascribed to everyone, or even to all free people, but only to those who are freed from necessary tasks. Those who perform necessary tasks for an individual are slaves; those who perform them for the community are vulgar craftsmen and hired laborers.

If we carry our investigation a bit further, it will be evident how things stand in these cases. In fact, it is clear from what we have already said.[35] For since there are several constitutions, there must also be several kinds of citizens, particularly of citizens who are being ruled. Hence in some constitutions vulgar craftsmen and hired laborers must be citizens, whereas in others it is impossible—for example, in any so-called aristocracy in which offices are awarded on the basis of virtue and merit. For it is impossible to engage in virtuous pursuits while living the life of a vulgar craftsman or a hired laborer.[36]

In oligarchies, however, while hired laborers could not be citizens (since participation in office is based on high property assessments), vulgar craftsmen could be, since in fact most craftsmen become rich (though in Thebes there used to be a law that anyone who had not kept away from the market for ten years could not participate in office).[37]

In many constitutions, however, the law even goes so far as to admit some foreigners as citizens; for in some democracies the descendant of a citizen mother is a citizen, and in many places the same holds of bastards too. Nevertheless, since it is because of a shortage of legitimate citizens that they make such people citizens (for it is because of underpop-

---

35. At III.1.
36. Explained somewhat at 1260ª38–ᵇ1, 1337ᵇ4–21.
37. Aristotle thinks that oligarchies *should* impose restrictions of this sort on vulgar craftsmen (1321ª26–29).

ulation that they employ laws in this way), when they are well supplied with a crowd of them, they gradually disqualify, first, those who have a slave as father or mother, then those with citizen mothers, until finally they make citizens only of those who come from citizens on both sides.

It is evident from these considerations, therefore, that there are several kinds of citizens, and that the one who participates in the offices is 35 particularly said to be a citizen, as Homer too implied when he wrote: "like some disenfranchised alien."[38] For people who do not participate in the offices *are* like resident aliens. When this is concealed, it is for the sake of deceiving coinhabitants.[39]

As to whether the virtue expressed by a good man is to be regarded as 40 the same as that of an excellent citizen or as different, it is clear from 1278^b what has been said that in one sort of city-state both are the same person, while in another they are different. And that person is not just anyone, but the statesman, who has authority or is capable of exercising authority in the supervision of communal matters, either by himself or with others. 5

Chapter 6

Since these issues have been determined, the next thing to investigate is whether we should suppose that there is just one kind of constitution or several, and, if there are several, what they are, how many they are, and how they differ.

A constitution is an organization of a city-state's various offices but, particularly, of the one that has authority over everything. For the governing class has authority in every city-state, and the governing class is 10 the constitution.[40] I mean, for example, that in democratic city-states the people have authority, whereas in oligarchic ones, by contrast, the few have it, and we also say the constitutions of these are different. And we shall give the same account of the other constitutions as well.

First, then, we must set down what it is that a city-state is constituted 15 for, and how many kinds of rule deal with human beings and communal life. In our first discussions, indeed, where conclusions were reached

---

38. *Iliad* IX.648, XVI.59. Achilles is complaining that this is how Agamemnon is treating him.
39. See 1264^a19–22.
40. Aristotle is relying on his doctrine that "a city-state and every other composite system is most of all the part of it that has the most authority" (*NE* 1168^b31–33).

about household management and rule by a master, it was also said that
a human being is by nature a political animal.[41] That is why, even when
20   they do not need one another's help, people no less desire to live together, although it is also true that the common benefit brings them together, to the extent that it contributes some part of living well to each.
This above all is the end, then, whether of everyone in common or of
each separately.[42] But human beings also join together and maintain political communities for the sake of life by itself. For there is perhaps
25   some share of what is NOBLE in life alone, as long as it is not too over-
burdened with the hardships of life. In any case, it is clear that most
human beings are willing to endure much hardship in order to cling to
life, as if it had a sort of joy inherent in it and a natural sweetness.

But surely it is also easy to distinguish at least the kinds of rule people
30   talk about, since we too often discuss them in our own external works.[43]
For rule by a master, although in truth the same thing is beneficial for
both natural masters and natural slaves, is nevertheless rule exercised
35   for the sake of the master's own benefit, and only coincidentally for that
of the slave.[44] For rule by a master cannot be preserved if the slave is destroyed. But rule over children, wife, and the household generally,
which we call household management, is either for the sake of the ruled
or for the sake of something common to both. Essentially, it is for the
40   sake of the ruled, as we see medicine, physical training, and the other
1279ᵃ crafts to be, but coincidentally it might be for the sake of the rulers as
well. For nothing prevents the trainer from sometimes being one of the
athletes he is training, just as the captain of a ship is always one of the
5   sailors. Thus a trainer or a captain looks to the good of those he rules,
but when he becomes one of them himself, he shares coincidentally in
the benefit. For the captain is a sailor, and the trainer, though still a
trainer, becomes one of the trained.

Hence, in the case of political office too, where it has been established
on the basis of equality and similarity among the citizens, they think it
10   right to take turns at ruling. In the past, as is natural, they thought it

41. See Introduction xlviii–lix.
42. Aristotle argues for this in VII.1–3.
43. The reference may be to lost works of Aristotle intended for a wider audi-
     ence than the *Politics*. See, e.g., *EE* 1217ᵇ22–23.
44. The master has a reason to keep his slaves alive and healthy, but only be-
     cause it is in his own interest as a master to do so (1252ᵃ31–34,
     1254ᵇ15–1255ᵃ3, 1255ᵇ5–15).

right to perform public service when their turn came, and then to have someone look to *their* good, just as they had earlier looked to his benefit when they were in office. Nowadays, however, because of the profits to be had from public funds and from office, people want to be in office continuously, as if they were sick and would be cured by being always in office. At any rate, perhaps the latter would pursue office in that way.   *15*

It is evident, then, that those constitutions that look to the common benefit turn out, according to what is unqualifiedly just, to be correct, whereas those which look only to the benefit of the rulers are mistaken and are deviations from the correct constitutions. For they are like rule   *20* by a master, whereas a city-state is a community of free people.

Chapter 7

Now that these matters have been determined, we must next investigate how many kinds of constitutions there are and what they are,[45] starting first with the correct constitutions. For once they have been defined, the deviant ones will also be made evident.

Since "constitution" and "governing class" signify the same thing,[46]   *25* and the governing class is the authoritative element in any city-state, and the authoritative element must be either one person, or few, or many, then whenever the one, the few, or the many rule for the common benefit, these constitutions must be correct. But if they aim at the private benefit, whether of the one or the few or the MULTITUDE, they are devi-   *30* ations (for either the participants[47] should not be called citizens, or they should share in the benefits).

A monarchy that looks to the common benefit we customarily call a kingship; and rule by a few but more than one, an aristocracy (either because the best people rule, or because they rule with a view to what is   *35* best for the city-state and those who share in it). But when the multitude governs for the common benefit, it is called by the name common to all CONSTITUTIONS, namely, *politeia*. Moreover, this happens reasonably. For while it is possible for one or a few to be outstandingly virtuous, it is difficult for a larger number to be accomplished in every virtue, but it   *40* can be so in military virtue in particular. That is precisely why the class   *1279ᵇ*

---

45. See 1274ᵇ32–33 and note.
46. See 1278ᵇ11 and note.
47. Rejecting with the mss. the insertion of *mē*.

of defensive soldiers, the ones who possess the weapons, has the most authority in this constitution.[48]

5 Deviations from these are tyranny from kingship, oligarchy from aristocracy, and democracy from polity. For tyranny is rule by one person for the benefit of the monarch, oligarchy is for the benefit of the rich, and democracy is for the benefit of the poor. But none is for their common profit.

Chapter 8

10 We should say a little more about what each of these constitutions is. For certain problems arise, and when one is carrying out any investigation in a philosophical manner, and not merely with a practical purpose in view, it is appropriate not to overlook or omit anything, but to make the truth
15 about each clear.

A tyranny, as we said, exists when a monarchy rules the political community like a master; in an oligarchy those in authority in the constitution are the ones who have property. A democracy is the opposite; those who do not possess much property, and are poor, are in authority. The
20 first problem concerns this definition. Suppose that the MAJORITY were rich and had authority in the city-state; yet there is a democracy whenever the majority has authority. Similarly, to take the opposite case, suppose the poor were fewer in number than the rich, but were stronger and had authority in the constitution; yet when a small group has authority it is said to be an oligarchy. It would seem, then, that these constitutions
25 have not been well defined. But even if one combines being few with being rich in one case, and being a majority with being poor in the other, and describes the constitutions accordingly (oligarchy as that in which the rich are few in number and hold the offices, and democracy as that in
30 which the poor are many and hold them), another problem arises. For what are we to call the constitutions we just described, those where the rich are a majority and the poor a minority, but each has authority in its

48. The constitution is a POLITY, which is governed by the HOPLITE class. It is the correct form of government by the many because its governing class are as virtuous as possible, since they possess military virtue, which is the one virtue that is broadly sharable. That is why Aristotle agrees that it is reasonable to call the correct form of government by the many a polity. On military virtue, see 1271[a]41–[b]2.

own constitution—if indeed there is no other constitution besides those just mentioned?[49]

What this argument seems to make clear is that it is a coincidence that the few have authority in oligarchies and the many in democracies, a re- 35 sult of the fact that everywhere the rich are few and the poor many. That is why, indeed, the reasons just mentioned are not the reasons for the differences. What does distinguish democracy and oligarchy from one another is poverty and wealth: whenever some, whether a minority or a 40 majority, rule because of their wealth, the constitution is necessarily an 1280ᵃ oligarchy, and whenever the poor rule, it is necessarily a democracy. But it turns out, as we said, that the former are in fact few and the latter many. For only a few people are rich, but all share in freedom; and these 5 are the reasons they both dispute over the constitution.[50]

Chapter 9

The first thing one must grasp, however, is what people say the defining marks of oligarchy and democracy are, and what oligarchic and democratic justice are. For [1] they all grasp justice of a sort,[51] but they go only to a certain point and do not discuss the whole of what is just in the most authoritative sense. For example, justice seems to be EQUALITY, and it is, 10 but not for everyone, only *for equals*. Justice also seems to be inequality, since indeed it is, but not for everyone, only *for unequals*.[52] They disregard the "for whom," however, and judge badly. The reason is that the judgment concerns themselves, and most people are pretty poor judges about what is their own.[53] 15

So since what is just is just *for certain people*, and consists in dividing things and people in the same way (as we said earlier in the *Ethics*),[54] they agree about what constitutes equality in the thing but disagree about it in the people. This is largely because of what was just mentioned, that they judge badly about what concerns themselves, but also 20

49. Presumably, the six listed in the previous chapter.
50. See 1290ᵃ30–ᵇ20.
51. As the remainder of the chapter will establish. The inserted numbers help reveal the structure of what is, even for Aristotle, a rather complexly structured argument.
52. Democrats give the first definition; oligarchs the second (1266ᵇ38–1267ᵃ2, 1267ᵃ37–41). See Introduction lxv–lxviii.
53. See 1287ᵃ41–ᵇ3.
54. *NE* V.3.

because, since they are both speaking up to a point about justice of a sort, they think they are speaking about what is unqualifiedly just. For one lot thinks that if they are unequal in one respect (wealth, say) they are wholly unequal, whereas the other lot thinks that if they are equal in one respect (freedom, say) they are wholly equal. But about the most authoritative considerations they do not speak.

25   For suppose people constituted a community and came together for the sake of property; then their participation in a city-state would be proportional to their property, and the oligarchic argument would as a result seem to be a powerful one. (For it is not just that someone who has contributed only one mina to a sum of one hundred minas should have equal shares in that sum, whether of the principal or of the interest, with
30   the one who has contributed all the rest.) But suppose [2] they do not do so only for the sake of life, but rather for the sake of living well, since otherwise there could be a city-state of SLAVES or animals, whereas in fact there is not, because these share neither in HAPPINESS nor in a life guided by DELIBERATIVE CHOICE.

And suppose [3] they do not do so for the sake of an alliance to safeguard themselves from being wronged by anyone, nor [4] to facilitate ex-
35   change and mutual assistance, since otherwise the Etruscans and the Carthaginians, and all those who have treaties with one another would virtually be citizens of one city-state. To be sure, they have import agreements, treaties about refraining from injustice, and formal docu-
40   ments of alliance, but no offices common to all of them have been established to deal with these matters; instead each city-state has different
1280ᵇ   ones. Nor are those in one city-state concerned with what sort of people the others should be, or that none of those covered by the agreements should be unjust or vicious in any way, but only that neither city-state acts unjustly toward the other. But those who are concerned with good
5   government give careful attention to political virtue and vice.[55] Hence it is quite evident that the city-state (at any rate, the one truly so called and not just for the sake of argument) must be concerned with virtue. For otherwise the community becomes an alliance that differs only in location from other alliances in which the allies live far apart, and law be-
10   comes an agreement, "a guarantor of just behavior toward one another," as the sophist Lycophron[56] said, but not such as to make the citizens good and just.

55. See 1281ᵃ4–8, 1340ᵇ41–1341ᵃ3, and 1254ᵇ27–32 with 1334ᵃ11–40.
56. Lycophron is known only from the writings of Aristotle. He may have belonged to the school of Gorgias.

It is evident that this is right. For even if [5] one were to bring their territories together into one, so that the city-state of the Megarians was attached to that of the Corinthians by walls, it still would not be a single city-state. Nor would it be so if their citizens intermarried, even though *15* this is one of the forms of community characteristic of city-states. Similarly, if there were some who lived separately, yet not so separately as to share nothing in common, and had laws against wronging one another in their business transactions (for example, if one were a carpenter, another a farmer, another a cobbler, another something else of that sort, and *20* their number were ten thousand), yet they shared nothing else in common besides such things as exchange and alliance—not even in this case would there be a city-state.

What, then, is the reason for this? Surely, it is not because of the non-proximate nature of their community. For suppose they joined together while continuing to share in that way, but each nevertheless treated his *25* own household like a city-state, and the others like a defensive alliance formed to provide aid against wrongdoers only. Even then this still would not be thought a city-state by those who make a precise study of such things, if indeed they continued to associate with one another in the same manner when together as when separated.

Evidently, then, a city-state is not [5] a sharing of a common location, and does not exist for the purpose of [4] preventing mutual wrongdoing *30* and [3] exchanging goods. Rather, while these must be present if indeed there is to be a city-state, when all of them *are* present there is still not yet a city-state, but [2] only when households and families live well as a community whose end is a complete and self-sufficient life. But this will not be possible unless they do inhabit one and the same location and *35* practice intermarriage. That is why marriage connections arose in city-states, as well as brotherhoods, religious sacrifices, and the LEISURED PURSUITS of living together. For things of this sort are the result of friendship, since the deliberative choice of living together constitutes friendship. The end of the city-state is living well, then, but these other things are for the sake of the end. And a city-state is the community of families and villages in a complete and self-sufficient life, which we say *40* is living happily and NOBLY. *1281ᵃ*

So political communities must be taken to exist for the sake of noble actions, and not for the sake of living together. Hence those who contribute the most to *this* sort of community have a larger share in the city-state than those who are equal or superior in freedom or family but infe- *5* rior in political virtue, and those who surpass in wealth but are surpassed in virtue.

It is evident from what has been said, then, that [1] those who dispute
10   about constitutions all speak about a *part* of justice.

Chapter 10

There is a problem as to what part of the state is to have authority, since
surely it is either the multitude, or the rich, or decent people, or the one
who is best of all, or a tyrant. But all of these apparently involve difficulties. How so? If the poor, because they are the greater number, divide up
15   the property of the rich, isn't that unjust? "No, by Zeus, it isn't, since it
seemed just to those in authority." What, then, should we call extreme injustice? Again, if the majority, having seized everything, should divide up
the property of the minority, they are evidently destroying the city-state.
But virtue certainly does not ruin what has it, nor is justice something
20   capable of destroying a city-state. So it is clear, then, that this law[57] cannot be just. Besides, everything done by a tyrant must be just as well; for
he, being stronger, uses force, just as the multitude do against the rich.
25   But is it just, then, for the rich minority to rule? If they too act in the
same way, plundering and confiscating the property of the multitude,
and this is just, then the other case is as well. It is evident, therefore, that
all these things are bad and unjust.

But should decent people rule and have authority over everything? In
that case, everyone else must be deprived of honors by being excluded from
30   political office. For offices are positions of honor, we say, and when the same
people always rule, the rest must necessarily be deprived of honors.

But is it better that the one who is best should rule? But this is even
more oligarchic, since those deprived of honors are more numerous.

Perhaps, however, someone might say that it is a bad thing in general
35   for a human being to have authority and not the LAW, since he at any rate
has the passions that beset the soul. But if law may be oligarchic or democratic, what difference will that make to our problems? For the things
we have just described will happen just the same.

Chapter 11

As for the other cases, we may let them be the topic of a different discussion.[58] But the view that the multitude rather than the few best peo-

---

57. The law requiring wealth to be divided up.
58. See III.12–13.

ple should be in authority would seem to be held, and while it involves a   *40*
problem, it perhaps also involves some truth. For the many, who are not
as individuals excellent men, nevertheless can, when they have come together, be better than the few best people, not individually but collec-   *1281ᵇ*
tively, just as feasts to which many contribute are better than feasts provided at one person's expense. For being many, each of them can have
some part of virtue and practical wisdom, and when they come together,
the multitude is just like a single human being, with many feet, hands,   *5*
and senses, and so too for their character traits and wisdom. That is why
the many are better judges of works of music and of the poets. For one of
them judges one part, another another, and all of them the whole
thing.[59]

It is in this way that excellent men differ from each of the many, just   *10*
as beautiful people are said to differ from those who are not beautiful,
and as things painted by craft are superior to real things: they bring together what is scattered and separate into one—although, at least if
taken separately, this person's eye and some other feature of someone
else will be more beautiful than the painted ones.

Whether this superiority of the many to the few excellent people can   *15*
exist in the case of every people and every multitude is not clear.
Though presumably, by Zeus, it is clear that in some of them it cannot
possibly do so, since the same argument would apply to beasts. For what
difference is there, practically speaking, between some people and
beasts? But nothing prevents what has been said from being true of *some*   *20*
multitude.

By means of these considerations, too, one might solve the problem
mentioned earlier and also the related one of what the free should have
authority over, that is to say, the multitude of the citizens who are not
rich and have no claim whatsoever arising from virtue. For it would not   *25*
be safe to have them participate in the most important offices, since, because of their lack of justice and practical wisdom, they would inevitably
act unjustly in some instances and make mistakes in others. On the other
hand, to give them no share and not to allow them to participate at all
would be cause for alarm. For a state in which a large number of people
are excluded from office and are poor must of necessity be full of enemies. The remaining alternative, then, is to have them participate in de-   *30*
liberation and judgment, which is precisely why Solon and some other

---

59. A panel chosen by lot selected the three best comedies and tragedies at the
    annual theater festivals in Athens.

legislators arrange to have them elect and INSPECT officials, but prevent them from holding office alone.[60] For when they all come together their
35   perception is adequate, and, when mixed with their betters, they benefit their states, just as a mixture of roughage and pure food-concentrate is more useful than a little of the latter by itself.[61] Taken individually, however, each of them is an imperfect judge.

But this organization of the constitution raises problems itself. In the first place, it might be held that the same person is able to judge whether
40   or not someone has treated a patient correctly, and to treat patients and cure them of disease when it is present—namely, the doctor. The same would also seem to hold in other areas of experience and other crafts.
1282ᵃ   Therefore, just as a doctor should be inspected by doctors, so others should also be inspected by their peers. But "doctor" applies to the ordinary practitioner of the craft, to a master craftsman, and thirdly, to someone with a general EDUCATION in the craft. For there are people of
5   this third sort in (practically speaking) all the crafts. And we assign the task of judging to generally educated people no less than to experts.

Moreover, it might be held that election is the same way, since choosing correctly is also a task for experts: choosing a geometer is a task for expert geometers, for example, and choosing a ship's captain is a task for
10   expert captains. For even if some laymen are also involved in the choice of candidates in the case of some tasks and crafts, at least they do not play a larger role than the experts. According to this argument, then, the multitude should not be given authority over the election or inspection of officials.

But perhaps not all of these things are correctly stated, both because
15   according to the earlier argument the multitude may not be too servile, since each may be a worse judge than those who know, but a better or no worse one when they all come together; and because there are some crafts in which the maker might not be either the only or the best judge—the ones where those who do not possess the craft nevertheless have knowledge of its products. For example, the maker of a house is not
20   the only one who has some knowledge about it; the one who uses it is an even better judge (and the one who uses is the household manager). A captain, too, judges a rudder better than a carpenter, and a guest, rather than the cook, a feast.[62]

60. See 1274ᵃ15–21.
61. See *GA* 728ᵃ26–30.
62. See 1277ᵇ25–30.

This problem might be held to be adequately solved in such a way. But there is another connected with it. For it is held to be absurd for inferior people to have authority over more important matters than decent people do. But inspections and elections of officials are very important things. And in some constitutions, as we said, these are assigned to the people, since the assembly has authority over all such matters. And yet those with low property assessments and of whatever age participate in the assembly, and in deliberation and decision, whereas those with high property assessment are the treasurers and generals and hold the most important offices.

But one can, in fact, also solve this problem in the same way. For perhaps these things are also correctly organized. For it is neither the individual juror, nor the individual councilor, nor the individual assemblyman who is ruling, but the court, the council, and the people, whereas each of the individuals mentioned is only a part of these. (By "part" I mean the councilor, the assemblyman, and the juror.) Hence it is just for the multitude to have authority over the more important matters. For the people, the council, and the court consist of many individuals, and their collective property assessment is greater than the assessment of those who, whether individually or in small groups, hold the important offices. So much for how these matters should be determined.

As to the first problem we mentioned,[63] it makes nothing else so evident as that the laws, when correctly established, should be in authority, and that the ruler, whether one or many, should have authority over only those matters on which the LAWS cannot pronounce with precision, because it is not easy to make universal declarations about everything.

It is not yet clear, however, what correctly established laws should be like, and the problem stated earlier remains to be solved.[64] For the laws must necessarily be bad or good, and just or unjust, at the same time and in the same way as the constitutions. Still, at least it is evident that the laws must be established to suit the constitution. But if this is so, it is clear that laws that accord with the correct constitutions must be just, and those that accord with the deviant constitutions not just.

Chapter 12

Since in every science and craft the end is a good, the greatest and best good is the end of the science or craft that has the most authority of all

25

30

35

40

1282^b

5

10

15

63. The one raised at 1281^{a}11 of who should have authority in the city-state.
64. See 1281^{a}34–39.

of them, and this is the science of statesmanship. But the political good
is justice, and justice is the common benefit. Now everyone holds that
what is just is some sort of equality, and up to a point, at least, all agree
with what has been determined in those philosophical works of ours
dealing with ethical issues.[65] For justice is something to someone, and
they say it should be something equal to those who are equal. But equality in what and inequality in what, should not be overlooked. For this involves a problem and political philosophy.

Someone might say, perhaps, that offices should be unequally distributed on the basis of superiority in any good whatsoever, provided the
people did not differ in their remaining qualities but were exactly similar, since where people differ, so does what is just and what accords with
merit. But if this is true, then those who are superior in complexion, or
height, or any other good whatsoever will get more of the things with
which political justice is concerned. And isn't that plainly false? The
matter is evident in the various sciences and capacities. For among flute
players equally proficient in the craft, those who are of better birth do
not get more or better flutes, since they will not play the flute any better
if they do. It is the superior performers who should also get the superior
instruments. If what has been said is somehow not clear, it will become
so if we take it still further. Suppose someone is superior in flute playing, but is very inferior in birth or beauty; then, even if each of these (I
mean birth and beauty) is a greater good than flute playing, and is proportionately more superior to flute playing than he is superior in flute
playing, he should still get the outstanding flutes. For the superiority in
wealth and birth would have to contribute to the performance, but in
fact they contribute nothing to it.

Besides, according to this argument every good would have to be
commensurable with every other. For if being a certain height counted
more,[66] height in general would be in competition with both wealth and
freedom. So if one person is more outstanding in height than another is
in virtue, and if height in general is of more weight than virtue, then all
goods would be commensurable. For if a certain amount of size is better
than a certain amount of virtue, it is clear that some amount of the one is
equal to some amount of the other. Since this is impossible, it is clear
that in political matters, too, it is reasonable not to dispute over political
office on the basis of just any sort of inequality. For if some are slow run-

65. The reference seems to be to *NE* 1131[a]9–[b]24.
66. Reading *mallon* with the mss. for the conjectural *enamillon.*

ners and others fast, this is no reason for the latter to have more and the former less: it is in athletic competitions that such a difference wins honor. The dispute must be based on the things from which a city-state is constituted. Hence the well-born, the free, and the rich reasonably lay 15 claim to office. For there must be both free people and those with assessed property, since a city-state cannot consist entirely of poor people, any more than of slaves. But if these things are needed in a city-state, so too, it is clear, are justice and political[67] virtue, since a city-state cannot be managed without these. Rather, without the former a city-state can- 20 not exist, and without the latter it cannot be well managed.

Chapter 13

As regards the existence of a city-state, all, or at any rate some, of these would seem to have a correct claim in the dispute. But as regards the good life, education and virtue would seem to have the most just claim of all in the dispute, as was also said earlier.[68] But since those equal in 25 one thing only should not have equality in everything, nor inequality if they are unequal in only one thing, all constitutions of this sort must be deviant.

We said before[69] that all dispute somewhat justly, but that not all do so 30 in an unqualifiedly just way. The rich have a claim due to the fact that they own a larger share of the land, and the land is something common, and that, in addition, they are usually more trustworthy where treaties[70] are concerned. The FREE and the well-born have closely related claims, for those who are better born are more properly citizens than those of ignoble birth, and good birth is honored at home by everyone. Besides, 35 they have a claim because better people are likely to come from better people, since good birth is virtue of family.[71] Similarly, then, we shall say that virtue has a just claim in the dispute, since justice, we say, is a communal virtue, which all the other virtues necessarily accompany.[72] But the majority too have a just claim against the minority, since they are 40

---

67. Reading *politikēs* with Ross, Schütrumpf, and some mss. Alternatively (Dreizehnter and some mss.): "military (*polemikēs*)."
68. At 1281ª1–8.
69. At 1280ª7–25.
70. *sumbolaia:* or contracts.
71. A slightly different definition is given at 1294ª21.
72. Because justice is complete virtue in relation to another person (*NE* 1129ᵇ25–1130ª5).

stronger, richer, and better, when taken as the majority in relation to the minority.

If they were all present in a single city-state, therefore (I mean, for ex-
1283ᵇ ample, the good, the rich, the well-born, and a political multitude in addition), will there be a dispute as to who should rule or not? Within each of the constitutions we have mentioned, to be sure, the decision as
5   to who should rule is indisputable, since these differ from one another because of what is in authority; for example, because in one the rich are in authority, in another the excellent men, and each of the others differs the same way. But be that as it may, we are investigating how the matter is to be determined when all these are present simultaneously. Suppose,
10 for example, that those who possess virtue are extremely few in number, how should the matter be settled? Should their fewness be considered in relation to the task? To whether they are able to manage the city-state? Or to whether there are enough of them to constitute a city-state by themselves?

But there is a problem that faces all who dispute over political office.
15 Those who claim that they deserve to rule because of their wealth could be held to have no justice to their claim at all, and similarly those claiming to do so because of their family. For it is clear that if someone is richer again than everyone else, then, on the basis of the same justice, this one person will have to rule them all. Similarly, it is clear that some-one who is outstanding when it comes to good birth should rule those who dispute on the basis of freedom. Perhaps the same thing will also
20 occur in the case of virtue where aristocracies are concerned. For if one man were better than the others in the governing class, even though they were excellent men, then, on the basis of the same justice, this man should be in authority. So if the majority too should be in authority be-cause they are superior to the few, then, if one person, or more than one
25 but fewer than the many, were superior to the others, these should be in authority rather than the multitude. All this seems to make it evident, then, that none of the definitions on the basis of which people claim that they themselves deserve to rule, whereas everyone else deserves to be ruled by them, is correct. For the multitude would have an argument of some justice even against those who claim that they deserve to have au-
30 thority over the governing class because of their virtue, and similarly against those who base their claim on wealth. For nothing prevents the multitude from being sometimes better and richer than the few, not as individuals but collectively.
35 Hence the problem that some people raise and investigate can also be

dealt with in this way. For they raise the problem of whether a legislator who wishes to establish the most correct laws should legislate for the benefit of the better citizens or that of the majority, when the case just mentioned occurs. But what is correct must be taken to mean what is equitable; and what is equitable in relation to the benefit of the entire   *40* city-state, and the common benefit of the citizens. And a citizen gener-ally speaking is someone who participates in ruling and in being ruled, although in each constitution he is someone different. It is in the best   *1284ᵃ* one, however, that he is the one who has the power and who deliberately chooses to be ruled and to rule with an eye to the virtuous life. But if there is one person or more than one (though not enough to make up a complete city-state) who is so outstanding by reason of his superior   *5* virtue that neither the virtue nor the political power of all the others is commensurable with his (if there is only one) or theirs (if there are a number of them), then such men can no longer be regarded as part of the city-state. For they would be treated unjustly if they were thought to merit equal shares, when they are so unequal in virtue and political power. For anyone of that sort would reasonably be regarded as a god   *10* among human beings. Hence it is clear that legislation too must be con-cerned with those who are equals both in birth and in power, and that for the other sort there is no law, since they themselves are law. For, indeed, anyone who attempted to legislate for them would be ridiculous, since they would presumably respond in the way Antisthenes tells us the lions   *15* did when the hares acted like popular leaders and demanded equality for everyone.[73]

That is why, indeed, democratically governed city-states introduce ostracism. For of all city-states these are held to pursue equality most, and so they ostracize those held to be outstandingly powerful (whether because of their wealth, their many friends, or any other source of polit-   *20* ical power), banishing them from the city-state for fixed periods of time.[74] The story goes, too, that the Argonauts left Heracles behind for this sort of reason: the Argo refused to carry him with the other sailors on the grounds that his weight greatly exceeded theirs.[75] That is also   *25*

---

73. The lions' reply was: "Where are your claws and teeth?" See Aesop, *Fables* 241. Antisthenes was a follower of Socrates and a founder of the school of philosophers known as the Cynics.
74. Ostracism, or banishment without loss of property or citizenship for ten (later five) years, was introduced into Athens by Cleisthenes. See *Ath.* XXII.
75. Athena had built a board into the Argo that enabled it to speak.

why those who criticize tyranny or the advice that Periander gave Thrasybulus should not be considered to be unqualifiedly correct in their censure. For they say that Periander said nothing to the messenger who had been sent to him for advice, but leveled a cornfield by cutting
30   off the outstandingly tall ears. When the messenger, who did not know why Periander did this, reported what had happened, Thrasybulus understood that he was to get rid of the outstanding men.[76]

This advice is not beneficial only to tyrants, however, nor are tyrants the only ones who follow it. The same situation holds too in oligarchies
35   and democracies. For ostracism has the same sort of effect as cutting down the outstanding people or sending them into exile. But those in control of power treat city-states and nations in the same way. For example, as soon as Athens had a firm grip on its imperial rule, it humbled
40   Samos, Chios, and Lesbos,[77] in violation of the treaties it had with them; and the king of the Persians often cut the Medes and Babylonians down
1284ᵇ to size, as well as any others who had grown presumptuous because they had once ruled empires of their own.

The problem is a general one that concerns all constitutions, even the correct ones. For though the deviant constitutions use such methods
5   with an eye to the private benefit, the position is the same with those that aim at the common good. But this is also clear in the case of the other crafts and sciences. For no painter would allow an animal to have a disproportionately large foot, not even if it were an outstandingly beautiful one, nor would a shipbuilder allow this in the case of the stern or
10   any of the other parts of the ship, nor will a chorus master tolerate a member of the chorus who has a louder and more beautiful voice than the entire chorus. So, from this point of view, there is nothing to prevent monarchs from being in harmony with the city-state they rule when they resort to this sort of practice, provided their rule benefits their
15   city-states. Where acknowledged sorts of superiority are concerned, then, there is some political justice to the argument in favor of ostracism.

It would be better, certainly, if the legislator established the constitution in the beginning so that it had no need for such a remedy. But the next best thing is to try to fix the constitution, should the need arise,

76. Periander was tyrant of Corinth (625–585). Thrasybulus was tyrant of Miletus. The full story is told by Herodotus V.92, who reverses the roles of Periander and Thrasybulus.
77. The most powerful city-states in the Athenian alliance.

with a corrective of this sort. This is not what actually tended to happen
in city-states, however. For they did not look to the benefit of their own   *20*
constitutions, but used ostracism for purposes of faction. It is evident,
then, that in each of the deviant constitutions ostracism is privately ad-
vantageous and just, but it is perhaps also evident that it is not unqualifiedly just.

    In the case of the best constitution, however, there is a considerable   *25*
problem, not about superiority in other goods, such as power or wealth
or having many friends, but when there happens to be someone who is
superior in virtue. For surely people would not say that such a person
should be expelled or banished, but neither would they say that they
should rule over him. For that would be like claiming that they deserved   *30*
to rule over Zeus, dividing the offices.[78] The remaining possibility—and
it seems to be the natural one—is for everyone to obey such a person
gladly, so that those like him will be permanent kings in their city-states.

Chapter 14

After the matters just discussed, it may perhaps be well to change to an   *35*
investigation of kingship, since we say that it is one of the correct constitutions. What we have to investigate is whether or not it is beneficial for
a city-state or territory which is to be well managed to be under a kingship, or under some other constitution instead, or whether it is beneficial for some but not for others. But first it must be determined whether   *40*
there is one single type of kingship or several different varieties.

    In fact this is easy to see—that kingship includes several types, and   *1285ª*
that the manner of rule is not the same in all of them. For kingship in
the Spartan constitution, which is held to be the clearest example of
kingships based on law, does not have authority over everything, but
when the king leaves the country, he does have leadership in military af-   *5*
fairs. Moreover, matters relating to the gods are assigned to the kings.
[1] This type of kingship, then, is a sort of permanent autocratic generalship. For the king does not have the power of life and death, except
when exercising a certain sort of kingship,[79] similar to that exercised in
ancient times on military expeditions, on the basis of the law of force.[80]
Homer provides a clear example. Agamemnon put up with being abused   *10*

---

78. So that he ruled and was ruled in turn.
79. Reading *en tini basileia(i)* with the mss.
80. It permitted summary execution without trial.

in the assemblies, but when they went out to fight he had the power even
of life and death. At any rate, he says: "Anyone I find far from the battle
. . . shall have no hope of escaping dogs and vultures, for I myself shall
put him to death."[81] This, then, is one kind of kingship—a generalship
15   for life. Some of these are based on lineage, others elective.

[2] But there is another kind of monarchy besides this, which is like
kingships that exist among some non-Greeks. The powers all these have
are very like those tyrants have, but they are based on law and are hereditary. Because non-Greeks are by nature more slavish in their character
20   than Greeks, those in Asia being more so than those in Europe, they tolerate rule by a master without any complaint. So for this sort of reason
these kingships are tyrannical, but they are stable because hereditary
and based on law. Their bodyguards are kingly and not tyrannical for the
25   same reason. For the citizens guard their kings with their weapons,
whereas a foreign contingent guards tyrants. For kings rule willing subjects on the basis of law, whereas the latter rule unwilling ones. Thus the
former have bodyguards drawn from the citizens, whereas the latter
have their bodyguards to protect them against the citizens.[82]

These, then, are two kinds of monarchy. [3] But there is another,
30   which existed among the ancient Greeks, those they call dictators. Put
simply, this is an elected tyranny, which differs from non-Greek kingship not because it is not based on law but only because it is not hereditary. Some hold this office for life, others for a fixed time or purpose. For
35   example, the Mytileneans once elected Pittacus to defend them against
the exiles led by Antimenides and the poet Alcaeus.[83] Indeed, it is Alcaeus who makes it clear in one of his drinking songs that they did elect
Pittacus tyrant. He complains that "They set up base-born Pittacus as
tyrant of that gutless and ill-omened city-state, with great praise from
1285ᵇ   the assembled throng."[84] These are and were tyrannical because like the
rule of a master, but kingly because elective and voluntary.[85]

[4] A fourth kind of kingly monarchy, which existed in the heroic pe-
5   riod,[86] was voluntary, elective, and established on the basis of law. For

81. *Iliad* II.391–393. The last line Aristotle quotes is not in our text.
82. See Plato, *Republic* 567a–568a.
83. On Pittacus, see 1274ᵇ18–23 and note. Alcaeus (born c. 620) was a lyric poet
    from Mytilene in Lesbos. Antimenides was his brother.
84. Diehl I.427, fr. 87.
85. Some non-Greek kingships were also of this sort; see 1295ᵃ11–14.
86. The period described in the Homeric poems.

because the first of the line were benefactors of the multitude in the crafts or war, or through bringing them together or providing them with land, they became kings over willing subjects, and their descendants took over from them. They had authority in regard to leadership in war, and religious sacrifices not requiring priests. They also decided legal   *10* cases, some doing so under oath, and others not (the oath consisted in lifting up the scepter). In ancient times, they ruled continuously over the affairs of the city-state, both domestic and foreign. But later, when the kings themselves relinquished some of these prerogatives, and oth-   *15* ers were taken away by the crowd in various city-states, only the sacrifices were left to the kings, and even where there was a kingship worthy of the name, it was only leadership in military affairs conducted beyond the frontiers that the king held on to.

There are, then, these four kinds of kingship. One belongs to the   *20* heroic age: this was over willing subjects and served certain fixed purposes; the king was general and judge and had authority over matters to do with the gods. The second is the non-Greek kind, which is rule by a master based on lineage and law. The third is so-called dictatorship,   *25* which is elective tyranny. Fourth among them is Spartan kingship, which, simply put, is permanent generalship based on lineage. These, then, differ from one another in this way.

[5] But there is a fifth kind of kingship, when one person controls everything in just the way that each nation and each city-state controls   *30* the affairs of the community. It is organized along the lines of household management. For just as household management is a sort of kingship over a household, so this kingship is household management of one or more city-states or nations.

Chapter 15

Practically speaking, then, there are just two kinds of kingship to be examined, namely, the last one and the Spartan. For most of the others lie in between them, since they control less than absolute kingship but   *35* more than Spartan kingship. So our investigation is pretty much about two questions: First, whether or not it is beneficial for a city-state to have a permanent general (whether chosen on the basis of family or by turns). Second, whether or not it is beneficial for one person to control everything. In fact, however, the investigation of this sort of gener-   *1286ᵃ* alship has the look of an investigation of LAWS rather than of constitutions, since this is something that can come to exist in any constitution.

So the first question may be set aside. But the remaining sort of king-
5   ship *is* a kind of constitution. Hence we must study it and go through
the problems it involves.

The starting point of the investigation is this: whether it is more beneficial to be ruled by the best man or by the best laws. Those who think
it beneficial to be ruled by a king hold that laws speak only of the uni-
10   versal, and do not prescribe with a view to actual circumstances. Consequently, it is foolish to rule in accordance with written prescriptions in
any craft, and doctors in Egypt are rightly allowed to change the treatment after the fourth day (although, if they do so earlier, it is at their
own risk). It is evident, for the same reason, therefore, that the best con-
15   stitution is not one that follows written laws.[87] All the same, the rulers
should possess the universal reason as well. And something to which the
passionate element is entirely unattached is better than something in
which it is innate. This element is not present in the law, whereas every
20   human soul necessarily possesses it.

But perhaps it ought to be said, to oppose this, that a human being
will deliberate better about particulars. In that case, it is clear that the
ruler must be a legislator, and that laws must be established, but they
must not have authority insofar as they deviate from what is best, though
they should certainly have authority everywhere else. As to what the law
cannot decide either at all or well, should the one best person rule, or
25   everyone? For as things stand now, people come together to hear cases,
deliberate, and decide, and the decisions themselves all concern particulars. Taken individually, any one of these people is perhaps inferior to
the best person. But a city-state consists of many people, just like a feast
to which many contribute, and is better than one that is a unity and sim-
30   ple. That is why a crowd can also judge many things better than any single individual. Besides, a large quantity is more incorruptible, so the
multitude, like a larger quantity of water, are more incorruptible than
the few. The judgment of an individual is inevitably corrupted when he
is overcome by anger or some other passion of this sort, whereas in the
same situation it is a task to get all the citizens to become angry and
35   make mistakes at the same time.

Let the multitude in question be the free, however, who do nothing
outside the law, except about matters the law cannot cover—not an easy
thing to arrange where numbers are large.[88] But suppose there were a

87. Aristotle returns to this argument at 1287ª33–1287ᵇ5.
88. See 1279ª39–ᵇ4, 1278ª6–11.

number who were both good men and good citizens, which would be more incorruptible—one ruler, or a larger number all of whom are good? Isn't it clear that it would be the larger number? "But such a group will split into factions, whereas the single person is free of fac- 1286^b
tion." One should no doubt oppose this objection by pointing out that they may be excellent in soul just like the single person.

So then, if the rule of a number of people, all of whom are good men, is to be considered an aristocracy, and the rule of a single person a king-ship, aristocracy would be more choiceworthy for city-states than king-   5
ship (whether the rule is supported by force or not),[89] provided that it is possible to find a number of people who are similar. Perhaps this too is the reason people were formerly under kingships—because it was rare to find men who were very outstanding in virtue, particularly as the city-states they lived in at that time were small. Besides, men were made kings because of benefactions, which it is precisely the task of good men   10
to confer. When there began to be many people who were similar in virtue, however, they no longer put up with kingship, but looked for something communal and established a polity. But when they began to acquire wealth from the common funds, they became less good, and it was from some such source, so one might reasonably suppose, that oli-garchies arose; for they made wealth a thing of honor.[90] Then from oli-   15
garchies they changed first into tyrannies, and from tyrannies to democ-racy. For by concentrating power into ever fewer hands, because of a shameful desire for profit, they made the multitude stronger, with the result that it revolted and democracies arose. Now that city-states have become even larger, it is perhaps no longer easy for any other constitu-   20
tion to arise besides democracy.[91]

But now if one does posit kingship as the best thing for a city-state, how is one to handle the matter of children? Are the descendants to rule as kings too? If they turn out as some have, it would be harmful. "But perhaps, because he is in control, he will not give it to his children." But   25
this is hardly credible. For it is a difficult thing to do, and demands greater virtue than human nature allows.

89. The "force" in question is probably the citizen bodyguards, which Greek kings typically possessed (1285^a25–27, 1286^b27–40), and which could be used in a tyrannical fashion.
90. Because the end that oligarchy sets for itself is wealth. See 1311^a9–10; Plato, *Republic* 554a, Introduction, lxv–lxvi.
91. For somewhat different explanations of the changes constitutions undergo, see 1297^b16–28, 1316^a1–$^b27$.

There is also a problem concerning force, and whether anyone who is
going to rule as king should have some force in attendance with which
he can compel anyone who does not wish to obey his rule. If not, how
30   can he possibly manage his office? For even if he were a king exercising
authority in accord with the law, and never acted in accordance with his
own wishes contrary to the law, it would still be necessary for him to
have some power with which to protect the laws. In the case of this sort
of king,[92] it is perhaps not difficult to determine the solution. He *should*
35   have a force, but a force of such a kind as to be stronger than an individual, whether by himself or together with many, but weaker than the multitude. This is the way the ancients gave bodyguards when they selected
someone from the city-state to be what they called a dictator or tyrant;
and when Dionysius[93] asked for bodyguards, someone advised the Syra-
40   cusans to give him bodyguards of this sort.

Chapter 16

Now that we have reached this point the next topic must be that of the
1287ᵃ   king who does everything according to his own wish, so we must investigate this. For the so-called king according to law does not, as we said,
amount to a kind of constitution, since a permanent generalship can
5   exist in any constitution (for example, in a democracy and an aristocracy), and many places put one person in control of managing affairs.
There is an office of this sort in Epidamnus, indeed, and to a lesser extent in Opus as well.

But as regards so-called absolute kingship (which is where the king
rules everything in accord with his own wish), some hold that it is not
10   even in accordance with nature for one person, from among all the citizens, to be in control, when the city-state consists of similar people. For
justice and merit must be by nature the same for those who are by nature
similar. Hence, if indeed it is harmful to their bodies for equal people to
have unequal food or clothing, the same holds, too, where offices are
15   concerned. The same also holds, therefore, when equal people have what
is unequal. Which is precisely why it is just for them to rule no more
than they are ruled, and, therefore, to do so in turn. But this is already
law; for the organization *is* law.[94] Thus it is more choiceworthy to have

92. One who rules in accordance with the laws.
93. Dionysius I. See 1259ᵃ28–36 and note.
94. The organization of ruling and being ruled in turn, which has to be regu-
    lated by statute. See also 1326ᵃ29–30.

law rule than any one of the citizens. And, by this same argument, even
if it is better to have certain people rule, they should be selected as   *20*
guardians of and assistants to the laws. For there do have to be some
rulers; although it is not just, they say, for there to be only one; at any
rate, not when all are similar. Moreover, the sort of things at least that
the law seems unable to decide could not be discovered by a human
being either. But the law, having educated the rulers for this special purpose, hands over the rest to be decided and managed in accordance with   *25*
the most just opinion of the rulers. Moreover, it allows them to make any
corrections by introducing anything found by experience to be an improvement on the existing laws. Anyone who instructs LAW to rule would
seem to be asking GOD and the understanding alone to rule;[95] whereas
someone who asks a human being asks a wild beast as well. For appetite   *30*
is like a wild beast, and passion perverts rulers even when they are the
best men. That is precisely why law is understanding without desire.

The comparison with the crafts, that it is bad to give medical treatment in accordance with written prescriptions and more choiceworthy
to rely on those who possess the craft instead, would seem to be false.
For doctors never do things contrary to reason because of friendship,   *35*
but earn their pay by healing the sick. Those who hold political office,
on the other hand, do many things out of spite or in order to win favor.
And indeed if people suspected their doctors of having been bribed by
their enemies to do away with them, they would prefer to seek treatment
derived from books. Moreover, doctors themselves call in other doctors   *40*
to treat them when they are sick, and trainers call in other trainers when   *1287ᵇ*
they are exercising, their assumption being that they are unable to judge
truly because they are judging about their own cases, and while in pain.
So it is clear that in seeking what is just they are seeking the mean; for
the law is the mean.[96] Again, laws based on custom are more authoritative and deal with matters that have more authority than do written laws,   *5*
so that even if a human ruler is more reliable than written laws, he is not
more so than those based on custom.

Yet, it is certainly not easy for a single ruler to oversee many things;
hence there will have to be numerous officials appointed under him.
Consequently, what difference is there between having them there from
the beginning and having one person appoint them in this way? Besides,   *10*

95. See Introduction §6.
96. The mean here being impartial treatment rendered according to the written
   rules of a craft by someone exercising trained judgment.

as we said earlier,[97] if it really is just for the excellent man to rule because he is better, well, two good ones are better than one. Hence the saying "When two go together . . . ," and Agamemnon's prayer, "May ten such counselors be mine."[98]

15   Even nowadays, however, officials, such as jurors, have the authority to decide some things the law cannot determine. For, as regards those matters the law can determine, certainly no one disputes that the law itself would rule and decide best. But because some matters can be covered by the laws, while others cannot, the latter lead people to raise and

20   investigate the problem whether it is more choiceworthy for the best law to rule or the best man (since to legislate about matters that call for deliberation is impossible). The counterargument, therefore, is not that it is not necessary for a human being to decide such matters, but that there

25   should be many judges, not one only. For each official judges well if he has been educated by the law. And it would perhaps be accounted strange if someone, when judging with one pair of eyes and one pair of ears, and acting with one pair of feet and hands, could see better than many people with many pairs, since, as things stand, monarchs provide

30   themselves with many eyes, ears, hands, and feet. For they appoint those who are friendly to their rule and to themselves as co-rulers. Now if they are not friendly in this way, they will not do as the monarch chooses. But suppose they are friendly to him and his rule—well, a friend is someone similar and equal, so if he thinks they should rule, he must think that those who are equal and similar to him should rule in a similar fashion.

These, then, are pretty much the arguments of those who dispute
35   against kingship.

Chapter 17

But perhaps these arguments hold in some cases and not in others. For what is by nature both just and beneficial is one thing in the case of rule by a master, another in the case of kingship, and another in the case of rule by a statesman (nothing is by nature both just and beneficial in the

40   case of a tyranny, however, nor in that of the other deviant constitutions, since they come about contrary to nature). But it is surely evident from what has been said that in a case where people are similar and equal, it is
1288ᵃ neither beneficial nor just for one person to control everything. This

97. At 1286ᵇ3–5.
98. *Iliad* X.224 and II.372.

holds whether there are no laws except the king himself, or whether there are laws; whether he is a good person ruling good people, or a not good one ruling not good ones; and even whether he is their superior in virtue—except in one set of circumstances. What these circumstances are must now be stated—although we have in a way already stated it.[99]   5

First, we must determine what kind of people are suited to kingship, what to aristocracy, and what to polity. A multitude should be under kingship when it naturally produces a family that is superior in the virtue appropriate to political leadership. A multitude is suited to aristocracy when it naturally produces a multitude[100] capable of being ruled   10 with the rule appropriate to free people by those who are qualified to lead by their possession of the virtue required for the rule of a statesman. And a multitude is suited to polity when there naturally arises in it a warrior multitude[101] capable of ruling and being ruled, under a law which distributes offices to the rich on the basis of merit. Whenever it happens, then, that there is a whole family, or even some one individual   15 among the rest, whose virtue is so superior as to exceed that of all the others, it is just for this family to be the kingly family and to control everything, and for this one individual to be king. For, as was said earlier, this not only accords with the kind of justice customarily put forward by those who establish constitutions, whether aristocratic, oli-   20 garchic, or even democratic (for they all claim to merit rule on the basis of superiority in something, though not superiority in the same kind of thing), but also with what was said earlier.[102] For it is surely not proper to kill or to exile or to ostracize an individual of this sort, nor to claim   25 that he deserves to be ruled in turn. For it is not natural for the part to be greater than the whole, but this is what happens in the case of someone who has this degree of superiority. So the only remaining option is for such a person to be obeyed and to be in control not by turns but unqualifiedly.[103]

Kingship, then, and what its varieties are, and whether it is beneficial   30 for city-states or not, and if so, for which and how, may be determined in this way.

---

99. At 1284ª3–ᵇ35.
100. Reading *plēthos* with Dreizehnter and the mss.
101. Reading *plēthos polemikon* with Dreizehnter and the mss.
102. At 1284ᵇ25–34.
103. The argument in this paragraph is discussed in the Introduction §8.

Chapter 18

We say that there are three correct constitutions, and that the best of them must of necessity be the one managed by the best people. This is the sort of constitution in which there happens to be either one particular person or a whole family or a number of people whose virtue is superior to that of all the rest, and where the latter are capable of being ruled and the former of ruling with a view to the most choiceworthy life. Furthermore, as we showed in our first discussions,[104] the virtue of a man must of necessity be identical to that of a citizen of the best city-state. Hence it is evident that the ways and means by which a man becomes excellent are the same as those by which one might establish a city-state ruled by an aristocracy or a king, and that the education and habits that make a man excellent are pretty much the same as those that make him statesmanlike or kingly.[105]

Now that these matters have been determined, we must attempt to discuss the best constitution, the way it naturally arises and how it is established. Anyone, then, who intends to do this must conduct the investigation in the appropriate way.[106]

---

104. III.4–5.
105. See Introduction xxv–xxvi.
106. This sentence appears again in a slightly different form as part of the opening sentence of Book VII. It is bracketed as incomplete by Ross.

BOOK IV[1]

Chapter 1

Among all the crafts and sciences that are concerned not only with a   *10*
part but that deal completely with some one type of thing, it belongs to
a single one to study what is appropriate for each type. For example:
what sort of physical training is beneficial for what sort of body, that is to
say, what sort is best (for the sort that is appropriate for the sort of body
that is naturally best and best equipped is necessarily best), and what
single sort of training is appropriate for most bodies (since this too is a   *15*
task for physical training). Further, if someone wants neither the condition nor the knowledge required of those involved in competition, it belongs no less to coaches and physical trainers[2] to provide this capacity
too. We see a similar thing in medicine, ship building, clothing manufac-
ture, and every other craft.   *20*

Consequently, it is clear that it belongs to the same science[3] to study:
[1] What the best constitution is, that is to say, what it must be like if it is
to be most ideal, and if there were no external obstacles. Also [2] which
constitution is appropriate for which city-states. For achieving the best
constitution is perhaps impossible for many; and so neither the unquali-   *25*
fiedly best constitution nor the one that is best in the circumstances
should be neglected by the good legislator and true statesman. Further,
[3] which constitution is best given certain assumptions. For a statesman
must be able to study how any given constitution might initially come

---

1. The end of III.18 prepares us for a discussion of the best constitution, but IV
   does not contain one. Indeed, the opening sentence of IV.2 seems to suggest
   that the best constitution has already been discussed. This is to some extent
   true, because much is said about the best constitution in discussing both
   other people's candidates for that title and aristocracy and kingship
   (1289^{b}30–32). But Aristotle's own candidate is not formally discussed until
   VII–VIII.
2. See 1338^{b}6–8.
3. Namely, STATESMANSHIP.

into existence, and how, once in existence, it might be preserved for the
30   longest time. I mean, for example, when some city-state happens to be
governed neither by the best constitution (not even having the necessary
resources) nor by the best one possible in the existing circumstances, but
by a worse one. Besides all these things, a statesman should know [4]
which constitution is most appropriate for all city-states. Consequently,
35   those who have expressed views about constitutions, even if what they
say is good in other respects, certainly fail when it comes to what is useful. For one should not study only what is best, but also what is possible,
and similarly what is easier and more attainable by all. As it is, however,
some seek only the constitution that is highest and requires a lot of re-
40   sources, while others, though they discuss a more attainable sort, do
away with the constitutions actually in place, and praise the Spartan or
some other. But what should be done is to introduce the sort of organi-
1289ᵃ   zation that people will be easily persuaded to accept and be able to participate in,[4] given what they already have, as it is no less a task to reform
a constitution than to establish one initially, just as it is no less a task to
correct what we have learned than to learn it in the first place. That is
5   why, in addition to what has just been mentioned, a statesman should
also be able to help existing constitutions, as was also said earlier.[5] But
this is impossible if he does not know [5] how many kinds of constitutions there are. As things stand, however, some people think that there is
just one kind of democracy and one of oligarchy. But this is not true. So
10   one must not overlook the varieties of each of the constitutions, how
many they are and how many ways they can be combined.[6] And [6] it is
with this same practical wisdom[7] that one should try to see both which
laws are best and which are appropriate for each of the constitutions. For
laws should be established, and all do establish them, to suit the constitution and not the constitution to suit the laws. For a constitution is the
15   organization of offices in city-states, the way they are distributed, what
element is in authority in the constitution, and what the end is of each of
the communities.[8] Laws, apart from those that reveal what the constitu-

---

4. Reading *koinōnein* with Dreizehnter and many mss. Alternatively (Ross):
   "will easily be able to use for the first time (*kainizein*)."
5. At 1288ᵇ28–39.
6. For an explanation, see 1290ᵇ25–1293ᵃ34, 1317ᵃ18–1318ᵃ3.
7. Since practical wisdom is the same state of the soul as statesmanship (*NE*
   1141ᵇ23–24), Aristotle switches labels here.
8. See Introduction lxv–lxvi.

tion is, are those by which the officials must rule, and must guard against
those who transgress them. Clearly, then, a knowledge of the varieties of   20
each constitution and of their number[9] is also necessary for establishing
laws. For the same laws cannot be beneficial for all oligarchies or for all
democracies—if indeed there are several kinds, and not one kind of
democracy nor one kind of oligarchy only.   25

Chapter 2

Since our initial inquiry concerning constitutions,[10] we distinguished
three correct constitutions (kingship, aristocracy, polity) and three deviations from them (tyranny from kingship, oligarchy from aristocracy,
and democracy from polity), and since we have already discussed aristocracy and kingship, for studying the best constitution is the same as   30
discussing these names,[11] since each of them tends to be established on
the basis of virtue furnished with resources; and since further, we have
determined how aristocracy and kingship differ from one another, and
when a constitution should be considered a kingship,[12] it remains to deal   35
with the constitution that is called by the name common to all CONSTI-
TUTIONS, and also with the others—oligarchy, democracy, and tyranny.

It is also evident which of these deviations is worst and which second
worst. For the deviation from the first and most divine constitution
must of necessity be the worst.[13] But kingship either must be in name   40
only and not in fact or must be based on the great superiority of the person ruling as king. Hence tyranny, being the worst, is furthest removed   1289^b
from being a constitution; oligarchy is second worst (since aristocracy is
very far removed from this constitution); and democracy the most moderate. An earlier thinker[14] has already expressed this same view, though   5

9. Reading *arithmon* with the mss.
10. A reference to Book III.6–8.
11. *tōn onomatōn*: See 1276^{b}11–13 and note.
12. I follow Lord in taking *basilean nomizein* in this way. Alternatively: "when to
have a kingship." When to have a kingship is discussed in III.17; when to
consider a constitution a kingship is discussed in III.14–16. It is unclear
why having discussed the former topic (as opposed to the latter) would help
support the conclusion Aristotle draws in the next sentence.
13. Kingship is presumably "most divine" because Zeus rules the other gods
with kingly rule (1252^{a}24–27). Tyranny "worst" for the reasons given in V.8.
See also *NE* 1160^{a}31–^{b}22.
14. Plato, *Statesman* 302e–303b.

he did not look to the same thing we do. For he judged that when all these constitutions are good (for example, when an oligarchy is good, and also the others), democracy is the worst of them, but that when they are bad, it is the best. But we say that these constitutions are all of them mistaken, and that it is not right to speak of one kind of oligarchy as bet-
10   ter than another, but as less bad.

But let us leave aside the judgment of this matter for the present. Instead, we must determine: [1] First, how many varieties of the constitutions there are (if indeed there are several kinds of democracy and oli-garchy). Next, [2] which kind is most attainable, and which most
15   choiceworthy after the best constitution (if indeed there is some other constitution which, though aristocratic and well constituted, is at the same time appropriate for most city-states), and also which of the other constitutions is more choiceworthy for which people (for democracy is perhaps more necessary than oligarchy for some, whereas for others the
20   reverse holds). After these things, [3] how someone who wishes to do so should establish these constitutions (I mean, each kind of democracy or oligarchy). Finally, when we have gone as far as we can to give a succinct account of each of these topics, [4] we must try to go through the ways in which constitutions are destroyed and those in which they are pre-
25   served, both in general and in the case of each one separately, and through what causes these most naturally come about.

Chapter 3

The reason why there are several constitutions is that every city-state has several parts.[15] For in the first place, we see that all city-states are composed of households; and, next, that within this multitude there
30   have to be some who are rich, some who are poor, and some who are in the middle; and that of the rich and of the poor, the one possessing weapons and the other without weapons. We also see that the people comprise a farming part, a trading part, and a vulgar craftsman part. And among the notables there are differences in wealth and in extent of their property—as, for example, in the breeding of horses, since this is
35   not easy for those without wealth to do. (That is why, indeed, there were oligarchies among those city-states in ancient times whose power lay in

---

15. Aristotle gives a number of different (but perhaps equivalent) explanations of why there are different kinds of constitutions (IV.6, 1301ª25–33, 1301ᵇ29–1302ª2, VI.1–7).

their cavalry, and who used horses in wars with their neighbors—as, for example, the Eretrians did, and the Chalcidians, the Magnesians on the river Menander, and many of the others in Asia.) There are also differ- *40* ences based on birth, on virtue, and on everything else of the sort that we characterized as part of a city-state in our discussion of aristocracy, *1290ª* since there we distinguished the number of parts that are necessary to any city-state.[16] For sometimes all of these parts participate in the constitution, sometimes fewer of them, sometimes more.

It is evident, therefore, that there must be several constitutions that *5* differ in kind from one another, since these parts themselves also differ in kind. For a constitution is the organization of offices, and all consitutions distribute these either on the basis of the power of the participants, or on the basis of some sort of equality common to them (I mean, for example, of the poor or of the rich, or some equality common to *10* both).[17] Therefore, there must be as many constitutions as there are ways of organizing offices on the basis of the superiority and varieties of the parts.

But there are held to be mainly two constitutions: just as the winds are called north or south, and the others deviations from these, so there are also said to be two constitutions, democracy and oligarchy. For aris- *15* tocracy is regarded as a sort of oligarchy, on the grounds that it is a sort of rule by the few, whereas a so-called polity is regarded as a sort of democracy,[18] just as the west wind is regarded as northerly, and the east as southerly.[19] According to some people, the same thing also happens in the case of harmonies, which are regarded as being of two kinds, the Do- *20* rian and the Phrygian, and the other arrangements are called either Phrygian types or Dorian types. People are generally accustomed, then, to think of constitutions in this way. But it is truer and better to distinguish them, as we have, and say that two constitutions (or one) are well formed, and that the others are deviations from them, some from the *25* well-mixed "harmony," and others from the best constitution, the more

16. Probably a reference to 1283ª14–26, but VII.7–9 also contains a discussion of this topic.
17. For example, equality in virtue, wealth, or freedom.
18. Because a polity is a kind of majority rule (1279ª37–39).
19. Winds are "generally classified as north or south. West winds are counted as northerly, since they blow from where the sun sets and are therefore colder; east winds are counted as southerly, since they blow from where the sun rises and are warmer. Winds are thus called northerly or southerly on the basis of this division between cold and hot or warm" (*Mete*. 364ª18–27).

tightly controlled ones and those that are more like the rule of a master being more oligarchic, and the unrestrained and soft ones democratic.[20]

Chapter 4

30   One should not assert (as some are accustomed to do now)[21] that democracy is simply where the multitude are in authority (for both in oligarchies and everywhere else, the larger part is in authority).[22] Nor should an oligarchy be regarded as being where the few are in authority over the constitution. For if there were a total of thirteen hundred people, out of which a thousand were rich people who give no share in office
35   to three hundred poor ones, no one would say that the latter were democratically governed even if they were free and otherwise similar to the rich. Similarly, if the poor were few, but stronger than the rich, who were a majority, no one would call such a constitution an oligarchy if the others, though rich, did not participate in office. Thus it is better to say
40   that a democracy exists when the free are in authority and an oligarchy
1290^b exists when the rich are; but it happens that the former are many and the latter few, since many are free but few are rich. Otherwise there would be an oligarchy if offices were distributed on the basis of height (as is
5   said to happen in Ethiopia) or on the basis of beauty, since beautiful people and tall ones are both few in number.

    Yet these[23] are not sufficient to distinguish these constitutions. Rather, since both democracy and oligarchy have a number of parts, we must further grasp that it is not a democracy if a few free people rule
10   over a majority who are not free, as, for example, in Apollonia on the Ionian Gulf and in Thera. For in each of these city-states the offices were held by the well born, the descendants of the first colonists, although they were few among many. Nor is it an oligarchy[24] if the rich rule be-
15   cause they are the multitude, as was formerly the case in Colophon, where the majority possessed large properties before the war against the

---

20. The example of music results in this extended musical metaphor in which "harmony" (*harmonia*) is used as a metaphor for a balanced mixture in a constitution. The well-mixed constitution is identified in IV.9.
21. See Plato, *Statesman* 291d.
22. See 1294^a11–14 for an explanation.
23. Namely, wealth and freedom.
24. Reading *oligarchia* with Ross. Alternatively (Dreizehnter and the mss.): "democracy (*dēmos*)."

Lydians.[25] Rather, it is a democracy when the free and the poor who are a majority have the authority to rule, and an oligarchy when the rich and well born, who are few, do.[26]

It has been stated, then, that there are a number of constitutions and why this is so. But let us now say why there are more than the ones mentioned,[27] what they are, and how they arise, taking as our starting point what was agreed to earlier.[28] For we are agreed that every city-state has not only one part but several.

If we wanted to grasp the kinds of animals, we would first determine what it is necessary for every animal to have: for example, certain of the sense organs; something with which to work on and absorb food (such as a mouth and a stomach); and also parts by which it moves. If these were the only parts, but they had varieties (I mean, for example, if there were several types of mouths, stomachs, and sense organs, and also of locomotive parts), then the number of ways of combining these would necessarily produce a number of types of animals. For the same animal cannot have mouths or ears of many different varieties. Hence, when these have been grasped, all the possible ways of pairing them together will produce kinds of animals, that is to say, as many kinds of animals as there are combinations of the necessary parts.[29] It is the same way with the constitutions we have mentioned. For city-states are constituted not out of one but many parts, as we have often said.

One of these parts is [1] the multitude concerned with food, the ones called farmers. A second is [2] those called vulgar craftsman. They are concerned with the crafts without which a city-state cannot be managed (of these some are necessary, whereas others contribute to luxury or fine living). A third is [3] the traders (by which I mean those engaged in selling and buying, retail trade, and commerce). A fourth is [4] the hired laborers. A fifth is [5] the defensive warriors, which are no less necessary than the others, if the inhabitants are not to become the slaves of any aggressor. For no city-state that is naturally slavish can possibly deserve to

25. See Herodotus I.14.
26. See 1279^{b}39–1280^{a}6.
27. The reference could be to (1) the list of six constitutions given at 1289^{a}26–30, (2) the shorter list said to constitute the present agenda at 1289^{a}35–38, or (3) oligarchy and democracy, which are the dominant focus of discussion after 1289^{b}6.
28. In IV.3.
29. Type, kind, and variety are the *genos*, *eidos*, and *diaphora*, the genus, species, and differentia, of Aristotelian biology.

be called a city-state at all; for a city-state is self-sufficient, whereas
10   something that is slavish is not self-sufficient.

That is why what is said in the *Republic*,[30] though sophisticated, is not
adequate. For Socrates says that a city-state is constituted out of four absolutely necessary classes, and these, he says, are weavers, farmers, shoemakers, and house builders. Then, on the grounds that these are not
self-sufficient, he adds blacksmiths, people to look after the necessary
15   livestock, and those engaged in retail trade and commerce. All these become the full complement of his first city-state—as if every city-state
were constituted for the sake of providing the necessities, not for the
sake of what is noble, and had equal need of both shoemakers and farmers. Nor does he assign it defensive warriors until, with the expansion of
20   its territory, it encroaches on that of its neighbors, and gets involved in a
war. Yet even in these communities of four (or however many) classes,
there must be someone to assign and decide what is just.[31] So if indeed
one should regard the soul as a more important part of an animal than
the body, then, in the case of city-states too, one should regard things of
25   the following sort to be parts, rather than those dealing with our necessary needs: the warriors; those who participate in administering judicial
justice; and also those who deliberate, since deliberation is a task for political understanding. It does not matter to the argument whether these
tasks belong to separate people or the same ones, since in fact it often
happens that the same people both possess weapons and engage in farm-
30   ing. Consequently, if both the former and the latter are to be regarded as
parts of a city-state, it is evident that those who possess weapons, at any
rate, must be a part of a city-state.[32]

[7] Seventh are those who perform PUBLIC SERVICE by means of their
property.[33] This is the class we call the rich. [8] Eighth are the civil ser-
35   vants, those who serve in connection with the various offices, since a
city-state cannot exist without officials. There must, therefore, be some
who are able to rule and perform this public service for the city-state

---

30. At 369d–371e.
31. See 1253a37–39, 1328b13–15.
32. The former are those that deal with our necessary needs; the latter, the war-
     riors, etc. What is evident is that a city-state must at least have warriors
     among its parts. But it will often need a navy as well. See VII.5 for further
     discussion.
33. The unidentified sixth part may be the class of priests (listed as an impor-
     tant part of any city-state at 1328b11–13). But it is also possible that the long
     aside about the *Republic* has caused Aristotle to go astray in his numbering.

either continuously or in turn. There remain those we happened to distinguish just now, those who deliberate and decide the claims of people involved in disputes. Therefore, if these things must indeed take place in city-states, and do so in a way that is noble and just, there must also be some who share in the virtue of statesmen.[34]

As for the other capacities, many hold that they can belong to the same people; for example, that it is possible for the same people to be warriors, farmers, and craftsmen, and both deliberators and judges besides. And everyone claims to possess the virtue[35] too, and thinks he is capable of ruling in most offices. But for the same people to be both rich and poor is impossible. Hence these in particular, the rich and the poor, are held to be parts of a city-state. Besides, the fact that the former are usually few in number and the latter many makes it seem that among the parts of the city-state these two are opposites. Consequently, constitutions are established on the basis of the superiority of these, and there are held to be two constitutions, democracy and oligarchy.[36]

That there are a number of constitutions, then, and why this is so has been stated earlier. But we may now say that there are also several kinds of democracy and oligarchy.[37] This is in fact evident from what has been said. For there are several kinds both of the people and of the so-called notables.[38] For example, of the people, one is the farmers; another, those concerned with the crafts; the kind involved in trading, which is engaged in buying and selling; and the kind concerned with the sea—of which part is the navy, part is engaged in wealth acquisition, part in ferrying passengers, and part in fishing. (In many places, a particular one of these amounts to a large crowd; for example, fishermen in Tarentum and Byzantium, navy men in Athens, traders in Aegina and Chios, and ferrymen in Tenedos.) In addition to these, there are the manual laborers, those who have too little property to enable them to be at leisure; the free people who are not of citizen parentage on both sides; and whatever

34. Deliberating in a way that is noble and just requires practical wisdom, the virtue peculiar to a statesmen (1277^{b}25–26, *NE* 1141^{b}23–24).
35. Presumably, that of statesmen.
36. A type (genus) is divided into kinds (species) on the basis of opposite varieties (differentia). If these characteristics are themselves indivisible, there will then be just two kinds (species). See *PA* 643^{a}31–^{b}8, especially 643^{a}7–8. The sorts of superiority claimed by the rich and the poor are wealth and freedom respectively.
37. See VI.1–7.
38. See 1289^{b}27–1290^{a}13.

other kind of multitude there may be. The notables are distinguished by
wealth, good birth, virtue, education, and the other characteristics that
are ascribed on the basis of the same sort of difference.

30   [1] The first democracy, then, is the one that is said to be most of all
based on equality. For the law in this democracy says that there is equality when the poor enjoy no more superiority than the rich and neither is
in authority but the two are similar. For if indeed freedom and equality
are most of all present in a democracy, as some people suppose,[39] this
35 would be most true in the constitution in which everyone participates in
the most similar way. But since the people are the majority, and majority
opinion has authority, this constitution is necessarily a democracy. This,
then, is one kind of DEMOCRACY.[40]

      [2] Another is where offices are filled on the basis of property assess-
ments, although these are low, and where anyone who acquires the req-
40 uisite amount may participate, whereas anyone who loses it may not. [3]
Another kind of democracy is where all uncontested citizens[41] partici-
1292ᵃ pate, and the law rules. [4] Another kind of democracy is where everyone
can participate in office merely by being a citizen,[42] and the law rules.

      [5] Another kind of democracy is the same in other respects, but the
5   multitude has authority, not the law. This arises when DECREES have authority instead of laws; and this happens because of POPULAR LEADERS.
For in city-states that are under a democracy based on law, popular leaders do not arise. Instead, the best citizens preside.[43] Where the laws are
10 not in authority, however, popular leaders arise. For the people become a
monarch, one person composed of many, since the many are in authority
not as individuals, but all together. When Homer says that "many-
headed rule is not good,"[44] it is not clear whether he means this kind of
rule, or the kind where there are a number of individual rulers. In any
15 case, a people of this kind, since it is a monarchy, seeks to exercise
monarchic rule through not being ruled by the law, and becomes a master. The result is that flatterers are held in esteem, and that a democracy
of this kind is the analog of tyranny among the monarchies. That is also
why their characters are the same: both act like masters toward the bet-

---

39. For example, Plato, *Republic* 557a–c, 562b–563d.
40. This kind does not appear on the other lists Aristotle gives in IV.5 and VI.4.
41. Those whose citizen birth is clear (1292ᵇ35–36, 1275ᵇ22–26).
42. A larger class participates in (4) than in (3) (1275ᵇ34–1276ᵃ6).
43. That is to say, are the most powerful (1308ᵃ22).
44. *Iliad* II.204.

ter people; the decrees of the one are like the edicts of the other; a popular leader is either the same as a flatterer or analogous. Each of these *20*
has special power in his own sphere, flatterers with tyrants, popular
leaders with a people of this kind. They are responsible for decrees
being in authority rather than laws because they bring everything before
the people. This results in their becoming powerful because the people *25*
have authority over everything, and popular leaders have it over the people's opinion, since the multitude are persuaded by them. Besides, those
who make accusations against officials say that the people should decide
them. The suggestion is gladly accepted, with the result that all offices
are destroyed.

One might hold, however, that it is reasonable to object that this kind *30*
of democracy is not a CONSTITUTION at all, on the grounds that there is
no constitution where the laws do not rule. For the law should rule uni-
versally over everything, while offices and the constitution[45] should decide particular cases. So, since democracy is one of the constitutions, it *35*
is evident that this sort of arrangement, in which everything is managed
by decree, is not even a democracy in the most authoritative sense, since
no decree can possibly be universal.[46]

The kinds of democracy, then, should be distinguished in this way.

Chapter 5

Of the kinds of oligarchy, [1] one has offices filled on the basis of such a
high property assessment that the poor, even though they are the major- *40*
ity, do not participate, but anyone who does acquire the requisite
amount may participate in the constitution. [2] In another the offices are
filled on the basis of a high assessment and they themselves elect some- *1292ᵇ*
one to fill any vacancy. If they elect from among all of these,[47] it is held
to be more aristocratic; if from some specified people, oligarchic.[48] [3] In

---

45. Reading *tēn politeian* with Dreizehnter and the mss. The oddity of the claim
    that the constitution decides particular cases is reduced if we remember that
    "the governing class is the constitution" (1278ᵇ11). In the kind of democ-
    racy under discussion, the people are the governing class.
46. With the explicable exception of absolute kingship (III. 17), a genuine CON-
    STITUTION is defined by and governed in accordance with LAWS, which, un-
    like DECREES, must be universal. Hence a democracy governed by decrees is
    arguably not a constitution.
47. All who have the assessed amount of property.
48. See 1300ᵃ8–ᵇ7 for an explanation.

5   another kind of oligarchy a son succeeds his father. [4] In a fourth what
was just mentioned occurs, and not the law but the officials rule. This is
to oligarchies what tyranny is to monarchies, and to the democracy we
10   spoke of last among democracies. Such an oligarchy is called a dynasty.

These, then, are the kinds of oligarchy and democracy. But one must
not overlook the fact that it has happened in many places that constitutions which are not democratic according to their laws are none the less
governed democratically because of custom and training. Similarly, in
15   other places, the reverse has happened: the constitution is more democratic in its laws, but is governed in a more oligarchic way as a result of
custom and training. This happens especially after there has been a
change of constitution. For the change is not immediate, but people are
content at first to take from others in smaller ways. Hence the pre-exist-
20   ing laws remain in effect, although those who have changed the constitution are dominant.

Chapter 6

It is evident from what has been said that there are this many kinds of
democracy and oligarchy. For either all of the aforementioned parts of
the people must participate in the constitution, or some must and others
25   not. [1] So when the part that farms and that owns a moderate amount of
property has authority over the constitution, it is governed in accordance with the laws. For they have enough to live on as long as they keep
working, but they cannot afford any leisure time. So they put the law in
charge and hold only such assemblies as are necessary. And the others
may participate when they have acquired the property assessment de-
30   fined by the laws. Hence all those who have acquired it may participate.
For, generally speaking, it is oligarchic when not all of these may participate, though not if what makes being at leisure impossible is the absence
of revenues.[49] This, then, is one kind of democracy and these are the reasons for it.

[2] Another kind arises through the following distinction. For it is
35   possible for everyone of uncontested birth to participate, but for only
those who have leisure actually to do so. Hence in this kind of democracy the laws rule because there is no revenue. [3] A third kind is when

---

49. The text is uncertain. Reading *to de exeinai, scholazein d'adunatein, prosodōn
mē ousōn, ou.*

all who are free may participate in the constitution, but, for the reason just mentioned, they do not participate, so that law necessarily rules in this kind also. [4] A fourth kind of democracy was the last to arise in city-states. For because city-states have become much larger than the original ones and possess abundant sources of revenue, everyone shares in the constitution, and so the multitude preponderates. And they all do participate and govern, because even the poor are able to be at leisure, since they get paid. A multitude of this sort is particularly leisured, indeed, since care for their own property does not impede them. But it does impede the rich, who often fail to take part in the assembly or serve on juries as a result. Hence the multitude of poor citizens come to have authority over the constitution and not the laws. The kinds of democracy, then, are such and so many because of these necessities.

40

*1293*ᵃ

5

10

As for the kinds of oligarchy, [1] when a number of people own property, but a smaller amount—not too much—this is the first kind of oligarchy. For anyone who acquires the amount may participate. And because of the multitude participating in the governing class, law is necessarily in authority, not human beings. For it is necessary for them to consent to having the law rule and not themselves, the more removed they are from exercising monarchy, and the more they have neither so much property that they can be at leisure without worrying nor so little that they need to be supported by the city-state.

15

20

[2] But if the property owners are fewer and their properties greater than those mentioned before, the second kind of oligarchy arises. For, being more powerful, the property owners expect to get more. Hence they themselves elect from among the rest of the citizens those who are to enter the governing class. But as they are not yet powerful enough to rule without law, they pass a law of this sort.⁵⁰

25

[3] But if they tighten this process by becoming fewer and owning larger properties, the third stage of oligarchy is reached, where they keep the offices in their own hands, but do so in accordance with a law requiring deceased members to be succeeded by their sons. [4] But when they now tighten it excessively through their property holdings and the number of their friends, a dynasty of this sort approximates a monarchy, and human beings are in authority, not law. This is the fourth kind of oligarchy, corresponding to the final kind of democracy.

30

---

50. Permitting already existing members of the ruling oligarchy to elect new members.

Chapter 7

35   There are also two constitutions besides democracy and oligarchy, one of
which is mentioned by everyone and which we said was one of the four
kinds of constitutions. The four they mention are monarchy, oligarchy,
democracy, and, fourth, so-called aristocracy. There is a fifth, however,
which is referred to by the name shared by all constitutions: the one
40   called a *politeia* (polity). But because it does not occur often, it gets overlooked by those who try to enumerate the kinds of constitutions, and, like
1293ᵇ   Plato,[51] list only the four in their discussion of constitutions.

It is well to call the constitution we treated in our first discussions an
aristocracy.[52] For the only constitution that is rightly called an aristocracy is the one that consists of those who are unqualifiedly best as regards
virtue, and not of those who are good men only given a certain assump-
5   tion. For only here is it unqualifiedly the case that the same person is a
good man and a good citizen. But those who are good in other constitutions are so relative to their constitutions. Nevertheless, there are some
constitutions that differ both from constitutions that are oligarchically
governed and from so-called polity, and are called aristocracies. For a
constitution where officials are elected not only on the basis of wealth
10   but also on the basis of merit differs from both of these and is called aristocratic. For even in those constitutions where virtue is not a concern of
the community, there are still some who are of good repute and held to
be decent. Hence wherever a constitution looks to wealth, virtue, and the
15   people (as it does in Carthage), it is aristocratic,[53] as also are those, like
the constitution of the Spartans, which look to only two, virtue and the
people, and where there is a mixture of these two things, democracy and
virtue. There are, then, these two kinds of aristocracy besides the first,
which is the best constitution; and there is also a third, namely, [4] those
20   kinds of so-called polity that lean more toward oligarchy.

Chapter 8

It remains for us to speak about so-called polity and about tyranny. We
have adopted this arrangement, even though neither polity nor the aris-

---

51. See *Republic* VIII–IX.
52. Perhaps a reference to 1276ᵇ34–1277ª1, 1278ª17–21, 1278ᵇ1–5, 1279ª34–37,
    1286ᵇ3–7, 1288ª37–1288ᵇ2.
53. See 1273ª21–ᵇ1.

tocracies just mentioned are deviant, because in truth they all fall short
of the most correct constitution, and so are counted among the devia- *25*
tions, and these deviations are deviations from them, as we mentioned in
the beginning.[54] On the other hand, it is reasonable to treat tyranny last,
since it is least of all a constitution, and our inquiry is about constitutions. So much for the reason for organizing things in this way. *30*

But we must now set forth our views on polity. Its nature should be
more evident now that we have determined the facts about oligarchy and
democracy. For polity, to put it simply, is a mixture of oligarchy and
democracy. It is customary, however, to call those mixtures that lean toward democracy polities, and those that lean more toward oligarchy aris- *35*
tocracies, because education and good birth more commonly accompany
those who are richer. Besides, the rich are held to possess already what
unjust people commit injustice to get, which is why the rich are referred
to as noble-and-good men, and as notables. So since aristocracies strive *40*
to give superiority to the best citizens, oligarchies too are said to consist
primarily of noble-and-good men. And it is held to be impossible for a
city-state to be well governed if it is not governed aristocratically, but by *1294ᵃ*
bad people, and equally impossible for a city-state that is not well governed to be governed aristocratically. But GOOD GOVERNMENT does not
exist if the laws, though well established, are not obeyed. Hence we must
take good government to exist in one way when the established laws are
obeyed, and in another when the laws that are in fact obeyed are well es- *5*
tablished (for even badly established laws can be obeyed). The second
situation can come about in two ways: people may obey either the best
laws possible for them, or the unqualifiedly best ones.

Aristocracy is held most of all to exist when offices are distributed on
the basis of virtue. For virtue is the defining mark of aristocracy, wealth *10*
of oligarchy, and freedom of democracy. But MAJORITY opinion is found
in all of them. For in oligarchy and aristocracy and in democracies, the
opinion of the major part of those who participate in the constitution
has authority. Now in most city-states the kind of constitution is
wrongly named, since the mixture aims only at the rich and the poor, at *15*
wealth and freedom. For among pretty much most people the rich are
taken to occupy the place of noble-and-good men. But there are in fact
three grounds for claiming equal participation in the constitution: freedom, wealth, and virtue. (The fourth, which they call good birth, is a *20*

54. At 1279ᵇ4–6, 1289ᵃ26–ᵇ5.

consequence of two of the others, since good birth is a combination of old money and virtue.) Hence it is evident that the mixture of the two, the rich and the poor, ought to be called polity, whereas a mixture of the three most of all the others (except for the true and first kind) deserves to be called an aristocracy.

25   We have said, then, that there are other kinds of constitutions besides monarchy, democracy, and oligarchy. And it is evident what they are, how aristocracies differ among themselves, and polities from aristocracy; and that they are not far apart from one another.

Chapter 9

After what has been said, let us next discuss how, in addition to democ-
30 racy and oligarchy, so-called polity arises, and how it should be estab-
lished. At the same time, however, the defining principles of democracy and oligarchy will also become clear. For what we must do is get hold of the division of these, and then take as it were a token from each to put together.[55]

35   There are three defining principles of the combination and mixture: [1] One is to take legislation from both constitutions. For example, in the case of deciding court cases, oligarchies impose a fine on the rich if they do not take part in deciding court cases, but provide no payment for
40 the poor, whereas democracies pay the poor but do not fine the rich. But what is common to both constitutions and a mean between them is doing both. And hence this is characteristic of a polity, which is a mix-
1294ᵇ ture formed from both. This, then, is one way to conjoin them. [2] An-
other is to take the mean between the organizations of each. In democra-
cies, for example, membership in the assembly is either not based on a property assessment at all or on a very small one, whereas in oligarchies it is based on a large property assessment. The common position here is to require neither of these assessments but the one that is in a mean be-
5 tween the two of them. [3] A third is to take elements from both organi-
zations, some from oligarchic law and others from democratic law. I mean, for example, it is held to be democratic for officials to be chosen

55. That is to say, the defining characteristics of a democracy must be divided off from those of an oligarchy, and then a characteristic from the former must be put together with an appropriately matching one from the latter. A token (*sumbolon*) was one half of a coin used to identify its possessor to the person with the other half.

by lot, and oligarchic by election; democratic not on the basis of a property assessment, oligarchic on such a basis. It is aristocratic, therefore, 10 and characteristic of a polity[56] to take one element from one and another from the other, by making officials elected, as in an oligarchy, but not on the basis of a property assessment, as in a democracy.

This, then, is the way to mix them. But the defining principle of a good mixture of democracy and oligarchy is when it is possible to speak of the same constitution both as an oligarchy and as a democracy. For it 15 is clear that speakers speak of it in this way because the mixture is a good one. The mean too is like this, since each of the extremes is visible in it. This is precisely how it is with the Spartan constitution. For many people attempt to speak of it as if it were a democracy, because it has many democratic elements in its organization. First, for example, there is the 20 way sons are brought up. Those of the rich are brought up like those of the poor, and are educated in a way that the sons of the poor could be. Similarly, at the next age, when they have become men, it is the same way. For nothing distinguishes a rich person from a poor one: the food at 25 the messes is the same for everyone, and the rich wear clothes that any poor person could also provide for himself. A further democratic element is that of the two most important offices, the people elect candidates to one and participate in the other; for they elect the senators and 30 participate in the overseership. But other people call the Spartan constitution an oligarchy on account of its having many oligarchic elements. For example, all the officials are chosen by vote and none by lot; a few have authority to impose death and exile; and there are also many other such elements. In a constitution that is well mixed, however, both elements should be held to be present—and neither; and it should survive 35 because of itself and not because of external factors, and because of itself, not because a majority wishes it (since that could happen in a bad constitution too), but because none of the parts of the city-state as a whole would even want another constitution.[57]

We have now described how a polity should be established and likewise those constitutions that are termed aristocracies.[58] 40

---

56. See 1273ª4–5 and note.
57. See 1270ᵇ21–22 and note.
58. "Those that are termed aristocracies" presumably refers to polities that lean toward oligarchy (1293ᵇ33–38). Hence by telling us how to establish a well-mixed polity, Aristotle can legitimately claim to have told us how to establish such aristocracies: just add more oligarchic elements and fewer democratic ones (1295ª31–34).

Chapter 10

1295ᵃ   It remained for us to speak about tyranny, not because there is much to say about it, but so that it can take its place in our inquiry, since we assign it too a place among the constitutions. Now we dealt with kingship in our first discussions[59] (when we investigated whether the kind of

5   kingship that is most particularly so called is beneficial for city-states or not beneficial, who and from what source should be established in it, and in what manner). And we distinguished two kinds of tyranny while we were investigating kingship, because their power somehow also overlaps

10   with kingship, owing to the fact that both are based on law. For some non-Greeks choose [1] autocratic monarchs, and in former times among the ancient Greeks there were [2] people called dictators who became monarchs in this way. There are, however, certain differences between

15   these; but both were kingly in as much as they were based on law, and involved monarchical rule over willing subjects; but both were tyrannical, in as much as the monarchs ruled like masters in accordance with their own judgment.[60] But [3] there is also a third kind of tyranny, which is held to be tyranny in the highest degree, being a counterpart to absolute kingship. Any monarchy is necessarily a tyranny of this kind if the monarch rules in an unaccountable fashion over people who are similar

20   to him or better than him, with an eye to his own benefit, not that of the ruled. It is therefore rule over unwilling people, since no free person willingly endures such rule.

The kinds of tyranny are these and this many, then, for the aforementioned reasons.

Chapter 11

25   What is the best constitution, and what is the best life for most city-states and most human beings, judging neither by a virtue that is beyond the reach of ordinary people, nor by a kind of education that requires natural gifts and resources that depend on luck, nor by the ideal constitution, but by a life that most people can share and a constitution in

30   which most city-states can participate? For the constitutions called aristocracies, which we discussed just now,[61] either fall outside the reach of

---

59. At III.14–17.
60. See III.14.
61. At 1293ᵇ7–21.

most city-states or border on so-called polities (that is why the two have to spoken about as one).

Decision about all these matters depends on the same elements. For if what is said in the *Ethics* is right, and a happy life is the one that expresses virtue and is without impediment, and virtue is a mean, then the middle life, the mean that each sort of person can actually achieve, must be best.[62] These same defining principles must also hold of the virtue and vice of a city-state or a constitution, since a constitution is a sort of life of city-state.

In all city-states, there are three parts of the city-state: the very rich, the very poor; and, third, those in between these. So, since it is agreed that what is moderate and in a mean is best, it is evident that possessing a middle amount of the GOODS of luck is also best. For it most readily obeys reason, whereas whatever is exceedingly beautiful, strong, well born, or wealthy, or conversely whatever is exceedingly poor, weak, or lacking in honor, has a hard time obeying reason. For the former sort tend more toward ARROGANCE and major vice, whereas the latter tend too much toward malice and petty vice; and wrongdoing is caused in the one case by arrogance and in the other by malice.[63] Besides, the middle classes are least inclined either to avoid ruling or to pursue it, both of which are harmful to city-states.

Furthermore, those who are superior in the goods of luck (strength, wealth, friends, and other such things) neither wish to be ruled nor know how to be ruled (and this is a characteristic they acquire right from the start at home while they are still children; for because of their luxurious lifestyle they are not accustomed to being ruled, even in school). Those, on the other hand, who are exceedingly deprived of such goods are too humble. Hence the latter do not know how to rule, but only how to be ruled in the way slaves are ruled, whereas the former do not know how to be ruled in any way, but only how to rule as masters rule. The result is a city-state consisting not of free people but of slaves and masters, the one group full of envy and the other full of arrogance. Nothing is further removed from a friendship and a community that is political. For community involves friendship, since enemies do not wish to share even a journey in common. But a city-state, at least, tends to consist as much as possible of people who are equal and similar, and this condition belongs particularly to those in the middle. Consequently, this city-state,

Chapter 11 column markers: 35, 40, 1295[b], 5, 10, 15, 20, 25

---

62. See *NE* 1140ª25–26, 1101ª14–16, Introduction xxxv–xxxix.
63. See 1271ª17, *Rh*. 1389ᵇ7–8, 1378ᵇ26–1379ª9, 1390ª17–18.

the one constituted out of those from which we say the city-state is naturally constituted, must of necessity be best governed. Moreover, of all
citizens, those in the middle survive best in city-states. For neither do
30   they desire other people's property as the poor do, nor do other people
desire theirs, as the poor desire that of the rich. And because they are
neither plotted against nor engage in plotting, they live out their lives
free from danger. That is why Phocylides did well to pray: "Many things
are best for those in the middle. I want to be in the middle in a city-
state."[64]

It is clear, therefore, that the political community that depends on
35   those in the middle is best too, and that city-states can be well governed
where those in the middle are numerous and stronger, preferably than
both of the others, or, failing that, than one of them. For it will tip the
balance when added to either and prevent the opposing extremes from
arising.[65] That is precisely why it is the height of good luck if those who
40   are governing own a middle or adequate amount of property, because
1296ᵃ   when some people own an excessive amount and the rest own nothing,
either extreme democracy arises or unmixed oligarchy or, as a result of
both excesses, tyranny. For tyranny arises from the most vigorous kind
of democracy and oligarchy,[66] but much less often from middle constitu-
5   tions or those close to them. We will give the reason for this later when
we discuss changes in constitutions.[67]

That the middle constitution is best is evident, since it alone is free
from faction. For conflicts and dissensions seldom occur among the citizens where there are many in the middle. Large city-states are also freer
from faction for the same reason, namely, that more are many in the
10   middle. In small city-states, on the other hand, it is easy to divide all the
citizens into two, so that no middle is left and pretty well everyone is either poor or rich. Democracies are also more stable and longer lasting
than oligarchies because of those in the middle (for they are more nu-
15   merous in democracies than in oligarchies and participate in office
more), since when the poor predominate without these, failure sets in
and they are quickly ruined. The fact that the best legislators have come
from the middle citizens should be regarded as evidence of this. For

---

64. Diehl I.50, fr. 10. Phocylides was a sixth century poet from Miletus.
65. By joining the poor it prevents extreme oligarchy; by joining the rich it pre-
    vents extreme democracy.
66. See 1312ᵇ34–38, 1310ᵇ3–4.
67. Perhaps a reference to 1308ᵃ18–24.

Solon was one of these, as is clear from his poems, as were Lycurgus (for he was not a king), Charondas, and pretty well most of the others.   *20*

It is also evident from these considerations why most constitutions are either democratic or oligarchic. For because the middle class in them is often small, whichever of the others preponderates (whether the property owners or the people), those who overstep the middle way con- *25* duct the constitution to suit themselves, so that it becomes either a democracy or an oligarchy. In addition to this, because of the conflicts and fights that occur between the people and the rich, whenever one side or the other happens to gain more power than its opponents, they establish neither a common constitution nor an equal one, but take their *30* superiority in the constitution as a reward of their victory and make in the one case a democracy and in the other an oligarchy. Then too each of those who achieved leadership in Greece[68] has looked to their own con- stitutions and established either democracies or oligarchies in city- states, aiming not at the benefit of these city-states but at their own. As a *35* consequence of all this, the middle constitution either never comes into existence or does so rarely and in few places. For among those who have previously held positions of leadership, only one man[69] has ever been persuaded to introduce this kind of organization, and it has now become customary for those in city-states not even to wish for equality, but ei- *40* ther to seek rule or to put up with being dominated.   *1296ᵇ*

What the best constitution is, then, and why it is so is evident from these considerations. As for the other constitutions (for there are, as we say, several kinds of democracies and of oligarchies), which of them is to be put first, which second, and so on in the same way, according to *5* whether it is better or worse, is not hard to see now that the best has been determined. For the one nearest to this must of necessity always be better and one further from the middle worse—provided one is not judging on the basis of certain assumptions. I say "on the basis of cer- tain assumptions," because it often happens that, while one constitution is more choiceworthy, nothing prevents a different one from being more *10* beneficial for some.

Chapter 12

The next thing to go through after what has been said is which constitu- tion and which kind of it is beneficial for which and which kind of peo-

---

68. Democratic Athens and oligarchic Sparta.
69. Identity unknown.

ple. First, though, a general point must be grasped about all of them,
namely, that the part of a city-state that wishes the constitution to con-
15 tinue must be stronger than any part that does not.[70] Every city-state is
made up of both quality and quantity. By "quality," I mean FREEDOM,
wealth, education, and good birth; by "quantity," I mean the superiority
of size. But it is possible that the quality belongs to one of the parts of
20 which a city-state is constituted, whereas the quantity belongs to another. For example, the low-born may be more numerous than the well-
born or the poor more numerous than the rich, but yet the one may not
be as superior in quantity as it is inferior in quality. Hence these have to
be judged in relation to one another. Where the multitude of poor peo-
25 ple is superior in the proportion mentioned,[71] there it is natural for a
democracy to exist, with each particular kind of democracy corresponding to the superiority of each particular kind of the people. For example,
if the multitude of farmers is predominant, it will be the first kind of
democracy; if the vulgar craftsmen and wage earners are, the last kind;
30 and similarly for the others in between these. But where the multitude
of those who are rich and notable is more superior in quality than it is
inferior in quantity, there an oligarchy is natural, with each particular
kind of oligarchy corresponding to the superiority of the multitude of
oligarchs, in the same way as before.[72]

But the legislator should always include the middle in his constitu-
35 tion: if he is establishing oligarchic laws, he should aim at those in the
middle, and if democratic ones, he must bring them in by these laws.
And where the multitude of those in the middle outweighs either both
of the extremes together, or even only one of them, it is possible to have
40 a stable constitution. For there is no fear that the rich and the poor will
1297ᵃ conspire together against these, since neither will ever want to serve as
slaves to the other; and if they look for a constitution that is more common than this, they will find none. For they would not put up with ruling in turn, because they distrust one another; and an ARBITRATOR is
5 most trusted everywhere, and the middle person is an arbitrator. The
better mixed a constitution is, the more stable it is. But many of those
who wish to establish aristocratic constitutions make the mistake not

70. See 1270ᵇ21–22 and note.
71. So that the poor are more superior in quantity than they are inferior in qual-
    ity.
72. The various kinds of democracy and oligarchy referred to are specified in
    IV.6.

only of granting more to the rich, but also of deceiving the people. For sooner or later, false goods inevitably give rise to a true evil; for the acquisitive behavior of the rich does more to destroy the constitution than that of the poor.[73]

Chapter 13

The devices used in constitutions to deceive the people are five in number, and concern the assembly, offices, the courts, weapons, and physical training. [1] As regards the assembly: allowing all citizens to attend assemblies, but either imposing a fine only on the rich for not attending, or a much heavier one on them. [2] As regards offices: not allowing those with an assessed amount of property to swear off,[74] but allowing the poor to do so. [3] As regards the courts: fining the rich for not serving on juries, but not the poor, or else imposing a large fine on the former and a small one on the latter, as in the laws of Charondas. In some places, everyone who has enrolled may attend the assembly and serve on juries, but once they have enrolled, if they do not attend or serve, they are heavily fined. The aim is to get people to avoid enrolling because of the fine, and not to serve or to attend because of not being enrolled. They legislate in the same way where possessing hoplite arms and physical training are concerned. [4] For the poor are permitted not to possess weapons, but the rich are fined if they do not; [5] and if they do not train, there is no fine for the former, but the latter are fined. That way the rich will participate because of the fine, whereas the poor, not being in danger of it, will not participate.

These legislative devices are oligarchic; in democracies there are opposite devices. For the poor are paid to attend the assembly and serve on juries, and the rich are not fined for failing to. If one wants to mix justly, then, it is evident that one must combine elements from either side, and pay the poor while fining the rich. For in this way everyone would participate, whereas in the other way the constitution comes to belong to one side alone. The constitution should consist only of those who possess weapons; but it is impossible unqualifiedly to define the size of the relevant property assessment, and say that it must be so much. One

---

73. See 1307[a]12–20.
74. To take an oath that holding the office would be unduly burdensome for financial or other reasons.

should instead look for what amount[75] is the highest that would let those
5 who participate in the constitution outnumber those who do not, and fix
on that. For the poor are willing to keep quiet even when they do not
participate in office, provided no one treats them arrogantly or takes
away any of their property (not an easy thing, however, since those who
10 do participate in the governing class are not always cultivated people).
People are also in the habit of shirking in time of war if they are poor
and do not receive provisions; but if food is provided, they will fight.[76]

In some places, the constitution consists not only of those who are
serving as hoplites but also of those who have served as hoplites in the
past. In Malea, the constitution consisted of both, although the officials
15 were elected from among the active soldiers. Also the first constitution
that arose among the Greeks after kingships also consisted of the defensive warriors.[77] Initially, it consisted of the cavalrymen, since strength
and superiority in war lay in them. For a hoplite force is useless without
20 organized formations, and experience in such things and organizations
did not exist among the ancients. Hence their strength lay in their cavalry. But as city-states grew larger and those with hoplite weapons became a stronger force, more people came to participate in the constitution. That is precisely why what we now call polities used to be called
25 democracies. But the ancient constitutions were oligarchic and kingly,
and quite understandably so. For because of their small population they
did not have much of a middle class, so that, being small in number and
poor in organization, the people put up with being ruled.

We have said, then, [1] why there are several constitutions—[1.1] why
30 there are others besides those spoken of (for democracy is not one in
number, and similarly with the others), [1.2] what their varieties are, and
[1.3] why they arise. In addition, [2] we have said which constitution is
best, for the majority of cases, and [3] among the other constitutions
which suits which sort of people.

Chapter 14

As regards what comes next, let us once again discuss constitutions gen-
35 erally and each one separately, taking the starting point that is appropri-

75. Reading *poion* with Dreizehnter and the mss.
76. This sentence and its predecessor explain why the costs of excluding a poor
minority from participation, whether in terms of social unrest or ability to
fight a war, need not be prohibitively high.
77. See 1286^b11–13.

ate to the subject. All constitutions have three parts by reference to which an excellent legislator must study what is beneficial for each of them. When these parts are in good condition, the constitution is necessarily in good condition, and constitutions necessarily differ from one another as a result of differing in each of these parts. One of the three *40* parts [1] deliberates about public affairs; the second [2] concerns the offices, that is to say, which offices there should be, with authority over *1298ª* what things, and in what way officials should be chosen;[78] and the third [3] is what decides lawsuits.[79] [1] The deliberative part has authority in relation to war and peace, the making and breaking of alliances, and laws; and in relation to death, exile, and the confiscation of property; *5* and in relation to the selection and inspection of officials. It is necessary that these matters for decision [1.1] be assigned either all to all citizens, or [1.2] all to some (to some single office, for example, or to several, or some to some and others to others), or [1.3] some to all and some to some.

[1.1] For all to deliberate about all issues is characteristic of a democracy, since this is the equality the people seek. But there are several ways *10* of having all deliberate. [1.1.1] One way is in turn rather than all together, as in the constitution of Telecles of Miletus.[80] There are other constitutions too in which deliberation is carried out by boards of officials meeting jointly, and all enter office in turn from the tribes and from *15* the smallest parts of the city-state, until all have been gone through. In these cases all meet together only to consider legislation and matters pertaining to the constitution, and to listen to official announcements. [1.1.2] Another way is where they all meet, but only for choosing offi- *20* cials, for legislation, matters of war and peace, and for inspections; and other matters are deliberated on by the officials chosen to deal with the particular area in question, these being chosen from all the citizens either by election or by lot. [1.1.3] Another way is for the citizens to meet together about offices and inspections, and to deliberate about[81] war and *25* alliance, and for other matters to be dealt with by offices of which as few as possible are filled by election, these being the ones where it is neces-

---

78. Discussed in IV.15.
79. Discussed in IV.16.
80. Otherwise unknown.
81. A reference to legislation has perhaps been accidentally omitted at this point, as Newman suggests.

sary to have knowledgeable people holding office.[82] [1.1.4] A fourth way
is for all to meet and deliberate about all matters, while the office decides
30   nothing, but prepares issues for decision only. This is the way in which
the final kind of democracy is actually managed, the one we say is analogous to a dynastic oligarchy or a tyrannical monarchy.[83]

All these ways, then, are democratic. But [1.2] for some people to deliberate about all matters is oligarchic. And here too there are several va-
35   rieties. [1.2.1] For when they are chosen on the basis of more moderate
property assessments, and there are more of them because of the moderateness of the assessments, and where they follow the law and do not attempt to make changes that it forbids, and where everyone who has the
assessed amount may participate—such a constitution is certainly an
oligarchy, but, on account of its moderateness, one with the character of
40   a polity. [1.2.2] When not everyone participates in deliberation but only
1298ᵇ   those elected, and when, as before, they rule in accordance with law, it is
oligarchic. [1.2.3] When those who have authority over deliberation
elect themselves, and when son succeeds father, and they have authority
over the laws, this organization is necessarily most oligarchic. [1.3] But,
5   when some have authority over some matters—for example, when all
have it over war and peace and inspections, whereas officials who are
elected, not[84] chosen by lot, have it in the other areas, it is an aristocracy
or[85] a polity. But if it happens that elected officials have authority in
some areas, whereas officials chosen by lot, either simply or from a pre-
selected group, have it in others, or if elected officials and officials chosen by lot share authority, some of these are features of an aristocratic
10   constitution and others of polity itself.

This is the way, then, that the deliberative part is distinguished in relation to the various constitutions, and each constitution administers
matters in accord with the determinations mentioned.

In the kind of democracy that is most particularly held to be a democracy nowadays (I mean the kind in which the people have authority over
15   even the laws), it is beneficial from the point of view of improving deliberation to do precisely the same thing as is done in oligarchies in regard

---

82. Democratic constitutions favored election by lot, but were willing to make
an exception when the office (for example, a generalship) required expert
knowledge (1317ᵇ20–21).
83. See 1292ª4–30.
84. Alternatively (Dreizehnter and the mss.): "elected or (*ē*) chosen by lot."
85. Reading *ē* with Dreizehnter.

to the courts. For they establish a fine for those people they want to have on juries to ensure that they serve (whereas democrats pay the poor). The same should be done in the case of assemblies too, for they will deliberate better if they all deliberate together, the people with the notables, and the latter with the multitude. It is beneficial too if those who do the deliberating are elected, or chosen by lot, in equal numbers from these parts. And even if the democrats among the citizens[86] are greatly superior in numbers, it is beneficial not to provide pay for all of them, but only for a number to balance the number of notables, or to exclude the excess by lot.

In oligarchies, however, it is beneficial either to select some additional people from the multitude of citizens to serve as officials or to establish a board of officials like the so-called preliminary councilors or law-guardians that exist in some constitutions, and then have the assembly deal only with issues that have been considered by this board. In this way, the people will share in deliberation, but will not be able to abolish anything connected to the constitution. It is also beneficial to have the people vote only on decrees brought before them that have already undergone preliminary deliberation, or on nothing contrary to them, or else to let all advise and have only officials deliberate. One should in fact do the opposite of what happens in polities.[87] For the multitude should have authority when vetoing measures but not when approving them; in the latter case, they should be referred back to the officials instead. For in polities, they do the contrary, since the few have authority when vetoing decrees but not when passing them; decrees of the latter sort are always referred to the majority instead.

This, then, is the way the deliberative part, the part that has authority over the constitution, should be determined.[88]

Chapter 15

[2] Next after these things comes the division of the offices.[89] For this part of a constitution too has many varieties: how many offices there are; with authority over what things; with regard to time: how long each

---

86. Reading *politōn* with Ross rather than *politikōn* ("statesmen") with Dreizehnter and the mss.
87. Or constitutions generally.
88. Reading *dei . . . diōristhai* with Dreizehnter.
89. This topic is further discussed in VI.8.

office is to last (some make it six months, some less, some make it a year, some a longer period); and whether they are to be held permanently or for a long time, or neither of these, but instead to be held by the same person several times, or not even twice but only once; and further, as re-
10 gards the selection of officials: from whom they should come, by whom, and how. For one should be able to determine how many ways all these can be handled, and then fit the kinds of offices to the kinds of constitutions for which they are beneficial.

15 But even to determine what should be called an office is not easy. For a political community needs many sorts of supervisors, so that not everyone who is selected by vote or by lot can be regarded as an official. In the first place, for example, there are the priests: for a priesthood must be regarded as something other than and apart from the political offices. Besides, patrons of the theater and heralds are elected, ambas-
20 sadors too. But some sorts of supervision *are* political, either concerned with all the citizens involved in a certain activity (as a general supervises those who are serving as soldiers) or some part of them (for example, the supervisors of women or children). Some are related to household management (for corn rationers are often elected),[90] while others are subordinate, and are of the sort that, when there are the resources, are assigned to slaves.

Simply speaking, however, the offices most properly so called are
25 those to which are assigned deliberation, decision, and issuing orders about certain matters, especially the latter, since issuing orders is most characteristic of office. This problem makes scarcely any difference in practice, but since terminological disputes have not been resolved, there
30 is some theoretical work yet to be done.

One might rather raise a problem with regard to any constitution about what sorts of offices and how many of them are necessary for the existence of a city-state,[91] and which sorts, though not necessary, are yet useful with a view to an excellent constitution, but one might particularly raise it with regard to constitutions in small city-states. For in large
35 city-states one can and should assign a single office to a single task. For because there are many citizens, there are many people to take up office, so that some offices are held again only after a long interval and others are held only once. Also every task is better performed when its supervi-

---

90. In times of scarcity or when a gift of corn had been given to the city-state, a corn rationer (*sitometrēs*) was elected to distribute it among the citizens.
91. Listed in VI.8.

sion is handled as a single matter rather than as one matter among many.[92] In small city-states, however, many offices have to be co-assigned to a few people, since underpopulation makes it hard to have a lot of people in office; for who will succeed them in their turn? But sometimes small city-states need the same offices and laws as large ones, except that the latter need the same ones often, whereas the former need them only at long intervals. That is why, indeed, nothing prevents their assigning many types of supervision at the same time (for they will not impede one another), and why, because of underpopulation, they must make their boards of officials like spit-lamps.[93]

If, then, we can say how many offices every city-state must have, and how many it need not but should have, it will be easier, in the light of this, to determine which offices it is appropriate to combine into a single office. It is also appropriate not to overlook the question of which matters should be supervised by many boards of officials on a local basis, and which a single office should everywhere have authority over. For example, good order: should a market supervisor have authority over this in the marketplace, and another official in another place, or the same one everywhere? Should the offices be distinguished by their tasks or by the people they deal with? I mean, for example, whether there should be a single office for good order, or one for children and another for women. And with regard to the constitutions too, whether the types of offices also differ in each, or not at all. For example, whether in a democracy, an oligarchy, an aristocracy, and a monarchy, the same offices have authority, even though they are not composed of equal or similar people, but from different sorts in different constitutions (the generally educated in aristocracies, the rich in oligarchies, and the free in democracies), or whether certain offices exist precisely because constitutions differ, with sometimes the same offices and sometimes different ones being beneficial (since it is appropriate for the same office to be large in some places and small in others).

Some offices are indeed peculiar to particular constitutions, for example, that of the preliminary councilors.[94] For it is undemocratic, whereas a council is democratic, since there must be some body of this sort to

1299[b]

5

10

15

20

25

30

---

92. A common claim, see 1252[b]1–5, 1273[b]9–15; also Plato, *Republic* 370a–b, 374a–c, 394e, 423c–d, 433a, 443b–c, 453b.
93. A spit-lamp (*obeliskoluchnion*) was a military tool which could be used either as a roasting spit or as a lamp holder.
94. See 1298[b]26–1299[a]2.

take care of preliminary deliberation on behalf of the people, so that
they can do their work. This is oligarchic if the councilors are few in
number; but the preliminary councilors are necessarily few in number,

35　and so this arrangement is oligarchic. Where both these offices exist,
however, the preliminary councilors are established as a check on the
councilors; for a councilor is democratic, a preliminary councilor, oligarchic. But the power of the council is also destroyed in those kinds of
democracies in which the people themselves come together and transact

1300ᵃ　all business. This is the usual result when those who attend the assembly
either are rich or receive pay,⁹⁵ since they then have the leisure to meet
often and decide everything themselves. The supervisor of children, the
supervisor of women, and any other office that has authority over this

5　sort of supervision, is an aristocratic feature, not democratic (for how
can one prevent the women of the poor from going outdoors?) or oligarchic (since the women of oligarchs live luxuriously).⁹⁶

So much about these matters for now, but as regards the selection of
officials, we must try to go through things from the beginning. Differ-

10　ences here lie in three defining principles, the combination of which
necessarily yields all the different ways. Of these three, the first is [2.1]
who selects the officials, second, [2.2] from whom, and, lastly, [2.3] in
what way. Of each of these there are three different varieties. Either

15　[2.1.1] all the citizens select or [2.1.2] some do; and they select either
[2.2.1] from all or [2.2.2] from certain specified people (determined by a
property assessment, for example, or by birth, virtue, or some other
such feature, as in Megara where they selected from those who had returned from exile together and fought in alliance against the people);⁹⁷
and they select either [2.3.1] by election or [2.3.2] by lot; and, again,
these may be paired—I mean that [2.1.3] all may select for some offices

20　and some for others, [2.2.3] some offices may be selected for from all and
others from some, and [2.3.3] some may be selected for by lot and others
by election.⁹⁸

95. Reading *tis ēi ē misthos* with Lord and the mss.
96. Well-off women in Athens were kept in a kind of purdah in the houses first
of their fathers and then of their husbands, and were seldom allowed to be
seen in public. Poor ones had to work in the fields or other public places. On
oligarchic women see 1269ᵇ12–39.
97. It is uncertain when this event took place. What seem to be further references to it occur at 1302ᵇ30–31, 1304ᵇ34–39.
98. The nine varieties are: (2.1.1) all select, (2.1.2) some select, (2.1.3) all select
for some offices and some select for others; (2.2.1) all are selectable, (2.2.2)

In the case of each of these varieties, there are four[99] different ways to proceed. Either all select from all by election or all select from all by lot[100] (and[101] from all either by sections—by tribe, for example, or by deme or clan, until all the citizens have been gone through—or from all on every occasion); or from some by election or from some by lot;[102] or partly in the first way and partly in the second. Again, if only some do the selecting, they may do so either from all by election or from all by lot; or from some by election or from some by lot; or partly in the first way and partly in the second—that is to say, for some from all by election and for some by lot.[103] This gives rise to twelve ways, setting aside two of the combinations.[104] Three of these ways of selecting are democratic, namely, when all select from all by election, by lot, or by both (that is, for some offices by election and for some by lot). But when not all select at the same time, but do so for all from all or from some, whether by election, lot, or both, or from all for some offices and from some for others, whether by election, lot, or both (by "both," I mean some by lot and others by election)—it is characteristic of a polity. When some appoint from all, whether by election, lot, or both (for some offices by lot for others by vote), it is oligarchic—although it is more oligarchic to do so by both. But when some offices are selected for from all and others from some or when some are selected for by election and some by vote, this is

25

30

35

40

---

some are selectable, (2.2.3) all are selectable for some offices and some are selectable for others; (2.3.1) selection is by lot, (2.3.2) selection is by election, (2.3.3) selection is by lot for some offices and by election for others.

99. Reading *tettares* with the mss in place of Ross's conjectural *hex*. The text of this entire paragraph is difficult, and many reorganizations and emendations have been proposed.

100. Deleting the material added by Ross.

101. Deleting *ei*, which Newman brackets.

102. Adding *ē ek tinōn hairesei ē ek tinōn klērō(i)*, which also appears at ᵃ28–29.

103. Deleting the material added by Ross.

104. The twelve ways referred to are: (1) all select from all by election; (2) all select from all by lot; (3) all select from some by election; (4) all select from some by lot; (5) all select from all partly by election and partly by lot; (6) all select from some partly by election and partly by lot; (7) some select from all by election; (8) some select from all by lot; (9) some select from some by election; (10) some select from some by lot; (11) some select from all partly by election and partly by lot; (12) some select from some partly by election and partly by lot. The two omitted combinations are: (2.1.3) all select for some offices and some select for others, and (2.2.3) all are selectable for some offices and some are selectable for others.

1300ᵇ   characteristic of an aristocratic polity. When some select from some by
election, it is oligarchic; also when some select from some by lot (even
though this does not happen), and when some select from some in both
ways. But when some select from all, and when all select from some by
election, it is aristocratic.

5   These, then, are the number of ways of selecting for offices, and this
is how they are distinguished in relation to the constitutions. It will become evident which ways are beneficial for which constitutions, and how
selections are to be made, when we determine the powers of the offices,
and which these are. By the "power of an office" I mean, for example,
10   having authority over revenues or authority over defense. For the kind of
power of a generalship, for example, is different from that of authority
over marketplace contracts.

Chapter 16

Of the three parts,[105] it remains to speak about [3] the judicial. And we
must grasp the ways that it can be organized by following the same supposition as before. The differences between courts are found in three
15   defining principles: from whom; about what; and how. From whom: I
mean whether they are selected from all or from some. About what: how
many kinds of courts are there. How: whether by lot or by election.

First, then, let us distinguish how many kinds of courts there are.
They are eight in number. One is [i] concerned with inspection. Another
20   [ii] deals with anyone who wrongs the community.[106] Another [iii] with
matters that affect the constitution. A fourth [iv] deals with officials and
private individuals in disputes about fines. A fifth [v] deals with private
transactions of some magnitude. Besides these there is [vi] a court that
deals with homicide and [vii] one that deals with aliens. The kinds of
homicide court, whether having the same juries or not, are: [vi.1] that
25   concerned with premeditated homicide, [vi.2] that concerned with involuntary homicide, [vi.3] that concerned with cases where there is
agreement on the fact of homicide but the justice of it disputed, and a
fourth [vi.4] concerned with charges brought against those who have
been exiled for homicide after their return (the court of Phreatto in

---

105. See 1297ᵇ36–1298ᵃ3.
106. "The man who is guilty of adultery or assault wrongs some definite per-
      son; the man who avoids military service wrongs the community" (*Rh.*
      1373ᵇ23–24).

Athens[107] is said to be an example), but such cases are rare at any time even in large city-states. The aliens' court has [vii.1] a part for aliens disputing with aliens and [vii.2] a part for aliens disputing with citizens. Besides all these, there is [viii] a court that deals with petty transactions: those involving one drachma, five drachmas, or a little more (for judgment must be given in these cases too, but it should not fall to a multitude of jurors to give it).

But let us set aside these courts as well as the homicide and aliens' courts and talk about the political ones, which, when not well managed, give rise to factions and constitutional changes. Of necessity, there are just the following possibilities: [3.1] All decide all the cases just distinguished, and are selected either [3.1.1] by lot or [3.1.2] by election; or [3.1] all decide all of them, and [3.1.3] some are selected by lot and some by election; or, [3.1.4] although dealing with the same case, some jurors may be selected by lot and some by election. Thus these ways are four in number. [3.2] There are as many again when selection is from only some of the citizens. For here again either [3.2.1] the juries are selected from some by election and decide all cases; or [3.2.2] they are selected from some by lot and decide all cases; or [3.2.3] some may be selected by lot and some by election; or [3.2.4] some courts dealing with the same cases may be composed of both members selected by lot and elected members. These ways, as we said, are the counterparts of the ones we mentioned earlier. [3.3] Furthermore, these same ones may be conjoined—I mean, for example, some may be selected from all, others from some, and others from both (as for example if the same court had juries selected partly from all and partly from some); and the selection may be either by lot or by election or by both.

We have now listed the possible ways the courts can be organized. Of these the first, [3.1] those which are selected from all and decide all cases, are democratic. The second [3.2], those which are selected from some and decide all cases, are oligarchic. The third [3.3], those which are partly selected from all and partly from some, are aristocratic or characteristic of a polity.

---

107. If someone exiled for involuntary homicide was charged with a second voluntary homicide, he could not enter Attica for trial, but he could offer his defense from a boat offshore at Phreatto, on the east side of Piraeus.

BOOK V

Chapter 1

20 Pretty well all the other topics we intended to treat have been discussed. Next, after what has been said, we should investigate: [1] the sources of change in constitutions, how many they are and of what sort; [2] what things destroy each constitution; [3] from what sort into what sort they principally change; further, [4] the ways to preserve constitutions in general and each constitution in particular; and, finally, [5] the means by which each constitution is principally preserved.[1]

25 We should take as our initial starting point that many constitutions have come into existence because, though everyone agrees about justice (that is to say, proportional EQUALITY), they are mistaken about it, as we also mentioned earlier.[2] For democracy arose from those who are equal in some respect thinking themselves to be unqualifiedly equal; for be-

30 cause they are equally free, they think they are unqualifiedly equal. Oligarchy, on the other hand, arose from those who are unequal[3] in some respect taking themselves to be wholly unequal; for being unequal in property, they take themselves to be unqualifiedly unequal. The result is that the former claim to merit an equal share of everything, on the grounds that they are all equal, whereas the latter, being unequal, seek to

35 get more (for a bigger share is an unequal one). All these constitutions possess justice of a sort, then, although unqualifiedly speaking they are mistaken. And this is why, when one or another of them does not participate in the constitution in accordance with their assumption,[4] they start faction. However, those who would be most justified in starting faction,

---

1. (4) The ways to preserve a constitution; (5) the steps or devices needed to implement them. See 1313^{a}34–^{b}32, 1319^{b}37–1320^{b}17.
2. At III.9.
3. Specifically, superior (1302^{b}26–27).
4. About the nature of proportional equality.

namely, those who are outstandingly virtuous, are the least likely to do   *40*
so.[5] For they alone are the ones it is most reasonable to regard as unqual-   *1301ᵇ*
ifiedly unequal. There are also certain people, those of good birth, who
suppose that they do not merit a merely equal share because they are unequal in this way. For people are thought to be noble when they have ancestral wealth and virtue behind them.

These, practically speaking, are the origins and sources of factions,   *5*
the factors that lead people to start it. Hence the changes that are due to
faction are also of two kinds. [1] For sometimes people aim to change the
established constitution to one of another kind—for example, from
democracy to oligarchy, or from oligarchy to democracy, or from these
to polity or aristocracy, or the latter into the former. [2] But sometimes
instead of trying to change the established constitution (for example, an   *10*
oligarchy or a monarchy), they deliberately choose to keep it, but [2.1]
want to have it in their own hands. Again, [2.2] it may be a question of
degree: where there is an oligarchy, the aim may be to make the governing class more oligarchic or less so; where there is a democracy, the aim   *15*
may be to make it more democratic or less so; and similarly, in the case of
the remaining constitutions, the aim may be to tighten or loosen them.[6]
Again, [2.3] the aim may be to change a certain part of the constitution,
for example, to establish or abolish a certain office, as some say Lysander
tried to abolish the kingship in Sparta, and King Pausanias the overseer-   *20*
ship.[7] In Epidamnus too the constitution was partially altered, since a
council replaced the tribal rulers, though it is still the case that only
those members of the governing class who actually hold office are
obliged to attend the public assembly when election to office is taking
place.[8] (Having a single supreme official was also an oligarchic feature of
this constitution.)   *25*

For faction is everywhere due to inequality, when unequals do not receive proportionately unequal things (for example, a permanent kingship is unequal if it exists among equals). For people generally engage in
faction in pursuit of equality. But equality is of two sorts: numerical

---

5. For the reason given at 1304ᵇ2–5.
6. The metaphor of tightening and loosening is introduced at 1290ᵃ22–29.
7. Lysander was a Spartan general and statesman who fought against Athens in
   the Peloponnesian war. He failed in his attempt to introduce elective monarchy in Sparta, and was killed in 395. Pausanias was largely responsible for the
   Greek victory over the Persians at the battle of Platea in 479.
8. This change may also be referred to at 1304ᵃ13–17.

30   equality and equality according to merit. By numerical equality I mean
being the same and equal in number or magnitude. By equality according to merit I mean what is the same and equal in ratio. For example,
three exceeds two and two exceeds one by a numerical amount. But four
exceeds two and two exceeds one in ratio. For two and one are equal
35   parts of four and two, since both are halves. But, though people agree
that what is unqualifiedly just is what is according to merit, they still
disagree, as we said earlier.[9] For some consider themselves wholly equal
if they are equal in a certain respect, whereas others claim to merit an
unequal share of everything if they are unequal in a certain respect.

That is also why two constitutions principally arise: democracy and
40   oligarchy. For good birth and virtue[10] are found in few people, whereas
wealth and freedom are more widespread. For no city-state has a hun-
1302ᵃ   dred good and well-born men, but there are rich ones[11] in many places.
But it is a bad thing for a constitution to be organized unqualifiedly and
entirely in accord with either sort of equality. This is evident from what
actually happens, since no constitution of this kind is stable. The reason
5   is that when one begins from an erroneous beginning, something bad inevitably results in the end. Hence numerical equality should be used in
some cases, and equality according to merit in others. Nevertheless,
democracy is more stable and freer from faction than oligarchy. For in
oligarchies, *two* sorts of faction arise, one among the oligarchs them-
10   selves and another against the people. In democracies, on the other
hand, the only faction is against the oligarchs, since there is none worth
mentioning among the people themselves.[12] Besides, a constitution
based on the middle classes is closer to a democracy than to an oligarchy,
15   and it is the most secure constitution of this kind.

Chapter 2

Since we are investigating the sources from which both factions and
changes arise in constitutions, we must first grasp their general origins
and causes. There are, roughly speaking, three of these, each of which
20   must first be determined in outline by itself. We must grasp [1] the condition people are in when they start faction, [2] for the sake of what, and,

9. At III.9.
10. The basis of aristocracy.
11. Omitting *kai aporoi* ("and poor ones") with Dreizehnter and the mss.
12. See 1296ᵃ13–18, where a somewhat different explanation is offered.

third, [3] what the origins are of political disturbances and factions among people.

[1] The principal general cause of people being in some way disposed to change their constitution is the one we have in fact already mentioned. For those who desire equality start faction when they believe that they are getting less, even though they are the equals of those who are getting more; whereas those who desire inequality (that is to say, superiority) do so when they believe that, though they are unequal, they are not getting more but the same or less. (Sometimes these desires are just, sometimes unjust.) For inferiors start factions in order to be equal, and equals do so in order to be superior. So much for the condition of those who start faction.

[2] The things over which they start such faction are profit, honor, *and* their opposites. For people also start faction in city-states to avoid dishonor and fines, either for themselves or for their friends.

[3] The causes and origins of the changes, in the sense of the factors that dispose people to feel the way we described about the issues we mentioned, are from one point of view seven in number and from another more. Two are the same as those just mentioned, but not in their manner of operation. For people are also stirred up by profit and honor not simply in order to get them for themselves, which is what we said before, but because they see others, whether justly or unjustly, getting more. Other causes are: ARROGANCE, fear, superiority, contempt, and disproportionate growth. Still other ones, although operating in another way, are electioneering, carelessness, gradual alteration, and dissimilarity.[13]

Chapter 3

The effect of arrogance and profit, and the way the two operate, are pretty much evident. For when officials behave arrogantly and become

25

30

35

40

1302[b]

5

13. The seven causes mentioned at [a]36–37 are profit, honor, arrogance, fear, superiority, contempt, and disproportionate growth in power. The two points of view are: (1) treating profit and honor as two causes each of which operates in two ways and (2) treating these two ways of operating as distinct causes. If (2) is adopted, there are then more than seven causes. Of the four causes mentioned in the final sentence, the first three (electioneering, carelessness, and gradual alteration) cause political change, but not by giving rise to faction in the way the initial seven (or nine) do (1303[a]13–14). The fourth (dissimilarity) also gives rise to faction, at least "until people learn to pull together" (1303[a]25–26).

acquisitive, people start faction with one another and with the constitutions that gave the officials authority. (Sometimes their ACQUISITIVE-NESS is at the expense of private properties, sometimes at that of public funds.)

10   It is also clear what honor is capable of, and how it causes faction. For people start faction both when they themselves are dishonored and when they see others being honored. This occurs unjustly when people are honored or dishonored contrary to their merit; justly, when it accords with merit.

Superiority causes faction when some individual or group of individ-
15   uals is too powerful for the city-state and for the power of the governing class. For the usual outcome of such a situation is a monarchy or a dynasty. That is why some places, such as Argos and Athens, have a practice of ostracism. Yet it is better to see to it from the beginning that no one can emerge whose superiority is so great than to supply a remedy af-
20   terwards.[14]

People start faction through fear both when they have committed injustice and are afraid of punishment and when they think they are about to suffer an injustice and wish to avoid becoming its victims. The latter occurred in Rhodes when the notables united against the people because of the lawsuits being brought against them.[15]

25   People also start faction and hostilities because of contempt. For example, this occurs in oligarchies when those who do not participate in the constitution are in a majority (since they consider themselves the stronger party),[16] and in democracies, when the rich are contemptuous of the disorganization and anarchy. Thus the democracy in Thebes collapsed because they were badly governed after the battle of Oenophyta,[17]
30   as was the democracy of the Megarians when they were defeated because of disorganization and anarchy.[18] The same happened to the democracy in Syracuse before the tyranny of Gelon,[19] and to the one in Rhodes prior to the revolt.[20]

Changes also occur in constitutions because of disproportionate

14. See 1284ª17–25; Introduction lxix–lxxii.
15. Presumably the event referred to at [b]32–33 and 1304[b]27–31.
16. In this case the majority are moved to engage in faction by the arrogance exhibited by the few in excluding them from office.
17. With Athens in 456.
18. Presumably the event referred to at 1300ª17–19 and 1304[b]34–39.
19. Gelon became tyrant in 485. See 1312[b]10–16.
20. Presumably the event referred to at [b]23–24 and 1304[b]27–31.

growth. For just as a body is composed of parts which must grow in pro- *35*
portion if balance is to be maintained (since otherwise it will be destroyed, as when a foot is four cubits [six feet] long, for example, and the
rest of the body two spans [fifteen inches]; or, if the disproportionate
growth is not only quantitative but also qualitative, its shape might
change to that of another animal),[21] so a city-state too is composed of *40*
parts, one of which often grows without being noticed—for example, *1303ª*
the multitude of the poor in democracies or polities. This sometimes
also happens because of luck. Thus a democracy took the place of a
polity in Tarentum when many notables were killed by the Iapygians
shortly after the Persian wars.[22] In Argos too, after the death of those cit- *5*
izens killed on the seventh[23] by the Spartan Cleomenes, the notables
were forced to admit some of their SUBJECT PEOPLES to citizenship; and
in Athens, when they had bad luck fighting on land, the notables were
reduced in number, because at the time of the war against Sparta those
serving in the army were drawn from the citizen service-list.[24] This sort *10*
of change also occurs in democracies, though to a lesser extent. For
when the rich become more numerous or their properties increase in
size, democracies change into oligarchies or polities.

But constitutions also change without the occurrence of faction, both
because of electioneering, as happened in Heraea (for they replaced
election with selection by lot for this reason, that those who election- *15*
eered were elected), and also because of carelessness, when people who
are not friendly to the constitution are allowed to occupy the offices with
supreme authority. Thus the oligarchy in Oreus was overthrown when

---

21. At *GA* 768ᵇ27–37, Aristotle describes a disease, "satyriasis," which pro-
    duces changes in a human face, so that it comes to resemble the face of an
    animal. He does not think, however, that an animal (or any of its parts) can
    actually change into an animal (or a part of an animal) of another species
    (see the discussion of so-called monsters at *GA* 769ᵇ10–30, especially,
    ᵇ16–17).
22. This war, which took place in 473, involved "the greatest slaughter of the
    Greeks that we know of" (Herodotus VII.170).
23. Apollo was believed to have been born on the seventh day of the month, and
    was specially honored at Sparta on that day. Cleomenes I was a Spartan king
    c. 519–487. See Herodotus VI.57.
24. Lists were kept of those citizens eligible for service in the cavalry, hoplites,
    or navy. During the Peloponnesian war (431–404), the army was recruited
    from the wealthier citizens, whereas in Aristotle's day it often consisted of
    mercenaries.

Heracleodorus became one of the officials and established a polity, or rather a democracy, in place of the oligarchy.[25]

20   Moreover, constitutions change because of small alterations. I mean that often a great change in the laws occurs unnoticed when a small alteration is overlooked. In Ambracia, for example, the property-assessment was small, but in the end people with no property came to hold office, because there is little or no difference between small and none.

25   Ethnic difference also causes faction, until people learn to pull together. For just as a city-state does not arise from any chance multitude,[26] neither does it arise in a chance period of time. That is why most of those who have admitted co-settlers or late-settlers have experienced faction. The Achaeans co-settled Sybaris with the Troezenians, but later, when the Achaeans became more numerous, they expelled the

30   Troezenians (this was the cause of the curse that fell on the Sybarites).[27] In Thurii too, Sybarites came into conflict with their co-settlers; for when they claimed to merit a larger share on the grounds that the country was theirs, they were expelled. In Byzantium, the late-settlers were discovered plotting against the original settlers and were forcibly expelled.[28] The Antissaeans forcibly expelled the Chian exiles they had ad-

35   mitted. The Zanclaeans were themselves expelled by the Samians they had admitted.[29] The Apolloniates on the Black Sea became factionalized after admitting late-settlers. The Syracusans became factionalized and fought with one another when they granted citizenship to foreigners

1303ᵇ   and mercenaries after the period of the tyrants.[30] The Amphipolitans admitted late-settlers from Chalcis and were almost all expelled by them.[31]

In oligarchies, as we said earlier, the many start faction on the grounds

25. The events in Heraea are otherwise unknown. The changes in Oreus, also called Hestiaea (1303ᵇ33), occurred in 377 when it revolted from the Spartans and joined the Athenian Confederacy.

26. See 1290ᵇ38–1291ᵇ13, 1326ª16–25, 1328ᵇ16–17.

27. The expelled Troezenians were received at Croton, which destroyed Sybaris in 510. The precise nature of the curse is unknown, but to drive out fellow colonists would have been viewed as a great sacrilege.

28. Nothing is known about this conflict, or about the one in Antissa mentioned in the next sentence.

29. The conflict at Zancle is described in Herodotus VI.22–24.

30. That is to say, after the fall of Thrasybulus in 467.

31. Also referred to at 1306ª2–4. The original Athenian settlers were driven out and Amphipolis was incorporated into the powerful Chalcidian Confederacy in around 370.

that they are treated unjustly because they do not participate equally, in spite of being equal. In democracies, the notables do so because they do participate equally, in spite of not being equal.[32] 5

City-states also occasionally become factionalized because of their location, when their territory is not naturally suitable for a city-state that is a unity. In Clazomenae, for example, the inhabitants of Chytrus came into conflict with those on the island, as did the inhabitants of Colophon and those of Notium.[33] At Athens, too, the people are not all similar, but 10 those in Piraeus are more democratic than those in the town. For just as in battles, where crossing even small ditches breaks up the phalanx, so every difference seems to result in factional division. The greatest factional division is probably between virtue and vice; next that between 15 wealth and poverty; and so on for the others, including the one we have just discussed, with each one greater than the next.

Chapter 4

Factions arise *from* small issues, then, but not *over* them; it is over important issues that people start faction. Even small factions gain greater power, however, when they arise among those in authority,[34] as happened in Syracuse in ancient times. For the constitution underwent change be- 20 cause two young men in office started a faction about a love affair.[35] While the first was away, the second, though his comrade, seduced his boyfriend. The first, enraged at him, retaliated by inducing the second's wife to commit adultery. The upshot was that they drew the entire governing class into their quarrel and split it into factions. That is precisely 25 why one should be circumspect when such things are beginning, and break up the factions of leaders and powerful men. For the error arises at the beginning, and "well begun is half done," as the saying goes. Consequently, even a small error at the beginning is comparable in effect to all 30 the errors made at the later stages.[36]

32. This paragraph seems out of place here.
33. Part of Clazomenae was on the mainland, part on an island. Notium was the seaport of Colophon.
34. See Plato, *Republic* 545c–d.
35. Thought to have occurred during the oligarchy of the Gamori, which was overthrown by the people shortly before Gelon's seizure of power in 485 (referred to at 1302ᵇ31).
36. Alternatively: "An error here is in the ruler (ARCHĒ). But 'the ruler (*archē*) is half of the whole,' as the saying goes. Hence a small error there is comparable in effect to all the errors made throughout the other parts (*merē*)."

Factions among the notables generally cause the whole city-state to
join in. For example, this happened in Hestiaea after the Persian wars
when two brothers quarreled over the division of their inheritance. The
poorer one, claiming that his brother had not declared the true value of
35   the property or of the treasure his father had found, enlisted the aid of
the people; and the other, who had much property, enlisted the aid of
the rich.[37] In Delphi, too, a quarrel arising from a marriage was the origin of all the subsequent factions. The bridegroom came to fetch the
1304ª   bride, but some accident occurred that he interpreted as a bad omen,
and he left without her. Her family considered that they had been
treated arrogantly, so they planted some sacred objects on him while he
was sacrificing, and then killed him as a temple robber. In Mytilene, a
conflict concerning heiresses was the source of many misfortunes, par-
5   ticularly, the war with the Athenians, in which Paches captured their
city-state.[38] For a rich citizen named Timophanes left behind two
daughters, and when Dexander, who wanted to obtain them for his sons,
had his suit rejected, he started a faction and incited the Athenians,
10   whose agent[39] he was, to interfere. Among the Phocians, an heiress was
the source of a conflict involving Mnaseas the father of Mnason and Eu-
thycrates the father of Onomarchus. This conflict was the beginning of
the sacred war for the Phocians.[40] In Epidamnus the constitution was
changed because of a marriage. For a man had betrothed his daughter,
15   and the father of the one to whom he had betrothed her became an official and imposed a fine on him, whereupon the first allied himself with
all those who were outside the constitution on the grounds that he had
been insulted.

Constitutions also change into oligarchies, democracies, or polities
when some office or part of the city-state acquires prestige or increases
in size. For example, the Council of the Areopagus, which won prestige
20   in the Persian wars, was held to have made the Athenian constitution

---

37. Referred to as Oreus at 1303ª18. Nothing else is known about this event,
which must have occurred prior to the absorption of Hestiaea by Athens in
446.
38. See Thucydides III.2–50.
39. An agent (*proxenos*), like a consul or ambassador, was the representative of
one city-state to another, but he was a citizen of the latter, not the former.
40. With Thebes (355–347), relating to control of the temple of Apollo at Delphi, which was situated on Phocian territory. The War was ended by Philip
of Macedon. Mnason seems to have been a friend of Aristotle's.

tighter;[41] in return, the seafaring crowd, who were responsible for victory at Salamis, and so for hegemony based on sea power, made the democracy more powerful.[42] In Argos the notables, having acquired prestige in connection with the battle against the Spartans at Mantinea, undertook to overthrow the democracy. In Syracuse the people, having been responsible for victory in the war against the Athenians, changed the constitution from a polity to a democracy. In Chalcis the people, with the aid of the notables, overthrew the tyrant Phoxus, and then immediately took control of the constitution. Similarly, in Ambracia the people joined with the opponents of Periander to expel him and afterwards took the constitution into their own hands.[43] Generally speaking, then, this should not be overlooked—that the people responsible for a city-state's power, whether private individuals, officials, tribes, or, in a word, a part or multitude of any sort, start faction. For either those who envy them for being honored start a faction, or they themselves, because of their superior achievement, are unwilling to remain as mere equals.

Constitutions also undergo change when parts of a city-state that are held to be opposed, such as the rich and the people, become equal to one another, and there is little or no middle class. For if either of the parts becomes greatly superior, the other will be unwilling to risk going up against their manifestly superior strength. That is why those who are outstandingly virtuous do not cause any faction, practically speaking, for they are few against many.

In general, then, the origins and causes of conflict and change are of this sort in all constitutions. But people change constitutions sometimes through force, sometimes through deceit. Force may be used right at the beginning or later on. Deceit is also employed in two ways. Sometimes they first deceive the others into consenting to a change in the constitution and then later keep hold of it by force when the others no longer consent. Thus the Four Hundred[44] deceived the Athenian people by telling them that the King of Persia would provide money for the war

41. That is to say, less democratic (1290ª22–29). Prior to the mid fifth century the Areopagus consisted of wealthy citizens of noble birth and was a powerfully oligarchic component of the Athenian constitution.

42. The navy was recruited from the poorest classes and was a powerfully democratic force in Athenian politics. See 1321ª13–14; Plato, *Republic* 396a–b, *Laws* 707b–c.

43. In *c*. 580. Further details are given at 1311ª39–ᵇ1.

44. The oligarchy which replaced the democracy at Athens in 411, described in Thucydides VIII.45–98.

against the Spartans, and, having deceived them, tried to keep the con-
15 stitution in their own hands. At other times, they persuade them at the
beginning, and continue to persuade them later on and rule with their
consent.

Simply stated, then, changes generally occur in all constitutions as a
result of the factors that have been stated.

Chapter 5

We must now take each kind of constitution separately and study what
happens to it as a result of these factors.

20   Democracies undergo change principally because of the wanton behavior of popular leaders,[45] who sometimes bring malicious lawsuits
against individual property owners, causing them to join forces (for a
shared fear unites even the bitterest enemies), and at others, openly egg
on the multitude against them. One may see this sort of thing happening
25 in many instances. In Cos the democracy was overthrown when evil popular leaders arose (for the notables banded together),[46] and also in
Rhodes. For the popular leaders provided pay for public service and prevented the naval officials from getting what they were owed; the latter
were then forced to unite and overthrow the democracy because of the
30 lawsuits brought against them.[47] Right after the colony was settled, the
democracy in Heraclea was also overthrown because of its popular leaders. For the notables were treated unjustly by them and went into exile.
Later the exiles united, returned home, and overthrew the democracy.
35 The democracy in Megara[48] was overthrown in a somewhat similar way.
For the popular leaders expelled many of the notables in order to declare
the latters' wealth public property, until they made numerous exiles.
The exiles then returned, defeated the people in battle, and established
an oligarchy.[49] A similar thing happened to the democracy in Cyme,

---

45. See 1292^{a}2–38, 1320^{a}4–17; Plato, *Republic* 565a–c.
46. Nothing is known about these events, but some have thought them to be
    connected with the defection of Cos from the Athenian Confederacy in 357.
47. The popular leaders used money owed to the naval officials (*triērarchoi*) for
    outfitting ships to pay the poor for public service on juries and the like. The
    officials were then sued by the creditors they were unable to pay.
48. Probably the colony of Megara on the Black Sea, founded in the middle of
    the sixth century. If so, it is a very early example of a democratic city-state.
49. Also referred to at 1302^{b}31.

which was overthrown by Thrasymachus.[50] Study would show that   *1305ª*
changes occur pretty much this way in the case of other city-states as
well. For popular leaders sometimes treat the notables unjustly in order
to curry favor with the people and force them to combine, by redistrib-
uting their properties or their income by means of PUBLIC SERVICES; and   *5*
sometimes they bring slanderous accusations against the rich so as to be
in a position to confiscate their property.

In ancient times, whenever the same person was both a popular leader
and a general, democracies changed to tyrannies. For the vast majority
of ancient tyrants started as popular leaders.[51] The reason this happened
then but not now is that then popular leaders came from the ranks of   *10*
those who held the office of general (for men were not yet skilled at public speaking). Now, however, with the development of rhetoric, capable
speakers become popular leaders. But because of their inexperience in
military matters, they do not try to become tyrants, although this may
have occurred in some places.

Tyrannies also arose more frequently in the past than they do now be-   *15*
cause important offices were in the hands of particular individuals, as in
Miletus, where one arose out of the presidency, because the president
had authority over many important matters.[52] Furthermore, city-states
were not large then and the people lived on their farms and were busy
with their work, so whenever democratic leaders became skilled war-   *20*
riors they attempted to establish a tyranny. They all did this after gain-
ing the people's trust, and this trust was based on their hatred of the
rich.[53] Thus Pisistratus started a faction against the plains-dwellers,[54] as
did Theagenes in Megara, because he slaughtered the rich men's cattle
when he caught them grazing by the river.[55] And Dionysius was judged   *25*
to merit the tyranny for prosecuting Daphnaeus and the rich. Because of
his hostility he was trusted as a man of the people.[56]

50. Nothing is known about this event.
51. See Plato, *Republic* 564d–566d.
52. Thought to be a reference to the tyranny of Thrasyboulus. See Herodotus
    I.20.
53. See 1310ᵇ14–16.
54. Pisitratus, the leader of the democratic "hill-dwellers," was later tyrant at
    Athens (561–527). The "plains-dwellers" were wealthy land owners. See
    Ath. XIII.4–XVII.2; Herodotus I.56–64.
55. Nothing is known about the events referred to.
56. Dionysius I prosecuted the Syracusan general Daphneus for failing to save
    Agrigentum from capture by the Carthaginians. See Diodorus Siculus
    XIII.86–96.

Democracies also change from the traditional kind to the newest kind. For when officials are elected, but not on the basis of a property assess-
30   ment, and the people do the electing, those seeking office, in order to curry favor, bring matters to this point, that the people have authority even over the laws. A remedy that prevents this, or diminishes its effect, is to have the tribes nominate the officials rather than the people as a whole.

Pretty well all the changes in democracies, then, happen for these rea-
40   sons.

Chapter 6

Oligarchies principally undergo change in two ways that are most evi-
dent. [1.1] The first is when they treat the multitude unjustly.[57] For any leader is adequate for the task when that happens, particularly if he comes from the ranks of the oligarchs themselves, like Lygdamis of Naxos, who actually became tyrant of the Naxians later on.[58] There are
1305ᵇ   also several other varieties of faction that originate with other people.[59] [1.2] For sometimes the overthrow comes from the rich themselves, though not the ones in office, when those holding the offices are very
5   few. This occurred in Massilia, Istrus, Heraclea, and other city-states, where those who did not participate in office agitated until first elder brothers and then younger ones were admitted. (For in some city-states, a father and son, and in others, an elder and younger brother, may not hold office simultaneously.) In Massilia, the oligarchy became more like
10   a polity; the one in Istrus ended in a democracy; and the one in Heraclea went from a small number to six hundred. [1.3] The oligarchy in Cnidus also changed when the notables became factionalized because so few participated in office, and, as was mentioned, if a father participated, his
15   son could not, nor, if there were several brothers, could any but the eldest alone. For while they were engaged in faction, the people intervened in the conflict, picked one of the notables as their leader, attacked, and were victorious (for what is factionalized is weak). And in Erythrae in ancient times, during the oligarchy of the Basilids, even though those with authority over the constitution governed well, the people neverthe-
20   less resented being ruled by a few and changed the constitution.[60]

---

57. The other is not discussed until 1305ᵇ22.
58. He became tyrant *c.* 540. See *Ath.* XV; Herodotus I.61, 64.
59. Other than the oligarchs themselves.
60. Nothing is known about these events. The revolt at Cnidus is referred to again at 1306ᵇ3–5.

[2] Oligarchies undergo change from within, however, [2.1] through the rivalry of those seeking popular leadership. This popular leadership is of two sorts. [2.1.1] One exists among the oligarchs themselves, since a popular leader can arise even when they are very few. For example, among the Thirty in Athens, Charicles and his followers became power- 25 ful by currying favor with the Thirty; and likewise in the time of the Four Hundred with Phrynichus and his followers.[61] [2.1.2] Another sort is where the oligarchs curry favor with the crowd. For example, in Lar- isa the guardians of the constitution[62] sought popularity with the crowd because it elected them. But the same holds in all oligarchies where 30 those who elect to office are not those from whom the officials are drawn, but offices are filled either from those with high property assess- ments or those who belong to certain political clubs, and the electors are either those who possess hoplite weapons or (as in Abydus) the people. It also happens wherever law courts are not drawn from the governing class; for by currying favor in order to influence judicial decisions the oligarchs change the constitution. This is what occurred in Heraclea on 35 the Black Sea.[63] [2.1.3] Moreover, it occurs when some draw the oli- garchy into fewer hands. For those who want equality are forced to bring in the people to assist them.

[2.2] Changes in oligarchy also occur when they spend their private resources on loose living. For such people seek to stir up change, and ei- 40 ther aim at tyranny themselves or help to institute it for someone else, as Hipparinus did for Dionysius in Syracuse.[64] In Amphipolis, a man 1306ᵃ named Cleotimus brought in late-settlers from Chalcis and, after they arrived, stirred up faction between them and the rich.[65] In Aegina, the man who negotiated with Chares tried to overthrow the constitution for 5 this sort of reason.[66] Sometimes such people try to make changes imme- diately; at other times they steal public funds. In the latter case, either they themselves or those who are opposed to their stealing start a faction against the oligarchs, which is what happened in Apollonia on the Black

---

61. The oligarchy of the Thirty Tyrants, of which Charicles was a member, was in control of Athens for a brief period in 404/3. The oligarchy of the Four Hundred gained control there in 411. See *Ath.* XXVIII–XXXVIII.

62. See 1268ª22, note.

63. Nothing is known about this event.

64. In 406–405.

65. Nothing is known about this event.

66. Chares was an Athenian general at the head of a troop of mercenaries sta- tioned in Corinth in 367 (a likely date for his negotiations).

Sea.[67] An oligarchy that is of one mind, however, is not easily destroyed
10   from within. The constitution in Pharsalus provides evidence of this;
for though the oligarchs are few in number, they have authority over
many because they treat one another well.[68]

[2.3] Oligarchies are also overthrown when another oligarchy is
formed within the oligarchy. This happens when, though the entire governing class consists of only a few people, not all of them participate in
15   the most important offices. This occurred once in Elis. The constitution
was in the hands of a few, but very few of them became senators. For the
senators, who numbered only ninety, held permanent office, and were
elected in a manner characteristic of a dynasty, like the one used to elect
the senators in Sparta.[69]

20   [2.4] Change in oligarchies occurs both in wartime and in peacetime.
[2.4.1] It occurs in wartime when the oligarchs are forced by their distrust of the people to employ mercenaries. For the man placed in charge
of them often becomes a tyrant, like Timophanes in Corinth.[70] And if
several men are placed in charge of them, they often set up a dynasty for
themselves. Sometimes fear of these consequences leads the oligarchs to
25   give a share of the constitution to the multitude, because they are forced
to make use of the people. [2.4.2] In peacetime, mutual distrust sometimes leads the oligarchs to put their defense in the hands of mercenaries and a neutral official, and he then occasionally gains authority over
both sides. This happened in Larisa at the time of the rule of Simus the
30   Aleuad, and in Abydos at the time of the political clubs, one of which
was that of Iphiades.[71]

[2.5] Factions also arise over marriages and lawsuits when some members of an oligarchy are scorned by others and are driven to start a faction. For example, the cases mentioned earlier in which marriage was
the cause.[72] And Diagoras overthrew the oligarchy of the cavalrymen in

67. The thieves attack the oligarchs to avoid punishment; their opponents do so
    if they sanction the theft of public funds. Nothing is known about the event
    referred to.
68. Nothing is known about this oligarchy.
69. See 1271ª9–18.
70. Timophanes became tyrant in 350, during the war with Argos, and was later
    killed by his brother Timolean. See Plutarch, *Timoleon* IV.4–8.
71. The Aleuds were a great Thessalian family. The Simus referred to is most
    probably the one who helped bring Thessaly into subjection to Philip of
    Macedon in 342. Nothing is know about the events in Abydos.
72. At 1303ᵇ37–1304ª17.

Eretria because he was treated unjustly in connection with a marriage. 35
The faction in Heraclea and Thebes arose over a decision in a law court,
when Eurytion (in Heraclea) and Archias (in Thebes) were justly but
factiously punished for adultery by the courts. For motivated by factional rivalry, their enemies had them bound in the pillory in the mar- 1306^b
ketplace.[73]

[2.6] Many have also been overthrown by those in the constitution
who became resentful because the oligarchies were too much like the
rule of a master, as, for example, the one in Cnidus and the one in
Chios.[74] 5

But changes also occur because of accidents both in so-called polities
and in oligarchies, where eligibility for the council, the courts, and the
other offices is based on a property assessment. For often the first assessment is set to suit existing circumstances, so that only a few will participate in the oligarchy and only the middle classes in the polity. But 10
when peace or some other sort of good luck leads to prosperity, properties come to be assessed at many times their original value, so that all the
citizens participate in all the offices. Sometimes the change happens
gradually and is unnoticed; at other times it happens quickly. 15

Oligarchies change and factionalize, then, for these sorts of reasons.
But, generally speaking, both democracies and oligarchies sometimes
change not into the opposing kinds of constitutions but into others of
the same type; for example, from democracies and oligarchies based on
law into those with complete authority,[75] and vice versa. 20

Chapter 7

[1] In aristocracies factions arise because few people participate in office, which is just what is said to change oligarchies as well,[76] because
aristocracy too is oligarchy of a sort. For the rulers are few in both,
though not for the same reason. At any rate, that is why an aristocracy 25
too is thought to be a kind of oligarchy. [1.1] Such conflict is particularly
inevitable [1.1.1] when there is a group of people who consider themselves equal in virtue to the ruling few—for example, the so-called Sons

---

73. Nothing is known about these events. Pillory was not a punishment com-
    monly inflicted on notables.
74. See 1305^{b}12–18. Nothing is known about the events in Chios.
75. See 1292^{a}4–6 (democracies), 1292^{b}5–10 (oligarchies).
76. At 1306^{a}13–22.

30   of the Maidens at Sparta (for they were descended from the Equals),
who were discovered in a conspiracy and sent off to colonize Tarentum;[77] or [1.1.2] when powerful men who are inferior to no one in virtue
are dishonored by others who are more esteemed, as Lysander was by
the kings; or [1.1.3] when a man of courage does not participate in office,
like Cinadon, who instigated the rebellion against the Spartiates in the
35   reign of Agesilaus;[78] or, again, [1.2] when some people are very poor and
others very rich, a situation which is particularly prevalent in wartime,
and also happened in Sparta at the time of the Messenian war (this is
clear from the poem of Tyrtaeus called "Good Government"),[79] for
1307ᵃ   those who were hard pressed because of the war demanded a redistribution of the land; or, again, [1.3] when there is a powerful man capable of
becoming still more powerful, who instigates conflict in order to become
sole ruler, as Pausanias (who was general during the Persian war) is held
5   to have done in Sparta, and Annon in Carthage.[80]

[2] Polities and aristocracies are principally overthrown, however, because of a deviation from justice within the constitution itself. For what
begins the process in a polity is failing to get a good mixture of democracy and oligarchy, and in an aristocracy, failing to get a good mixture of
these and virtue as well, but particularly the two. I mean by the two
10   democracy and oligarchy, since these are what polities and most so-
called aristocracies try to mix. For aristocracies differ from what are
termed polities in this,[81] and this is why the former of them are less and

77. The Equals (*homoioi*) were Spartan citizens, born of citizen parents, who
possessed sufficient wealth to enable them to participate in the communal
meals (see 1271ᵃ25–37). Various ancient accounts are given of the Sons of
the Maidens: they were the offspring of Spartans degraded to the rank of
helots for failing to serve in the First Messanian War; they were the illegitimate sons of young unmarried Spartan women who were encouraged to increase the population during that war; or they were the sons of adulterous
Spartan women conceived while their husbands were fighting in that war.
They founded Tarentum in 708.
78. Lysander was a Spartan general whose plans were thwarted by king Pausanius in 403, and later by king Agesilaus. Cinadon's rebellion of 398 was discovered and he was executed. See Xenophon, *Hellenica* II.4.29; Plutarch,
Lysander XXIII.
79. See Diehl I.7–9, fr. 2–5. Tyrtaeus was a seventh century Spartan elegiac
poet.
80. Annon's identity is uncertain. He may be the Carthaginian general of that
name who fought against Dionysius II in Sicily, *c.* 400.
81. In their way of mixing democracy and oligarchy.

the latter more stable. For those constitutions that lean more toward oligarchy get called aristocracies, whereas those that lean more toward the *15* multitude get called polities. That is why, indeed, the latter sort are more secure than the former. For the majority of citizens are the more powerful party and they are quite content with an equal share; whereas if the rich are granted superiority by the constitution, they act arrogantly and try to get even more for themselves.

Generally speaking, whichever direction a constitution leans is the di- *20* rection in which it changes when either party grows in power, for example, polity into democracy and aristocracy into oligarchy. Or it changes in the opposite direction; for example, aristocracy changes into democracy (when the poorer people pull it toward its opposite because they are being unjustly treated), and polity changes into oligarchy. For the only *25* stable thing is equality in accordance with merit and the possession of private property. The aforementioned change[82] occurred at Thurii. Because the property assessment for holding office was rather high, a change was made to a smaller one and to a larger number of offices. But because the notables illegally acquired all the land (for the constitution *30* was still too oligarchic), they were able as a result to get more. But the people, who had received military training during the war, proved stronger than the garrison troops, and forced those who had more than their fair share of the land to give it up.

Moreover, [3] because all aristocratic constitutions are oligarchic in character, the notables in them tend to get more. Even in Sparta, for ex- *35* ample, properties keep passing into fewer and fewer hands. The notables are also freer to do as they please and make marriage alliances as they please. The city-state of the Locrians was ruined, indeed, because a marriage alliance was formed with the tyrant Dionysius, something that would not have occurred in a democracy or a well-mixed aristocracy.[83]

[4] Aristocracies are particularly apt to change imperceptibly by being *40* overturned little by little. This is precisely what was said earlier as a gen- *1307ᵇ* eral point about all constitutions,[84] namely, that even a small thing can cause them to change. For once one thing relating to the constitution is

82. From aristocracy to democracy. Nothing is known for certain about the events referred to.
83. Locri accepted a marriage alliance with Dionysius I, who was tyrant of Syracuse 367–356, 346–343. Later (starting in 356) it suffered under the oppressive tyranny of the offspring of this marriage, Dionysius II.
84. At 1303ᵃ20–1304ᵇ18.

abandoned, people can more easily change something slightly larger
5   next time, until they alter the entire order. This also happened to the
constitution of Thurii. For the law allowed the same man to be general
only after a four-year interval. But when some of the young men showed
military ability and became popular with the multitude of garrison
troops, they came to have contempt for the men who were in charge of
10   affairs, and thought that they themselves could easily prevail. They first
undertook to abrogate this law, so as to make it possible for the same men
to serve as generals continuously, for they saw that the people would
vote for them with enthusiasm. The officials in charge of such matters,
the so-called councilors, were at first inclined to oppose this. But they
15   were won over, because they thought that once this law was changed, the
rest of the constitution would be left alone. Later, however, when they
wished to prevent other things from being changed, they were unable to
do anything more, and the entire organization of the constitution was
changed into a dynasty ruled by those men who had begun the process
of stirring up change.[85]

All constitutions are subject to change, however, (sometimes from
20   outside, sometimes from within) when there is a constitution of the opposite type either nearby or far away but powerful. This is what happened in the time of the Athenian and Spartan empires. For the Athenians overthrew oligarchies everywhere, and the Spartans democracies.[86]

Pretty well all the origins of change and faction in constitutions have
25   now been discussed.

Chapter 8

Our next topic is the preservation of constitutions generally and each
kind of constitution separately. [1] It is clear, in the first place, that if we
know what destroys a constitution, we also know what preserves it. For
opposites are productive of opposite things, and destruction is opposite
30   to preservation. In well-mixed constitutions, then, if care should be
taken to ensure that no one breaks the law in other ways, small violations
should be particularly guarded against. For illegality creeps in unnoticed, in just the way that property gets used up by frequent small expenditures: the expense goes unnoticed because it does not occur all at
35   once. For the mind is led to reason fallaciously by them, as in the so-

85. Nothing else is known about these events.
86. During the Peloponnesian war. See 1296ª32–ᵇ1, 1312ª39–ᵇ4.

phistical argument "if each is small, all are also." In one way this is true; in another false: the whole composed of all the parts is not small, but it is composed of small parts. One thing to guard against, then, is destruction that has a starting point of this sort.

[2] Secondly, we must not put our faith in the devices that are designed to deceive the multitude, since they are shown to be useless by the facts. (I mean the sort of devices used in constitutions that we discussed earlier.)[87]

[3] Next, we should notice that not only some aristocracies but also some oligarchies survive, not because their constitutions are secure, but because those in office treat well both those outside the constitution and those in the governing class. They do this by not being unjust to the nonparticipants and by bringing their leading men into the constitution; by not being unjust to those who love honor by depriving them of honor, or to the many by depriving them of profit; and by treating each other, the ones who do participate, in a democratic manner. For what democrats seek to extend to the multitude, namely, equality, is not only just for those who are similar but also beneficial. That is why, if the governing class is large, many democratic legislative measures prove beneficial, for example, having offices be tenable for six months in order that all those who are similar can participate in them. For those who are similar are already a people of a sort, which is why popular leaders arise even among them, as we mentioned earlier.[88] Furthermore, oligarchies and aristocracies of this sort are less likely to fall into the hands of dynasties. For officials who rule a short time cannot so easily do wrong as those who rule a long time. For this is what causes tyrannies to arise in oligarchies and democracies, since in both constitutions, the ones who attempt to establish a tyranny are either the most powerful (popular leaders in democracies, dynasts in oligarchies) or those who hold the most important offices, and hold them for a long time.

[4] Constitutions are preserved not only because of being far away from what destroys them, but sometimes too because they are nearby.[89] For fear makes people keep a firmer grip on the constitution. Hence those who are concerned about their constitution should excite fears and make faraway dangers seem close at hand, so that the citizens will de-

87. At IV.13. Aristotle seems to encourage the use of just such a device at 1308ᵃ28–30.
88. At 1305ᵇ23–27.
89. See 1307ᵇ19–21.

fend the constitution and, like sentries on night-duty, never relax their
guard.

[5] Moreover, one should try to guard against the rivalries and factions of the notables, both by means of the laws and by preventing those
who are not involved in the rivalry from getting caught up in it themselves. For it takes no ordinary person to recognize an evil right from the
beginning but a man who is a statesman.

[6] As for change from an oligarchy or a polity because of property assessments—if it occurs while the assessments remain the same but
money becomes more plentiful, it is beneficial to discover what the total
communal assessment is compared with that of the past; with that of last
year's in city-states with annual assessment, with that of three or five
years ago in larger city-states. If the total is many times greater or many
times less than it was when the rates qualifying someone to participate
in the constitution were established, it is beneficial to have a law that
tightens or relaxes the assessment; tightening it in proportion to the increase if the total has increased, relaxing it or making it less if the total
has decreased. For when oligarchies and polities do not do this, the result is that if the total has decreased, an oligarchy arises from the latter
and a dynasty from the former, and if it has increased, a democracy
arises from a polity and either a polity or a democracy from an oligarchy.

[7] It is a rule common to democracy, oligarchy, monarchy, and every
constitution not to allow anyone to grow too great or out of all due proportion, but to try to give small honors over a long period of time rather
than large ones quickly. For people are corrupted by major honors, and
not every man can handle good luck.[90] Failing that, constitutions should
at least try not to take away all at once honors that have been awarded all
at once, but to do so gradually. They should try to regulate matters by
means of the laws, indeed, so as to ensure that no one arises who is far
superior in power because of his friends or wealth. Failing that, they
should ensure that such men are removed from the city-state by being
ostracized.[91]

[8] But since people also attempt to stir up change because of their
private lives, an office should be set up to keep an eye on those whose
lifestyles are not beneficial to the constitution, whether to the democracy in a democracy, to the oligarchy in an oligarchy, or similarly for

90. See 1334[a]25–34, *NE* 1153[b]19–25.
91. See 1302[b]15–21.

each of the other constitutions. For the same reasons, one must guard against the prospering of the city-state one part at a time.[92] A remedy for this is always to place the conduct of affairs and the offices in the hands of opposite parts. (I mean that the decent are opposite to the multitude, the poor to the rich.) Another remedy is to try to mix the multitude of the poor with that of the rich or to increase the middle class, since this dissolves faction caused by inequality.

[9] But the most important thing in every constitution is for it have the laws and the management of other matters organized in such a way that it is impossible to make a profit from holding office.[93] One should pay particular heed to this in oligarchies. For the many are not as resentful at being excluded from office—they are even glad to be given the leisure to attend to their private affairs—as they are when they think that officials are stealing public funds. At any rate, they are then pained both at not sharing in office and at not sharing in its profits. Indeed, the only way it is possible for democracy and aristocracy to coexist is if someone instituted this,[94] since it would then be possible for both the notables and the multitude to have what they want. For allowing everyone to hold office is democratic, but having the notables actually hold the offices is aristocratic. But this is what will happen if it is impossible to profit from office. For the poor will not want to hold office, because there is no profit in it, but will prefer to attend to their private affairs, whereas the rich will be able to hold it, because they need no support from public funds. The result will be that the poor will become rich through spending their time working, and the notables will not have to be ruled by anybody and everybody. But to prevent public funds from being stolen, the transfer of the money[95] should take place in the presence of all citizens, and copies of the accounts should be deposited with each clan, company,[96] and tribe. And to ensure that people will hold office without seeking profit, there should be a law that assigns honors to reputable officials.

92. So that one part prospers while another does not.
93. See Plato, *Republic* 520e–521b.
94. That is to say, made it impossible for people to profit from holding office. A constitution in which aristocratic and democratic coexist is described in IV.9.
95. From an official leaving office to his successor.
96. A company (*lochos*) was originally a military classification, but here it refers to a civil administrative division of the city-state.

[10] In democracies, the rich should be treated with restraint, not
15   only by not having redistributions of their property but by not having
redistributions of their incomes either (as happens unnoticed in some
constitutions). It is also better to prevent the rich, even if they are willing to do so, from taking on expensive but useless public services, such
as equipping choruses, officiating at torch races, and other similar
things. In an oligarchy, on the other hand, one should take good care of
20   the poor, and distribute offices that yield some gain to them. If a rich
person treats them arrogantly, his punishment should be greater than if
he treated a member of his own class arrogantly. Inheritances should be
passed on not by bequest but by kinship, and the same person should
not receive more than one inheritance. In this way, property holdings
25   would be more equitable, and more of the poor could join the ranks of
the rich. It is beneficial, both in democracy and in oligarchy, to give either equality or preference in all other matters to those who participate
least in the constitution, the rich in a democracy and the poor in an oli-
30   garchy. But the offices of the constitution that have supreme authority
should be kept solely or largely in the hands of those who do participate
in the constitution.

Chapter 9

Those who are to hold the offices with supreme authority should possess three qualities: first, friendship for the established constitution;
35   next, the greatest possible capacity for the tasks of office; third, in each
constitution the sort of virtue or justice that is suited to the constitution
(for if what is just is not the same in all constitutions, there must be differences in the virtue of justice as well). But there is a problem. When all
of these qualities are not found in the same person, how is the choice to
40   be made? For example, if one man is an expert general but is vicious and
1309^b no friend to the constitution, whereas another is just and friendly to it,
how should the choice be made? It seems that one should consider two
things: which quality does everyone have a larger share in, and which a
smaller one? That is why, in the case of a generalship, one should consider experience more than virtue. For everyone shares in generalship
5   less, but in decency more. In the case of guardianship or stewardship, on
the other hand, the opposite holds. For these require more virtue than
the many possess, but the knowledge they require is common to all. One
might also raise the following problem. If someone has the capacity for
the tasks of office as well as friendship for the constitution, why does he

also need virtue, since even the first two will produce beneficial results? *10*
Or is it possible for someone who possesses these two qualities to be
weak-willed, so that just as people can fail to serve their own interests
well even though they have the knowledge and are friendly to themselves, so nothing prevents them from behaving in the same way where
the common interest is concerned?

Simply speaking, everything in laws that we say is beneficial to constitutions also preserves those constitutions, as does the most important *15*
fundamental principle, so often mentioned, of keeping watch to ensure
that the multitude that wants the constitution is stronger than the multitude that does not.[97]

In addition to all this, one thing must not be overlooked, which is in
fact overlooked by deviant constitutions: the mean. For many of the
things that are held to be democratic destroy democracies, and many *20*
that are held to be oligarchic destroy oligarchies. But those who think
that this[98] is the only kind of virtue push the constitution to extremes.
They do not know that constitutions are just like parts of the body. A
straight nose is the most beautiful, but one that deviates from being
straight and tends toward being hooked or snub can nevertheless still be
beautiful to look at. Yet if it is tightened still more toward the extreme, *25*
the part will first be thrown out of due proportion, and in the end it will
cease to look like a nose at all, because it has too much of one and too little of the other of these opposites. The same holds of the other parts as
well. This can also happen in the case of the constitutions. For it is pos- *30*
sible for an oligarchy or a democracy to be adequate even though it has
diverged from the best organization. But if someone tightens either of
them more, he will first make the constitution worse, and in the end it
will not be a constitution at all. That is why legislators and statesmen *35*
should not be ignorant about which democratic features preserve a
democracy and which destroy it, or which oligarchic features have these
effects on an oligarchy. For neither of these constitutions can exist and
survive without rich people and the multitude, but when a leveling of
property occurs, the resulting constitution is necessarily of a different
kind. Hence by destroying these classes through extreme legislation, *40*
they destroy their constitution. *1310ᵃ*

A mistake is made in both democracies and oligarchies. In democracies popular leaders make it where the multitude have authority over the

---

97. See 1270ᵇ21–22 and note.
98. Virtue as they conceive of it. See Introduction lxvi–lxviii.

laws. For they divide the city-state in two by always fighting with the
5   rich, yet they should do the opposite, and always be regarded as spokesmen for the rich. In oligarchies, the oligarchs should be regarded as
spokesmen for the people, and should take oaths that are the opposite of
the ones they take nowadays. For in some oligarchies, they now swear
"and I will be hostile to the people and will plan whatever wrongs I can
10 against them." But they ought to hold and to seem to hold the opposite
view, and declare in their oaths that "I will not wrong the people."[99]

But of all the ways that are mentioned to make a constitution last, the
most important one, which everyone now despises, is for citizens to be
educated in a way that suits their constitutions. For the most beneficial
15 laws, even when ratified by all who are engaged in politics, are of no use
if people are not habituated and educated in accord with the constitution—democratically if the laws are democratic and oligarchically if
they are oligarchic. For if weakness of will indeed exists in a single individual, it also exists in a city-state. But being educated in a way that suits
20 the constitution does not mean doing whatever pleases the oligarchs or
those who want a democracy. Rather, it means doing the things that will
enable the former to govern oligarchically and the latter to have a democratic constitution. In present-day oligarchies, however, the sons of the
rulers live in luxury, whereas the sons of the poor are hardened by exercise and toil, so that the poor are more inclined to stir up change and are
25 better able to do so. In those democracies that are held to be particularly
democratic, the very opposite of what is beneficial has become established. The reason for this is that they define freedom incorrectly. For
there are two things by which democracy is held to be defined: by the
majority being in supreme authority and by freedom. For justice is held
30 to be equality; equality is for the opinion of the multitude to be in authority; and freedom is doing whatever one likes. So in democracies of
this sort everyone lives as he likes, and "according to his fancy," as Euripides says.[100] But this is bad. For living in a way that suits the constitu-
35 tion should be considered not slavery, but salvation.[101]

Such, then, simply speaking, are the sources of change and destruction in constitutions, and the factors through which they are preserved
and maintained.

---

99. See Aristotle's advice to tyrants at 1314ª29–1315ᵇ10.
100. Nauck 646, fr. 891. See 1316ᵇ24, 1319ᵇ30; Plato, *Republic* 557b.
101. See Introduction lxii–lxiv.

Chapter 10

It remains to go through monarchy too, both the sources of its destruction and the means by which it is naturally preserved. What happens in   *40* the case of kingships and tyrannies is pretty much similar to what we said happens in constitutions. For kingship is akin to aristocracy, and   *1310ᵇ* tyranny is a combination of ultimate oligarchy and ultimate democracy.[102] That is why, indeed, tyranny is also the most harmful to those it rules, seeing that it is composed of two bad constitutions and involves   *5* the deviations and errors of both.

Each of these kinds of monarchy comes to be from directly opposite circumstances. For kingship came into existence to help the decent against the people,[103] and a king is selected from among the decent men   *10* on the basis of a superiority in virtue, or in the actions that spring from virtue, or on the basis of a superiority of family of this sort. A tyrant, on the other hand, comes from the people (that is to say, the multitude) to oppose the notables, so that the people may suffer no injustice at their hands. This is evident from what has happened. For almost all tyrants began as popular leaders who were trusted because they abused the no-   *15* tables. For some tyrannies were established in this way in city-states that had already grown large. Other earlier ones arose when kings departed from ancestral customs and sought to rule more in the manner of a master. Others were established by people elected to the offices that have supreme authority; for in ancient times, the people appointed "doers of   *20* the people's business" and "sacred ambassadors" to serve for long periods of time.[104] Still others arose in oligarchies that gave a single elected official authority over the most important offices. For in all these ways people could easily become tyrants if only they wished, because of the power they already possessed through the kingship or through other   *25*

---

102. Kingship corresponds to aristocracy because both are based on virtue or merit (1289ᵃ30–35, 1310ᵇ32–34). Ultimate oligarchy is dynasty (1293ᵃ30–34); the ultimate democracy is where the people are in authority rather than the laws (1293ᵃ1–10). On the nature of tyranny as a mixture of these two forms, see 1296ᵃ3–4, 1312ᵇ34–38.

103. Reading *epi ton dēmon*. The help he provides is not partisan, however, but just to both parties (1310ᵇ40–1311ᵃ2). Alternatively (Dreizehnter and the mss.): "to provide help from the people (*apo tou dēmou*) for the decent."

104. See 1308ᵃ19–24. "Doers of the people's business" (*dēmiourgoi*) existed in many Greek city-states; "sacred ambassadors" (*theōroi*) were sent to attend religious games and festivals and to consult oracles.

high office. Thus Pheidon of Argos and others became tyrants having already ruled as kings; the Ionian tyrants and Phalaris as a result of their high office; and Panaetius in Leontini, Cypselus in Corinth, Pisistratus in Athens, Dionysius in Syracuse, and likewise others, from having been popular leaders.[105]

Kingship is, then, as we said,[106] an organization like aristocracy, since it is based on merit, whether individual or familial virtue, or on benefactions, or on these together with the capacity to perform them. For all those who obtained this office either had benefited or were capable of benefiting their city-states or nations. Some, like Codrus, saved their people from enslavement in war; others, like Cyrus, set them free; others acquired or settled territory, like the kings of the Spartans, Macedonians, and Molossians.[107] A king tends to be a guardian, seeing to it that property owners suffer no injustice and the people no arrogance. But tyranny, as has often been said,[108] never looks to the common benefit except for the sake of private profit. A tyrant aims at what is pleasant; a king at what is noble; and that is why it is characteristic of a tyrant to be most acquisitive of wealth[109] and of a king to be most acquisitive of what is noble. Also, a king's bodyguard consists of citizens, whereas a tyrant's consists of foreigners.[110]

That tyranny has the vices of both democracy and oligarchy is evident. From oligarchy comes its taking wealth to be its end (for, indeed, only in this way can the tyrant possibly maintain his bodyguard and his luxury), and its mistrust of the multitude (which is why, indeed, tyrants deprive them of weapons). It is common to both constitutions (oligarchy and tyranny) to ill-treat the multitude, drive them out of the town, and disperse them. From democracy, on the other hand, comes its hostility

105. Pheidon as tyrant in the middle of the seventh century. Phalaris was a notoriously cruel sixth-century tyrant of Agrigentum in Sicily. For Pisistratus, see 1305^{a}23–24 note. Cypselus was tyrant of Corinth *c.* 655–625. Dionysius is Dionysius I.

106. At 1310^{b}2–3.

107. Codrus was a legendary early king of Athens. According to one traditional account he was already king when he gave his life to prevent Athens from Dorian invasion. Cyrus was the first ruler of the Persian empire (559–529); he freed Persia from the Medes in 559. Neoptolemus, the son of Achilles, conquered the Molossians and became their king.

108. For example, at 1279^{b}6–10, 1295^{a}17–22.

109. On the connection between wealth and the pursuit of pleasure, see 1257^{b}40–1258^{a}5.

110. See 1285^{a}24–29.

to the notables, its destruction of them both by covert and overt means, and its exiling of them as rivals in the craft of ruling and impediments to its rule. For it is from the notables that conspiracies arise, since some of them wish to rule themselves, and others not to be enslaved. Hence too the advice that Periander gave to Thrasybulus when he cut down the   20
tallest ears of corn, namely, that it is always necessary to do away with the outstanding citizens.[111]

As has pretty much been said, then, one should consider the sources of change both in CONSTITUTIONS and in monarchies to be the same. For it is because of injustice, fear, and contemptuous treatment that   25
many subjects attack monarchies. In the case of injustice, arrogance is the principal cause, but sometimes too the seizure of private property. The ends sought are also the same there as in tyrannies and kingships, since monarchs possess the great wealth and high office that everyone   30
desires.

In some cases, attack is directed against the person of the rulers; in others, against their office. Those caused by arrogance are directed against the person. Arrogance has many forms, but each of them is a cause of anger; and most angry people act out of revenge, not ambition.   35
For example, the attack on the Pisistratids took place because they abused Harmodius' sister and showed contempt for Harmodius himself (for Harmodius attacked because of his sister, and Aristogeiton because of Harmodius).[112] People plotted against Periander, tyrant of Ambracia, because once when he was drinking with his boyfriend, he asked   40
whether he was pregnant by him yet. Philip was attacked by Pausanias   1311[b]
because he allowed him to be treated arrogantly by Attalus and his coterie.[113] Amyntas the Little was attacked by Derdas because he boasted of having deflowered him.[114] The same is true of the attack on Evagoras of Cyprus by a eunuch;[115] he felt arrogantly treated because Evagoras'   5
son had taken away his wife.

Many attacks have also occurred because of the shameful treatment of other people's bodies by certain monarchs. The attack on Archelaus[116]

111. See 1284[a]26–33.
112. The attack on the Athenian Pisistratid tyranny in 514 is discussed in *Ath*. XVIII, Herodotus V.55–65, Thucydides VI.54–9.
113. Philip of Macedon was murdered by Pausanius (a young Macedonian) in 330.
114. Amyntas and Dardas are otherwise unknown.
115. Evagoras ruled Salamis in Cyprus from 411 until his death in 374.
116. King of Macedon 413–399. See Plutarch, *Amatorius* 23.

by Crataeas is an example. For Crataeas always felt disgust at their sexual
10   relations, so that even a lesser excuse than the fact that Archelaus did not
give him one of his daughters in marriage, though he had agreed to do
so, would have been enough. (Instead, when hard pressed in the war
against Sirras and Arrabaeus, Archelaus gave his elder daughter to the
king of Elimeia and the younger one to his own son Amyntas, thinking
that this would be likely to prevent Amyntas from quarreling with his
15   son by Cleopatra.) In any case, the source of Crataeas' estrangement was
his disgust at his sexual activities with Archelaus. Hellanocrates of Larisa joined him in the attack for the same reason. For because Archelaus
deflowered him and then persistently refused to return him to his home
as promised, he thought that the king's sexual relations with him were
20   motivated by arrogance rather than sexual desire. Python and Heraclei-
des of Aenus, on the other hand, killed Cotys[117] to avenge their father.
But Adamas revolted on the grounds of arrogant treatment, because he
had been castrated by him when he was a boy.

Many people, outraged by blows to their bodies, have, on the grounds
of arrogant treatment, killed or tried to kill those responsible, even those
25   who held office or were associated with kingly dynasties. For example,
when the Penthilids of Mytilene[118] went around beating up people with
clubs, Megacles and his friends attacked and killed them. Later, Smerdis
killed Penthilus because he had dragged him away from his wife and
30   beaten him. Decamnichus became leader of the revolt against Archelaus
and was the first to incite his adversaries. The reason for his anger was that
Archelaus had handed him over to the poet Euripides for flogging (Euripides had been enraged by a remark he had made about his bad breath).
35   Many others have been killed or plotted against for reasons such as these.

Similar attacks also occur out of fear, which is a cause of change in
monarchies and constitutions, as we mentioned.[119] For example, Artapanes
killed Xerxes because he feared that he would be accused in connection
with the murder of Darius. Artapanes had hanged him without being or-
dered to do so by Xerxes, thinking he would be pardoned, since Xerxes
would not remember what orders he had given on account of his dining.[120]

117. King of Thrace 382–358.
118. The ruling family in the early Mytilenian oligarchy, which claimed descent
       from Penthilus, an illegitimate son of Orestes.
119. At 1311ª25.
120. Xerxes was king of Persia; Darius was his son; Artapanes (or Artabanus)
       was the captain of Xerxes' bodyguard. Presumably, Xerxes usually drank
       heavily at dinner.

Other attacks on monarchs have been motivated by contempt. Thus, *40*
if what the storytellers say is true, a man killed Sardanapalus[121] out of
contempt because he saw him carding wool with the women (though if *1312ᵃ*
this is not true of Sardanapalus, it might well be true of someone else).
And Dion attacked Dionysius the Younger out of contempt, when he
saw that the citizens had the same reactions to his always being drunk.[122] *5*
Even a monarch's friends sometimes attack him out of contempt. For
the fact that they are trusted makes them contemptuous and confident
they will not be discovered. And those who think they have the power to
take over as ruler attack out of contempt in a way. For it is because of
their power and the contempt for the danger their power gives them that *10*
they are ready to try their luck. That is why generals attack their monarchs. For example, Cyrus attacked Astyages out of contempt both for
his lifestyle and for his power, which had declined while he was living in
luxury. And Seuthes the Thracian attacked Amadocus while he was his
general.[123]

Others attack monarchs from several of these motives, as Mithridates *15*
attacked Ariobarzanes out of contempt and out of a desire for profit.[124]
Attempts of this sort are made principally by those of a bold nature who
are assigned to military office by their monarch. For boldness is courage
combined with power, and it is because of both of these that people attack and think that they will easily prevail.[125] *20*

In cases where the attack is motivated by love of honor, however, the
explanation is of a different sort from those previously discussed. For
some attack tyrants because they see great profit and high office in store
for themselves, but this is not why someone whose attack is motivated by
love of honor deliberately chooses to take the risk. The former attack for *25*
the reasons mentioned, but the latter do so for the same reason that they
would do any other extraordinary deed that made a name for themselves
and made them notable in the eyes of others: because they want not

121. The last king of the Assyrian empire at Nineveh.
122. See 1312ᵇ16–18; Plutarch, *Dion* 22–51.
123. Astyages was the last king of the Medes (594–559). Cyrus was his grand-
     son as well as his general. See Herodotus I.107–30. Amadocus was king of
     the Odrysians. The events in Thrace are otherwise unknown.
124. Perhaps the Ariobarzanes who was satrap of the Persian province of Pontus
     from 363 to 336, and was succeeded by his son Mithridates II.
125. This sentence seems to have been transposed from the end of the previous
     paragraph, or, as Newman suggests, from directly following the word
     "drunk" (*methuonta*) at ᵃ6.

30 monarchy but fame. Nevertheless, very few people are impelled by this sort of motive, since it presupposes a total disregard for their own safety in the event that the action is not successful. They must be guided by the same fundamental principle as Dion (something that is not easy for most people). For Dion accompanied by a small force marched against

35 Dionysius, saying that whatever point he was able to reach, he would be satisfied to have completed that much of the enterprise, and that if, for example, he were killed after having just set foot on land, he would have a noble death.

Like each of the other constitutions, one way a tyranny is destroyed is

40 from the outside, if there is a more powerful constitution opposed to
1312ᵇ it.[126] For the wish to destroy a tyranny will clearly be present, because the deliberate choices of the two are opposed; and people always do what they wish when they have the power. The constitutions opposed to tyranny are democracy, kingship, and aristocracy. Democracy is opposed to it as "potter to potter" (as Hesiod puts it),[127] since the extreme sort of

5 democracy is also a tyranny.[128] Kingship and aristocracy are opposed to it because of opposition of constitution. That is why the Spartans overthrew a large number of tyrannies, as did the Syracusans while they were well governed.

Another way a tyranny is destroyed is from within, when those participating in it start a faction. This happened in the tyranny of the family of

10 Gelon and, in our own time, in that of the family of Dionysius. The tyranny of Gelon was destroyed when Thrasyboulus, the brother of Hiero, curried favor with Gelon's son and led him into a life of sensual pleasure, in order that he himself might rule. The family got together to destroy not the entire tyranny, but Thrasyboulus.[129] But those who

15 joined them seized the opportunity and expelled all of them. Dion, who was related by marriage to Dionysius, marched against him, won over the people, and expelled him, but was himself killed afterwards.

The two principal motives people have for attacking tyrannies are hatred and contempt. Of them, hatred always attaches to tyrants, but many

126. See 1307ᵇ19–25.
127. *Works and Days* 25.
128. See 1292ª2–38.
129. Gelon was tyrant of Syracuse (485–478). He was succeeded by his brother Hiero who died in 467. Thrasyboulus succeeded in becoming tyrant of Syracuse on Hiero's death. He had been in control for just ten months when the tyranny was overthrown in 466. See 1315ᵇ34–39.

overthrows are due to contempt. Evidence of this is the fact that most of   20
those who won the office of tyrant held onto it, whereas their successors
almost all lost it right away. For living lives of indulgence, they easily became contemptible and gave others ample opportunity to attack them.   25
Anger must also be considered a part of the hatred, since in a way it
gives rise to the same sorts of actions. Often, in fact, it is more conducive to action than hatred. For angry people attack more vehemently
because passion does not employ rational calculation. People are particularly apt to be led by their angry spirit on account of arrogant treatment. This was the cause of both the overthrow of the Pisistratid   30
tyranny and that of many others. But hatred employs calculation more
than anger does. For anger involves pain, and pain makes rational calculation difficult; but hatred does not involve pain.

To speak summarily, however, the causes that we said destroy unmixed or extreme oligarchies and extreme democracies should also be   35
regarded as destroying tyranny. For these are in fact divided tyrannies.[130]

Kingship is destroyed least by outside factors, which is also why it is
long-lasting. The sources of its destruction generally come from within.
It is destroyed in two ways: first, when those who participate in the kingship start faction, and, second, when the kings try to manage affairs in a   1313[a]
more tyrannical fashion, claiming that they deserve to have authority
over more areas than is customary, and to be beyond the law. Kingships
no longer arise nowadays, but if any do happen to occur, they tend more
to be tyrannical monarchies.[131] This is because kingship is rule over willing subjects and has authority over more important matters. But nowa-   5
days there are numerous men of equal quality, although none so outstanding as to measure up to the magnitude and dignity of the office of
king. Hence people are unwilling to put up with this sort of rule. And if
someone comes to exercise it, whether through force or deceit, this is
immediately held to be a tyranny.

In the case of kingships based on lineage, there is something besides   10
the factors already mentioned that should be considered a cause of their
destruction, namely, the fact that many kings easily become objects of
contempt and behave arrogantly, even though they exercise kingly office,
not tyrannical power. For then overthrow is easy. For a king whose sub-

---

130. Tyrannies in which power is not in just one person's hands.
131. *monarchiai kai turannides mallon*: I follow Pellegrin in treating the phrase as
a *hendiadys*.

jects are unwilling immediately ceases to be a king whereas a tyrant can
15   rule even unwilling subjects.

Monarchies are destroyed for these reasons, then, and for others of
the same sort.

Chapter 11

It is clear, to put it simply, that monarchies are preserved by the opposite
causes.[132] But kingships in particular are preserved by being made more
20   moderate. For the fewer areas over which kings have authority, the
longer must their office remain intact. For they themselves become less
like masters, more equal in their characters, and less envied by those
they rule. That is also why the kingships of the Molossians lasted a long
time, and that of the Spartans as well. In the latter case it was because
25   the office was divided into two parts from the beginning, and again because Theopompus, besides moderating it in other ways, instituted the
office of the overseers.[133] By diminishing the power of the kingship he
increased its duration, so that in a way he made it greater, not lesser. He
is supposed to have given precisely this answer, indeed, when his wife
30   asked him whether he was not ashamed to hand over a lesser kingship to
his sons than the one he had inherited from his father: "Certainly not,"
he said, "for I am handing over one that will be longer lasting."

Tyrannies[134] are preserved in two quite opposite ways. One of them is
35   traditional and is the way most tyrants exercise their rule. Periander of
Corinth is said to have instituted most of its devices, but many may also
be seen in the Persian empire. These include the device we mentioned
some time ago[135] as tending to preserve a tyranny (to the extent that it
40   can be preserved): [1] cutting down the outstanding men and eliminat-
ing the high-minded ones. Others are: [2] Prohibiting messes, clubs, ed-
1313b   ucation, and other things of that sort. [3] Keeping an eye on anything
that typically engenders two things: high-mindedness and mutual trust.
[4] Prohibiting schools and other gatherings connected with learning,[136]

132. Opposite to the causes that preserve them.
133. Theopompus was King of Sparta (*c.* 770–720). The overseers acted as a
check on the monarchy (1270b6–17).
134. It is useful to compare Aristotle's forthcoming account of tyranny with that
given in Plato, *Republic* 562a–569c.
135. At 1311a15–22.
136. A broad characterization intended to cover formal schools (like Aristotle's
own Lyceum), symposia, and conversations like those of Socrates that take
place in the agora and gymnasia.

and doing everything to ensure that people are as ignorant of one another as possible, since knowledge tends to give rise to mutual trust. [5] Requiring the residents to be always in public view and to pass their time at the palace gates.[137] For their activities will then be hard to keep secret and they will become humble-minded from always acting like slaves. [6] Imposing all the other restrictions of a similar nature that are found in Persian and non-Greek tyrannies (for they are all capable of producing the same effect).

[7] Another is trying to let nothing done or said by any of his subjects escape notice, but to retain spies, like the so-called women informers of Syracuse, or the eavesdroppers that Hiero[138] sent to every meeting or gathering. For people speak less freely when they fear the presence of such spies, and if they do speak freely, they are less likely to go unnoticed. [8] Another is to slander people to one another, setting friend against friend, the people against the notables, and the rich against themselves. [9] It is also tyrannical to impoverish the people, so that they cannot afford a militia and are so occupied with their daily work that they lack the leisure for plotting. The pyramids of Egypt, the Cypselid monuments, the construction of the temple of Olympian Zeus by the Pisistratids, and the works on Samos commissioned by Polycrates are all examples of this.[139] For all these things have the same result, lack of leisure and poverty for the ruled. [10] And there is taxation, as in Syracuse, when, during the reign of Dionysius,[140] taxation ate up a person's entire estate in five years. [11] A tyrant also engages in warmongering in order that his subjects will lack leisure and be perpetually in need of a leader. And while a kingship is preserved by its friends, it is the mark of a tyrant to distrust his friends, on the grounds that while all his subjects wish to overthrow him, these are particularly capable of doing so.[141]

All the practices found in the extreme kind of democracy are also characteristic of a tyranny: [12] the dominance of women in the household, in order that they may report on the men, and [13] the license of slaves for the same reason. For slaves and women not only do not plot against tyrants but, because they prosper under them, are inevitably well

---

137. So as to be at the tyrant's beck and call.
138. Tyrant of Syracuse 478–467.
139. The Cypselids were tyrants of Corinth. Polycrates was a sixth-century tyrant of Samos.
140. Dionysius I (409–367).
141. When ability and wish coincide, action usually follows (1312^b1–3).

disposed toward tyrannies and toward democracies as well (for the people too aspire to be a monarch). That is why a flatterer is honored in
both constitutions—in democracies, the popular leader (for the popular
40   leader is a flatterer of the people), in tyrannies, those who are obse-
quious in their dealings with the tyrant, which is precisely a task for flat-
1314ª tery. For that is also why tyranny loves vice. For tyrants delight in being
flattered. But no free-minded person would flatter them. On the contrary, decent people act out of friendship, not flattery.[142] The vicious are
5   also useful for vicious tasks—"nail to nail," as the saying goes.[143] And it
is characteristic of a tyrant not to delight in anyone who is dignified or
free-minded. For a tyrant thinks that he alone deserves to be like that.
But anyone who is a rival in dignity or free-mindedness robs tyranny of
its superiority and its status as a master of slaves, and so tyrants hate him
as a threat to their rule. And it is also characteristic of a tyrant to have
foreigners rather than people from the city-state as dinner guests and
10   companions, on the grounds that the former are hostile to him, whereas
the latter oppose him in nothing.

These devices are characteristic of tyrants and help preserve their
rule, but there is no vice they leave out. They all fall into three cate-
15   gories, broadly speaking. For tyranny aims at three things: first, that the
ruled think small, for a pusillanimous person would plot against no
one;[144] second, that they distrust one another, for a tyranny will not be
overthrown until some people trust each other. This is also why tyrants
attack decent people. They view them as harmful to their rule not only
20   because they refuse to be ruled as by a master, but also because they
command trust among both themselves and others, and do not inform
on one another or on anyone else. Third, that the ruled be powerless to
act. For no one tries to do what is impossible, and so no one tries to over-
25   throw a tyranny if he lacks the power. Thus the wishes of tyrants may be
reduced in fact to these three defining principles, since all tyrannical
aims might be reduced to these three tenets: that the ruled not trust one
another; that they be powerless; that they think small.

142. A true friend loves one for one's own qualities; a flatterer is someone who
seems to do this but does not. If decent people seem friendly it will be because they are so, not because they are engaging in flattery (*Rh.*
1371ª17–24).
143. More usually, "nail is driven out by nail," but here something like "it takes
a nail to do a nail's work."
144. See *NE* 1123ᵇ9–26, 1125ª19–27.

This, then, is one way in which the preservation of tyrannies comes about. The other involves precautions that are pretty much the opposite *30* of those just discussed. One may grasp it by considering the destruction of kingships. For just as one way to destroy a kingship is to make its rule more tyrannical, so one way to preserve a tyranny is to make it more like a kingship. One thing only must be safeguarded, the tyrant's power, so *35* he can rule not just willing subjects but unwilling ones as well. For if this power is lost, the tyranny is also.[145] But while this must remain a basic principle, a tyrant should perform or seem to perform everything else in a noble, kingly fashion.

First, then, [1] he should seem to take care of public funds. He should *40* not squander them on gifts that enrage the multitude, taking money *1314ᵇ* from people who are laboring and toiling in penury, and lavishing it on prostitutes, foreigners, and craftsmen. He should also render an account of funds received and expended, as some tyrants in the past have done. *5* For in this way, he will give the impression of managing the city-state like the head of a household rather than a tyrant. He should not be afraid of running short of funds, since he has authority over the city-state. At any event, it is even more beneficial for tyrants who are often away on foreign campaigns to do this[146] than to amass a great hoard of wealth and leave it behind. For those who guard the city-state will be *10* less likely to seize his things. A tyrant on a foreign campaign has more to fear from such guards, indeed, than from the citizens. For the citizens accompany him, while the guards stay behind. Next, it should appear that taxes and public services exist for the purposes of administration, *15* and to meet the needs of military emergencies. In a word: a tyrant should pose as a guardian and steward of the public funds, not of his own private estate.

[2] He should also appear not harsh but dignified, the kind of person who inspires awe rather than fear in those who meet him. But this is not easily achieved if he is contemptible. That is why even if a tyrant ne- *20* glects the other virtues, he must cultivate military virtue[147] and get himself a reputation for it.

Furthermore, [3] not only should he himself avoid any appearance of behaving arrogantly toward any teenage boys and girls among his sub-

---

145. Since tyranny differs from kingship in being rule over unwilling subjects.
146. Of rendering public accounts and seeming to take care of public funds.
147. The mss. have "political virtue (*politikē aretē*)."

25   jects, but neither should any of his followers. The women of his household should also be similarly respectful toward other women, as the arrogant behavior of women has caused the downfall of many tyrannies.
Where bodily pleasures are concerned, the tyrant should do the opposite of what some in fact do. For they not only begin their debaucheries
30   at dawn and continue them for days on end, but they also wish to be seen
doing so by others, in order that they may be admired as happy and
blessed. But above all the tyrant should be moderate in such matters, or
failing that, he should at least avoid exhibiting his indulgence to others.
For it is not easy to attack or despise a sober or wakeful man, but it is
35   easy to attack or despise a drunk or drowsy one.

[4] A tyrant must do the opposite of pretty well all the things we mentioned a while back.[148] For he must lay out and beautify the city-state as
if he were a household steward rather than a tyrant.

Again, [5] a tyrant should always be seen to be very zealous about
matters concerning the gods, but without appearing foolish in the
process. For people are less afraid of suffering illegal treatment at the
40   hands of such people. And if they regard their ruler as a god-fearing
1315ᵃ   man who pays heed to the gods, they plot against him less, since they
think that he has the gods on his side.

[6] A tyrant should so honor those who prove to be good in any area
5   that they do not expect that they would be more honored by citizens living under their own laws. He should bestow such honors himself, but
punishments should be administered by other officials and by the
courts. But it is a precaution common to every sort of monarchy not to
make any one man important, but where necessary to elevate several, so
that they will keep an eye on one another. If it happens to be necessary to
make one man important, however, at all events it should not be some-
10   one of courageous character. For men of this sort are the most enterpris-
ing in any sphere of action. And if it is considered necessary to remove
someone from power, his prerogatives should be taken away gradually,
not all at once.

[7] A tyrant should refrain from all forms of arrogance, and from two
15   in particular: corporal punishment and arrogance toward adolescents.
This is particularly true where those who love honor are concerned. For
while lovers of money resent contemptuous acts affecting their property, honor lovers and decent human beings resent those involving dis-

148. At 1313ᵃ34–1313ᵇ32.

honor. Hence either he should not treat people in these ways or else he   20
should appear to punish like a father, not out of contempt; and to engage
in sexual relations with young people out of sexual desire, and not as if it
were a prerogative of his office. And as a general rule, he should com-
pensate apparent dishonors with yet greater honors. Of those who make
attempts on his life, a tyrant should most fear and take the greatest pre-   25
cautions against those who are ready to sacrifice their own lives to destroy him. Hence he should be particularly wary of people who think
that he has behaved arrogantly toward them or those they happen to
cherish. For people who attack out of anger are careless of themselves.
As Heraclitus said, "Anger is a hard enemy to combat, because it pays   30
for what it wants with life."[149]

[8] Since city-states consist of two parts, poor and rich, it is best if
both believe that they owe their safety to the tyrant's rule, and that neither is unjustly treated by the other because of it. But whichever of them
is the stronger should be particularly attached to his rule, so that with   35
his power thus increased he will not need to free slaves or confiscate
weapons. For the latter of the two parts added to his force will be enough
to make them stronger than attackers.

But it is superfluous to discuss all such measures in detail. For their   40
aim is evident. A tyrant should appear to his subjects not as a tyrant but
as a head of household and a kingly man, not as an embezzler but as a   *1315*[b]
steward. He should also pursue the moderate things in life, not excess,
maintaining close relations with the notables, while playing the popular
leader with the many. For as a result, not only will his rule necessarily be
nobler and more enviable, but since he rules better people who have not
been humiliated he will not end up being hated and feared. And his rule   5
will be longer lasting, and his character will either be nobly disposed to
virtue or else half good, not vicious but half vicious.   10

Chapter 12

Yet, the shortest-lived of all constitutions are oligarchy and tyranny. For
the longest lasting tyranny was that of Orthagoras and his sons in
Sicyon. It lasted a hundred years.[150] This was because they treated their

---

149. Diels-Kranz B85. Heraclitus of Ephesus (*c.* 540–480) was one of the
    greatest of the Presocratic philosophers.
150. The tyranny was founded in 670. Cleisthenes was grandson of Orthagoras
    and grandfather of the Athenian reformer of the same name.

15   subjects moderately and were subservient to the laws in many areas;
Cleisthenes, in particular, was also not easy to despise because of his
ability in battle; and they acted as popular leaders by looking after the
people's interests in various ways. At any rate, Cleisthenes is said to have
given a crown to the judge who denied him victory in a competition.
And some say that the seated figure in the marketplace is a statue of the
20   man who gave the verdict. They also say that Pisistratus[151] once allowed
himself to be summoned for trial before the Areopagus.

The second longest tyranny was that of the Cypselids in Corinth,
which lasted seventy-three years and six months. For Cypselus was
25   tyrant for thirty years, Periander for forty and a half, and Psammeticus,
the son of Gorgus, for three.[152] The reasons it lasted are also the same.
Cypselus was a popular leader who went without a bodyguard throughout his rule; and Periander, though he became tyrannical, was able in
battle.[153]

The third was that of the Pisistratids in Athens. But it was not contin-
30   uous. For Pisistratus went into exile twice, so that in a period of thirty-
three years he was tyrant for seventeen. Since his sons ruled for eighteen
years, the tyranny lasted for thirty-five years altogether.

The longest lasting of the remaining tyrannies was the one associated
35   with Gelon and Hiero at Syracuse. Yet even this did not last long, just
eighteen years total. For Gelon was tyrant for seven and died in the
eighth; Hiero for ten; whereas Thrasyboulus was expelled after ten
months. But the majority of tyrannies have all been quite short-lived.

40   The various causes that destroy constitutions and monarchies, and
also those that preserve them, have now pretty well all been discussed.

1316ᵃ   In the *Republic* Socrates discusses change, but he does not discuss it
well. For in the case of the first and best constitution he does not discuss
the change peculiar to it. For he claims that its cause is that nothing is
permanent, but that everything undergoes a sort of cyclical change, and
5   that the origin of this lies in the elements four and three, which "married with five, give two harmonies," whenever the number of this figure
becomes cubed. His idea is that nature sometimes produces people who
are mediocre and stronger than education.[154] Perhaps he is not wrong in
10   saying this, since there may be some people who are ineducable and can-

151. Tyrant at Athens (561–527).
152. Gorgus was Periander's successor.
153. Therefore, difficult to despise.
154. See *Republic* 545c ff.

not become good men. But how could this sort of change be any more peculiar to the constitution he says is best than common to all the others and to everything that comes into existence? Yes, and is it during this period of time,[155] due to which, as he says, everything changes, that even things that did not begin to exist at the same time change at the same time? If something comes into existence on the day before the completion of the cycle, for example, does it still change at the same time as everything else? Furthermore, why does the best constitution change into a constitution of the Spartan sort? For all constitutions more often change into their opposites than into the neighboring one.[156] The same remark also applies to the other changes. For he says that the Spartan constitution changes to an oligarchy, then to a democracy, then to a tyranny. Yet change may also occur in the opposite direction. For example, from democracy to oligarchy, and to it more than to monarchy.

Moreover, he does not tell us whether tyranny undergoes change, or what causes it to change, if it does. Nor does he tell us what sort of constitution it changes into. The reason for this is that he could not easily have told us, since the matter is undecidable, although according to him it should change into his first or best constitution, since that would make the cycle continuous. But in fact tyranny can also change into another tyranny, as the constitution at Sicyon changed from the tyranny of Myron to that of Cleisthenes; into oligarchy, like that of Antileon in Chalcis; into democracy, like that of Gelon and his family at Syracuse; and into aristocracy, like that of Charillus in Sparta [or the one in Carthage].[157]

Change also occurs from oligarchy to tyranny, as happened in most of the ancient oligarchies in Sicily: in Leontini, it was to the tyranny of Panaetius; in Gela, to that of Cleander; in Rhegium, to that of Anaxilaus; and similarly in many other city-states.[158] It is also absurd to hold that a constitution changes into an oligarchy because the office holders are money lovers and acquirers of wealth,[159] and not because those who are far superior in property holdings think it unjust for those who do not

15

20

25

30

35

40

1316[b]

155. Reading *dia tou chronou* with the mss.
156. See 1307[a]20–27.
157. The bracketed clause may well be an interpolation, as Rackham suggests. 1272[b]24–33 states that Carthage never had a tyranny or any significant faction; 1316[b]5–6 states that it never suffered change.
158. Nothing is known of Antileon. On Cleander, see Herodotus VII.154–55, and on Anaxilaus, VI.23, VII.165, 170.
159. As Socrates does at *Republic* 555d ff.

own anything to participate equally in the city-state with those who do.
And in many oligarchies office holders are not only not allowed to acquire wealth, but there are laws to prevent it. On the other hand, in
5   Carthage, which is governed timocratically,[160] the officials do engage in
acquiring wealth, and it has not yet undergone change.

It is also absurd to claim that an oligarchic city-state is really two city-
states, one of the rich and one of the poor.[161] For why is this any more
true of it than of the Spartan constitution, or any other constitution
where the citizens do not all own an equal amount of property or are not
10   all similarly good men? And even when no one becomes any poorer than
he was, constitutions still undergo change from oligarchy to democracy,
if the poor become a majority, or from democracy to oligarchy, if the
rich happen to be more powerful than the multitude, and the latter are
careless, while the former set their mind to change. Also, though there
are many reasons why oligarchies change into democracies, Socrates
15   mentions but one: poverty caused by riotous living and paying interest
on loans[162]—as if all or most of the citizens were rich at the start. But
this is false. Rather, when some of the leading men lose their properties,
they stir up change; but when some of the others do so, nothing terrible
happens. And even when change does occur, it is no more likely to result
20   in a democracy than in some other constitution. Besides, if people have
no share in office or are treated unjustly or arrogantly, they start factions
and change constitutions, even if they have not squandered all their
property through being free to do whatever they like (the cause of
which, Socrates says, is too much freedom).[163]
25   Although there are many kinds of oligarchies and democracies,
Socrates discusses their changes as if there were only one of each.

---

160. Reading *timokrateumenē(i)* with Newman. Alternatively (Ross, Dreizehnter and the mss.): "governed democratically *dēmokratoumenē(i)*." See
1272[b]24–33. Oligarchs are timocrats or honor lovers.
161. As Socrates does at *Republic* 551d.
162. See *Republic* 555c ff.
163. See *Republic* 555d, 563d–564d. Socrates makes excessive liberty the mark
of a democratic, not an oligarchic city-state. Perhaps on the basis of
564[a]10–[b]2, Aristotle seems to be taking Socrates' explanation of how prop-
ertyless people arise in democracies to apply to oligarchies too.

BOOK VI

Chapter 1

We have already discussed[1] the number and varieties of the deliberative *30*
and authoritative elements of constitutions, the ways of organizing offices and courts, which is suited to which constitution, and also what the
origins and causes are of the destruction and preservation of constitutions.[2] But since it turned out that there are several kinds of democra- *35*
cies, and similarly of the other constitutions, we would do well to consider whatever remains to be said about these, and to determine which
ways of organizing things are appropriate for and beneficial to each of
them.

Moreover, we have to investigate the combinations of all the ways of *40*
organizing the things we mentioned. For these, when coupled, cause
constitutions to overlap, resulting in oligarchic aristocracies and democ- *1317ᵃ*
ratically inclined polities. I mean those couplings which should be investigated but at present have not been. For example, where the deliberative
part and the part that deals with the choice of officials are organized oligarchically, but the part that deals with the courts is aristocratic; or *5*
where the part that deals with the courts and the deliberative part are
oligarchic, and the part that deals with the choice of officials is aristocratic; or where, in some other way, not all the parts appropriate to the
constitution are combined.[3]

We have already discussed[4] the question of which kind of democracy
is suited to which kind of city-state; similarly, which kind of oligarchy is *10*
suited to which kind of people; and which of the remaining constitutions is beneficial for which. Still, since we should make clear not only
which kind of constitution is best for a city-state, but also how it and the

---

1. At IV.14–16.
2. At V.1–12.
3. These combinations are not discussed in the *Politics* as we have it.
4. At IV.12.

175

15   other kinds should be established, let us briefly go through this. We may
begin with democracy, since that will at the same time throw some light
on the opposite constitution, the one some call oligarchy.

      To carry out this inquiry, we need to grasp all the features that are de-
20   mocratic and that are held to go along with democracy. For it is as a result of the way these are combined that the various kinds of democracy
arise, and more than one variety of each kind of democracy. For there
are *two* reasons why there are several kinds of democracy. The first is the
one mentioned earlier,[5] that there are different kinds of people. For
25   there is the multitude of farmers, that of vulgar craftsmen, and that of
laborers. And when the first of these is added to the second, and the
third again to both of them, it not only affects the quality of the democracy for better or worse, it also changes its kind. But the second reason
is the one we are discussing now. For the features that go along with
30   democracy and are held to be appropriate to this kind of constitution,
when they are differently combined, cause democracies to differ, since a
few of these features will go with one kind of democracy, more with a
second, and all of them with a third. It is useful to be familiar with each
of them, whether for the purpose of establishing whichever kind of
democracy one happens to want, or for that of reforming an existing
35   kind. For those who are establishing a constitution try to combine all the
features that are in keeping with its fundamental principle. But they err
in doing so, as was pointed out earlier in our discussions of what causes
the destruction and preservation of constitutions.[6]

      Let us now discuss the fundamental principles, character, and aims of
the various kinds of democracy.

Chapter 2

40   The fundamental principle of the democratic constitution is freedom.
For it is commonly asserted that freedom is shared only in this sort of
1317ᵇ   constitution, since it is said that all democracies have it as their aim. One
component of freedom is ruling and being ruled in turn. For democratic
justice is based on numerical equality, not on merit.[7] But if this is what
5   justice is, then of necessity the multitude must be in authority, and

---

5. At 1291ᵇ14–28, IV.6, 1296ᵇ24–31.
6. At 1309ᵇ20–1310ª2, 1310ª12–36.
7. Numerical EQUALITY (*to ison kata arithmon*) involves equal participation in
political office by each citizen, and so an interchange of ruling and being

whatever seems right to the majority, this is what is final and this is what is just, since they say that each of the citizens should have an equal share. The result is that the poor have more authority than the rich in democracies. For they are the majority, and majority opinion is in authority. This, then, is one mark of freedom which all democrats take as a 10 goal of their constitution. Another is to live as one likes. This, they say, is the result of freedom, since that of slavery is not to live as one likes. This, then, is the second goal of democracy. From it arises the demand not to be ruled by anyone, or failing that, to rule and be ruled in turn. In 15 this way the second goal contributes to freedom based on equality.

From these presuppositions and this sort of principle arise the following democratic features: [1] Having all choose officials from all. [2] Having all rule each and each in turn rule all. [3] Having all offices, or all 20 that do not require experience or skill, filled by lot. [4] Having no property assessment for office, or one as low as possible. [5] Having no office, or few besides military ones, held twice or more than a few times by the same person. [6] Having all offices or as many as possible be short-term. [7] Having all, or bodies selected from all, decide all cases, or most of 25 them, and the ones that are most important and involve the most authority, such as those having to do with the inspection of officials, the constitution, or private contracts. [8] Having the assembly have authority over everything or over all the important things, but having no office with authority over anything or over as little as possible. The council is the most 30 democratic office in city-states that lack adequate resources to pay everyone, but where such resources exist even this office is stripped of its power. For when the people are well paid, they take all decisions into their own hands (as we said in the inquiry preceding this one).[8] [9] Having pay provided, preferably for everyone, for the assembly, courts, and 35 public offices, or failing that, for service in the offices, courts, council, and assemblies that are in authority, or for those offices that require their holders to share a mess. Besides, since oligarchy is defined by family, wealth, and education, their opposites (low birth, poverty, and vulgarity) 40 are held to be characteristically democratic.[9] [10] Furthermore, it is democratic to have no office be permanent; and if such an office happens

---

ruled (see 1261[a]30–[b]6), it does not seem necessarily to involve equality of property, since none of the ways of establishing it discussed in VI.3 involves a redistribution of property.

8. At 1299[b]38–1300[a]4.

9. Dreizehnter brackets this sentence as an interpolation.

to survive an ancient change, to strip it of its power, at least, and have it filled by lot rather than by election.

These, then, are the features commonly found in democracies. And from the type of justice that is agreed to be democratic, which consists in everyone having numerical equality, comes what is held to be most of
5   all a democracy and a rule by the people, since equality consists in the poor neither ruling more than the rich nor being alone in authority, but in all ruling equally on the basis of numerical equality, since in that way they would consider equality and freedom to be present in the constitu-
10 tion.

Chapter 3

The next problem that arises is how they will achieve this equality. Should they divide assessed property so that the property of five hundred citizens equals that of a thousand others, and then give equal power to the thousand as to the five hundred?[10] Or is this not the way to produce numerical equality? Should they instead divide as before, then take
15 an equal number of citizens from the five hundred as from the thousand and give them authority over the elections and the courts? Is this the constitution that is most just from the point of view of democratic justice? Or is it the one based on quantity? For democrats say that whatever seems just to the greater number constitutes justice,[11] whereas oligarchs say that it is whatever seems just to those with the most property. For
20 they say that quantity of property should be the deciding factor. But both views are unequal and unjust. For if justice is whatever the few decide, we have tyranny, since if one person has more than the others who are rich, then, from the point of view of oligarchic justice, it is just for him alone to rule.[12] On the other hand, if justice is what the numerical
25 majority decide, they will commit injustice by confiscating the property of the wealthy few (as we said earlier).[13]

What sort of equality there might be, then, that both would agree on is something we must investigate in light of the definitions of justice

10. We have two groups, one of five hundred (the rich), another of one thousand (the poor), each of which has the same amount of property. If we so distribute political power that each group has the same amount, have we treated both the rich and the poor as numerical equality demands?
11. See 1317^b5–7
12. See 1283^b13–27.
13. At 1281^a14–28.

they both give. For they both say that the opinion of the MAJORITY of the citizens should be in authority. So let this stand, though not fully. Instead, since there are in fact two classes in a city-state, the rich and the poor, whatever is the opinion of both or of a majority of each should have authority. But if they are opposed, the opinion of the majority (that is to say, the group whose assessed property is greater) should prevail. Suppose, for example, that there are ten rich citizens and twenty poor ones, and that six of the rich have voted against fifteen of the poorer ones, whereas four of the rich have sided with the poor, and five of the poor with the rich. When the assessed properties of both the rich and the poor on each side are added together, the side whose assessed property is greater should have authority. If the amounts happen to be equal, this should be considered a failure for both sides, as it is at present when the assembly or the court is split, and the question must be decided by lot or something else of that sort.

Even if it is very difficult to discover the truth about what equality and justice demand, however, it is still easier than to persuade people of it when they have the power to be ACQUISITIVE. For equality and justice are always sought by the weaker party; the strong pay no heed to them.

Chapter 4

Of the four kinds of democracy, the first in order is the best, as we said in the discussions before these.[14] It is also the oldest of them all. But I call it first as one might distinguish people. For the first or best kind of people is the farming kind, and so it is also possible to create a democracy where the multitude live by cultivating the land or herding flocks. For because they do not have much property, they lack leisure and cannot attend meetings of the assembly frequently. And because they do not[15] have the necessities, they are busy at their tasks and do not desire other people's property. Indeed, they find working more pleasant than engaging in politics and holding office, where no great profit is to be had from office, since the many seek money more than honor. Evidence of this is that they even put up with the ancient tyrannies, and continue to put up with oligarchies, so long as no one prevents them from working or takes anything away from them. For in no time some of them become

14. At 1291ᵇ30–1292ᵃ38, 1292ᵇ25–1293ᵃ10.
15. Reading *mē* with the mss.

20 rich, while the others at least escape poverty. Besides, having authority over the election and inspection of officials will give them what they need, if they do have any love of honor. In fact, in some democracies, the multitude do not participate in the election of officials; instead, electors are selected from all the citizens by turns, as in Mantinea; yet if they
25 have authority over deliberation, they are content. (This arrangement too should be regarded as a form of democracy, as it was at Mantinea.)

That is why, indeed, in the aforementioned kind of democracy, it is both beneficial and customary for all the citizens to elect and inspect officials and sit on juries, but for the holders of the most important offices
30 to be elected from those with a certain amount of assessed property (the higher the office, the higher the assessment), or alternatively for officials not to be elected on the basis of property assessments at all, but on the basis of ability. People governed in this way are necessarily governed well; the offices will always be in the hands of the best, while the people will consent and will not envy the decent; and this organization is neces-
35 sarily satisfactory to the decent and reputable people, since they will not be ruled by their inferiors, and will rule justly because the others have authority over the inspection of officials. For to be under constraint, and not to be able to do whatever seems good, is beneficial, since freedom to
40 do whatever one likes leaves one defenseless against the bad things that
1319ᵃ exist in every human being. So the necessary result, which is the very one most beneficial in constitutions, is that the decent people rule without falling into wrongdoing and the multitude are in no way short-changed.

It is evident, then, that this is the best of the democracies, and also the
5 reason why: that it is because the people are of a certain kind. And for the purpose of establishing a farming people, some of the laws that existed in many city-states in ancient times are extremely useful, for example, prohibiting the ownership of more than a certain amount of land under any circumstances, or else more than a certain amount situated between a given place and the city-state's town. And there used to be a
10 law in many city-states (at any rate, in ancient times) forbidding even the sale of the original allotments of land,[16] and also one, said to derive from Oxylus,[17] with a similar sort of effect, forbidding lending against more than a certain portion of each person's land. Nowadays, however, one should also attempt reform by using the law of the Aphytaeans, as it too

16. See 1266ᵇ19–24 for some examples.
17. Oxylus was an ancient king and legislator in Elis.

is useful for the purpose under discussion. For though the citizens of   *15*
Aphytis are numerous and have little land, they all engage in farming,
because property assessments are based not on whole estates[18] but on
such small subdivisions of them that even the poor can exceed the assessment.

After the multitude of farmers, the best sort of people consists of
herdsmen, who get their living from livestock. For herding is in many   *20*
respects similar to farming, and where military activities are concerned,
they are particularly well prepared, because they are physically fit and
able to live in the open. The other multitudes, of which the remaining
kinds of democracies are composed, are almost all very inferior to these.   *25*
For their way of life is bad, and there is no element of virtue involved in
the task to which the multitude of vulgar craftsmen, tradesmen, and laborers put their hand.[19] Furthermore, because they wander around the
marketplace and town, practically speaking this entire class can easily attend the assembly. Farmers, on the other hand, because they are scat-   *30*
tered throughout the countryside, neither attend so readily nor have the
same need for this sort of meeting. But where the lay of the land is such
that the countryside is widely separated from the CITY-STATE, it is even
easier to create a democracy that is serviceable and a CONSTITUTION. For   *35*
the multitude are forced to make their settlements out in the country
areas, so that, even if there is a whole crowd that frequents the marketplace, one should simply not hold assemblies in democracies without the
multitude from the country.

How, then, the best or first kind of democracy should be established
has been described. But how the others should be established is also evident. For they should deviate in order from the best kind, always ex-   *40*
cluding a worse multitude.[20]

The ultimate democracy, because everyone participates in it, is not   *1319^b*
one that every city-state can afford;[21] nor can it easily endure, if its laws
and customs are not well put together. (The factors that cause the de-

18. That is, the original allotments.
19. Explained at 1260^a39–^b1, 1337^b4–21.
20. The best kind of democracy includes only the best multitude (the farmers)
   and excludes the multitude that is only slightly worse (the herdsmen); the
   next best kind includes the herdsmen but excludes the next worst multitude
   (the craftsmen); and so on. Thus at each stage a worse multitude is excluded.
21. For one thing, only a wealthy city-state can afford to provide the payment
   needed to enable everyone to participate (1293^a1–10).

struction of this and other constitutions have pretty well all been dis-
5   cussed earlier.)[22] With a view to establishing this sort of democracy and
making the people powerful, the leaders usually admit as many as possible to citizenship, including not only the legitimate children of citizens
but even the illegitimate ones, and those descended from citizens on
only one side (I mean their mother's or their father's). For this whole
10 class are particularly at home in this sort of democracy. This, then, is
how popular leaders usually establish such a constitution; yet they
should add citizens only up to the point where the multitude outnumber
the notables and middle classes, and not go beyond this. For when they
do overshoot it, they make the constitution more disorderly and provoke
15 the notables to such an extent that they find the democracy hard to endure (which was in fact the cause of the faction at Cyrene).[23] For a small
class of worthless people gets overlooked, but as it grows larger it gets
more noticed.
20   Also useful to a democracy of this kind are the sorts of institutions
that Cleisthenes used in Athens when he wanted to increase the power of
the democracy, and that those setting up the democracy used at
Cyrene.[24] For different and more numerous tribes and clans should be
created, private cults should be absorbed into a few public ones, and
25 every device should be used to mix everyone together as much as possible and break up their previous associations. Furthermore, all tyrannical
institutions are held to be democratic. I mean, for example, the lack of
supervision of slaves (which may really be beneficial to a democracy up
to a certain point), or of women or children,[25] and allowing everyone to
30 live as he likes. For many people will support a constitution of this sort,
since for the many it is more pleasant to live in a disorderly fashion than
in a temperate one.

Chapter 5

For a legislator, however, or for those seeking to establish a constitution
of this kind, setting it up is not the most important task nor indeed the

22. In V.5.
23. Perhaps the revolution of 401 in which five hundred rich people were put to
death.
24. The reforms of Cleisthenes are described in *Ath*. XXI. The reference to the
democracy at Cyrene may be to the one established there in 462.
25. On this sort of supervision, see 1300^a4-8, $1322^b37-1323^a6$. The advantage
of not having it in a democracy is explained at 1313^b32-39, 1323^a3-6.

only one, but rather ensuring its preservation. For it is not difficult for   *35*
those who govern themselves in any old way to continue for a day or
even for two or three days. That is why legislators should make use of
our earlier studies of what causes the preservation and destruction of
constitutions, and from them try to institute stability, carefully avoiding
the causes of destruction, while establishing the sort of LAWS, both written and unwritten, which best encompass the features that preserve con-   *40*
stitutions. They should consider a measure to be democratic or oli-   *1320ᵃ*
garchic not if it will make the city-state be as democratically governed or
as oligarchically governed as possible, but if it will make it be so for the
longest time.

Popular leaders nowadays, however, in their efforts to curry favor with
the people, confiscate a lot of property by means of the courts. That is   *5*
why those who care about the constitution should counteract this by
passing a law that nothing confiscated from a condemned person should
become common property, but sacred property instead. For wrongdoers
will be no less deterred, since they will be fined in the same way as before, whereas the crowd will less frequently condemn defendants, since   *10*
they will gain nothing by doing so. Public lawsuits too should always be
kept to an absolute minimum, and those who bring frivolous ones
should be deterred by large fines.²⁶ For they are usually brought against
notables, not democrats; but all the citizens should be well disposed toward the constitution, or, failing that, they should at least not regard   *15*
those in authority as their enemies.²⁷

Since the ultimate democracies have large populations that cannot easily attend the assembly without wages, where they also happen to have a
dearth of revenues, this is hostile to the notables. For the wages have to be
obtained from taxes, confiscations of property, and corrupt courts—   *20*
things that have already brought down many democracies. Where revenues are lacking, then, few assemblies should be held, and courts with
many jurors should be in session for only a few days. For this helps reduce
the fears of the notables about expense, provided the rich are not paid for   *25*
jury service but only the poor. It also greatly improves the quality of decisions in lawsuits; for the rich are unwilling to be away from their private
affairs for many days, but are willing to be so for brief periods.

Where there are revenues, however, one should not do what popular
leaders do nowadays. For they distribute any surplus, but people no   *30*

---

26. See 1268ᵇ25 and note.
27. See 1270ᵇ21–22 and note.

sooner get it than they want the same again. Helping the poor in this way, indeed, is like pouring water into the proverbial leaking jug.[28] But the truly democratic man should see to it that the multitude are not too poor (since this is a cause of the democracy's being a corrupt one). Measures must, therefore, be devised to ensure long-term prosperity. And,
35 since this is also beneficial to the rich, whatever is left over from the revenues should be collected together and distributed in lump sums to the poor, particularly if enough can be accumulated for the acquisition of a plot of land, or failing that, for a start in trade or farming. And if this cannot be done for all, distribution should instead be by turns on the
1320ᵇ basis of tribe or some other part. In the meantime the rich should be taxed to provide pay for necessary meetings of the assembly, while being released from useless sorts of public service.

It is by governing in this sort of way that the Carthaginians have won
5 the friendship of their people, since they are always sending some of them out to their subject city-states to become rich.[29] But it is also characteristic of notables who are cultivated and sensible to divide the poor amongst themselves and give them a start in some line of work. It is a good thing too to imitate the policy of the Tarentines, who retain the goodwill of the multitude by giving communal use of their property to
10 the poor.[30] They also divide all their offices into two classes, those that are elected and those chosen by lot: those by lot, so the people participate; those elected, so they are governed better. But this can also be done by dividing the same office between those people chosen by lot and
15 those elected.

We have said, then, how democracies should be established.

Chapter 6

It is also pretty well evident from these remarks how oligarchies should be established. For each oligarchy should be assembled from its oppo-
20 sites, by analogy with the opposite democracy, as in the case of the best mixed and first of the oligarchies. This is the one very close to so-called

28. See 1267ᵇ1–5. Forty-nine of Danaus' fifty daughters murdered their husbands on their wedding night and were punished in Hades by having endlessly to fill leaking jugs with water.
29. Compare 1273ᵇ18–24.
30. See 1263ª35–40 where this policy is attributed to the Spartans, who were the ancestors of the Tarentines.

polity. Here the property assessments should be divided in two, some
being made smaller and some larger, the smaller ones making people eligible for the necessary offices,[31] the larger ones, for the offices with
more authority. Anyone who acquires a qualifying property should be al-   25
lowed to participate, and the assessment should be used to admit a sufficiently large number of the people that those who participate in the constitution will be stronger than those who do not, and those who do share
should always be drawn from the better part of the people.[32]

The next kind of oligarchy should be established in a similar way, except that the qualifications for citizenship should be slightly tighter.[33]   30
But as for the kind of oligarchy opposite to the ultimate democracy,
which is the most dynastic and tyrannical of oligarchies, the worse it is,
the more guarding it requires. For just as bodies that are in good health
or ships with crews that are in fine shape for a voyage can undergo a
large number of mishaps without being destroyed, whereas diseased   35
bodies and ships with loose timbers and worthless crews cannot survive
even a small number, so too the worst constitutions need the most
guarding. Democracies are generally kept safe by their large citizen pop-   1321ᵃ
ulations (for this is the opposite of justice based on merit), but it is clear
that an oligarchy should, on the contrary, secure its preservation by
being well organized.

Chapter 7

Since there are four principal parts of the multitude (farmers, vulgar   5
craftsmen, tradesmen, and hired laborers), and four useful in war (cavalry, HOPLITES, light infantry, and naval forces), where the country happens to be suitable for cavalry, natural conditions favor the establish-
ment of a powerful oligarchy. For the security of the inhabitants
depends on horse power, and horse breeding is the privilege of those   10
who own large estates.[34] Where the country is suitable for hoplites, on
the other hand, conditions favor the next kind of oligarchy, since hoplites are more often rich than poor.[35]

---

31. Those required for the very existence of a city-state (1283ᵃ17–22, VI.9).
32. From the farmers first, then from the herdsmen, then from the artisans, and
    so on. See 1319ᵃ39–ᵇ1 and note.
33. See 1290ᵃ22–29 and note.
34. See 1289ᵇ33–40.
35. Since heavy armor is expensive.

Light infantry and naval forces, however, are entirely democratic. Therefore, as things stand, wherever there are large numbers of these,
15 and there is faction, the oligarchs often get the worst of it. As a cure for this, one should adopt the practice of military commanders who couple an appropriate contingent of light infantry to their forces of cavalry and hoplites. This is the way the people prevail over the rich during factional
20 conflict (or light infantry can easily take on cavalry and hoplites). Therefore, oligarchs who establish such a force drawn from them are establishing a force against themselves. But since there is a difference of age, and some are older and others younger, they should have their own sons trained in unarmed and lightly armed combat while they are young, so
25 that when they have been taken out of the ranks of the boys they will themselves be skilled practitioners of these tasks.

The multitude should be given a share in the governing class, either in the way mentioned earlier,[36] to those who own an assessed amount of property, or, as in Thebes, to those who have kept out of vulgar occupations for a given period of time,[37] or, as in Massilia, to those who are
30 judged to merit it, whether they come from inside or outside the governing class.

Furthermore, the offices with the most authority, which those in the constitution must hold, should also have public services attached to them, so that the people will be willing not to participate in them, and will sympathize with officials who have paid a heavy price for office. It is also appropriate that, on entering office, they should offer magnificent
35 sacrifices and provide something for the community, so that the people, through sharing in the festivities, and seeing the city-state adorned here with votive statues and there with buildings, will be glad to see the constitution endure. In addition, the notables will have memorials of their
40 expenditure. As things stand, however, those connected with oligarchies do the opposite of this, because they seek profit no less than honor. That is precisely why it is well to call them small democracies.[38]
1321ᵇ   This, then, is the way to determine how democracies and oligarchies should be established.

---

36. At 1320ᵇ25–29.
37. See 1278ᵃ25–26.
38. "Small": because ruled by the few instead of the many; "democracies": because the few pursue money just like the many (see 1318ᵇ16–17).

Chapter 8

After what has just been said, the next topic, as was mentioned earlier,[39] is the matter of correctly distinguishing what pertains to the offices, how many they are, what they are, and what they are concerned with. For 5 without the necessary offices a city-state cannot exist, and without those concerned with proper organization and order it cannot be well managed. Furthermore, in small city-states the offices are inevitably fewer, while in larger ones they are more numerous, as was also said earlier.[40]　10 Consequently, the question of which offices it is appropriate to combine and which to keep separate should not be overlooked.

The first of the necessary offices, then, deals with [1] the supervision of the market, where there must be some office to supervise contracts and maintain good order. For in almost all city-states people have to be able to buy and sell in order to satisfy each other's necessary needs. This 15 is also the readiest way to achieve self-sufficiency, which is thought to be what leads people to join together in one constitution.[41]

Another kind of supervision, connected to this one and close to it, is [2] the supervision of public and private property within the town, so that it may be kept in good order; also, the preservation and repair of decaying buildings and roads, the supervision of property boundaries, so 20 that disputes do not arise over them, and all other sorts of supervision similar to these. Most people call this sort of office town management, though its parts are more than one in number. More populous city-states assign different officials to these; for example, wall repairers, well 25 supervisors, and harbor guards.

Another office is also necessary and closely akin to this one, since it deals with [3] the same areas, though it concerns the country and matters outside the town. In some places its holders are called country managers, in others foresters.

These, then, are three kinds of supervision that deal with necessities. 30 Another is [4] the office that receives public funds, safeguards them, and distributes them to the various branches of the administration. Its holders are called receivers or treasurers.

Another office is [5] that where private contracts and the decisions of

---

39. At 1298ᵃ1–3, IV.15.
40. At 1299ᵃ31–ᵇ30.
41. See 1278ᵇ18–30.

35   law courts must be recorded. Indictments and initiations of judicial proceedings should also be recorded with these officials. In some places this
office too is divided into several parts, in others a single office has authority over all these matters. The officials are called sacred recorders,
supervisors, and recorders.

40   The next after this, and pretty well the most necessary and the most
difficult of the offices, is [6] the one concerned with actions against
those who have been convicted in court, and those whose names are

1322ª posted for fines, and with the custody of their persons. It is a difficult office because it provokes a lot of hatred. So where it is not possible to
make large profits from it, either people are unwilling to hold it, or those
who do hold it are unwilling to act in accordance with the laws. It is a

5   necessary office because there is no benefit in having lawsuits about matters of justice if they do not achieve their end. Consequently, if people
cannot live in a community with each other when lawsuits do not take
place,[42] they cannot do so either where no actions are taken. That is why
it is better for this not to be a single office but to consist of several people drawn from different courts, and why one should try to divide up the

10   tasks connected with posting the list of debtors in a similar way. Furthermore, officials too[43] should take some actions; in particular, incom-
ing officials should take those imposed by outgoing ones, and, in the
case of sitting officials, one should pass sentence and another take the
action. For example, the town managers should take the action imposed
by the market supervisors, while other officials take those imposed by
the town managers. For the less hatred there is toward those who exact

15   the penalty, the more the actions will achieve their end. To have the
same people both pass sentence and carry it out certainly doubles the
hatred; and to have the same people carry out every sentence makes
them inimical to everyone. In many places, the office that keeps prisoners in custody is different from the one that carries out the sentence, as

20   in the case of the office of the so-called Eleven in Athens.[44] Hence it is
also better to split it up, and to use the same device in its case too, since
it is no less necessary than the previous one. Decent people particularly

42. See 1253ª29–39.
43. In addition to those normally assigned the task.
44. Prisoners were kept in custody pending punishment; prison itself was not
used as a punishment. The Eleven, who were in charge of the custody of
prisoners, did carry out executions, but not other sentences. Thus they did to
some degree exemplify the separation Aristotle is praising. But because they
do not perfectly exemplify it, many editors consider the clause in which they
are mentioned to be a marginal gloss which has made its way into the text.

avoid it, however, and giving bad ones authority over it is not safe, since they are more in need of guarding than capable of guarding others. That is why there should not be a single office in charge of guarding prisoners, nor the same office continuously. Instead, prisoners should be supervised by different people in turn, chosen from among the young men, in places where there is a regiment of cadets or guards,[45] or from the other officials.

These offices must be put first, then, as the most necessary. After these are others that are no less necessary, but ranked higher in dignity, since they require much experience and trustworthiness. The offices [7] that deal with the defense of the city-state are of this sort, and any that are organized to meet its wartime needs. In peacetime and wartime alike there should be people to supervise the defense of the gates and walls, and the inspection and organizing of the citizens. In some places there are more offices assigned to all these areas, in others there are fewer (in small city-states, for example, a single office deals with all of them). Such people are called generals or warlords. Furthermore, if there is a cavalry, a light infantry, archers, or a navy, an office is sometimes established for each of them. They are called admirals, cavalry commanders, or regimental commanders, whereas those in charge of the units under these are called warship commanders, company commanders, or tribal leaders, and so on for their subunits. But all of these together constitute a single kind, namely, supervision of military affairs. This, then, is the way things stand with regard to this office.

But since some if not all of the offices handle large sums of public money, there must be [8] a different office to receive and examine their accounts which does not itself handle any other matters. Some call these inspectors, accountants, auditors, or advocates.

Besides all these offices, there is [9] the one with the most authority over everything; for the same office often has authority over both implementing and introducing a measure, or presides over the multitude where the people have authority. For there must be some body to convene the body that has authority over the constitution. In some places, they are called preliminary councilors, because they prepare business for the assembly.[46] But where the multitude are in authority they are usually called a council instead.

Margin references: 25, 30, 35, 1322ᵇ, 5, 10, 15

---

45. In Athens and other city-states young men served from the time they were eighteen until they were twenty in such regiments, which acted as police or civic guards.
46. See 1298ᵇ26–34.

This, then, is pretty much the number of offices that are political. But another kind of supervision is [10] that concerned with the worship of the gods: for example, priests, supervisors of matters relating to the
20   temples (such as the preservation of existing buildings, the restoration of decaying ones), and all other duties concerning the gods. Sometimes it happens, for example, in small city-states, that a single office supervises all this, but sometimes, apart from the priests, there are a number of others, such as supervisors of sacrifices, temple guardians, and sacred
25   treasurers. Next after this is the office specializing in the public sacrifices that the law does not assign to the priests; instead, the holders have the office from the communal hearth.[47] These officials are called archons by some, kings or presidents by others.

To sum up, then, the necessary kinds of supervision deal with the fol-
30   lowing: religious matters, military matters, revenues and expenditures, the market, town, harbors, and country; also matters relating to the courts, such as registering contracts, collecting fines, carrying out of
35   sentences, keeping prisoners in custody, receiving accounts, and inspecting and examining officials; and, finally, matters relating to the body that deliberates about public affairs.

On the other hand, peculiar to city-states that enjoy greater leisure and prosperity and that also pay attention to good order are [11] the offices dealing with the supervision of women, [12] the guardianship of the laws, [13] the supervision of children, [14] authority over the gymnasia, and
1323ᵃ   also [15] the supervision of gymnastic or Dionysiac contests,[48] as well as of any other such public spectacles there may happen to be. Some of these are obviously not democratic, for example, the supervision of women and that of children, for the poor have to employ their women
5   and children as servants, because of their lack of slaves.

There are three offices that city-states use to supervise the selection of the officials who are in authority: [16] the office of law guardian, [17] that of preliminary councilor, and [18] the council. The office of law guardian is aristocratic, that of preliminary councilor oligarchic, and a council, democratic.
10   Pretty well all the offices have now been discussed in outline.

---

47. The communal hearth (*koinē hestia*) derives from the hearth in the king's palace which had both a practical and a magico-religious significance.
48. The dramatic festivals in which tragic and comedic poets competed.

Book VII

Chapter 1

Anyone who intends to investigate the best constitution in the proper way must first determine which life is most choiceworthy, since if this remains unclear, what the best constitution is must also remain unclear. For it is appropriate for those to fare best who live in the best constitution their circumstances allow—provided nothing contrary to reasonable expectation occurs. That is why we should first come to some agreement about what the most choiceworthy life is for practically speaking everyone,[1] and then determine whether it is the same for an individual as for a community, or different.

Since, then, I consider that I have already expressed much that is adequate about the best life in the "external" works,[2] I propose to make use of them here as well. For since, in the case of one division at least, there are three groups—external GOODS, goods of the body, and goods of the soul—surely no one would raise a dispute and say that not all of them need be possessed by those who are BLESSEDLY HAPPY. For no one would call a person blessedly happy who has no shred of courage, temperance, justice, or practical wisdom, but is afraid of the flies buzzing around him, stops at nothing to gratify his appetite for food or drink, betrays his dearest friends for a pittance, and has a mind as foolish and prone to error as a child's or a madman's. But while almost all accept these claims, they disagree about quantity and relative superiority. For they consider any amount of virtue, however small, to be sufficient, but seek an unlimitedly excessive amount of wealth, possessions, power, reputation, and the like.

We, however, will say to them that it is easy to reach a reliable conclusion on these matters even from the facts themselves. For we see that the

1. At 1324ᵃ18–19 it is allowed that participating in a city-state may not be most choiceworthy for *absolutely* everyone.
2. See 1278ᵇ31 note.

40   virtues are not acquired and preserved by means of external goods, but
the other way around,[3] and we see that a happy life for human beings,
1323ᵇ   whether it consists in pleasure or virtue or both, is possessed more often
by those who have cultivated their characters and minds to an excessive
degree, but have been moderate in their acquisition of external goods,
than by those who have acquired more of the latter than they can possi-
5   bly use, but are deficient in the former. Moreover, if we investigate the
matter on the basis of argument, it is plain to see. For external goods
have a limit, as does any tool, and all useful things are useful for something; so excessive amounts of them must harm or bring no benefit to
their possessors.[4] In the case of each of the goods of the soul, however,
10   the more excessive it is, the more useful it is (if these goods too should
be thought of as useful, and not simply as noble).

It is generally clear too, we shall say, that the relation of superiority
holding between the best condition of each thing and that of others corresponds to that holding between the things whose conditions we say
15   they are. So since the soul is UNQUALIFIEDLY more valuable, and also
more valuable to us, than possessions or the body, its best states must be
proportionally better than theirs. Besides, it is for the sake of the soul
that these things are naturally choiceworthy, and every sensible person
20   should choose them for its sake, not the soul for theirs.

We may take it as agreed, then, that each person has just as much happiness as he has virtue, practical wisdom, and the action that expresses
them. We may use GOD as evidence of this. For he is blessedly happy, not
because of any external goods but because of himself and a certain qual-
25   ity in his nature.[5] This is also the reason that good luck and happiness
are necessarily different. For chance or luck produces goods external to
the soul, but no one is just or temperate as a result of luck or because of
luck.[6]

30   The next point depends on the same arguments. The happy city-state
is the one that is best and acts nobly. It is impossible for those who do
not do noble deeds to act nobly; and no action, whether a man's or a city-
state's, is noble when separate from virtue and practical wisdom. But the

---

3. The point is probably not that virtue invariably makes you rich, but that,
without virtue, wealth and the rest can do you as much harm as good.
4. See 1256ᵇ35–36, 1257ᵇ28.
5. See Introduction xliii–xlv. Luck (*tuchē*) and chance (*to automaton*) and the
difference between them are discussed in *Ph.* II.4–6.
6. See *NE* 1153ᵇ19–25.

courage, justice, and practical wisdom of a city-state have the same capacity and are of the same kind as those possessed by each human being   *35*
who is said to be just, practically wise, and temperate.

So much, then, for the preface to our discussion.[7] For we cannot avoid
talking about these issues altogether, but neither can we go through all
the arguments pertaining to them, since that is a task for another type of
study.[8] But for now, let us assume this much, that the best life, both for   *40*
individuals separately and for city-states collectively, is a life of virtue
sufficiently equipped with the resources[9] needed to take part in virtuous
actions. With regard to those who dispute this, if any happen not to be   *1324ᵃ*
persuaded by what has been said, we must ignore them in our present
study, but investigate them later.

Chapter 2

It remains to say whether the happiness of each individual human being   *5*
is the same as that of a city-state or not. But here too the answer is evident, since everyone would agree that they are the same. For those who
suppose that living well for an individual consists in wealth will also call
a whole city-state blessedly happy if it happens to be wealthy. And those
who honor the tyrannical life above all would claim that the city-state   *10*
that rules the greatest number[10] is happiest. And if someone approves of
an individual because of his virtue, he will also say that the more excellent city-state is happier.

Two questions need to be investigated, however. First, which life is
more choiceworthy, the one that involves taking part in politics with
other people and participating in a city-state, or the life of an alien cut   *15*
off from the political community? Second, and regardless of whether
participating in a city-state is more choiceworthy for everyone or for
most but not for all, which constitution, which condition of the city-
state, is best? This second question, and not the one about what is   *20*
choiceworthy for the individual, is a task for political thought or theory.
And since that is the investigation we are now engaged in, whereas the
former is a further task, our task is the second question.[11]

---

7. VII.1–3 is all prefatory, as 1325ᵇ33 makes clear.
8. Namely, ethics.
9. That is, external GOODS.
10. Presumably, the greatest number of other city-states.
11. See Introduction xlvi–xlviii.

    It is evident that the best constitution must be that organization in
25 which anyone might do best and live a blessedly happy life. But the very
    people who agree that the most choiceworthy life is the life of virtue are
    the ones who dispute about whether it is the political life of action that is
    worthy of choice or rather the one released from external concerns—a
    contemplative life, for example, which some say is the only life for a
    philosopher. For it is evident that almost all of those, past or present,
    with the greatest love for the honor accorded to virtue have chosen be-
30 tween these two lives (I mean the political life and the philosophic one).
    And it makes no small difference on which side the truth lies, since any-
    one with sound practical wisdom at least must organize his affairs by
    looking to the better target—and this applies to human beings individu-
    ally and to the constitution communally.

35   Some people think that ruling over one's neighbors like a master in-
    volves one of the greatest injustices, and that rule of a statesman, though
    it involves no injustice, does involve an impediment to one's own well-
    being. Others think almost the opposite, they say that an active, political
40 life is the only one for a man, since the actions expressing each of the
    virtues are no more available to private individuals than to those engaged
1324ᵇ in communal affairs and politics. Some give this reply, then, but others
    claim that only a constitution that involves being a master or tyrant is
    happy.

        For some people, indeed, the fundamental aim of the constitution and
    the laws just is to rule their neighbors like a master. That is why, even
5   though most customs have been established pretty much at random in
    most cases, anywhere the laws have to some extent a single aim, it is al-
    ways domination. So in Sparta and Crete the educational system and
    most of the laws are set up for war. Besides, all the nations that have the
10 power to be ACQUISITIVE honor military power—for example, the
    Scythians, Persians, Thracians, and Celts. Indeed, some of them even
    have laws designed to foster military virtue. It is said that in Carthage,
    for example, they receive armlets as decorations for each campaign in
15 which they take part. There was once a law in Macedonia too that any
    man who had not killed an enemy must wear a halter for a belt. Among
    the Scythians, when the cup passes around at a feast, those who have not
    killed an enemy are not permitted to drink from it. And among the
    Iberians, a warlike race, they place small obelisks in the earth around a
20 man's tomb to show the number of enemies he has killed. And there are
    many other similar practices among other peoples, some prescribed by
    law, others by custom.

Yet to anyone willing to investigate the matter, it would perhaps seem quite absurd if the task of a statesman involved being able to study ways to rule or master his neighbors, whether they are willing or not. For how *25* could this be a political or legislative task, when it is not even lawful? But to rule not only justly but also unjustly is unlawful, whereas it is quite possible to dominate unjustly. Certainly, this is not what we see in the other sciences; for it is not the doctor's or captain's task to use force on *30* his patients or passengers if he cannot persuade them. Yet many seem to think that statesmanship is the same as mastership,[12] and what they all say is unjust or nonbeneficial when it is done to them, they are not ashamed to do to others. For they seek just rule for themselves, but pay *35* no attention to justice in their dealings with others. It is absurd to deny, however, that one thing is fit to be a master and another not fit to be a master.[13] So, if indeed one is that way, one should not try to rule as a master over everyone, but only over those who are fit to be ruled by a master. Similarly, one should not hunt human beings for a feast or sacrifice, but only animals that are fit to be hunted for these purposes: and *40* that is any wild animal that is edible.

Furthermore, it is possible for even a single city-state to be happy all by itself, provided it is well governed, since it is possible for a city-state *1325ª* to be settled somewhere by itself and to employ excellent laws. And *its* constitution will not be organized for the purposes of war or of dominating its enemies (for we are assuming that it has none).

It is clear, therefore, that all military practices are to be regarded as *5* noble, not when they are pursued as the highest end of all, but only when they are pursued for the sake of the highest end. The task of an excellent legislator, then, is to study how a city-state, a race of men, or any other community can come to have a share in a good life and in the happiness that is possible for them. There will be differences, of course, in *10* some of the laws that are instituted, and if there are neighboring peoples, it belongs to legislative science to consider what sorts of military training are needed in relation to which sorts of people and which measures are to be used in relation to each.

But the question of which end the best constitution should aim at will receive a proper investigation later.[14] *15*

12. See 1252ª7–16 and note.
13. Reading *despozon* with Lord and the mss.
14. VII.13–15.

Chapter 3

We must now reply to the two sides who agree that the virtuous life is most choiceworthy, but disagree about how to practice it. For some rule out the holding of political office and consider that the life of a free person is both different from that of a statesman and the most choiceworthy one of all. But others consider that the political life is best, since it is impossible for someone inactive to do or act well, and that doing well and happiness are the same. We must reply that they are both partly right and partly wrong. On the one hand, it is true to say that the life of a free person is better than that of a master. For there is certainly nothing grand about using a slave as a slave, since ordering people to do necessary tasks is in no way noble. None the less, it is wrong to consider that every kind of rule is rule by a master. For the difference between rule over free people and over slaves is no smaller than the difference between being naturally free and being a natural slave. We have adequately distinguished them in our first discussions.[15] On the other hand, to praise inaction more than action is not correct either. For happiness is ACTION, and many noble things reach their end in the actions of those who are just and temperate.

Perhaps someone will take these conclusions to imply, however, that having authority over everyone is what is best. For in that way one would have authority over the greatest number of the very noblest actions. It would follow that someone who has the power to rule should not surrender it to his neighbor but take it away from him, and that a father should disregard his children, a child his father, a friend his friend, and pay no attention to anything except ruling. For what is best is most choiceworthy, and doing well is best.

What they say is perhaps true, if indeed those who use force and commit robbery will come to possess the most choiceworthy thing there is. But perhaps they cannot come to possess it, and the underlying assumption here is false. For someone cannot do noble actions if he is not as superior to those he rules as a husband is to his wife, a father to his children, or a master to his slaves. Therefore, a transgressor could never make up later for his deviation from virtue. For among those who are similar, ruling and being ruled in turn is just and noble, since this is equal or similar treatment. But unequal shares for equals or dissimilar ones for similars is contrary to nature; and nothing contrary to nature is

15. I.4–7.

noble. Hence when someone else has superior virtue and his power to do   *10*
the best things is also superior, it is noble to follow and just to obey him.
But he should possess not virtue alone, but also the power he needs to do
these things.

If these claims are correct, and we should assume that happiness is
doing well, then the best life, whether for a whole city-state collectively
or for an individual, would be a life of action. Yet it is not necessary, as   *15*
some suppose, for a life of action to involve relations with other people,
nor are those thoughts alone active which we engage in for the sake of
action's consequences; the study and thought that are their own ends
and are engaged in for their own sake are much more so. For to do or act   *20*
well is the end, so that ACTION of a sort is the end too. And even in the
case of actions involving external objects, the one who does them most
fully is, strictly speaking, the master craftsman who directs them by
means of his thought.[16]

Moreover, city-states situated by themselves, which have deliberately
chosen to live that way, do not necessarily have to be inactive, since activity can take place even among their parts. For the parts of a city-state   *25*
have many sorts of communal relationships with one another.[17] Similarly, this holds for any human being taken singly. For otherwise GOD
and the entire universe could hardly be in a fine condition; for they have
no external actions, only the internal ones proper to them.

It is evident, then, that the same life is necessarily best both for each   *30*
human being and for city-states and human beings collectively.

Chapter 4

Since what has just been said about these matters was by way of a preface, and since we studied the various constitutions earlier,[18] the starting
point for the remainder of our investigation is first to discuss the condi-   *35*
tions that should be presupposed to exist by the ideal city-state we are
about to construct. For the best constitution cannot come into existence
without commensurate resources. Hence we should presuppose that
many circumstances are as ideal as we could wish, although none should

---

16. See 1253[b]27–1254[a]8.
17. Normally, however, a city-state is politically active when it exercises leader-
    ship over other city-states or has other sorts of political relations with them
    (see 1327[b]4–6).
18. In Book II.

be impossible. I have in mind, for example, the number of citizens and
40 the size of the territory.[19] For other craftsmen—for example, a weaver or
a shipbuilder—should also be supplied with suitable material to work
1326ᵃ on, and the better the material that has been prepared, the finer the
product of their craft must necessarily be. So too a statesman or legislator should be supplied with proper material in a suitable condition.

5   First among the political resources needed for a city-state is the multitude of people. How many should there be of them, and of what sort?
Similarly for the territory, how large should it be, and of what nature?
Most people suppose that a happy city-state must be a great one, but
even if what they suppose is true, they are ignorant of the quality that
10 makes a city-state great or small. For they judge a city-state to be great if
the number of its inhabitants is large, whereas they ought to look not to
number but to ability. For a city-state too has a task to perform, so that
the city-state that is best able to complete it is the one that should be
considered greatest.[20] Similarly, one should say that Hippocrates[21] is a
15 greater doctor than someone who exceeds him in physical size, not a
greater human being.

       Yet even if one had to judge the greatness of a city-state by looking to
the multitude, this should not be any chance multitude (for city-states
inevitably contain a large number of slaves, resident aliens, and foreign-
20 ers), but rather to those who are *part* of it, that is to say, those who form
one of the parts from which a city-state is properly constituted.[22] For
possessing a superior number of these is the sign of a great city-state. A
city-state that can send a large number of vulgar craftsmen out to war,
on the other hand, but only a few hoplites, cannot possibly be great. For
a great city-state is not the same as a densely populated one.

25   Furthermore it is evident from the facts at least that it is difficult,
perhaps impossible, for an overly populated city-state to be well governed. At any rate, among those that are held to be nobly governed, we
see none that fails to restrict the size of its population. Argument also
convinces us that this is clearly so. For law is a kind of organization,[23]
30 and good government must of necessity be good organization. But an
excessively large number of things cannot share in organization. For that

19. See 1265ᵃ17–18.
20. See *NE* 1098ᵃ7–20.
21. A famous fifth-century doctor from the island of Cos.
22. See VII.8.
23. Compare 1287ᵃ18.

would be a task for a divine power, the sort that holds the entire universe together. For beauty is usually found in number and magnitude. Hence a city-state whose size is fixed by the aforementioned limit must also be the most beautiful. But the size of city-state, like everything else, has a *35* certain scale: animals, plants, and tools. For when each of them is neither too small nor too excessively large, it will have its own proper capacity; otherwise, it will either be wholly deprived of its nature or be in poor condition. For example, a ship that is one span [seven and a half inches] long will not be a ship at all, nor will one of two stades [twelve *40* hundred feet]; and as it approaches a certain size, it will sail badly, because it either is still too small or still too large. Similarly for a city-state: *1326ᵇ* one that consists of too few people is not SELF-SUFFICIENT (whereas a city-state is self-sufficient), but one that consists of too many, while it is self-sufficient in the necessities, the way a nation is, is still no city-state, since it is not easy for it to have a constitution. For who will be the general of its excessively large multitude, and who, unless he has the voice *5* of Stentor, will serve as its herald?[24]

Hence the first city-state to arise is the one composed of the first multitude large enough to be self-sufficient with regard to living the good life as a political community. It is also possible for a city-state that exceeds this one in number to be a greater city-state, but, as we said, this is *10* not possible indefinitely. The limit to its expansion can easily be seen from the facts. For a city-state's actions are either those of the rulers or those of the ruled. And a ruler's task is to issue orders and decide. But in order to decide lawsuits and distribute offices on the basis of merit, each *15* citizen must know what sorts of people the other citizens are. For where they do not know this, the business of electing officials and deciding lawsuits must go badly, since to act haphazardly is unjust in both these proceedings. But this is plainly what occurs in an overly populated city-state. Besides, it is easy for resident aliens and foreigners to participate *20* in the constitution, since the excessive size of the population makes escaping detection easy. It is clear, then, that the best limit for a city-state is this: it is the greatest size of multitude that promotes life's self-sufficiency and that can be easily surveyed as a whole. The size of the city-state, then, should be determined in this way. *25*

24. Stentor was a Homeric hero gifted with a very powerful voice.

Chapter 5

Similar things hold in the case of territory. For, as far as its quality is concerned, it is clear that everyone would praise the most self-sufficient. And as such it must produce everything, for self-sufficiency is having everything and needing nothing. In size or extent, it should be large
30 enough to enable the inhabitants to live a life of leisure in a way that is generous and at the same time temperate.[25] But whether this defining principle is rightly or wrongly formulated is something that must be investigated with greater precision later on, when we come to discuss the question of possessions generally—what it is to be well off where prop-
35 erty is concerned, and how and in what way this is related to its use. For there are many disputes about this question raised by those who urge us to adopt one extreme form of life or the other: penury in the one case, luxury in the other.[26]

The layout of the territory is not difficult to describe (although on
40 some points the advice of military experts should also be taken): it should be difficult for enemies to invade and easy for the citizens to get out to.[27] Moreover, just as the multitude of people should, as we said, be
1327ᵃ easy to survey as a whole, the same holds of the territory. For a territory easy to survey as a whole is easy to defend.

If the CITY-STATE is to be ideally sited, it is appropriate for it to be well situated in relation to the sea and the surrounding territory. One
5 defining principle was mentioned above: defensive troops should have access to all parts of the territory. The remaining defining principle is that the city-state should be accessible to transportation, so that crops, timber, and any other such materials the surrounding territory happens to possess can be easily transported to it.

Chapter 6

There is much dispute about whether access to the sea is beneficial or harmful to well-governed city-states. For it is said that entertaining for-

---

25. See 1265ᵃ31–38.
26. The general investigation advertised in this passage does not appear in the *Politics* as we have it. The defining principle mentioned is endorsed at 1265ᵃ28–38, 1266ᵇ24–31. The relationship between ownership of property and its use is discussed in 1262ᵇ37–1263ᵃ40.
27. *euexodon*: "get out of." But see 1327ᵃ6–7.

eigners as guests who have been brought up under different laws is
detrimental to good government, and that the overpopulation which results from having a multitude of traders who use the sea for importing   *15*
and exporting is contrary to being well governed.[28] But if these consequences are avoided, it is quite clear that it is better for a city-state and
its territory to have access to the sea, both for the purposes of safety and
to ensure a ready supply of necessities. For to be able to withstand war   *20*
more easily and ensure their own safety, the citizens should be capable of
defending themselves on both land and sea; and if they are unable to attack their assailants on both land and sea, at least they will be in a better
position to do so on one or the other, if they have access to both.   *25*

City-states must also import the commodities that are not available at
home and export those of which they have a surplus. For a city-state
should engage in trade for itself, not others.[29] Those who open their
market to everyone do so for the revenue. But a city-state that should not
be involved in this sort of acquisitiveness should have no market of this   *30*
sort.

Even nowadays we see many territories and city-states that have ports
or harbors naturally well situated in relation to the city-state, so that
they are neither too far away from it nor are yet parts of the same town
but are kept under its authority by walls and other similar defenses. So it   *35*
is evident that if any good comes from this sort of connection with a port
or harbor, it will be available to the city-state, whereas if there is anything harmful, it can be prevented by means of laws that specify or define the sorts of people that should or should not have dealings with one
another.

As far as naval forces are concerned, it is quite clear that it is best to   *40*
have a certain amount of them. For a city-state should be formidable on
both land and sea, able to defend not just itself but some of its neighbors
as well. But when it comes to the number and size of these forces, we   *1327ᵇ*
have to consider the city-state's way of life. If it is going to have a political life and one of leadership, it must possess naval as well as other forces   *5*
adequate for its actions. But there is no need for city-states to suffer the
overpopulation associated with including a crowd of sailors, since they
should not be part of the city-state. For the marines who are part of the
infantry are free, and it is they who are in authority and command the   *10*
crew. And if the city-state contains a multitude of SUBJECT PEOPLES and

28. See VI.4.
29. See 1277ᵃ33–ᵇ7, 1337ᵇ17–21.

farmers, there cannot be any shortage of sailors. We see this happening in certain city-states even now—for example, in the city-state of Heraclea. For it can man many triremes, despite being more modest in size

15   than many other city-states.

Matters regarding territory, harbors, city-states, the sea, and naval force, then, should be determined in this way.

Chapter 7

We spoke earlier about what limit there should be on the number of citizens.[30] Let us now discuss what sort of natural qualities they should have.

20   One may pretty much grasp what these qualities are by looking at those Greek city-states that have a good reputation, and at the way the entire inhabited world is divided into nations. The nations in cold regions, particularly Europe, are full of spirit but somewhat deficient in intelligence and craft knowledge. That is precisely why they remain

25   comparatively free, but are apolitical and incapable of ruling their neighbors. Those in Asia, on the other hand, have souls endowed with intelligence and craft knowledge, but they lack spirit. That is precisely why they are ruled and enslaved. The Greek race, however, occupies an intermediate position geographically, and so shares in both sets of characteristics.

30   teristics. For it is both spirited and intelligent. That is precisely why it remains free, governed in the best way, and capable, if it chances upon a single constitution, of ruling all the others.[31] Greek nations also differ from one another in these ways. For some have a nature that is one-

35   sided, whereas in others both of these capacities are well blended. It is evident, then, that both spirit and intelligence should be present in the natures of people if they are to be easily guided to virtue by the legislator.

Some say that guardians should have precisely this quality: they must be friendly to those they know and fierce to those they do not,[32] and that

40   spirit is what makes them be friendly. For spirit is the capacity of the soul by which we feel friendship. A sign of this is that our spirit is roused

---

30. In VII.4.
31. Aristotle cannot be supposing that all of Greece might form a single city-state; it was far too large for that. Presumably, then, he is supposing that it might consist of different city-states that are friendly to one another because (unlike Sparta and Athens) they have the same kind of constitution.
32. Plato, *Republic* 375b–376c.

more against associates and friends who we think have slighted us than 1328ᵃ
against strangers. Hence, when Archilochus was complaining about his
friends, it was appropriate for him to say to his spirit: "It is you who are
choked with rage against your friends."[33] Ruling and being free invari- 5
ably derive from this capacity; for spirit is both imperious and in-
domitable. But it is not correct to claim that guardians should be harsh
to those they do not know, since one should not treat anyone in this way.
Nor are magnanimous people naturally harsh, except to wrongdoers, 10
though they are harsher to companions they think are wronging them,
as we said earlier. And it is reasonable that this should be so. For in addition to the wrong they have suffered, they consider themselves to have
been deprived of the benefit companions owe to one another. Hence the
sayings: "Wars among brothers are harsh" and "Those who have loved 15
excessively will hate excessively, too."[34]

Enough has now been determined about the people who should participate in politics, their number and their natural qualities, and about
the size and type of the city-state's territory. We should not expect theoretical discussions to provide the same precision as what comes through 20
perception.[35]

Chapter 8

Since, as in the case of every other naturally constituted whole, the
things that it cannot exist without are not all parts of it, clearly the
things that are necessary for the existence of a city-state should not be 25
assumed to be parts of it either, and likewise for any other community
that constitutes a single type of thing. For communities should have one
thing that is common and the same for all their members, whether they
share in it equally or unequally: for example, food, a piece of territory, or
something else of this sort. But whenever one thing is for the sake of another and the other is the end for whose sake it is, they have nothing in
common except that one produces and the other gets produced. I mean,
for example, the relationship of every tool or craftsman to the work pro- 30
duced. For the house and the builder have nothing in common. Rather,

---

33. Diehl I.230, fr. 67b. Archilochus was a seventh-century poet from Paros.
34. The first quotation is from Euripides (Nauck 672, fr. 975); the second
(Nauck 854, fr. 78) is from an unknown author.
35. Presumably, because no theoretical discussion can take account of all the
empirical details (observation or perception must provide these).

the builder's craft is for the sake of the house. That is why, though city-states need property, property is not a part of a city-state. Among the
35   parts of property are many living things, but a city-state is a community of similar people aiming at the best possible life.

Since happiness is the best thing, however, and it is some sort of activation or complete exercise of virtue,[36] and since, as it happens, some people are able to share in happiness, whereas others are able to do so only to a small degree or not at all, it is clear that this is why there are
40   several kinds and varieties of city-state and a plurality of constitutions. For it is by seeking happiness in different ways and by different means
1328ᵇ that individual groups of people create different ways of life and different constitutions.[37]

But we must also investigate the question of how many of these things there are that a city-state cannot exist without. For what we are calling the parts of a city-state would of necessity be included among them. So we must determine the number of tasks there are, since this will make
5   the answer clear. First, there should be a food supply. Second, crafts (for life needs many tools). Third, weapons; for the members of the community must also have weapons of their own, both in order to rule (since there are people who disobey) and in order to deal with outsiders who
10   attempt to wrong them. Fourth, a ready supply of wealth, both for internal needs and for wars. Fifth, but of primary importance, the supervision of religious matters, which is called a priesthood. Sixth, and most necessary of all, judgment about what is beneficial and what is just in their relations with one another.[38] These, then, are the tasks that need to
15   be done in practically speaking every city-state. For a city-state is not just any chance multitude, but one that is self-sufficient with regard to life, as we say; and if any of these tasks is lacking, a community cannot be unqualifiedly self-sufficient. Hence a city-state must be organized
20   around these tasks. So there should be a multitude of farmers to provide the food, craftsmen, soldiers, rich people, priests, and people to decide matters of necessity and benefit.[39]

---

36. See Introduction xxxi–xxxv.
37. Compare IV.3, IV.6, 1301ᵃ25–33, 1301ᵇ29–1302ᵃ2, VI.1–7.
38. Deliberative judgment concerns what is beneficial, judicial judgment what is just or unjust (see 1328ᵇ6–7).
39. What is necessary is what justice requires (see 1328ᵇ14).

Chapter 9

Having determined these matters, it remains to investigate whether everyone should share in all the tasks we mentioned (for it is possible for all the same people to be farmers, craftsmen, deliberators and judges), or whether different people should be assigned to each of them, or whether some tasks are necessarily specialized, whereas others can be shared by everyone. But it is not the same in every constitution. For it is possible, as we said,[40] for everyone to share every task, or for not everyone to share in every task, but certain people in certain ones. For these differences too make constitutions differ. In democracies everyone shares in everything, whereas in oligarchies it is the opposite.

Since we are investigating the best constitution, however, the one that would make a city-state most happy—and happiness cannot exist apart from virtue, as was said earlier—it evidently follows that in a city-state governed in the finest manner, possessing men who are unqualifiedly just (and not given certain assumptions[41]), the citizens should not live the life of a vulgar craftsman or tradesman. For lives of these sorts are ignoble and inimical to virtue. Nor should those who are going to be citizens engage in farming, since leisure is needed both to develop virtue and to engage in political actions.

But since the best city-state contains both a military part and one that deliberates about what is beneficial and makes judgments about what is just, and since it is evident that these, more than anything else, are parts of the city-state, should these tasks also be assigned to different people, or are both to be assigned to the same people? This is also evident, because in one way the tasks should be assigned to the same people, and in another they should be assigned to different ones. For since the best time for each of the two tasks is different, in that one requires practical wisdom and the other physical strength, they should be assigned to different people. On the other hand, since those capable of using and resisting force cannot possibly tolerate being ruled continuously, for this reason the two tasks should be assigned to the same people. For those who control the weapons also control whether a constitution will survive or not. The only course remaining, then, is for the constitution to assign both tasks to the same people, but not at the same time. Instead, since it

40. For example, II.1–5.
41. For example, those that a deviant constitution makes about the nature of justice. See Introduction, lxvi–lxvii.

15   is natural for physical strength to be found among younger men and
      practical wisdom among older ones, it is beneficial and just to assign the
      tasks to each group on the basis of age, since this division is based on
      merit.

          Moreover, the property should belong to them. For the citizens must
      be well supplied with resources, and these people are the citizens. For
      the class of vulgar craftsmen does not participate in the city-state, nor
20   does any other class whose members are not "craftsmen of virtue."[42]
      This is clear from our basic assumption. For happiness necessarily ac-
      companies virtue, and a city-state must not be called happy by looking at
      just a part, but by looking at all the citizens.[43] It is also evident that the
25   property should be theirs, since the farmers must be either slaves or
      non-Greek subject peoples.

          Of the things we listed earlier, then, only the class of priests remains.
      Its organization is also evident. No farmer or vulgar craftsman should be
      appointed a priest, since it is appropriate for the gods to be honored by
30   citizens. But because the political or citizen class is divided into two
      parts, the military and the deliberative, and because it is appropriate for
      those who have retired because of age to render service to the gods and
      find rest, the priesthoods should be assigned to them.

          We have now discussed the things without which a city-state cannot
35   be constituted, and how many parts of a city-state there are. Farmers,
      craftsmen, and the laboring class generally are necessary for the exis-
      tence of city-states, but the military and deliberative classes are a city-
      state's parts. Each of these classes is separate from the others, some per-
      manently, others by turns.

Chapter 10

      Those who philosophize about constitutions, whether nowadays or in
40   recent times, seem not to be the only ones to recognize that a city-state
      should be divided into separate classes, and that the military class
1329⁵ should be different from the class of farmers. For it is still this way even

---

42. Plato, *Republic* 500d.
43. The best constitution must be happy; a constitution is happy if all its parts
    are; happiness goes along with virtue; so all the parts must have virtue; vul-
    gar craftsmen cannot have virtue; hence they cannot be happy; hence they
    cannot be parts of the best constitution.

today in Egypt and Crete, Sesostris having made such a law for Egypt, so it is said, and Minos for Crete.[44]

MESSES also seem to be an ancient organization; they arose in Crete 5 during the reign of Minos, but those in Italy are much older. Local historians say that the Oenotrians changed their name to Italians when a certain Italus who settled there became their king. It was because of him that the promontory of Europe that lies between the Gulfs of Scylletium 10 and Lametius (which are a half-day's journey apart) was given the name Italy.[45] It was Italus, they say, who made the nomadic Oenotrians into farmers, enacted laws for them, and first introduced messes. That is why 15 some of his descendants still use messes even today, as well as some of his other laws. Those living near Tyrrhenia were the Opicians, who were then (as now) called Ausonians; those living near Iapygia and the Ionian 20 Gulf, in a region called Siritis, were the Chonians, who were related to the Oenotrians by race. So it was in this region that messes were first organized. The separation of the political multitude into classes, on the other hand, originated in Egypt, for the kingship of Sesostris is much earlier than that of Minos. We should take it, indeed, that pretty well 25 everything else too has been discovered many times, or rather an infinite number of times, in the long course of history. For our needs are likely to teach the necessities, and once they are present, the things that add refinement and luxury to life quite naturally develop.[46] Hence we should suppose that the same is true of matters pertaining to constitutions. 30 That all such matters are ancient is indicated by the facts about Egypt. For the Egyptians are held to be the most ancient people, and they have always had laws and a political organization. Therefore, one should make adequate use of what has been discovered, but also try to investigate whatever has been overlooked. 35

We said earlier that the territory should belong to those who possess weapons and participate in the constitution; we explained why the class of farmers should be different from them; and we discussed how much territory there should be and of what sort. Our first task now is to discuss the distribution of land, who the farmers should be, and what sort of people they should be. We do not agree with those who claim that 40

44. See Herodotus II.164–67; Plato, *Timaeus* 24b. Sesostris or Senusret III was king of Egypt *c.* 2099–2061.
45. The area referred to is the "toe" of modern Italy between the Gulfs of Squillace and Eufemia.
46. See 1264ᵃ5 and note.

property should be communally owned, but it should be commonly
1330ᵃ used, as it is among friends, and no citizen should be in need of sustenance.[47] As for messes, everyone agrees that it is useful for well-orga-
nized city-states to have them. (Our own reasons for agreeing with this
5   will be stated later.)[48] All the citizens should participate in these meals,
even though it is not easy for the poor to contribute the required amount
from their private resources and maintain the rest of their household as
well. Furthermore, expenses relating to the gods should be shared in
common by the entire city-state.

So the territory must be divided into two parts, one of which is com-
10   munal and another that belongs to private individuals. And each of these
must again be divided in two: one part of the communal land should be
used to support public services to the gods, the other to defray the cost
of messes; one part of the private land should be located near the frontiers, the other near the city-state, so that, with two allotments assigned
15   to each citizen, all of them may share in both locations. This not only accords with justice and equality, but ensures greater unanimity in the face
of wars with neighbors. For wherever things are not this way, some citizens make light of feuds with bordering city-states, while others are
20   overly and ignobly concerned about them. That is why some city-states
have a law that prohibits those who dwell close to the border from participating in deliberations about whether to go to war with neighboring
peoples, because their private interests are thought to prevent them
from deliberating well. For these reasons, then, the land must be divided
in the way we described.

25   As for the farmers, ideally speaking, they should be racially heteroge-
neous and spiritless slaves, since they would then be useful workers, un-
likely to stir up change. As a second best, they should be non-Greek
subject peoples, similar in nature to the slaves just mentioned. Those
30   who work on private land should be the private possessions of the owners; those who work on the communal land should be communal property. Later we shall discuss how slaves should be treated and why it is
better to hold out freedom as a reward to all slaves.[49]

47. See 1263ᵃ21–41, Introduction lxxvi–lxxviii.
48. A promise unfulfilled in the *Politics* as we have it.
49. The promised further discussion is missing from the *Politics* as we have it.
    See *Oec*. 1344ᵇ11–21.

Chapter 11

We said earlier that a city-state should have as much access to land and sea, and indeed to its entire territory, as circumstances allow. As regards its own situation, one should ideally determine its site by looking to four factors.[50] The first is health, since it is a necessity. City-states that slope toward the east, that is, toward the winds that blow from the direction of the rising sun, are healthier. Those that slope away from the north wind are second healthiest, since they have milder winters. A further factor is that the city-state should be well sited for political and military activities. As regards military activities, the city-state should be easy for the citizens themselves to march out from but difficult for their enemies to approach and blockade. It should also possess a plentiful water supply of its own, especially springs. But if it does not, the construction of many large reservoirs for rain water has been found as a way to prevent the supply from running short when the citizens are kept away from their territory by war. Since we must of necessity consider the health of the inhabitants, and it depends on the city-state being well situated on healthy ground and facing in a healthy direction, and second, on using healthy water supplies, this too should be matter of more than incidental concern. For the things our bodies use most frequently and in the greatest quantity contribute most to health, and water and air are by nature of this sort. Hence if it happens that all the springs are not equally healthy or if the healthy ones are not abundant, well-planned city-states should keep apart those suitable for drinking from those used for other purposes.

The same type of fortification is not beneficial for all constitutions. For example, an acropolis [hill fort] is suitable for an oligarchy or a monarchy; one on level ground for a democracy. An aristocracy, on the other hand, should have neither of these, but rather a number of strongholds.

Where private dwellings are concerned, the modern Hippodamean[51] scheme of laying them out in straight rows is considered pleasanter and

(margin line numbers: 35, 40, 1330[b], 5, 10, 15, 20)

---

50. Reading *pros hautēn* at [a]36 with Dreizehnter and the mss. The four factors could be either fresh air, clean water, political requirements, and military requirements, or health (which is largely a matter of fresh air and clean water), political requirements, military requirements, and order or beauty (see 1330[b]31, 1331[a]12).

51. Hippodamus of Miletus: see II.8.

more useful for general purposes. But, when it comes to security in wartime, the opposite plan, which prevailed in ancient times, is thought
25　to be better. For it makes it difficult for foreign troops to enter[52] and for attackers to find their way around. Hence the best city-state should share in the features of both plans. This is possible if the houses are laid out like vine "clumps" (as some farmers call them),[53] that is, if certain parts and areas are laid out in straight rows, but not the city-state as a
30　whole. In this way, both safety and beauty will be well served.

Some people say[54] that city-states that lay claim to virtue should not have walls. But this is a very old-fashioned notion. Especially when it is plain to see that city-states that pride themselves on not having walls are refuted by the facts.[55] It may not be noble to seek safety behind fortified
35　walls against an evenly matched or only slightly more numerous foe, but it can and does happen that the superior numbers of the attackers are too much for human virtue[56] or the virtue of a small number of people. Hence if the city-state is to survive without suffering harm or arrogant
40　treatment, it should be left to military expertise to determine what the most secure kind of fortified walls are for it to have, particularly now
1331ᵃ　that the invention of projectiles and siege engines[57] has reached such a high degree of precision. To claim that city-states should not have surrounding walls is like flattening the mountains and trying to make the
5　territory easy to invade, or like not having walls for private houses, on the grounds that they make the inhabitants cowardly. Furthermore, we should not forget that the inhabitants of a city-state with surrounding walls can treat it either as having walls or as not having them, whereas the inhabitants of a city-state without walls lack this option. Given that
10　this is how things stand, a city-state not only should have surrounding walls, it should take care to ensure that they both enhance the beauty of the city-state and satisfy military requirements, especially those brought

52. Reading *duseisodos* with Richards, Ross, and others. Alternatively (mss.): "difficult to get out of" (*dusexodos*). See 1330ᵇ2–3.
53. A vine clump was laid out like the five spots on a die.
54. See Plato, *Laws* 778d–779b. The virtue in question is primarily courage (see 1331ᵃ6).
55. Probably an allusion to Sparta, which prided itself on having no walls, and suffered humiliating defeat in 369, when it was invaded by the Theban Epaminondas (1269ᵇ37).
56. The level of nonheroic virtue achievable by most humans (1295ᵃ25–31).
57. Catapults, siege towers, and battering rams had all been fairly recently introduced.

to light by recent discoveries. For just as attackers are always busily concerned with new ways to get the better of city-states, so too, though   *15*
some defensive devices have already been discovered, defenders should
keep searching for and thinking out new ones. For when people are well
prepared in the first place, no one even thinks of attacking them.

Chapter 12

Since the multitude of citizens should be assigned to messes, and the
walls should have guard houses and towers in suitable places, clearly   *20*
some messes should be provided in these guard houses. That, then, is
how one might arrange these matters. But as for the buildings assigned
to the gods, and the principal messes for officials, it is fitting for them to   *25*
be located together on a suitable site (except in the case of temples assigned a separate location by the law or the Delphic Oracle). This site
should be adequate for the display of virtue[58] and also better fortified
than the neighboring parts of the city-state.

Below this site, it is fitting to establish the kind of marketplace called   *30*
"free," and named as such in Thessaly.[59] This is one that should be kept
clear of all merchandise, and that no vulgar craftsmen, farmers, or the
like may enter unless summoned by officials. The place would have   *35*
added appeal if the gymnasia for adults were situated there. It is also fitting that these be organized by division into age groups. Some of the officials should spend their time with the younger men, while the older
men should spend time with the other officials. For being under the eyes
of the officials is what most engenders true shame, and the kind of fear   *40*
appropriate to free people. The marketplace for merchandise, on the
other hand, should be different from the free one. It should have a sepa-   *1331[b]*
rate site, conveniently located for collecting together goods sent in from
both land and sea.

Since the city-state's governing class[60] is divided into priests and officials, it is fitting too for the messes of the priests to be located in the
vicinity of the temples. As for the boards of officials that supervise con-   *5*

---

58. Reading *thesin* . . . *epiphaneian* with Thomas and Lord. Alternatively
(mss.): "This site should be adequately conspicuous as a place of virtue
(*epiphaneian* . . . *thesin*)."
59. Reading *onomazousin* at ª32 with Dreizehnter and the mss.
60. The mss. have *plēthos* ("multitude"); Newman's *proestos* ("the governing
class"), accepted by Ross and Pellegrin, gives a better sense.

tracts, legal indictments, summonses, and other administrative matters
of that sort, as well as those that deal with marketplace management and
so-called town management, they should have buildings near the mar-
10   ketplace or in some public meeting place in the vicinity of the "necessary" marketplace. For the upper marketplace is intended for leisurely
activities, the lower, for necessary ones.

   The organization of the country areas should mimic the one just described. For the officials that some call foresters and others country
15   managers must have messes and guard houses in order to promote security. Moreover, some temples dedicated to gods and others to heroes
have to be distributed throughout the countryside.

   It would be a waste of time, however, to speak about such things in
20   detail here. For they are not hard to think out, just hard to do. Speaking
about them is a task for ideal theory; the task of good luck is to bring
them about.[61] Hence any further discussion of them may be set aside for
the present.

Chapter 13

But we must now discuss the constitution itself, and from which and
what sorts of people a city-state should be constituted if it is to be a
25   blessedly happy and well governed. In all cases, well-being consists in
two things: setting up the aim and end of action correctly and discovering the actions that bear on it. These factors can be in harmony with one
30   another or in disharmony. For people sometimes set up the end well but
fail to achieve it in action; and sometimes they achieve everything that
promotes the end, but the end they set up is a bad one. Sometimes they
make both mistakes. For example, in medicine it sometimes happens
that doctors are neither correct in their judgment about what condition
35   a healthy body should be in, nor successful in producing the condition
they have set up as their end. In the crafts and sciences both of these
have to be under control, the end and the actions directed toward it. It is
evident that everyone aims at living well and at happiness. But while
40   some can achieve these ends, others, whether because of luck or because
of something in their nature, cannot. For we also need resources in order
1332ᵃ to live a good life, although we need fewer of them if we are in a better
condition, more if we are in a worse one. Others, though they could

61. See 1332ᵃ28–32 for a more careful statement.

achieve happiness, search for it in the wrong place from the outset. But since we are proposing to look at the best constitution, and this is the one under which a city-state will be best governed, and since a city-state is best governed under a constitution that would above all make it possible for the city-state to be happy, it is clear that we should not overlook the question of what happiness actually is.

We say, and we have given this definition in our ethical works (if anything in those discussions is of service), that happiness is a complete activation or use of virtue, and not a qualified use but an unqualified one.[62] By "qualified uses" I mean those that are necessary; by "unqualified" I mean those that are NOBLE. For example, in the case of just actions, just retributions and punishments spring from virtue, but are necessary uses of it, and are noble only in a necessary way, since it would be more choiceworthy if no individual or city-state needed such things. On the other hand, just actions that aim at honors and prosperity are unqualifiedly noblest. The former involve choosing[63] something that is somehow bad, whereas the latter are the opposite: they construct and generate goods. To be sure, an excellent man will deal with poverty, disease, and other sorts of bad luck in a noble way. But blessed happiness requires their opposites. For according to the definition established in our ethical works, an excellent man is the sort whose virtue makes *unqualifiedly* good things good *for him*. Clearly, then, his use of them must also be unqualifiedly good and noble. That is why people think that external GOODS are the causes of happiness. Yet we might as well hold that a lyre is the cause of fine and brilliant lyre playing, and not the performer's craft. It follows, then, from what has been said, that some goods must be there to start with, whereas others must be provided by the legislator. That is why we pray that our city-state will be ideally equipped with the goods that luck controls (for we assume that luck does control them). When we come to making the city-state excellent, however, that is no longer a task for luck but one for scientific knowledge and deliberate choice. A city-state is excellent, however, because the citizens who participate in the constitution are excellent; and in our city-state all the

---

62. See *NE* 1098^{a}7–20, 1101^{a}14–17, 1102^{a}5–7.

63. Reading *hairesis* with the mss. Alternatively (Ross, Dreizehnter, and others): "destruction (*anairesis*)." Both punishment and retribution involve choosing to do bad things to someone in order to bring about a good or just end. These things must be done if justice is to be served, but no just person would choose to do them simply for their own sake.

CITIZENS participate in the constitution. The matter we have to investi-
35   gate, therefore, is how a man becomes excellent. For even if it is possible
for all the citizens to be collectively excellent without being so individually, the latter is still more choiceworthy, since if each is excellent, all are.

But surely people become excellent because of three things. The three
40   are nature, habit, and reason. For first [1] one must possess a certain nature from birth, namely, that of a human, and not that of some other animal. Similarly, one's body and soul must be of a certain sort. But in the
case of some of these qualities, there is no benefit in just being born with
1332ᵇ them, because they are altered by our habits. [2] For some qualities are
naturally capable of being developed by habit either in a better direction
or in a worse one. The other animals mostly live under the guidance of
nature alone, although some are guided a little by habit. [3] But human
beings live under the guidance of reason as well, since they alone have
5   reason. Consequently, all three of these factors need to be harmonized
with one another.[64] For people often act contrary to their habits and
their nature because of reason, if they happen to be persuaded that some
other course of action is better.

We have already determined[65] the sorts of natures people should have
if it is to be easy for the legislator to take them in hand. Everything
thereafter is a task for EDUCATION. For some things are learned by habit-
10   uation, others by instruction.

Chapter 14

Since every political community is composed of rulers and ruled, we
must investigate whether rulers and ruled should be the same or differ-
15   ent throughout life. For clearly their education must correspond to this
division. Now if they differed from one another as much as gods and heroes are believed to differ from human beings, if the former were so
greatly superior, first in body and then in soul, that their superiority was
20   indisputable and manifest to those they ruled—it would clearly be altogether better if the same people always ruled and the others were always
ruled. But this is not easy to achieve, and there are not, as Scylax[66] says
there are in India, kings that are so superior to the ruled. Evidently,

---

64. See 1334ᵇ6–28 for further explanation.
65. At VII.7.
66. Scylax of Caryanda in Caria was a geographer of the late sixth century. See
     Herodotus 4.44.

then, and for many different reasons, it is necessary for all to share alike *25*
in ruling and being ruled in turn. For equality consists in giving the
same to those who are alike,[67] and it is difficult for a constitution to last
if its organization is contrary to justice. For the citizens being ruled will
be joined by those in the surrounding territory who want to stir up
change, and the governing class cannot possibly be numerous enough to *30*
be more powerful than all of them.

Surely it is indisputable, however, that the rulers should be different
from the ruled. Hence the legislator should investigate the question of
how this is to achieved, and how they should share with one another. We
discussed this earlier,[68] for nature itself settled the choice by making part *35*
of the same species younger and part older, the former fit to be ruled
and the latter to rule. For young people do not object to being ruled, or
think themselves better than their rulers, particularly when they are
going to be compensated for their contribution[69] when they reach the *40*
proper age. We must conclude, therefore, that rulers and ruled are in
one way the same and in another different. Consequently, their education too must be in one way the same and in another different. For if *1333ª*
someone is going to rule well, as the saying goes, he should first have
been ruled.[70]

As we said in our first discussions,[71] however, there is a kind of rule
that is for the sake of the ruler and a kind that is for the sake of the ruled.
The former, we say, is rule by a master, the latter rule over free people. *5*
Now some commands differ not with respect to the tasks they assign but
with respect to that for the sake of which they are done. That is why it is
noble even for free young men to perform many of the tasks that are held
to be appropriate for slaves. For the difference between noble and
shameful actions does not lie so much in the acts themselves as in their
ends, on that for the sake of which they are performed. Since we say that *10*
the virtue of a citizen or ruler is the same as that of the best man,[72] and
that the same man should be ruled first and a ruler later, the legislator

---

67. See 1261ª30–ᵇ5, 1325ᵇ7–10.
68. At 1329ª2–17.
69. The contribution (*eranos*) the young make is their obedience to their elders;
    they are compensated when they are older by being obeyed in turn.
70. See 1277ᵇ11–13 note.
71. At 1277ª29–1277ᵇ16, 1278ᵇ30–1279ª21.
72. True because Aristotle is discussing the best constitution. See III.4,
    1288ª37–39, 1293ᵇ5–6, 1316ᵇ9–10, 1332ª32–35.

should make it his business to determine how and through what prac-
15 tices men become good, and what the end of the best life is.

The SOUL is divided into two parts, one of which has reason intrinsically, whereas the other does not, but is capable of listening to it, and we
say that the virtues of the latter entitle a man to be called, in a certain
way, good. As to the question of which of these the end is more particu-
20 larly found in, to those who make the distinction we mentioned it is not
unclear what must be said. For the worse part is always for the sake of
the better, and this is as evident in the products of the crafts as it is in
those of nature. But the part that has reason is better; and it, in accordance with our usual way of dividing, is divided in two: for there is prac-
25 tical reason and theoretical reason. So it is clear that the rational part of
the soul must also be divided in the same manner. Actions too, we will
say, are divided analogously, and those that belong to the naturally better
part must be more choiceworthy to anyone who can carry out all or only
two of them.[73] For what is most choiceworthy for each individual is al-
30 ways this: to attain what is highest. But the whole of life too is divided
into work and leisure, war and peace, and of actions some are necessary
or useful, others noble. And the same choice must be made among these
as among the parts of the soul and their actions. War must be chosen for
35 the sake of peace, work for the sake of leisure, necessary and useful
things for the sake of noble ones.

A statesman must, therefore, look to all these things, particularly to
those that are better and those that are ends, and legislate in a way that
suits the parts of the soul and their actions. And he should legislate in
40 the same way where life and the divisions[74] of actions are concerned. For
one should be able to work or go to war, but even better able to remain at
1333ᵇ peace and leisure; able to perform necessary or useful actions, but better
able to perform noble ones. These then are the aims that should be kept
in view when educating citizens, both when they are still children and
5 whenever else they need education.

It is evident, however, that those Greeks who are currently held to be
best governed, and the legislators who established their constitutions,
did not organize the various aspects of their constitutions to promote
the best end. Nor did they organize their laws and educational system to
promote all the virtues, but instead were vulgarly inclined to promote

---

73. See Introduction xlvi–xlvii.
74. Reading *diaireseis* with Newman and the mss. The divisions are those re-
    ferred to in the opening sentence of the paragraph.

the ones held to be more useful and more conducive to acquisition.[75]   *10*
Some later writers have expressed the same opinion in the same spirit.
For they praise the Spartan constitution and express admiration for the
aim of its legislator, because his entire legislation was intended to promote conquest and war. What they say is easy to refute by argument, and
has now been refuted by the facts too. For most human beings are eager   *15*
to rule as masters over many because it provides a ready supply of the
goods of luck. And Thibron and all these other writers[76] are no different:
they admire the Spartan legislator because by training the Spartans to   *20*
face danger he enabled them to rule over many. And yet it is clear, now
that their empire is no longer in their hands at any rate, that the Spartans are not a happy people, and that their legislator is not a good one.
Moreover, it is absurd if it was by keeping to his laws and putting them
into practice without impediment that they lost their fine way of life.   *25*
They are also incorrect in their conception of the sort of rule a legislator
should be seen to honor. For rule over free people is nobler and more
virtuous than rule by a master. Besides, one should not consider a city-
state happy or praise its legislator because he trained it to conquer and   *30*
rule its neighbors, since such things involve great harm. For clearly any
citizen who is able to should also try to acquire the power to rule his own
city-state.[77] Yet this is precisely what the Spartans accused their king,
Pausanias, of doing, even though he held so high an office.[78]

    Arguments and laws of this sort are not worthy of a statesman, then,
nor are they beneficial or true. For the same things are best both for in-   *35*
dividuals and for communities, and it is these that a legislator should
implant in the souls of human beings. Training in war should not be undertaken for the sake of reducing those who do not deserve it to slavery,
but, first, to avoid becoming enslaved to others; second, to pursue a   *40*
position of leadership in order to benefit the ruled, not to be masters of
all of them; and, third, to be masters of those who deserve to be slaves.   *1334ᵃ*

    Both facts and arguments testify, then, that the legislator should give
more serious attention to how to organize his legislation, both the part
that deals with military affairs and the part that deals with other matters,

---

75. The constitutions held to be best governed include Sparta and Crete. The
    same criticism of them is leveled at 1271ᵃ41–ᵇ10, 1334ᵃ2–ᵇ5, 1324ᵇ5–11.
76. Thibron is otherwise unknown. The other writers referred to presumably
    include Xenophon.
77. See 1325ᵃ34–41.
78. See 1307ᵃ2–5.

5   for the sake of peace and leisure. For most city-states of the sort described remain secure while they are at war, but come to ruin once they
have acquired empire. Like an iron sword, they lose their edge when
they remain at peace. But the one responsible is their legislator, who did
10   not educate them to be able to be at leisure.

Chapter 15

Since it is evident that human beings have the same end, both individually and collectively, and since the best man and the best constitution
must of necessity have the same aim, it is evident that the virtues suitable for leisure should be present in both. For, as has been said repeat-
15   edly, peace is the end of war, and leisure of work. Some of the virtues
useful for leisure and LEISURED PURSUITS accomplish their task while
one is actually at leisure, but others do so while one is at work. For many
necessities must be present in order for leisure to be possible.[79] That is
why it is appropriate for our city-state to have temperance, courage, and
20   endurance. For as the proverb says, there is no leisure for slaves, and
people who are unable to face danger courageously are the slaves of their
attackers. Courage and endurance are required for work, philosophy for
leisure, and temperance and justice for both, but particularly for peace
25   and leisure. For war compels people to be just and temperate, but the
enjoyment of good luck and the leisure that accompanies peace tend to
make them arrogant. Much justice and temperance are needed, therefore, by those who are held to be doing best and who enjoy all the things
30   regarded as blessings; people like those, if there are any, who live in the
isles of the blessed,[80] as the poets call them. For they will be most in
need of philosophy, temperance, and justice the more they live at leisure
amidst an abundance of such goods. It is evident, then, why a city-state
35   that is to be happy and good should share in these virtues. For it is
shameful to be unable to make use of good things, but it is even more
shameful to be unable to make use of them in leisure time—to make it
plain that we are good men when working or at war, but slaves when at
peace and leisure. That is why one should not cultivate virtue as the city-
40   state of the Spartans does. For the difference between the Spartans and

79. And the acquisition and proper use of these goods requires the virtues connected with work.
80. See Hesiod, *Works and Days* 168–73.

others is not that they consider different things to be the greatest   *1334ᵇ*
goods, but that they believe that these goods are obtained by means of a
particular virtue. And because they consider these goods and the enjoyment of them to be better than the enjoyment of the virtues, [they train
themselves only in the virtue that is useful for acquiring them, and ignore the virtue that is exercised in leisure.] But it is evident from what
we have said, that [the latter virtue should be cultivated] on its own account. We must now study how and through what means this will come
about.[81]   5

We distinguished earlier[82] three requirements: nature, habit, and reason. We have already determined[83] the natural qualities our citizens
should have. It remains to study whether they are to be educated
through reason first or through habits. For the harmony between those
should be the best kind of harmony. For it is possible for someone's rea-   10
son to have missed the best supposition[84] and for him to be led similarly
astray by his habits.

This much at least is evident. First, procreation, like the production
of any other kind of thing, has a starting point, and some starting points
have ends that are the starting points of further ends. But reason and
understanding constitute our natural end.[85] Hence they are the ends   15
that procreation and the training of our habits should be organized to
promote. Second, just as soul and body are two, so we see that the soul
has two parts as well, one that is nonrational and one that has reason.
Their states are also two in number, desire and understanding. And just
as the development of the body is prior to that of the soul, so the nonra-   20
tional part is prior to the rational. This too is evident. For spirit, wish,
and also appetite are present in children right from birth, whereas reasoning and understanding naturally develop as they grow older.[86] That is
why supervision of the body comes first and precedes that of the soul;   25
then comes supervision of appetite or desire. But supervision of desire
should be for the sake of understanding, and that of the body for the
sake of the soul.

81. There is a gap in the text at 1334ᵇ4. The bracketed material is conjectural.
82. At 1332ᵃ38–ᵇ11.
83. At VII.7.
84. The correct supposition about what happiness is.
85. See Introduction §4–6.
86. See Plato, *Republic* 441a–b.

Chapter 16

Since, then, the legislator should see to it from the start that the bodies
30   of children being reared develop in the best possible way, he must first
supervise the union of the sexes, and determine what sorts of people
should have marital relations with one another, and when. In legislating
for this community,[87] he should have regard both to the people involved
and to their life spans, so that they reach the same stage of life at the
same time: that is to say, there should be no disharmony between their
35   procreative powers, as happens when the man is still capable of procreating but the woman is not, or when the woman is capable and the man
not, since these things cause conflicts and disagreements among couples.

Next, he should have regard to the difference in age between parents
and children. For children should not be too far removed in age from
40   their fathers, since the gratitude of children is of no benefit to older fathers, and the assistance of such fathers is of no benefit to their children.
1335ᵃ   But they should not be too close in age either, since this leads to many
difficulties. For there is less respect for them, as for contemporaries, and
the closeness in age leads to conflict over the management of the household.

Third, to return to the point at which we began this digression, the
5   legislator should ensure that the bodies of those who are born are as he
wishes.

These results can pretty well all be achieved by a single sort of supervision. For in the majority of cases, a man's fertility comes to an end at a
maximum age of seventy, and a woman's at fifty. Hence the beginning of
10   their sexual union should be so timed that they reach their decline simultaneously. The coupling of young people, however, is a bad thing
from the point of view of childbearing. For in all animals the young are
more likely to bear offspring that are imperfect, female, or undersized,
and so the same must occur in human beings as well. The following is
15   evidence of this. In all those city-states in which the coupling of young
men and women is the local custom, people's bodies are imperfect and
undersized. Second, young women have longer labors, and more of
them die in childbirth. According to some accounts, indeed, the well-
20   known oracle was given to the Troezenians not because of anything to do
with the harvest but because their custom of marrying off younger

---

87. The partnership or community consisting of husband and wife (1252ᵇ10).

women resulted in so many deaths.[88] Third, with regard to temperance or chastity, it is beneficial for women to be given in marriage when they are older, since women who have had sex when they are young are held to be more licentious. Fourth, if males have sex while their bodies[89] are still growing, this is held to impair their growth; for this growth too takes a definite period of time, after which it is no longer extensive.[90] It is fitting, therefore, for the women to be married at around the age of eighteen; the men at thirty-seven or a little before.[91] At those ages, sexual union will occur when their bodies are in their prime, and will end, conveniently for both, at the time when they cease to be fertile. As to difference in age between parents and children, if the children are born soon after marriage occurs, as can reasonably be expected, they will be at the beginning of their prime when their father's period of vigor has come to an end, at around the age of seventy.

We have said when sexual union should occur; as for the season, however, one should use the time many people use. For nowadays they correctly set aside the winter as the time to begin this sort of cohabitation. In addition, couples should study for themselves what is said by doctors and natural scientists about procreation. For doctors have adequately discussed the times that are right as regards the body, and natural scientists have discussed the winds, favoring northerly over southerly ones.[92]

As to the bodily characteristics in parents that are most beneficial to the offspring being produced, we must deal with that topic at greater length in our discussion of the supervision of children.[93] It is sufficient to speak of it in outline now. Neither the physical condition of athletes nor one that is overly reliant on medical treatment and poorly suited to exertion is useful from the point of view of health or procreation, or is

25

30

35

40

1335[b]

5

---

88. The scholiasts tell us that the oracle in question said: "Do not plow the young furrow."

89. Reading *sōmatos* with Pellegrin and some mss. In Aristotle's biological theory, male semen is a very concentrated or "concocted" blood product. Hence it takes a lot of nourishment to replace. If a young man has frequent sexual intercourse (as he no doubt would with a licentious young wife), his growth is likely to suffer, because the nourishment needed for it will be expended to produce semen. Alternatively (Ross, Dreizehnter, and others): "if males have sex while their semen (*spermatos*) is still growing."

90. Omitting *ē mikron* with Dreizehnter and Kraut.

91. Reading *ē mikron proteron* with Kraut.

92. See Plato, *Laws* 747d–e.

93. This promise is unfulfilled in the *Politics* as we have it.

the condition needed in a good citizen. But the condition that is a mean between these two *is* useful for these purposes. The proper physical condition, therefore, is one that is achieved by exertion, but not by violent exertion, and that promotes not just one thing, as the athletic
10   condition does, but the actions of free people. And these should be provided to women and men alike. Even pregnant women should take care of their bodies and not stop exercising or adopt a meager diet. The legislator can easily prevent them from doing these things by requiring them
15   to take a walk every day to worship the gods whose assigned prerogative is to watch over birth.[94] But in contrast with their bodies, it is appropriate for their minds to remain somewhat inactive.[95] For unborn children obviously draw resources from their mothers, just as plants do from the earth.

     As to the question of whether to rear offspring or expose them, there
20   should be a law against rearing deformed ones, but where it is because of the number of children, if it happens that the way custom is organized prohibits the exposure of offspring once they are born, a limit should be imposed on procreation.[96] And if some people have sex in violation of this regulation and conceive a child, it should be aborted before the
25   onset of sensation and life. For sensation and life distinguish what is pious from what is impious here.

     Since we have specified the earliest age at which men and women should begin their sexual union, we should also specify the appropriate length of time for them to perform public service by having children. For the offspring of parents who are too old, like those of parents who
30   are too young, are imperfect in both body and mind, and those of people who have actually reached old age are weak. Hence we should define the length of the time in question by reference to the time when the mind is in its prime. In most cases, this occurs around the fiftieth year, as some of the poets who measure age in periods of seven years have pointed
35   out.[97] Therefore, men who exceed this age by four or five years should be

---

94. For example, Artemis and Eileithuia. See Plato, *Laws* 789e.
95. Perhaps for the reason suggested at 1339[a]7–10.
96. Reading *ean . . . kōluē(i)* at [b]21–2 with Dreizehnter and *hōristhai dei* at [b]22 with Kraut. Exposure or abandonment of newborns was a fairly common form of birth control in ancient Greece. Aristotle does not approve of this practice, since he goes on to condemn the abortion of sentient fetuses. But, like Plato (*Republic* 459d–461c), he does require that deformed offspring be exposed, and that any offspring conceived in violation of the laws be aborted.
97. See Solon, Diehl I.31–32, fr. 17.

released from procreating for the community. If they have sex after that, it should be evident that it is for the sake of health, or for some other such reason.

As to having sex with another man or another woman when one is a husband or referred to as such, it should be regarded as shameful to be openly involved in any form of it with anyone. If a man is discovered   40
doing something of this sort during his period of procreation, he should
be punished with a loss of honor[98] appropriate to his offense.[99]   1336ᵃ

Chapter 17

It should be recognized that the sort of nourishment children are given once they are born makes a large difference to the strength of their bodies. It is evident to anyone who investigates the other animals or those   5
nations concerned to cultivate a military disposition that the nourish-
ment particularly suited to children's bodies has a lot of milk in it but very little wine, because of the diseases it produces.[100] Furthermore, it is also beneficial for them to make whatever movements are possible at that age. But to prevent curvature of the limbs, due to softness, there are cer-   10
tain mechanical devices, which some nations already employ, to keep   )
their bodies straight. It is beneficial, too, to habituate children to the cold right from the time they are small, since this is very useful both from the point of view of health and from that of military affairs. That is why many non-Greeks have the custom of submerging newborn chil-   15
dren in a cold river, whereas many others—for example, the Celts—
dress them in light clothing. For whenever it is possible to create habits, it is better to create them right from the start, but to do so gradually.

98. *atimia*: here used in the legal sense to refer to the loss of the rights and priv-
ileges possessed by citizens.
99. Athenian law *required* a man to divorce an adulterous wife. Since Aristotle
thinks that *all* adultery is wrong (*NE* 1107ᵃ9–17), he probably agreed that
this sort of legal sanction was appropriate. But on the topic of male adultery,
which is the only kind under discussion here, his views are more unconven-
tional. Male adultery was unregulated in Athens; Aristotle criminalizes it, at
least during the period in which the male is procreating as a public service.
No doubt the intention of the law is to restrict the number of illegitimate
children. Presumably, then, a man who commits homosexual adultery during this period will suffer a smaller loss of honor. Other reasons for a male to
avoid adultery are given in *Oec*. III.2.
100. See *HA* 588ᵃ3–8.

And because their bodily condition is hot, children are naturally suited
20　to being trained to bear the cold.[101]

In the first stage of life, then, it is beneficial to adopt this sort of supervision as well as any other similar to it. During the next stage, which
lasts until the age of five, it is not a good idea to have children engage in
any kind of learning or any necessary tasks, lest it interfere with their
25　growth. But they should engage in enough exercise to avoid physical
laziness, and this should be provided to them through play and other
such activities. But the games they play should not be either unfit for
free people or exerting or undisciplined. As for the kinds of stories and
30　fables children of this age should listen to, the officials called child supervisors should deal with that issue. For all such things should pave the
way for their later pursuits. Hence many of the games they play should
imitate the serious occupations of later life. Those in the *Laws* who prevent children from screaming and crying[102] are wrong to prohibit such
35　things, for they contribute to growth, since they are a sort of exercise for
the body. For holding the breath gives strength to those who are exerting
themselves,[103] and this is just what occurs in children when they are
screaming their lungs out.

The child supervisors should pay attention to the way the children
40　pursue leisure. In particular, they should ensure that they pursue it as
little as possible in the company of slaves. For, at this age, and until they
1336ᵇ　are seven, children must be educated in the household. So it is reasonable to expect that they will pick up some taint of servility from what
they see and hear even at that early age. The legislator should altogether
outlaw shameful talk[104] from the city-state, as he would any other
5　shameful thing, since by speaking lightly of a shameful activity one
comes closer to doing it. He should particularly outlaw it among children, so that they neither say nor hear anything of the sort. If it happens, none the less, that any free man who is not yet old enough to have
been given a seat at the messes is found saying or doing something for-
10　bidden, he should be punished by being dishonored or beaten. But if he
is older than this, he should be punished with those dishonors usually

---

101. The natural heat of children is discussed at *Rh.* 1389ª18–20 and *Pr.*
872ª3–8. See Plato, *Laws* 664e, 666a.

102. Plato, *Laws* 791d–792e.

103. See *GA* 737ᵇ36–738ª1.

104. *aischrologia*: obscene but also abusive language of various sorts (*NE*
1128ª9–32, *Rh.* 1405ᵇ8–16).

reserved for the unfree, because he has acted in a manner characteristic of slaves.

Since we are outlawing shameful talk, it is evident that we should also outlaw looking at unseemly pictures or stories. The officials should ensure, therefore, that there are no statues or pictures representing unseemly acts, except those kept in the temples of those gods at whose festivals custom permits even mockery to occur.[105] Custom allows men of suitable age to pay this sort of honor to the gods on behalf of themselves and of their wives and children. But younger people should not be permitted to witness iambus or comedy[106] until they have reached the age when it is appropriate for them to recline at the communal table and drink wine, and their education has rendered them immune to the harm such things can do.[107]

Our present discussion of this issue has been cursory. Later we must stop and determine it at greater length, first raising the problem of whether the attendance of the young at such performances should or should not be prohibited, and if so how it should be handled.[108] It was right to touch on it at this juncture, however, but only to the extent necessary for present purposes. Perhaps Theodorus,[109] the tragic actor, put the point rather well. He said that he never allowed any other actor, not even an incompetent one, to play a part before he did, because audiences become accustomed to the voice they hear first. The same is true of our relationships with people and things; whatever we encounter first we like better. That is why everything bad or vulgar should be alien to the young, particularly if it involves vice or malice.

When children reach the age of five, they should spend the two years till they are seven as observers of the lessons they themselves will eventually have to learn. There are then two stages in their education that should be distinguished, from age seven to puberty and from puberty to age twenty-one. For those who divide the stages of life into seven-year periods are for the most part correct. But one should be guided by a

15

20

25

30

35

40

---

105. Ritualized obscenity and mockery played a role in certain religious festivals honoring Dionysus, Demeter, and other gods.
106. Iambus is the name given to the mocking songs sung at certain religious festivals. Comedy, especially the so-called old comedy of such writers as Aristophanes, was often abusive and obscene.
107. Probably, at the age of twenty-one (1336^{b}40).
108. A promise unfulfilled in the remainder of the *Politics*.
109. A famous actor of the fourth century the quality of whose voice is praised at *Rh*. 1404^{b}22–24.

1337^a natural division, since every craft and every sort of education is intended to supplement nature. First, then, we should investigate whether
some organization should be established to deal with the children; second, whether it is beneficial for their supervision to be established by the
5   community or arranged on a private basis (as is the case in most city-
states nowadays); and third, what sort of supervision it should be.

BOOK VIII

Chapter 1

No one would dispute, therefore, that legislators should be particularly concerned with the education of the young, since in city-states where this does not occur, the constitutions are harmed. For education should suit the particular constitution. In fact, the character peculiar to each constitution usually safeguards it as well as establishes it initially (for example, the democratic character, a democracy; and the oligarchic one, an oligarchy), and a better character is always the cause of a better constitution. Besides, prior education and habituation are required in order to perform certain elements of the task of any capacity or craft. Hence it is clear that this also holds for the activities of virtue.

Since the whole city-state has one single end, however, it is evident that education too must be one and the same for all, and that its supervision must be communal, not private as it is at present, when each individual supervises his own children privately and gives them whatever private instruction he thinks best. Training for communal matters should also be communal.

At the same time, one should not consider any citizen as belonging to himself alone, but as all belonging to the city-state, since each is a part of the city-state.[1] And it is natural for the supervision of each part to look to the supervision of the whole. For this reason one might praise the Spartans, since they pay the most serious attention to their children, and do so as a community.

Chapter 2

It is evident, then, that there should be legislation regarding education, and that education should be communal. But the questions of what kind

---

1. See 1253ᵃ18–29, 1254ᵃ9–10, Introduction lxix–lxxii.

of education there should be and how it should be carried out should not
35   be neglected. In fact, there is dispute at present about what its tasks
are. For not all consider that the young should learn the same things,
whether to promote virtue or the best life; nor is it evident whether it is
more appropriate for education to develop the mind or the soul's character.[2]

Investigation of the education we see around us results in confusion,
40   since it is not at all clear whether people should be trained in what is
useful for life, in what conduces to virtue, or in something out of the ordinary. For all of these proposals have acquired some advocates. Besides,
there is no agreement about what promotes virtue. For, in the first place,
1337ᵇ people do not all esteem the same virtue, so they quite understandably
do not agree about the training needed for it.

That children should be taught those useful things that are really necessary, however, is not unclear. But it is evident that they should not be
taught all of them, since there is a difference between the tasks of the
5   free and those of the unfree, and that they should share only in such useful things as will not turn them into vulgar craftsmen. (Any task, craft,
10   or branch of learning should be considered vulgar if it renders the body
or mind of free people useless for the practices and activities of virtue.
That is why the crafts that put the body into a worse condition and work
done for wages are called vulgar; for they debase the mind and deprive it
of LEISURE.)

Even in the case of some of the sciences that are suitable for a free
15   person, while it is not unfree to participate in them up to a point, to
study them too assiduously or exactly is likely to result in the harms just
mentioned. What one acts or learns *for* also makes a big difference. For
what one does for one's own sake, for the sake of friends, or on account
of virtue is not unfree, but someone who does the same thing for others
20   would often be held to be acting like a hired laborer or a slave.

Chapter 3

The subjects that are now established tend in two directions, as was
mentioned earlier.[3] But generally speaking there are four that are customarily taught: reading and writing, gymnastics, music, and fourth (but

---

2. Aristotle's own answer is that education must develop both (1323ᵇ1–3).
3. In the mss. this sentence concludes VIII.2. Following Lord I have transposed
   it to the beginning of the present chapter. The subjects customarily taught

only occasionally), drawing. Reading, writing, and drawing are taught *25* because they are useful for life and have many applications; gymnastics is taught because it contributes to courage; but in the case of music a problem immediately arises. Nowadays, most people take part in music for the sake of pleasure. But those who originally included it as a part of education did so, as has often been said, because nature itself aims not *30* only at the correct use of work but also at the capacity for noble leisured activity.[4] Since this is the starting point for everything else,[5] I propose to discuss it once again.

If both are required, but leisured activity is more choiceworthy than work and is its end, we should try to discover what people should do for leisured activity. For surely they should not be amusing themselves, oth- *35* erwise amusement would have to be our end in life. But if that is impossible, and if amusements are more to be used while one is at work (for one who exerts himself needs relaxation, relaxation is the end of amusement, and work is accompanied by toil and strain), then we should, for this reason, permit amusement, but we should be careful to use it at the *40* right time, dispensing it as a medicine for the ills of work.[6] For this sort of motion of the soul is relaxing and restful because of the pleasure it involves.

Leisured activity is itself held to involve pleasure, happiness, and liv- *1338ª* ing blessedly. This is not available to those who are working, however, but only to those who are engaged in leisured activity. For one who is working is doing so for the sake of some end he does not possess, whereas happiness *is* an end that everyone thinks is accompanied not by *5* pain but by pleasure. This pleasure is not the same for everyone, however, but each takes it to be what suits himself and his condition, and the best person takes it to be the best pleasure, the one that comes from the noblest things.[7] It is evident, then, that we should learn and be taught certain things that promote leisured activity. And these subjects and *10*

---

presumably do not include anything out of the ordinary (1337ª42), so that the two directions referred to are (1) being useful for life and (2) conducing to virtue (1337ª41–42).

4. See 1271ª41–ᵇ10, 1333ª30–ᵇ5, 1334ª2–ᵇ28, *NE* 1177ᵇ2–18.

5. Noble leisured activity is a starting point (*ARCHĒ*) because it is happiness, the end for the sake of which we pursue all our other ends. Hence, until we have it in view, we cannot know what the best political system is, or what sort of education should be part of that system (see 1323ª14–21).

6. Compare *NE* 1176ᵇ9–1177ª11.

7. See *NE* 1176ª15–19.

studies are undertaken for their own sake, whereas those relating to work are necessary and for the sake of things other than themselves.

It is for this reason that our predecessors assigned music a place in education. They did not do so because they supposed: that it is necessary
15 for life (for it is nothing of the sort); or that, like reading and writing, it is useful for making money, managing a household, acquiring further learning, or for a large number of political activities; or that, like gymnastics, it promotes health and vigor, for we see that neither of these re-
20 sults from music. What remains, then, is that music is for pursuit in leisure, which is evidently the very reason our predecessors included it in education. For they give it a place among the LEISURED PURSUITS they considered appropriate for free people. Hence Homer's instruction to
25 "call the bard alone to the rich banquet." And he goes on to mention certain others who "call the bard that he may bring delight to all."[8] Elsewhere, Odysseus says that the best leisured pursuit is when men are enjoying good cheer and "the banqueters seated in due order throughout the hall, give ear to the bard."[9] It is evident, then, that there is a certain
30 kind of education that children must be given not because it is useful or necessary but because it is noble and suitable for a free person. But the number of subjects involved (whether one or many), what they are, and how they should be taught—these are questions that must be discussed later on.[10] But as things stand, a certain amount of progress has been
35 made, because we have some evidence from the ancients about the educational subjects they established, music being an obvious case in point.

Furthermore, it is clear that children should be taught some useful subjects (such as reading and writing) not only because of their utility, but also because many other areas of study become possible through
40 them. Similarly, they should be taught drawing not in order to avoid making mistakes in their private purchases or being cheated when buy-
1338ᵇ ing or selling products,[11] but rather because it makes them contemplate the beauty of bodies. It is completely inappropriate for magnanimous and free people to be always asking what use something is.[12]

---

8. *Odyssey* XVII. 382–5. The first line is not in the poem as we have it but seems to have followed line 382 in Aristotle's version.
9. *Odyssey* IX. 7–8.
10. This promise is not fulfilled in our *Politics*.
11. For example, so as to be able to understand an architect's plan, or sketch a piece of furniture one was commissioning.
12. Magnanimity is discussed in *NE* IV.3.

Since it is evident that education through habituation must come before education through reason, and that education of the body must come before education of the mind, it clearly follows that children must   5
be put in the hands of physical trainers who will bring their bodies into a certain condition, and coaches who will teach them to do certain physical tasks.

Chapter 4

At present, the city-states that are thought to be most concerned with children turn them into athletes, and thus distort the shape and devel-   10
opment of their bodies; whereas the Spartans, though they do not make this mistake, none the less brutalize their children through rigorous exertion, thinking that this will greatly enhance their courage. Yet, as we have said many times,[13] the supervision of children should not aim to promote just one virtue, especially not this one. But even if this one   15
were the aim, the Spartans do not succeed in producing it. For in other animals or in non-Greek nations, we do not find that courage goes along with the greatest savagery, but that it goes along with a tamer, lionlike character.[14] Many of these nations think nothing of killing and cannibal-   20
izing people—for example, the Achaeans and Heniochi, who live around the Black Sea. And there are similar peoples on the mainland, and others who are even worse. These nations are skilled in raiding, to be sure, but of courage they have no share.

Besides, we know that even the Spartans, who were superior to others as long as they alone persisted in their devotion to rigorous exertion, are   25
now inferior to others in both gymnastic and military contests. They were superior to others not because they trained their young people in that rigorous way, but only because they had training, while their adversaries had none.

So nobility, not brutality, should play the leading role here. For no wolf or other wild beast faces danger when it is noble to do so, but a good   30
man does. Those who throw the young into too much of this sort of rigorous exertion and leave them without training in what is necessary produce people who are truly vulgar. For they make them useful to states-

13. At 1271ª41–ᵇ10, 1333ᵇ5–10, 1334ª2–ᵇ28.
14. According to Aristotle, lions are "free, courageous, and nobly-bred" (*HA* 488ᵇ16–17), dangerous while feeding, but gentle when no longer hungry (629ᵇ8–9).

35   manship for one task only, and one at which they are worse than other
people, as our argument shows. One should judge the Spartans on the
basis not of their earlier deeds, but of their present ones. For now there
are people who rival them in education, whereas earlier there were none.

We have agreed, then, that we must make use of gymnastics, and how
it is to be employed. Until children reach puberty they should be given
40   lighter exercises, but a strict diet and strenuous exertions should be forbidden, so that nothing impedes their growth. It is no small indication
1339ᵃ   that such exertions can have this impeding effect that one finds only two
or three people on the list of Olympic victors who were victorious both
as men and as boys, because the training of the young, and the strenuous
exercises involved, robs them of their strength. But when they have
5   spent the three years after puberty on other studies,[15] it is appropriate
for them to spend the next period of their lives exerting themselves and
maintaining a strict diet. For one should not exert the mind and the
body at the same time, since these kinds of exertion naturally produce
opposite effects: exerting the body impedes the mind and exerting the
10   mind impedes the body.

Chapter 5

As for MUSIC, we have mentioned some of the problems in our earlier
discussion.[16] But it will be well to take them up again now and develop
them further, in order to provide a sort of prelude to the arguments that
might be made in an exposition of the subject. For it is not easy to de-
15   termine what the power of music is, or why one should take part in it. Is
it for the sake of amusement and relaxation, like sleep and drink? Sleep
and drink are not in themselves serious matters; they are pleasant, and at
the same time they "put an end to care," as Euripides says.[17] That is why
people include music in the same class as sleep and drink, indeed, and
20   treat them all in the same way. They also include dancing in this class.
Or should we believe instead that music contributes something to
virtue, on the grounds that, just as gymnastics gives us a body of a certain quality, so music has the power to give us a character of a certain
quality, by instilling the habits that enable us to enjoy ourselves in the
25   right way? Or does music contribute something to leisured pursuits and

15. See EDUCATION.
16. At 1337ᵇ25–1338ᵇ4.
17. *Bacchae* 381.

to practical wisdom (which must be set down as third among the possibilities that are mentioned)?

It is clear that the young should not be educated for the sake of amusement. For while they are learning they are not amusing themselves, since learning is a painful process. On the other hand, it is not appropriate to give children of that age leisured pursuits, since the end *30* (something complete) is not appropriate for someone who is incomplete.[18] But perhaps it might be held that the serious activities of children are undertaken for the sake of their amusement when they have become men and are complete. If that were true, however, why should they have to learn music themselves? Why shouldn't they be like the kings of the Persians and the Medes, and take part in musical learning and its pleasure through listening to others performing? Aren't those who have *35* made music their very task and craft bound to produce something better than those who devote only as much time to it as is needed to learn it? On the other hand, if they have to study music in depth, they would also have to take up the activity of cooking delicacies.[19] But that is absurd. *40*

The same problem arises, however, even if music is able to improve people's character. Why should they learn it themselves, rather than being like the Spartans, who enjoy the music of others in the right way and are able to judge it? For the Spartans do not learn it themselves, but *1339ᵇ* are still able, so they say, to determine which melodies are good and which are not.

The same argument also applies if music is to be used to promote *5* well-being and the leisured pursuits appropriate to someone who is free. Why should they learn it themselves rather than benefiting from the fact that others practice it? In this regard, we may consider the conception we have of the gods; for Zeus himself does not sing or accompany poets on the lyre. On the contrary, we even say that musicians are VULGAR CRAFTSMEN, and that a true man would not perform music unless he were drunk or amusing himself.

Perhaps we should investigate these matters later on, however.[20] The *10* question we must first investigate is whether music is to be included in education or not, and in which of the three areas we mentioned earlier

---

18. Children have not yet developed the VIRTUES and so are incapable of HAPPINESS and the leisured pursuits in which it consists.
19. If they need to study music in depth to appreciate it, they would, by the same token, have to become chefs to appreciate delicate food.
20. At VIII.6.

its power lies: amusement, education, or leisured pursuits. It seems reasonable to assign it to, and it seems to have a share in, all three. For
15   amusement is for the sake of relaxation, and relaxation is of necessity pleasant, since it is a sort of cure for the pain caused by one's exertions. It is generally agreed, moreover, that one's leisured pursuits should be not only noble but also pleasant, since happiness is both. But everyone
20   says that music is among the very greatest pleasures, whether it is unadorned or with voice accompaniment. At any rate, Museus says that "singing is the most pleasant thing for mortals."[21] That is why, because of its power to delight, it is reasonably included in social gatherings and among leisured pursuits.

One might suppose, then, that young people should be educated in
25   music for this reason too. For harmless pleasures are suitable not only because they promote the end of life, but because they promote relaxation too. But since people rarely achieve this end, whereas they do frequently relax and make use of amusements (not only because relaxation and amusements lead to other things, but also because of the pleasure they provide), it would be useful to allow the young to find rest from
30   time to time in the pleasures of music.

What has happened, however, is that people make amusement their end. For the end perhaps involves a certain pleasure (though not just any chance one), and in their search for it they mistake amusement for it, because it has a certain similarity to the end of action. For the end is not
35   choiceworthy for the sake of what will come later, and these sorts of amusements are not choiceworthy for what will come later, but because of things that have happened already (exertions and pains, for example). One might plausibly conclude, therefore, that this is the reason people try to achieve happiness by means of pleasant amusements. But people
40   do not take part in music for that reason alone, it seems, but also because it is useful for promoting relaxation.

Yet we must investigate whether this effect of music is not simply co-
1340ª incidental, whereas its true nature is more estimable than the usefulness we mentioned suggests, and whether one should not take part only in the common pleasure that derives from music (a pleasure everyone perceives, since it is of a natural sort, and so is agreeable to people of all ages
5   and characters), but see whether music influences one's character and soul in some way. This would be clear if one came to be of a certain qual-

21. Museus was a semi-legendary bard to whom a number of sayings and verses were attributed.

ity in one's character because of music. But that we do indeed come to be of a certain quality is evident on many different grounds, and not least from the melodies of Olympus.[22] For it is generally agreed that they cause souls to become inspired, and inspiration is an emotion that affects the character of one's soul.

Moreover, everyone who listens to representations comes to have the corresponding emotions, even when the rhythms and melodies these representations contain are taken in isolation.[23] And since music happens to be one of the pleasures, and virtue is a matter of enjoying, loving, and hating in the right way,[24] it is clear that nothing is more important than that one should learn to judge correctly and get into the habit of enjoying decent characters and noble actions. But rhythms and melodies contain the greatest likenesses of the true natures of anger, gentleness, courage, temperance, and their opposites, and of all the other components of character as well. The facts make this clear. For when we listen to such representations our souls are changed. But getting into the habit of being pained or pleased by likenesses is close to being in the same condition where the real things are concerned. For example, if someone enjoys looking at an image of something for no other reason than because of its shape or form, he is bound to enjoy looking at the very thing whose image he is looking at.

It happens, however, that other perceptible objects, such as those of touch or taste, contain no likenesses of the components of character, although the objects of sight contain faint ones. For there are a few shapes that do contain such likenesses, and[25] everyone perceives them. Still, they are not really likenesses of the components of character; rather, the shapes and colors that are produced are signs of characters, and are derived from a body in the grip of the emotions.[26] This is not to deny, however, that insofar as it also makes a difference which of these objects we look at, the young should look at the works of Polygnotus or any other painter or sculptor who deals with character, not those of Pauson.[27]

---

22. A Phrygian composer of the seventh century.
23. From the words. See 1339^{b}20–21, 1341^{b}23–24, Plato, *Laws* 669d–e.
24. See Introduction xxxv–xxxix.
25. Rejecting *ou* with Dreizehnter. Alternatively (Ross): "and not (*ou*) everyone."
26. Reading *apo tou sōmatos* at ^{a}34–35. Colors and shapes are likenesses of *emotions* etc. only by representing *people* expressing them.
27. "Polygnotus represented people as better than they actually were, Pauson represented them as worse" (*Po.* 1448^{a}5–6).

It is evident, however, that melodies themselves contain representations of the components of character. For, in the first place, harmonies
40 have divergent natures, so that listeners are affected differently and do not respond in the same way to each one. They respond to some (for ex-
1340ᵇ ample, the so-called Mixo-Lydian) in a more mournful and solemn way; to others (for example, the more relaxed modes), their response is more tender minded; their response to the Dorian (which is held to be the only mode that produces this effect) is particularly balanced and composed, whereas the Phrygian causes them to be inspired. These views
5 have been well discussed by those who have philosophized about this type of education,[28] since they base their arguments on the facts themselves. The same also holds of the different rhythms. Some have a steadying character, others get us moving; and some of these movements
10 are more slavish or boorish, whereas others are more free.

It is evident from all these considerations that music has the power to produce a certain quality in the character of our souls. And if it has this power, children should clearly be introduced to music and educated in it. Besides, education in music is appropriate to their youthful nature.
15 For on account of their age, the young are unwilling to put up with anything that is unsweetened with pleasure, and music is something naturally sweet. Also there seems to be a natural affinity for harmonic modes and rhythms. That is why many of the wise say the soul is a harmony, others that it has a harmony.[29]

Chapter 6

We must now discuss the problem we mentioned earlier of whether or
20 not the young ought to learn to sing and to play an instrument themselves. It is not difficult to see, of course, that if someone takes part in performance himself, it makes a great difference in the development of certain qualities, since it is difficult if not impossible for people to become excellent judges of performance if they do not take part in it. At
25 the same time, children should have something to keep them occupied,

28. Plato discusses the effects of the different harmonic modes in *Republic* 397a–401b, and refers to Damon (an important fifth-century writer on music and meter) for a fuller discussion of music.
29. Pythagoras held that the soul was a harmony (see *DA* 407ᵇ30–408ª28; Plato, *Phaedo* 85e–86d, 92a–95a), Plato that it had a harmony (*Republic* 443c–444e).

and the rattle of Archytas,[30] which is given to young children to keep them from breaking things in the house, should be considered a good invention, since youngsters cannot keep still. A rattle is suitable for children in their infancy, then, and education is a rattle for older children.　　*30*

These considerations make it evident that children should be educated in music so as to be able to take part in its performance. Moreover, it is not difficult to determine what is suitable or unsuitable for them at various ages, or to solve the problem raised by those who say that to care about performance is vulgar. For, first, since one should take part in performance in order to judge, for this reason they should engage in performance while they are young and stop performing when they are older,　　*35* but be able to judge which melodies are noble and enjoy them in the right way, because of what they learned while they were young. As for the objection raised by some people, that performing music makes one　　*40* vulgar, it is not difficult to refute, if we investigate the extent to which those being educated in political virtue should take part in performance, what sorts of melodies and rhythms they should take part in, and on　　*1341ᵃ* which sorts of instruments they should learn (since this too probably makes a difference). The refutation depends on these issues. For it is quite possible that certain styles of music *do* have the effect we mentioned. It is evident, then, that learning music should not be an impedi-　　*5* ment to later activities, or make children's bodies into those of vulgar craftsmen,[31] useless for military or political training, current employment, or later studies.[32]

This could be achieved where lessons in music are concerned if the students do not exert themselves to learn either what is needed for professional competition or the astonishing or out-of-the-ordinary works　　*10* which have now made their way into competitions and from there into education, but rather learn the ones not of this sort and only up to the point at which they are able to enjoy noble melodies and rhythms, instead of just the common sort of music, which appeals even to some of　　*15* the other animals, and to the majority of slaves and children as well.

It is also evident from these considerations what sorts of instruments should be used. Flutes[33] should not be introduced into their education,

---

30. Archytas of Tarentum, a Pythagorean philosopher of the first half of the fourth century.
31. See 1254ᵇ27–32, 1341ᵇ14–17.
32. Reading *chrēseis . . . mathēseis* with Dreizehnter.
33. An *aulos* ("flute" is the standard translation) is actually a reed instrument, rather like a modern oboe.

nor should the cithara, or any other professional instruments of that
sort. They should learn only those instruments that will make them
20   good listeners, whether to musical education or to education of any
other sort. Besides, the flute has more to do with religious frenzy than
with character, and so the correct occasions for its use are those where
observing has the power to purify rather than educate.[34] The fact that
playing the flute interferes with speech also tells against its use in edu-
25   cation.

For these reasons, our predecessors were right to reject the practice of
having the young or the free play the flute, even when they had played it
earlier. For when they came to have more leisure as a result of greater
prosperity, and took greater pride in their virtue, and had in addition re-
flected on their accomplishments both before and after the Persian
30   Wars, they seized indiscriminately on every sort of learning and pursued
them all. Hence they also included flute playing among their studies. In
Sparta, there was even a patron of the theater who played the flute himself to accompany his own chorus.[35] And in Athens flute playing became
35   such a local custom that most free people took part in it, as is clear from
the tablet Thrasippus, the theater patron, set up for Ecphantides.[36]
Later, when they were better able to distinguish what does promote
virtue from what does not, they rejected flute playing because of their
experience with it. And the same thing happened to many other ancient
40   instruments (for example, the pektis and the barbitos), those that enhance the pleasure of people who listen for embellishments[37] (the hepta-
gon, the trigona, and the sambukai), and all those requiring professional
1341ᵇ knowledge. The story told by the ancients about flutes is also plausible.
They say that Athena invented flutes, but discarded them. There is
nothing wrong with saying that the goddess did this out of annoyance at

---

34. In religious frenzy, as in wild dancing or competitive sports, we are able
safely to discharge powerfully violent or destructive emotions, so that we are
less likely to fall prey to them in real life. But we do not learn either how to
do or feel the ethically correct thing in the process. We undergo purification
(*katharsis*), but we are not educated (1342ᵃ1–16, 1336ᵇ14–17, 1340ᵃ8–12).

35. The patron (*choregos*) was usually a wealthy man who paid for the chorus as
part of his public service. The flute accompaniment was provided by a professional flute player, a vulgar craftsman, not someone rich and free.

36. Ecphantides was one of the earliest comic poets; Thrasippus is otherwise
unknown.

37. Reading *chrōmatōn* with Immisch and Kraut. The barbitos was a lyre; all the
others are harps of some sort.

how flute playing distorted her face, but the more likely explanation is   *5*
that the flute does nothing to develop the mind, whereas we attribute
scientific knowledge and craft to Athena.

We reject professional education in instruments, then, (and by professional education I mean the kind that aims at competition). For the   *10*
performer does not take part in this kind of education for the sake of his
own virtue[38] but to give his audience pleasure, and a boorish pleasure at
that. That is precisely why we judge this sort of activity to be more appropriate for hired laborers than for free men. For performers do indeed
become vulgar, since the end they aim at is a base one. The listener, be-   *15*
cause he is boorish himself, typically has an influence on the music, in
that he imparts certain qualities to the professionals who perform for
him, and to their bodies as well, because of the movements he requires
them to make.

Chapter 7

As for harmonies and rhythms and their role in education, we should
also investigate: whether all the harmonies and rhythms should be used,   *20*
or whether we should divide them; whether the same division should be
established for those who are at work on their education, or a third class
introduced.[39] Since we can certainly see that music consists of melody
making and rhythms, we should not neglect the power that each of these
has to promote education but ask whether we should prefer music that   *25*
has a good melody or the kind that has a good rhythm. But since I consider that current experts on music as well as those in philosophy[40] who
happen to be experienced in issues pertaining to musical education say
many good things on these topics, I shall refer anyone who wants a precise account of each particular to their works. Here, however, the discus-   *30*
sion concerns legislation, and we shall speak in outline only.

38. See 1277[b]1–7.
39. The opening sentence is difficult and many repunctuations and deletions
 have been proposed. I take the division referred to in the first question to be
 between (1) the class of rhythms and harmonies to be used in the best city-
 state for any purpose (for example, for purification or for listening to when
 at leisure) and (2) the class not to be used for any purpose. The second question asks whether the rhythms and harmonies in (1) are all to be used in education or whether a third class is needed, namely, (3) the class consisting of
 those members of (1) useful in education.
40. See 1340[b]6 note.

Since we accept the division made by some people in philosophy who divide melodies into those relating to character, action, and inspiration, claiming that the harmonies are by nature peculiarly suited to these par-
35   ticular melodies, one being suited to one melody, and another to another; and since we claim that music should not be used for the sake of one benefit but several—for it is for the sake of education and purification (I shall not elaborate on what I mean by purification here, but I shall return to it in my work on poetics and discuss it in greater detail),[41] and third,
40   for leisured pursuit, for rest, and for the relaxation of one's tensions—it
1342ª is evident that all the harmonies are to be used, but that they are not all to be used in the same way. The ones that most pertain to character should be used in education, whereas those that pertain to action or inspiration should be used for listening to while others perform them. For
5   any emotion that strongly affects some people's souls (for example, pity, fear, or inspiration) is present in everyone, although to a greater or lesser degree. For there are some who are prone to become possessed by this motion.[42] But under the influence of sacred melodies (when they make use of the ones that induce a frenzy in their souls), we see that they calm
10   down, as if they had received medical treatment and a purifying purgation. The same thing, then, must be experienced by those who are prone to pity or fear, by those who are generally emotional, and by others to the extent that they share in these emotions: they all undergo a kind of purification and get a pleasant feeling of relief. In a similar way, the purify-
15   ing[43] melodies provide harmless enjoyment for people.

That is why competitors who perform music for the theater should be permitted to use such harmonies and melodies. But since theater audiences are of two kinds, one free and generally educated, the other boorish and composed of vulgar craftsmen, hired laborers, and other people
20   of that sort, the latter too must be provided with competitions and spectacles for the purposes of relaxation. Just as there are souls that are distorted from the natural state, so too there are deviant harmonies and melodies that are strained and over-ornamented, and what gives each
25   person pleasure is what is akin to his nature. Hence those who compete before a theater audience of the second sort should be permitted to use the second type of music.

41. Purification (*katharsis*) is mentioned in the *Poetics* at 1449ᵇ26–28, but the reference here is probably to the lost second book.
42. See 1337ᵇ42.
43. Reading *kathartika* with Dreizehnter and the mss.

But, as we said,[44] the melodies and harmonies that pertain to character should be used for education. The Dorian is of this sort, as we said earlier,[45] but we should accept any other that passes the inspection carried out for us by those who share in the practice of philosophy and musical education. The Socrates of the *Republic* was not right to retain only the Phrygian along with the Dorian, however, particularly since he includes the flute among the instruments he rejects.[46] For the Phrygian has the same power among the harmonies that the flute has among the instruments, since both are frenzied and emotional. For all Bacchic frenzy and all motions of that sort[47] are more closely associated with the flute than with any of the other instruments, whereas among the harmonies, the Phrygian melodies are the ones that are suited to them. Poetry shows this clearly. For example, the dithyramb is generally held to be Phrygian. And experts on these matters cite many instances to prove this, notably the fact that when Philoxenus tried to compose a dithyramb—*The Mysians*—in Dorian, he could not do it, but the very nature of his material forced him back into Phrygian, which is the harmony naturally appropriate to it. As for the Dorian, everyone agrees that it is the steadiest and has a more courageous character than any other. Besides, we praise what is in a mean between two extremes, and say that it is what we should pursue. So, since the Dorian has this nature, when compared to the other harmonies, it is evident that Dorian melodies are more suitable for the education of younger people.

There are two things to aim at: what is possible and what is suitable. And each individual should undertake what is more possible and more suitable for him. But possibility and suitability are determined by one's stage of life. For example, it is not easy for people exhausted by age to sing harmonies that are strained—nature recommends the relaxed harmonies at their stage of life. That is why some musical experts rightly criticize Socrates because he rejected the relaxed harmonies for the purposes of education,[48] not because they have the power that drink has of producing Bacchic frenzy, but because like drink they make us weak. So, with an eye to that future stage of life—old age—children *should* take up

30

1342[b]

5

10

15

20

25

44. At 1342[a]3.
45. At 1340[a]38–[b]5.
46. Plato, *Republic* 399a–d.
47. See 1337[b]42.
48. Plato, *Republic* 398d–399a.

harmonies and melodies of this relaxed sort. Moreover, if there is a certain sort of harmony that is suited to childhood, because it has the power
to provide both order and education at the same time (as seems particularly true of the Lydian harmony), then it is evident that these three
things must be made the defining principles of education: the mean, the
possible, and the suitable.

GLOSSARY

ACQUISITIVENESS, GET MORE THAN *pleonexia, pleonektein*
Pleonektein means "get the better of" or "get or have a larger share," usually in the sense of a share that is larger than one's fair share (although 1302ª1 makes it clear that it is possible to get a larger share justly). The corresponding disposition, or character trait, is acquisitiveness, which, though not always a vice, none the less has a substantial potential to lead to vicious action—in particular (distributive) injustice.

ACTION *praxis*
Aristotle sometimes uses the term *praxis* and the cognate verb *prattein* to refer to any intentional action (*NE* 1111ª25–26), but he also uses it in a stricter, canonical sense (*Ph.* 197ᵇ1–11, *EE* 1224ª28–29) to refer only to what results in the appropriate way from DELIBERATE CHOICE. Canonical actions are explained by contrast with productions (*poiēseis*): "Producing is different from its end, but acting is not, since its end is acting well (*eupraxia*)" (*NE* 1140ᵇ6–7). When someone produces a chair, his end (the chair) is different from his production of it. For example, the chair comes into existence only when the production of it ceases. But when someone performs an action, his unqualified end is simply happiness or acting well, which is not different from his performance of the action as the chair is different from the production. For example, the action ceases to exist when the performance of it ceases. Because actions have no further end beyond acting well, they are for their own sakes or because of themselves; whereas productions, which have a further end, are for the sake of or because of their products. The NOBLE or LEISURED actions preferred by FREE people, in which happiness consists, are all actions or activities of the canonical sort.

aisumnētēs DICTATOR

ARCHĒ
In Aristotle's political science (statesmanship), an *archē* is the office held by an official or ruler, or the type of rule he exercises as a holder of that office. In his epistemology an *archē* is a first principle, an undemonstrated premise (often a definition) used to establish other things. In his metaphysics, an *archē* is an origin, starting point, or cause (often the thing in the world that a definition picks out).

aretē VIRTUE

ARISTOCRACY
A constitution whose citizens are virtuous men of practical wisdom (see Introduction §10). The best constitution described in Books VII–VIII is an aristocracy of this sort. Various lesser kinds of aristocracy are distinguished in IV.7.

ARROGANCE *hubris*
A kind of belittling (*oligōria*) or dishonoring "in which the sufferer is shamed, not so that some benefit may come to the doer, or because some harm has been done to him, but simply for the pleasure involved. . . . The cause of pleasure to those committing arrogance is that they think they become superior to others by ill-treating them. That is why the young and the rich are arrogant: by being arrogant they think they are being superior" (*Rh.* 1378^{b}23–29).

autarkeia SELF-SUFFICIENCY

AUTHORITY, AUTHORITATIVE *kurion, kuriōs*
For X to be *kurion* Y is for X to have authority or control or to be sovereign over Y. A *kurion* F is an F in the fullest or most authoritative (*kuriōs*) sense of the term.

banausos, banausos technitēs VULGAR, VULGAR CRAFTSMAN

barbaros NON-GREEK, barbaric

basileus KING

BLESSEDLY HAPPY *makarios*
Often Aristotle does not distinguish between a happy person and a blessedly happy one. But sometimes he marks off the blessedly happy person as enjoying a particularly high level of HAPPINESS untinged with misfortune and well equipped with external GOODS (*NE* 1101^{a}6–8, 1179^{a}1–9).

chernētēs MANUAL LABORER

chrēmatistikē WEALTH ACQUISITION

CITIZEN *politēs*
An UNQUALIFIED citizen (*politēs haplōs*) is someone who participates in judicial and deliberative office (see III.1–2, 5). But Aristotle also uses the term "citizen" in a broader sense. At 1332^{a}32–35, he contrasts citizens who participate in the constitution with a larger class of citizens who do not. At 1285^{a}25–29, he says that kings, unlike tyrants, have fellow citizens as their bodyguards, again implying that it is possible to be a citizen without participating in office (only the king is an unqualified citizen). At 1279^{a}31–32, he regards those who share in the benefits of office, but not in office itself, as citizens. At 1260^{b}15–20 and 1299^{a}20–23 women and children are implicitly included among the citizens. Presumably,

some of the apparent disunity in Aristotle's notion of a citizen is to be explained by the fact that a citizen is defined relative to a city-state and a constitution (1275^{a}33–^{b}21), so that a person might be referred to as a citizen if he counted as a citizen relative to *some* constitution. But it is also no doubt true that Aristotle sometimes uses the term in the loose and popular sense to apply to anyone who passes the sorts of pragmatic tests of citizenship mentioned in III.2 (for example, having parents who are citizens). In every constitution, the office holders and the unconditional citizens are the same. See MAJORITY.

CITY-STATE *polis*
A canonical city-state is a unique organization, something like a city and something like a state (hence both "city" and "state" are common — if not entirely happy—translations of "*polis*"). Unlike a typical contemporary city, a city-state enjoyed the political sovereignty characteristic of a modern state: it could possess its own army and navy, enter into alliances, make war, and so on. Unlike a typical contemporary state, it was a politically, religiously, and culturally unified community, and quite small-scale. A city-state is always identical to the totality of its citizens, in a way that states and cities are not. The territory of city-state included a single (typically) walled town (*astu*), with a citadel and a marketplace, which, as the political and governmental heart of a city-state, is itself often referred to as the city-state (Book VII provides many examples of this). But a city state also included the surrounding agricultural land, and the citizens lived bo n there and inside the town proper. Somewhat confusingly, Aristotle also uses the term "*polis*" to refer to large states that may comprise many cities or towns, or to those cities or towns themselves, even though neither of these is a canonical city-state. In this looser sense of the term, any state with a city or any city, however large, is a city-state.

Because a city-state is a multitude of citizens (1276^{b}10–11), Aristotle's conception of it inherits some of the complexity inherent in his notion of a CITIZEN. Because a city-state is a community of citizens sharing a constitution (1276^{b}1–2), city-states with different constitutions are also different (1276^{b}10). A city-state includes women, children, and slaves (1260^{b}8–20, 1269^{b}14–19, 1277^{a}5–12), but strictly speaking only the unqualified citizens who participate in judicial and deliberative office are genuine "parts" of it (1328^{a}21–^{b}2, 1329^{a}2–5, 19–22). A city-state, unqualifiedly speaking, is a political community consisting of free citizens governed by a constitution (1326^{b}5): a community of equals that aims at the best life possible (1328^{a}35–37). It is the natural community for human beings to live in (1253^{a}7–18, 1278^{b}19–25, *NE* 1162^{a}17–19, *EE* 1242^{a}22–27), since there, and only there, can they achieve the happiness that is their natural end. See Introduction §7; NATION, EDUCATION.

COLONY *apoikia*
When, for example, the population of a Greek city-state became too large for its available resources, it often sent some of its citizens out to colonize new territory

elsewhere. This colony was politically autonomous but typically retained some ties with its mother city-state. A Greek colony is thus quite different from what we call a colony.

COMMERCE *kapēlikē*

The craft that is part of WEALTH ACQUISITION, but not of HOUSEHOLD MANAGE-MENT (1257ᵃ41–1258ᵃ18), that produces wealth through EXCHANGE (1257ᵇ 20–22). It is concerned with money as opposed to natural WEALTH, and involves getting wealth at the expense of others. Usury is a part of it (1258ᵃ38–ᵇ2).

COMMUNITY, COMMUNAL, COMMON *koinonia, koinos*

A community consists of different people who engage in a common enterprise that involves sharing something in common (1260ᵇ39–40), and who are bound to one another by a sort of friendship and a sort of justice as a result. Thus a house-hold is a community, a CITY-STATE is a community, but so are a master and a slave, or the partners in a business transaction, or even fellow travelers. And all these communities are subordinate to the political community. See *NE* VII.9.

CONSTITUTION *politeia*

The United States Constitution is the highest law of the land. It is embodied in a document. A *politeia* is like that, but it isn't just a set of laws; instead it is the community of people whose laws those are. (The English word "constitution" has a parallel sense, as in "He has a strong constitution.") Aristotle gives a num-ber of characterizations of a *politeia* which show this clearly: A constitution is a sort of life of a city-state (1295ᵃ40–ᵇ1), an organization of its inhabitants (1274ᵇ38) and offices, especially those with authority over everything (1278ᵇ 8–10, 1289ᵃ15–18), its governing class (1278ᵇ11). However, Aristotle uses the term *politeia*, thus understood, in a number of different ways: (1) Sometimes it refers to a political system of any sort (1271ᵇ20 with 1272ᵇ9–11). (2) Sometimes it refers to a system of a particular sort, namely, a POLITY (1265ᵇ26–28, 1273ᵃ4–5, 1279ᵃ37–ᵇ4, 1286ᵇ13, 1289ᵇ28). (3) Most often, however, it refers to any political system defined by and governed in accordance with universal LAWS (1289ᵃ18–20).

CRAFT *technē*

Sometimes "*technē*" is a synonym for "*epistēmē*" (science). But strictly speaking a craft is a rational discipline concerned exclusively with production. It is con-trasted with PRACTICAL WISDOM, which is concerned with ACTION (*NE* 1140ᵇ3, 1153ᵃ25), and with theoretical science, which aims at knowledge alone, and is neither practical nor productive.

DECENCY, DECENT *epieikeia, epieikēs*

Decency is "a sort of justice" (*NE* 1138ᵃ3), and "decent" is often used as a near synonym of "good" (*NE* 1137ᵃ35–ᵇ2) or "virtuous." Decent people are often contrasted with the "many" or the majority.

DECREE *psēphisma*
Unlike a LAW, which is universal, a decree is adapted to particular circumstances (*NE* 1137ᵇ27–32). It says what is to be done in a particular case, and so is the last thing reached in a piece of deliberation (*NE* 1141ᵇ24–28). The political significance of decrees is discussed at 1292ᵃ4–37.

DELIBERATE CHOICE *prohairesis*
Wish (*boulēsis*) is a desire for the good (HAPPINESS) or what is taken to be such (*NE* 1113ᵃ23–25). Deliberation (*bouleusis*) is a process of practical reasoning through which we discover what we can do in order ᵇᵉst to promote our happiness in the particular circumstances we are in (*N.* 1111ᵇ26–30, 1112ᵇ12–16). An effective desire resulting from wish and based on deliberation to do what best promotes happiness is a deliberate choice (*NE* 1113ᵃ9–14). See also ACTION.

dēmagōgos POPULAR LEADER

DEME *dēmos*
A local territorial district, on the order of a village; its inhabitants or members.

DEMOCRACY *dēmokratia*
Democracy is a deviant form of the constitution Aristotle calls a *politeia* (POLITY). Unlike the latter, where the many rule in the interests of the entire city-state, a democracy is rule by the multitude for the benefit of the poor (1279ᵇ8–9). But this definition captures its essence only accidentally (1279ᵇ34–39): unqualifiedly speaking, democracy is rule of the poor for the sake of the poor (1280ᵃ2–3). It is the most moderate of the deviant constitutions (1289ᵇ4–5).

Aristotle recognizes a variety of democracies, distinguishing them in a number of different (and not obviously equivalent) ways: (1) At 1306ᵇ20–21, he distinguishes between (a) a democracy based on law and (b) one in which the people have complete authority. (2) At 1291ᵇ30–1292ᵃ38 he distinguishes five kinds of democracy: (a) the rich and the poor are equal by law and neither has authority; (b) offices are filled on the basis of a low property assessment; (c) all uncontested citizens participate and the law rules; (d) all citizens (contested or uncontested) participate and the law rules; (e) is the same as (d) except the citizens, not the laws, are in authority. (2a–d) are presumably subvarieties of (1a), whereas (2e) is identical to (1b). (3) At 1292ᵇ22–1293ᵃ12, on the other hand, just four kinds of democracy are listed, which seem to correspond to (2b–e). This list omits (2a), perhaps because it combines elements of democracy (rule by the many) and oligarchy (rule by the few) and so is more of a polity than a democracy—the distinctions here are somewhat fluid, as Aristotle recognizes (see 1293ᵇ33–38). (2a) is also omitted from the list given in VI.4. (4) The recipe given at 1319ᵃ39–ᵇ1 for generating the various kinds of democracies, which is based on the various kinds of common people distinguished at 1290ᵇ39–ᵃ10, does not seem to result in (2b–e) in any obvious way.

dēmos PEOPLE, DEMOCRACY, DEME.

diagōgē LEISURED PURSUIT

DICTATOR *aisymnētēs*
The holder of an elective TYRANNY based on LAW. See 1285ª30–b1, b25–26.

dunasteia DYNASTY

DYNASTY *dunasteia*
Hereditary OLIGARCHY in which not law but officials rule.

EDUCATION *paideia*
Aristotle thinks that education is of enormous political importance (1310ª12–14, 1332b10–11): a community could not really be a city-state if it did not train its citizens in virtue (1280b1–8); people are unified and made into a community by means of education (1263b36–37). Yet, in part because the *Politics* is incomplete (see 1326b32–39, 1330ª31–33, 1335b2–5, 1336b24–27, 1338ª32–34, 1341b19–23), it is difficult to get clear even about the elementary education described in VII.17–VIII.7. Four stages are, however, discernible in it: (1) The treatment of infants, and their informal training up to the age of 5, is sketchily described at 1336ª3–1336b35. (2) From ages 5 to 7, children observe the studies they will later learn for themselves (1336b35–37). (3) From ages 7 to 14, this includes "easier gymnastic exercises" (1338b40–42). (4) From ages 14 to 21, this includes (ages 17 to 21) arduous physical training combined with a strict diet (1339ª5–7), as well as three years (ages 14 to 17) of "other studies" (1339ª5).

The "other studies" mentioned in connection with (4) are not explicitly identified. They could be reading and writing, music, and drawing (1337b24–25). But then the only thing that children are taught in (3), a period of seven whole years, is light gymnastics. This is sufficiently implausible on its own terms (why postpone reading, writing, drawing, and music until age 14?) and a sufficiently large departure from common Greek practice and Plato's recommendations that we would expect Aristotle to acknowledge it as an innovation and defend it carefully. The fact that he does neither of these things suggests that he is in fact intending to follow tradition and include reading, writing, drawing, and music in (3).

If the "other studies" are not reading, writing, music, and drawing, however, what are they? There are a number of possibilities. In I.11, Aristotle says that a FREE person has theoretical knowledge of all of the practical aspects of WEALTH ACQUISITION (1258b9–11). And in various places he refers to what he calls a generally educated person (*pepaideumenos*). This is someone who studies practically all subjects, not to acquire expert scientific knowledge in all of them (which would be impossible), but in order to become a good judge (*PA* 639ª1–6, *NE* 1094b28–1095ª2). Generally educated in medicine, for example, he is as capable as an expert doctor (1282ª3–7) of judging whether or not someone has treated a disease correctly. Acquainted with many subjects, methodologies, and areas of study, he knows "what we should and should not seek to have demonstrated" (*Metaph.* 1106ª5–11) and "seeks exactness in each area to the extent that the subject-matter allows" (*NE* 1094ᵇ23–27).

Because he is able to judge the works and advice of experts, a generally educated person is free from the sort of intellectual enslavement to them that would otherwise be his lot. He knows who is and who isn't worth listening to on any matter and so can get good expert advice when he needs it. But he is also free from the inner enslavement that is all too often the lot of the narrow expert, whose imagination is straitjacketed by the one thing he knows too well. For, while he has indeed studied all the civilized sciences (liberal arts), he has done so only "up to a point," and not so assiduously or pedantically as "to debase the mind and deprive it of leisure" (1337ᵇ14–17). Presumably, then, the citizens of the best city-state, who are all civilized and generally educated men, must be trained in these subjects at some point, if not as part of (3), then later in their lives.

In VIII.3, we are promised a discussion of a kind of education "that sons must be given not because it is useful or necessary but because it is noble and suitable for a free person" (1338ª30–34). The promise is unfortunately not fulfilled in our *Politics,* but we do nevertheless have some clues to go on as to the nature of these studies. We know, for example, that music and drawing are both to be taught, in part because they are NOBLE and free and contribute to LEISURE (1338ª21–22, 1338ᵇ1–2). But we also know that many other subjects, particularly philosophy (1263ᵇ29–40, 1267ª10–12, 1334ª23) and other theoretical sciences, are crucial to spending one's leisure time well and achieving happiness. Since the end of a city-state is to enable its citizens to lead the good life and be happy, it must surely educate them in these subjects and sciences (see VII.15).

Finally, there is the vexed question of explicitly ethical or political training and education. Ethical training (in the shape of habituation) must take place before more formal education in ethics and statesmanship (for example, listening to Aristotle's own lectures in the Lyceum) can begin (*NE* 1095ᵇ4–8). 1336ª 23–34 suggests that some of this already occurs in (1). Formal ethical education is required, however, in order to develop the PRACTICAL WISDOM (including the knowledge of what happiness really is), which all the citizens of the best city-state must have if they are to rule successfully when their turn comes (*NE* 1103ª14–17). Such education presumably takes place after (4), but precisely when and in what form we can only guess (see 1333ᵇ3–5). Moreover, we know from the *Rhetoric* that training in rhetoric is crucial for political success in most city-states and that it too is part of general education (*Rh.* 1356ª7–9). It seems reasonable to conclude, therefore, that, in addition to ethical habituation, some training in the theoretical sciences must be included in (1)–(4) and that some further education in ethics, rhetoric, and perhaps in these sciences too must occur after (4). See also MESSES.

Just as important as the content of the education Aristotle advocates is the fact that he explicitly conceives of it not in the traditional Greek way as privately provided (1337ª18–26) but as *public* education suited to the constitution and provided to citizens by it (1260ᵇ15, 1337ª14). It is no surprise, therefore, that most of his remarks about the education provided in the best city-state concern the education of future unqualified citizens, all of whom are, of course, males. It seems certain, none the less, that he thinks that public education should also be provided to girls and WOMEN (1260ᵇ13–20, 1269ᵇ12–24, 1335ᵇ11–12). But since he thinks that male and female virtues are different (I.13), their education is bound to differ substantially.

eleutheros FREE

epieikēs DECENT, good

epistēmē SCIENCE

EQUALITY *to ison, isotēs*
Suppose a piece of land is divided into two parcels, X and Y, that are then distributed to two people, A and B, respectively. The distribution is just in Aristotle's view if the ratio between the *value* of X and the *value* of Y is the same as the ratio between the *merit* of A and the *merit* of B. That is to say, if

$$\text{Value (X)} / \text{Value (Y)} = \text{Merit (A)} / \text{Merit (B)}.$$

Aristocrats, oligarchs, and democrats agree about the conditions under which Value (X) = Value (Y), but they disagree about those under which Merit (A) = Merit (B). Democrats claim that all free citizens are equal in merit; aristocrats claim that merit is proportional to VIRTUE; oligarchs claim that it is proportional to wealth (*NE* 1131ª14–ᵇ23). Democratic equality seems to be numerical equality; and aristocratic and oligarchic equality seem to be equality according to merit or proportional equality (1301ᵇ29–30). Some of the problems involved in numerical equality are discussed in VI.3. See Introduction lxxv–lxxvi.

ergon TASK

ethnos NATION

eudaimonia HAPPINESS

eunomia, eunomeisthai GOOD GOVERNMENT

euthuna INSPECTION

excellent *spoudaios*

EXCHANGE *allattein, allagē, metablētikē*
The three parts of exchange are trading (whose subparts are ship owning, transport, and marketing), money lending, and wage earning (1258ᵇ20–27). The kinds of exchange that involve bartering surplus goods for other needed goods are natural and are not a part of WEALTH ACQUISITION (1257ª14–30). The other kinds are parts of COMMERCE.

FACTION, START A FACTION *stasis, stasiazein*
Internal political conflict (extending from tensions to actual civil war), typically between aristocrats, oligarchs, and democrats, which sometimes leads to the overthrow or modification of the constitution.

FREE free-minded, generous *eleutheros*
A free person is, in the first instance, someone who is not a SLAVE. In this sense the farmer citizens of a DEMOCRACY are free men. But a farmer must work in order to get the necessities; he is not a man of LEISURE. Therefore, there is another sense in which he is not free. A person who is free in this second sense has distinctive character traits, EDUCATION, and outlook. Unlike a slavish or VULGAR person, he is not obsessed with practical or useful things (1333^{b}9–10, 1338^{b}2–4), preferring NOBLE and unproductive ones (*NE* 1125^{a}11–12). His general education gives him a broad perspective on the world, rather than a narrow-minded or overly specialized one. Hence he is able to judge or assess the credibility and appropriateness of discussions belonging to different professions and disciplines in which he is not himself an expert (*PA* 639^{a}1–6). Only the free man has PRACTICAL WISDOM and the VIRTUES of character. Hence he alone has what it takes to be an unqualified citizen in the best kind of city-state (1329^{a}2–17). Since that city-state ensures that he has the resources needed for LEISURE (1329^{a}17–26), he does not need to work for a living, and so does not "live in dependence on another," which is another important mark of being free (*Rh.* 1367^{a}32–33). The art and MUSIC he enjoys, and the use he makes of his leisure, further distinguish him from those who are vulgar or uncivilized (1342^{a}19–32, 1334^{a}11–40, *Po.* 1461^{b}26–1462^{a}4). But even such a citizen is often under the authority of others, whom he must obey. There are thus substantial limitations on his freedom or self-determination. See Introduction §8.

GOD *theos*
The Aristotelian cosmos consists of a series of concentric spheres, with the earth at its center. God is an incorporeal being whose only activity is the STUDY or contemplation of himself (*Metaph.* 983^{a}6–7, 1072^{b}13–30, 1074^{b}33–1075^{a}5). Since this sort of activity is the highest kind of happiness (*NE* 1178^{a}6–10), God is described as being his own happiness (*EE* 1245^{b}16–29). His cosmological role is that of first mover, or first cause of motion in the universe. But he does not act on the universe to cause it to move; instead he moves it in the way that an object of love causes motion in the things that love or desire it (*DA* 415^{a}26–^{b}7). Hence he is also an unmoved mover (*Metaph.* 1072^{a}25–27). His role in the universe is like that of understanding (*nous*) in the human soul (*EE* 1248^{a}25–29).

GOOD, GOODS *agathon, agatha*
(1) A good F is one that possesses the features that enable it to perform well the TASK (*ergon*) characteristic and definitive of Fs. Thus a good man is someone who is able to perform well the rational activities that are characteristic and definitive of human beings (*NE* 1097^{b}24–1098^{a}20). He has human virtue. (2) The

ultimate good for human beings, the human good, is happiness. Other things we aim at are good to the degree that they promote our happiness (*NE* 1097ª15–ᵇ22). Things that promote an end other than happiness are good relative to that end, not unqualifiedly good (*NE* 1113ª15–33).

Aristotle divides the goods that typically promote happiness into three classes: external goods (also called resources or goods of luck), goods of the soul, and goods of the body (1323ª25–26, *NE* 1098ᵇ12–16). Goods of the soul are states (the virtues) and the activities that express them, for example, happiness. External goods and goods of the body, on the other hand, are capacities or tools that the virtuous person uses to achieve good ends, and the vicious bad ones (1323ᵇ7–12, *NE* 1129ª11–16).

Unlike the goods of the soul, external goods and goods of the body are the result of luck (1323ᵇ27–29, *NE* 1153ᵇ16–19). However, the sphere of luck can be reduced by craft, so that many external goods admit of at least limited human control (*NE* 1140ª17–20, *Metaph.* 981ª1–5). It is for these reasons, no doubt, and because our bodies are parts of us, that Aristotle sometimes seems to waver on whether to class goods of the body as internal goods or as external resources: "Goods of the body and of the psyche are internal; good birth, friends, money, and honor are external" (*Rh.* 1360ᵇ26–29; cf. *NE* 1178ᵇ33–35). For some goods of the body are, like goods of the psyche, less controlled by luck, while others, like some external goods, are more controlled by it.

External goods are also subject to another important kind of subdivision between those that people compete over, such as money, honors, and bodily pleasure, and those they do not compete for, such as friends, beauty, or good birth (*NE* 1169ª20–21). The former form the area of focus for many of the virtues of character. See Introduction xxxix.

GOOD GOVERNMENT, WELL GOVERNED *eunomia, eunomeisthai*
A city-state or constitution exhibits good government or is well governed if it has laws (*nomoi*) that are in fact obeyed, and these either are the best possible for that city-state or constitution or are unqualifiedly best (1294ª4–9).

GOVERNING CLASS *politeuma*
The group or class of CITIZENS that is eligible to hold office and has supreme authority in the city-state.

GYMNASTICS *gumnastikē*
Gymnastics includes general exercises aimed at physical fitness (*NE* 1138ª31, *EE* 1218ª35–36, 1227ᵇ27) and provided by a trainer (*gumnastikos*), as well as more focused education aimed to inculcate specific physical skills (including athletic and military ones) provided by a coach (*paidotribēs*) (1338ᵇ6–8). See also MUSIC.

haplōs UNQUALIFIED, unqualifiedly, simply

HAPPINESS *eudaimonia*

Happiness is the highest good for human beings. It is the end of the city-state as well as of all its individual citizens ($1323^b40-1324^a2$), the final end of all ACTION (*NE* 1102^a2-3, 1176^a30-31), and, though less directly, all production (*NE* 1139^a35-^b3). Aristotle sometimes speaks of happiness as being made up of other goods, and of those other goods as its parts (*NE* 1129^b17-19, *MM* 1184^a18-19, *Rh.* 1360^b19-26). This may explain why it is complete (choiceworthy because of itself and never because of something else (*NE* 1097^a30-34)), and self-sufficient (something that "all by itself makes a life choiceworthy and lacking in nothing" (*NE* 1097^a8-9)). But it is also clear that Aristotle thinks of these goods as being organized into a system, so that external GOODS and goods of the body are chosen for the sake of goods of the soul (1323^b18-21), and some goods of the soul are chosen (at least in part) for the sake of others. Thus both activity expressing practical wisdom and political activity, which are goods of the soul, are chosen for the sake of LEISURE and the activities of leisure (1334^a11-40, *NE* 1177^b2-18, *EE* 1249^b9-21). That is why the most important part of happiness consists in activities like MUSIC, PHILOSOPHY, and the contemplation of GOD (1267^a10-12, *NE* 1177^a27-^b1).

Even from this brief sketch, it is clear that Aristotelian happiness is not a feeling of contentment or pleasure, although pleasure and contentment are involved in it. It is really more a matter of living successfully by living a life in which really valuable things are achieved. For further discussion, see Introduction xxv–lix.

HOPLITE

A heavily armed infantryman. His equipment included a bronze helmet, body armor, a round shield (*hoplon*), a spear, and a sword. Since he had to provide this equipment at his own expense, only people at least moderately wealthy could afford to be hoplites. Poorer people rowed in the navy or served as light-armored troops. Wealthier citizens who could afford a horse fought in the cavalry. Citizen hoplites, organized in phalanxes, were the principal fighting force until mercenaries replaced them late in the fourth century.

HOUSEHOLD *oikos*. See Introduction l–li.

HOUSEHOLD MANAGEMENT *oikonomia*

Household management is the science that deals with the use of property (1256^a10-13). The natural part of PROPERTY ACQUISITION is a part of it (1256^b26-27), but COMMERCE is not. Other parts are mastership of slaves, marital science, and procreative science (see I.3, 12–13).

hubris ARROGANCE

INSPECTION *euthuna*

Inspection (scrutiny, auditing) was a device to ensure public control of officials. In Athens, an official was usually inspected at the end of his term of office. The first part of the inspection dealt with his handling of public funds, and was conducted by a board of ten accountants. The second part, conducted by a board of ten inspectors, dealt with other objections to his conduct while in office. The inspectors could dismiss the objections or pass them on to the courts.

kalon NOBLE, beautiful, good, fine

KING, KINGSHIP *basileus, basileia*
A kingship is a monarchical constitution that aims at the common benefit (1279^a32–34). The deviation from it is TYRANNY. Five kinds of kingship are discussed in III.14: (1) Spartan; (2) non-Greek; (3) DICTATORSHIP; (4) heroic; and (5) absolute. In II.15 (1285^b33–37), these are reduced to two fundamental kinds: Spartan and absolute. In III.16, Spartan kingship is removed from the list of genuine kinds of kingship, on the grounds that it is not a kind of constitution (1287^a3–4).

ktētikē PROPERTY ACQUISITION

kurion AUTHORITY

LAW *nomos*
Laws are universal commands (1269^a11–12, *NE* 1137^b13–14) typically backed by sanctions that compel compliance (*NE* 1180^a21). There are two kinds of law: specific (*idion*) and common (*koinon*). Specific law is the written law followed by some city-state; common law is unwritten but "agreed to among all" (*Rh.* 1368^b7–9). Common law is "based on nature" (*Rh.* 1373^b4–7, 1375^a32). Law "based on custom (*kata to ethos*)" is common law, as the fact that it is contrasted with written law strongly suggests (see *VV* 1250^b15–18). Specific law and common law can conflict, as they typically do, for example, in deviant constitutions (*Rh.* 1373^b9–13, 1375^a27–$^b8$), or they can have the same content.

Being ruled by law is generally better than being ruled by human beings, because the law is dispassionate (1286^a17–20, 1287^a28–32). None the less, the law cannot cover every eventuality and cannot dictate how it is to be applied in every particular case, so "the law educates the rulers specially for this task and then appoints them to decide and manage whatever it omits in accordance with their most just opinion" (1287^a25–27; see also *Rh.* 1374^a18–$^b23$).

Laws are sometimes contrasted with the constitution itself (1265^a1–3, 1286^a2–4). The nature of this contrast is explained at 1289^a15–25. Making laws that benefit a constitution is a task of statesmanship or practical wisdom (1289^a11–13).

LEISURE, LEISURED ACTIVITY *scholē, scholazein*
Leisure is usually contrasted with work (*ascholia*) or what one must do in order to acquire the necessities (1331^b10–13), and usually associated with what is NOBLE or FREE. Leisurely actions or activities are engaged in for their own sake, and not for the sake of something else. Thus there is a fair amount of overlap be-

tween our conception of leisure and Aristotle's. But whereas we are inclined to think that almost anything can be a leisured activity provided we enjoy it and do it for pleasure, Aristotle thinks that some actions or activities are objectively or intrinsically leisurely. These are the canonical ACTIONS or activities that are their own ends and that we perform only for their own sakes and never for the sake of something else. Political action is leisured to some extent, but philosophical contemplation is the only activity that is truly and fully leisured ($1267^a10–12$, *NE* $1177^b2–18$). This is why FREE people spend their time on politics and philosophy ($1255^b35–37$, $1324^a25–32$). See Introduction xxxv–xlviii.

LEISURED PURSUIT *diagōgē, diagōgē scholē*
A leisured pursuit is an activity appropriate to LEISURE time, such as music, philosophy, or mathematics (*Metaph.* $981^b13–25$).

leitourgia PUBLIC SERVICE

MAJORITY *pleion*
The notion of the majority is a complex one. The majority is always the majority of the citizens of a city-state, never the majority of its total population (which includes many noncitizens, such as slaves and resident aliens). Because of this it inherits some of the problems inherent in the notion of a CITIZEN. For example, when Aristotle tells us that the majority (or majority opinion) has authority in all constitutions ($1294^a11–14$), the majority he is referring to is the majority of unqualified citizens ($1275^a19–23$) who participate in the offices of the constitution. In the case of an aristocracy or an oligarchy, this may be a very small number of people. But when a democracy is characterized as control by the majority, the majority in question cannot be the majority of the unqualified citizens. If it were, the contrast between a democracy and the other types of constitutions would collapse. What Aristotle has in mind here is presumably the majority of those who pass the kinds of pragmatic tests for citizenship discussed in III.2, such as being born of citizen parents.

makarios BLESSEDLY HAPPY

MANUAL LABORER *chernētēs*
Sometimes the class of hired laborers, who are poor ($1291^b25–26$). Sometimes a broader class, which includes the VULGAR CRAFTSMEN ($1277^a38–^b1$), who may be quite wealthy ($1278^a24–25$).

MASTER, MASTERSHIP *despotēs, despotikē, despotikē epistēmē*
A master is someone who (in the best case) exercises the rule of a master (*despotikē*) over SLAVES (unfree and unwilling subjects) in accordance with the science of mastership (I.7).

MESSES *sussitia*
Sussitia are groups of people who regularly eat meals together, the places where such meals are eaten, or the meals themselves. They are organized by the city-

state, and often paid for from public funds. Despite the fact that Aristotle's promised discussion of this institution is missing (1330ᵃ4–5), it seems pretty clear from what he does say that though one of its functions was to feed the citizens (1330ᵃ1), another was to foster community among them. Thus having messes tends to foster the communal use of property, which Aristotle favors (1263ᵃ21–41, 1263ᵇ40–1264ᵃ1); and tyrants forbid messes because they do not want the citizens to know and trust one another (1313ᵃ41–ᵇ6). Moreover, there was often a symposium after the meal itself, at which there was music and discussion. It seems certain that Aristotle plans to have such symposia in his best city-state (1336ᵇ20–23, 1338ᵃ21–30). Some understanding of the political and educational significance of symposia can be gleaned from Plato, *Laws* I–II.

MIDDLE CONSTITUTION
Described in IV.11, the middle constitution is probably a POLITY. It is not the unqualifiedly best constitution, but it is the best one for most city-states and most people, because it requires fewer resources and less than perfectly virtuous citizens.

MONARCHY *monarchia*
Monarchy is one-person rule; KINGSHIP is its correct and TYRANNY its deviant form.

MONEY *nomisma*
First introduced to facilitate EXCHANGE of needed goods, it eventually becomes an unnatural form of WEALTH that is dealt with by a science of its own: COMMERCE. In addition to functioning as a medium of exchange, it serves as a unit of value, and as a way of storing wealth for future use. See I.9–10, Introduction liv–lv, lxxv–lxxvi.

MULTITUDE *plēthos*
Any large group of people, but often the poor citizens as opposed to the few rich ones.

MUSIC *mousikē*
Music consists of melodies (*melos*), or (occasionally) of the constituents of melodies other than the words (1341ᵇ23–24). Melodies (songs, poems) consist of words (*logos*), harmony (*harmonia*), and rhythm (*ruthmos*). A harmony or harmonic mode is an arrangement of tones of a particular sort (Dorian, Lydian, Mixo-Lydian, Phrygian). Sometimes, however, *melos* is itself used to refer to a harmony, and *harmonia* is used to refer to a way of tuning an instrument that suits it to a particular mode.

NATION *ethnos*
A nation occupied a larger territory than a city-state, had a larger population, and a less tight social organization. It need not have a single town or urban center, and may consist of many scattered villages.

NATURE, IS (EXISTS) BY NATURE, NATURAL *phusis*, *kata phusin*: see Introduction §4.

NOBLE *kalon*
The opposite of shameful (*aischron*). Something is noble if it is "both choice-worthy because of itself and praiseworthy" (*Rh.* 1366ª33–34). Hence what is noble is usually contrasted with what is merely useful (1323ᵇ11–12) or necessary (1325ª26–27, 1332ª7–17) or VULGAR (1333ᵇ9). "The virtues and the actions resulting from virtue" are the only unqualifiedly noble things (*EE* 1248ᵇ36–37). Since happiness is "a complete activation or employment of virtue," it consists in doing noble actions (1332ª9). FREE people prefer what is noble to everything else.

nomisma MONEY

nomos LAW, custom

OFFICE *ARCHĒ*, *timē*

olkos HOUSEHOLD

OLIGARCHY *oligarchia*
Rule by the few rich for the their own benefit (1280ª1–2), rule that "results from wealth and power" (*NE* 1161ª2–3). A deviation from ARISTOCRACY.

paideia EDUCATION

PEOPLE *dēmos*
Sometimes the entire body of citizens regardless of their social class (1268ª12), but often the poor or the common people. This ambiguity gives rise to a parallel ambiguity in DEMOCRACY (rule by the *dēmos*), which is either rule by the majority of citizens or rule by the poorer classes.

perioikoi SUBJECT PEOPLES

PHILOSOPHY *philosophia*: See Introduction §2.

phronēsis PRACTICAL WISDOM.

pleion MAJORITY

plēthos MULTITUDE

polis CITY-STATE

politeia CONSTITUTION, POLITY

politeuma GOVERNING CLASS

politikē STATESMANSHIP

politikos STATESMAN

POLITY *politeia*

Aristotle gives a number of different accounts of what a polity is: (1) a constitution ruled by the multitude for the common benefit (1279ᵃ37–39); (2) a mixed constitution (1293ᵇ33–34, 1294ᵃ22–23); (3) a constitution that depends on the middle class (1295ᵇ34–1296ᵃ9); (4) a constitution that depends on the hoplite or warrior class (1265ᵇ26–28, 1288ᵃ12–15, 1297ᵇ1–2). The nature of the mixture mentioned in (2) is also variously characterized: (2.1) a mixture of democracy and oligarchy (1293ᵇ34, 1307ᵃ10–12); (2.2) a mixture of the rich and the poor, wealth and freedom (1294ᵃ16–17); (2.3) a mixture of elements drawn from democratic and oligarchic constitutions (IV.9).

Aristotle never explicitly identifies a polity with the MIDDLE CONSTITUTION described in IV.11 (except perhaps at 1297ᵃ39–40), but for the following reasons it seems that the latter just is a (well-mixed) polity: (1) There are just six types of constitutions: kingship, aristocracy, polity, democracy, oligarchy, and tyranny (1289ᵃ26–30). Hence one would expect the middle constitution to be one of these. What could it be besides a polity? (2) A well-mixed polity is in the middle between an oligarchy and a democracy (1294ᵇ14–18); so is the middle constitution (1296ᵃ22–40). Since there cannot be two middles between two extremes, the middle constitution must be a well-mixed polity.

POPULAR LEADER *dēmagōgos*

Occasionally *dēmagōgos* is a neutral term used to describe an influential democratic leader such as Pericles (1274ᵃ10), but more often it has a negative connotation ("demagogue"), referring to those who curry favor with (*dēmagōgein*) the people and undermine the rule of LAW (1292ᵃ4–37) in order to gain power.

PRACTICAL WISDOM *phronēsis*: See Introduction §5.

PRIOR *proteron*

Aristotle recognizes many different ways in which one thing can be prior to another. The following are particularly relevant to the *Politics:* (1) X is prior *in nature* to Y if X can exist without Y, but Y cannot exist without X (*Metaph.* 1019ᵃ2–4). This is also sometimes referred to as priority in substance (*Metaph.* 1050ᵇ6–19, 1077ᵃ36–ᵇ11). (2) X is prior *in substance* to Y if and only if X is more nearly perfect or more complete than Y (*GA* 742ᵃ19–22, *Metaph.* 1050ᵃ4–ᵇ6, *Rh.* 1392ᵃ20–23). This is also sometimes referred to as priority in nature (*Ph.* 261ᵃ13–14, 265ᵃ22–24, *PA* 646ᵃ25–26, *Metaph.* 989ᵃ15–18). (3) X is prior in *definition* (or formula) to Y if and only if X is mentioned in the definition of Y but not Y in the definition of X (*Metaph.* 1035ᵇ4–6, 1049ᵇ12–17, 1077ᵇ3–4).

prohairesis DELIBERATE CHOICE

psēphisma DECREE

PROPERTY ACQUISITION *ktētikē*
The craft or science dealing with the acquisition but not the use of property.

PROPERTY ASSESSMENT *timēma*
A measure of wealth or property for the purposes of taxation or determining PUBLIC SERVICE, often used to determine citizenship or access to political office.

PUBLIC SERVICE *leitourgia*
Rich people in Athens were required to equip a trireme, or to pay for the production of a play at a theater festival, or the like as a public service. This was, in effect, a form of taxation on their wealth.

rule *ARCHĒ*

scholē, scholazein LEISURE, leisured activity

SCIENCE (*epistēmē*) See Introduction §2.

SELF-SUFFICIENCY *autarkeia*
Something is self-sufficient if it can carry out its TASK or fulfill its function by itself. Happiness is self-sufficient because by itself it makes life choiceworthy (*NE* 1097^{b}14–16). A city-state is self-sufficient, and more so than a household or village, because it enables its inhabitants not just to live but to fulfill their functions and live leisured, happy lives (1352^{b}27–1353^{a}1, 1326^{b}30–32).

SLAVE *doulos*
A slave is a piece of animate property who belongs wholly to a single master, not to a community (1278^{a}11–13). He is a tool, an extension of his master's body, for use in matters having to do not with production but with ACTION (I.4). Some people are *natural* slaves because their souls lack a deliberative part (1252^{a}31–34, 1254^{b}21–23, 1260^{a}12, 1280^{a}33–34). Hence they are not self-sufficient (1291^{a}10), cannot be happy (1280^{a}32–34), and are (generally) better off being under the authority of someone to whose reason they can listen. For many such people, though not perhaps for those who have been living as free people (1255^{a}1–3), slavery is coincidentally beneficial (1278^{b}32–37) and just. But it is neither just nor beneficial for merely *legal* slaves to be enslaved, unless perhaps they have been living as slaves for some time (1255^{a}1–3).

Many tensions and apparent inconsistencies have been detected in Aristotle's various remarks about slaves: It is just and beneficial for natural slaves to be enslaved, yet Aristotle thinks that all slaves, natural or legal, should be offered freedom as a reward for good service (1330^{a}31–33). Slaves lack deliberation and foresight, yet those who have the resources delegate the position of household manager (a position that seems to require both deliberative ability and foresight) to a steward who is himself (presumably) a slave (1255^{b}33–37). These tensions are real, no doubt, but they can be somewhat lessened if we bear in mind a few facts and distinctions. First, there are various kinds of slaves, some with a larger share in virtue (or reason) than others (1255^{b}27–29, 1260^{a}14–20, 1330^{a}30–31).

Second, there are also various kinds of free people; a VULGAR CRAFTSMAN is a free man who shares in virtue to the extent that he is a limited slave still to some extent under the authority of a master (1260ᵃ39–ᵇ7), but he is not a free CITIZEN in most constitutions (III. 5).

We are not likely to find congenial Aristotle's views on slaves, however consistent, but we should remember that they provide a basis for the ethical critique of contemporary Greek practices. How many actual Greek slaves, we might wonder, would turn out to be credibly categorized as natural ones?

SOUL *psuchē*: see Introduction xxxviii.

spoudaios excellent, good

stasis FACTION

STATESMAN *politikos*
A statesman ("politician," "political ruler" are common alternative translations) is a man of practical wisdom, capable of ruling free and equal subjects (1255ᵇ20) in accordance with the precepts of statesmanship (IV.1), and of being ruled by them in that way when his turn comes (1259ᵇ4–6).

STATESMANSHIP *politikē*: see Introduction xxv–xxvi.

STUDY, THEORETICAL *theōrein*, *theōria*, *theōrētikos*
The verb *theōrein* (to view or look at) often means to study or contemplate or engage in theoretical activity (see Introduction §6). The adjective *theōrētikos* is frequently contrasted with *praktikos* (practical, or pertaining to ACTION). But in Aristotle's technical sense, theorizing is more practical, more of a canonical ACTION, than such paradigm practical matters as engaging in politics or running a city-state (1325ᵇ16–21).

SUBJECT PEOPLES *perioikoi*
Perioikoi ("those who dwell around") were the subject peoples found in various Greek city-states such as Sparta and Crete. They sometimes paid taxes, or served in the army, or provided farm labor. They did not participate in government, but were not SLAVES, and could not be bought and sold.

sussitia MESSES

TASK *ergon*: see Introduction §4.

technitēs VULGAR CRAFTSMAN

thēs hired laborer

timēma PROPERTY ASSESSMENT

TYRANNY *tyrannis*
A deviant form of monarchy. It is rule of unwilling subjects (1313ᵃ14–16,

1314³34–38) by one master, who aims at his own advantage rather than that of the community as a whole (see 1279ᵇ6–7, 16–17). It is a mixture of extreme oligarchy and extreme democracy (1310ᵇ2–7) and so is the worst constitution of all, the one that is furthest from being a true constitution (see 1289ᵇ1–2, 1293ᵇ27–30, 1309ᵇ30–35). If a tyrant listens to a true statesman, however, he will rule in a more moderate way and will either be "nobly disposed to virtue or else half good, not vicious but half vicious" (1315ᵇ9–10). Types of tyranny discussed in III.14 and IV.10 include foreign kingship and DICTATORSHIP.

UNQUALIFIED, UNQUALIFIEDLY *haplōs*
Something is unqualifiedly F or simply F if it is F intrinsically (*kath' hauto*) or by nature (*phusei*); it is qualifiedly F if it is F only in relation to something else (*pros ti*) or coincidentally (*kata sumbebēkos*) or on the basis of an assumption (*pros hupothesin*) or from a perspective, or in some other qualified way (1274ᵇ14–20, 1293ᵇ3–7, 1328³38–39, *NE* 1139ᵇ1–3, 1151³35–ᵇ3, 1153³5–6, 1157ᵇ3–5).

VIRTUE *aretē*
If something is a knife (say) or a man, its *aretē* or virtue as a knife or a man is that state or property of it that makes it a good knife or a good man, able to perform its task or function well. The *aretē* of a knife might include having a sharp blade; the *aretē* of a man might include being intelligent, well born, just, or courageous. *Aretē* is thus broader than our notion of moral virtue. It applies to things (such as knives) that are not moral agents. And it applies to aspects of moral agents (such as intelligence or family status) that are not normally considered to be moral aspects of them. See Introduction xxxii.

VULGAR *banausos*
People or activities that are the opposite of NOBLE or FREE are vulgar or common.

VULGAR CRAFTSMAN *banausos, banausos technitēs*
Vulgar craftsmen have a rather odd position in Aristotle's scheme of things. They are free men, not slaves. Yet they seem to be further removed from virtue than slaves (1260³39–ᵇ1). The work they do prevents them from acquiring virtue and being happy (1337ᵇ4–21). Yet nothing in their nature fits them to do that work rather than some other kind (1260ᵇ1–2). This suggests that if they hadn't become vulgar craftsmen, they might have been capable of virtue and happiness.

WEALTH *chrēmata, ploutos*
Natural wealth consists of the tools required by household managers and statesmen (1256ᵇ36–37). Unnatural wealth is MONEY. See COMMERCE, HOUSEHOLD MANAGEMENT, WEALTH ACQUISITION.

WEALTH ACQUISITION *chrēmatistikē*
The craft or science of acquiring WEALTH. Because of complexity in the latter notion, there are at least two different kinds of wealth acquisition. The natural

kind is concerned with the acquisition (but not the use) of natural wealth, and is a part of (1253ᵇ12–13) or assistant to (1256ᵃ3–7) HOUSEHOLD MANAGEMENT. The unnatural kind of wealth acquisition is COMMERCE. And in I.11 a third kind that "comes between" these two is discussed; it deals with metals etc. extracted from the earth, and timber and other nonfoodstuffs grown on it (1258ᵇ27–31).

WOMAN, FEMALE *gunē, to thēlu*

By nature men are rulers and women are ruled; hence women are naturally inferior to men (1254ᵇ13–14, *Po*. 1454ᵃ20–22) and have different virtues from them (I.13). A woman can make deliberate choices, but the deliberative part of her SOUL is *akuron*, it lacks AUTHORITY (1260ᵃ12–13). Part of what this might imply is that a woman, having arrived through deliberation at what she judges is the best thing to do in particular circumstances, may sometimes do something else, because she tends to be less able to control her own appetites and emotions than a man. This would explain why those who are weak-willed are likened to women (*NE* 1150ᵃ32–ᵇ16). Notice, however, that having said that the deliberative element in women lacks authority, Aristotle goes on to talk about their fitness to command (1259ᵇ1–3). This makes it much more likely that what he thinks women lack is authority over *other people*, for females have less spirit or assertiveness than males (*HA* 608ᵃ33–ᵇ12, *PA* 661ᵇ33–34), and spirit is responsible for the ability to command (1328ᵃ6–7). Since these differences between men and women are natural, we would expect to find an explanation of them in Aristotle's embryology. But no such explanation is given. No doubt Aristotle is postulating some unknown biological basis for the differences he observes (or thinks he observes) between men and women, and between males and females of other species, rather than deriving the latter from the former.

Also relevant are Aristotle's views on the age at which women should marry, the factors that conduce to harmony in marriage (VII.16), (certain sorts of) male adultery (1335ᵇ38–1336ᵃ2), and public EDUCATION for women.

WORK *ascholia*: opposite of LEISURE.

BIBLIOGRAPHY

TEXTS, COMMENTARIES, AND TRANSLATIONS

AUBONNET, J. *Aristote: Politique*. Paris: Budé, 1960–89.

DREIZEHNTER, A. *Aristoteles Politica*. Munich: Wilhelm Fink, 1970.

KEYT, D. *Aristotle Politics Books V and VI*. Oxford: Clarendon Aristotle Series, forthcoming.

KRAUT, R. *Aristotle Politics Books VII and VIII*. Oxford: Clarendon Aristotle Series, 1998.

LORD, C. *Aristotle: The Politics*. Chicago: University of Chicago Press, 1984.

NEWMAN, W. L. *The Politics of Aristotle*. 4 vols. Oxford: Clarendon Press, 1887–92.

PELLEGRIN, P. *Aristote: Les Politiques*. 2 ed. Paris: Flammarion, 1993.

RACKHAM, H. *Aristotle: Politics*. Cambridge: Loeb Classical Library, 1944.

ROBINSON, R. *Aristotle Politics Books III and IV*. 2 ed. With a Supplementary Essay by D. Keyt. Oxford: Clarendon Aristotle Series, 1995.

ROSS, W. D. *Aristotelis Politica*. Oxford: Clarendon Press, 1957.

SAUNDERS, T. J. *Aristotle's Politics Books I and II*. Oxford: Clarendon Aristotle Series, 1995.

SCHÜTRUMPF, E. *Aristoteles: Politik Buch I*. Berlin: Akademie-Verlag, 1991.

———. *Aristoteles: Politik Buch II–III*. Berlin: Akademie-Verlag, 1991.

——— & HANS-JOACHIM GEHRKE. *Aristoteles: Politik Buch IV–VI*. Berlin: Akademie-Verlag, 1997.

SIMPSON, P. L. P. *The Politics of Aristotle*. Chapel Hill: The University of North Carolina Press, 1997.

———. *Aristotle's Politics: A Philosophical Commentary*. Chapel Hill: The University of North Carolina Press, 1998.

SINCLAIR, T. A. *Aristotle: The Politics*. Revised and represented by Trevor J. Saunders. Harmondsworth: Penguin Books, 1981.

SUSEMIHL, F. & R. D. HICKS. *The Politics of Aristotle: A Revised Text*. Books I–III & VII–VIII. London: Macmillan, 1894.

BACKGROUND

AUSTIN, N. M., & P. VIDAL-NAQUET. *Economic and Social History of Greece*. Berkeley: University of California Press, 1977.

BURKERT, W. *Greek Religion*. Cambridge: Harvard University Press, 1985.

DE STE. CROIX, G. E. M. *The Class Struggle in the Ancient Greek World*. Ithaca: Cornell University Press, 1981.

DOVER, K. J. *Greek Homosexuality*. Cambridge: Harvard University Press, 1978.

FERRAR, C. *The Origins of Democratic Thinking: The Invention of Politics in Classical Athens*. Cambridge: Cambridge University Press, 1988.

GRANT, M., & R. KITZINGER. *Civilization of the Ancient Mediterranean: Greece and Rome*. 3 vols. New York: Scribners, 1988.

HORNBLOWER, S., & A. SPAWFORTH. *The Oxford Classical Dictionary*. 3 ed. Oxford: Oxford University Press, 1996.

IRWIN, T. H. *Classical Thought*. Oxford: Oxford University Press, 1989.

JOINT ASSOCIATION OF CLASSICAL TEACHERS. *The World of Athens: An Introduction to Classical Athenian Culture*. Cambridge: Cambridge University Press, 1984.

GENERAL WORKS

ACKRILL, J. L. *Aristotle the Philosopher*. Oxford: Oxford University Press, 1981.

ANNAS, J. *The Morality of Happiness*. New York: Oxford University Press, 1993.

BARKER, E. *The Political Thought of Plato and Aristotle*. London: Methuen, 1906.

BARNES, J., ed. *The Cambridge Companion to Aristotle*. Cambridge: Cambridge University Press, 1995.

BODÉÜS, R. *The Political Dimensions of Aristotle's Ethics*. Albany: State University of New York Press, 1993.

BROADIE, S. *Ethics With Aristotle*. New York: Oxford University Press, 1991.

IRWIN, T. H. *Aristotle's First Principles*. Oxford: Clarendon Press, 1988.

KRAUT, R. *Aristotle on the Human Good*. Princeton: Princeton University Press, 1989.

————. *Aristotle's Political Philosophy: An Introduction and Defense*. Oxford: Clarendon Press, forthcoming.

LEAR, J. *Aristotle: The Desire to Understand*. Cambridge: Cambridge University Press, 1988.

MILLER JR., F. D. *Nature, Justice, and Rights in Aristotle's Politics*. Oxford: Clarendon Press, 1995.

MULGAN, R. G. *Aristotle's Political Theory: An Introduction for Students of Political Theory*. Oxford: Clarendon Press, 1977.

NUSSBAUM, M. *The Fragility of Goodness*. Cambridge: Cambridge University Press, 1986.

REEVE, C. D. C. *Practices of Reason: Aristotle's Nicomachean Ethics*. Oxford: Clarendon Press, 1992.

ROBINSON, T. A. *Aristotle in Outline*. Indianapolis: Hackett, 1995.

ROSS, W. D. *Aristotle*. London: Methuen, 1923.

SALKEVER, S. G. *Finding the Mean: Theory and Practice in Aristotelian Political Philosophy*. Princeton: Princeton University Press, 1990.

YACK, B. *The Problems of a Political Animal: Community, Justice and Conflict in Aristotelian Political Thought*. Los Angeles: University of California Press, 1993.

COLLECTIONS OF ESSAYS

Five useful collections of essays have recently appeared:

(1) BARNES, J., M. SCHOFIELD, R. SORABJI, eds. *Articles on Aristotle*. Vol. 2. *Ethics and Politics*. London: Duckworth, 1977. Contains the following essays on the *Politics:*

VON FRITZ, K., & E. KAPP. "The Development of Aristotle's Political Philosophy and the Concept of Nature," 113–34.

FORTENBAUGH, W. W. "Aristotle on Slaves and Women," 135–39.

FINLEY, M. I. "Aristotle and Economic Analysis," 140–58.

WHEELER, M. "Aristotle's Analysis of the Nature of Political Struggle," 159–69.

KELSEN, H. "Aristotle and the Hellenic-Macedonian Policy," 170–94.

DEFOURNEY, M. "The Aim of the State: Peace," 195–201.

WEIL, R. "Aristotle's View of History," 202–17.

(2) PATZIG, G., ed. *XI Symposium Aristotelicum: Aristoteles Politik*. Göttingen: Vanderhoeck & Ruprecht, 1990:

SCHOFIELD, M. "Ideology and Philosophy in Aristotle's Theory of Slavery," 1–27. Comments by C. H. KAHN, 28–31.

SEEL, G. "Die Rechtfertigung von Herrschaft in der 'Politik' des Aristoteles," 32–62. Comments by T. EBERT, 63–72.

IRWIN, T. H. "The Good of Political Activity," 73–98. Comments by G. STRIKER, 99–100.

BODÉÜS, R. "Savoir politique et savoir philosophique," 101–23.

PELLEGRIN, P. "Naturalité, excellence, diversité. Politique et biologie chez Aristote," 124–51.

NUSSBAUM, M. "Nature, Function, and Capability: Aristotle on Political Distribution," 153–86. Comments by D. CHARLES, 187–201.

LORD, C. "Politics and Education in Aristotle's 'Politics'," 203–15. Comments by D. A. REES, 216–19.

COOPER, J. M. "Political Animals and Civic Friendship," 220–41. Comments by J. ANNAS, 242–48.

BARNES, J. "Aristotle and Political Liberty," 249–63. Comments by R. SORABJI, 264–76.

EUCKEN, C. "Der aristotelische Demokratiebegriff und sein historisches Umfeld," 277–91. Comments by T. H. IRWIN 292–95.

NATALI, C. "Aristote et la chrématistique," 296–324.

BIEN, G. "Die Wirkungsgeschichte der aristotelischen 'Politik,'" 325–56. Comments by W. KULLMANN, 357–68.

KAHN, C. H. "The Normative Structure of Aristotle's 'Politics,'" 369–84.

(3) KEYT, D., & F. D. MILLER JR., eds. *A Companion to Aristotle's Politics*. Oxford: Blackwell, 1991:

BRADLEY, A. C. "Aristotle's Conception of the State," 13–56.

ROWE, C. "Aims and Methods in Aristotle's *Politics*," 57–74.

ADKINS, A. W. H. "The Connections Between Aristotle's *Ethics* and *Politics*," 75–93.

KULLMANN, W. "Man as a Political Animal in Aristotle," 94–117.

KEYT, D. "Three Basic Theorems in Aristotle's *Politics*," 118–41.

SMITH, N. D. "Aristotle's Theory of Natural Slavery," 142–56.

MEIKLE, S. "Aristotle and Exchange Value," 156–81.

STALLEY, R. F. "Aristotle's Criticism of Plato's *Republic*," 182–99.

IRWIN, T. H. "Aristotle's Defense of Private Property," 200–25.

FORTENBAUGH, W. W. "Aristotle on Prior and Posterior, Correct and Mistaken Constitutions," 238–78.

KEYT, D. "Aristotle's Theory of Distributive Justice," 238–78.

MILLER JR., F. D. "Aristotle on Natural Law and Justice," 279–306.

MULGAN, R. "Aristotle's Analysis of Oligarchy and Democracy," 307–22.

POLANSKY, R. "Aristotle on Political Change," 323–45.

DEPEW, D. J. "Politics, Music, and Contemplation in Aristotle's Ideal State," 346–80.

(4) LORD, C., & D. K. O'CONNOR, eds. *Essays on the Foundations of Aristotelian Political Theory.* Berkeley: University of California Press, 1991:

SALKEVER, S. K. "Aristotle's Social Science," 11–48.

LORD, C. "Aristotle's Anthropology," 49–73.

SHULSKY, A. "The 'Infrastructure' of Aristotle's *Politics*: Aristotle on Economics and Politics," 74–111.

OBER, J. "Aristotle's Political Sociology: Class, Status, and Order in the *Politics*," 112–35.

O'CONNOR, D. K. "The Aetiology of Justice," 136–65.

SALKEVER, S. K. "Women, Soldiers, Citizens: Plato and Aristotle on the Politics of Virility," 166–91.

NEWELL, W. R. "Superlative Virtue: The Problem of Monarchy in Aristotle's *Politics*," 192–211.

STRAUSS, B. S. "On Aristotle's Critique of Athenian Democracy," 212–33.

BODÉÜS, R. "Law and the Regime in Aristotle," 212–48.

(5) AUBENQUE, P., ed. *Aristote Politique: Etudes sur la Politique d'Aristote.* Paris: Presses Universitaires de France, 1993:

PELLEGRIN, P. "La *Politique* d'Aristote: unité et fracteurs," 3–34.

CAUJOLLE-ZASLAWSKY, F. "Citoyens à six mines," 35–48.

CANTO-SPERBER, M. "L'unité de l'Etat et les conditions du bonhéur public (Platon, *République*, V; Aristote, *Politique* II)," 49–72.

PETIT, A. "L'analyse aristotélicienne de la tyrannie," 73–92.

CHARLES-SAGET, A. "Guerre et Nature. Etude sur le sens du *Polémos* chez Aristote," 93–118.

ROMEYER DHERBEY, G. "Aristote et la poliorcétique *Politique*, VII, 11, 1330^{b}32–1331^{a}18)," 119–32.

LLOYD, G. E. R. "L'idée de nature dans le *Politique* d'Aristote," 135–60. Reprinted in English as "The Idea of Nature in the *Politics*," in his *Aristotelian Explorations* (Cambridge: Cambridge University Press), 184–204.

KULLMANN, W. "L'image de l'homme dans la pensée politique d'Aristote," 161–84.

MULLER, R. "La logique de la liberté dans la *Politique*," 185–208.

DEMONT, P. "Le loisir (*scholē*) dans la *Politique* d' Aristote," 209–30.

LABARRIÈRE, J-L. Le rôle de la *phantasia* dans la recherche du bien pratique," 231–52.

AUBENQUE, P. "Aristote et la démocracie," 255–62.

NARCY, M. "Aristote devant les objections de Socrate à la démocracie (*Politique*, III, 4 et 11)," 265–88.

WOLFF, F. "L'unité structurelle du livre II," 289–314.

LEANDRI, A. "L'aporie de la souveraineté," 315–30.

BODÉÜS, R. "Du quelques prémisses de la *Politique*," 331–50.

BUBNER, R. "Langage et politique," 351–66.

CASSIN, B. "*Logos* et politique. Politique, rhétorique et sophistique chez Aristote," 367–99.

RODRIGO, P. et TORDESSILLAS A. "Politique, ontologie, rhétorique: éléments d'une kairologie aristotélicienne?" 399–420.

BRAGUE, R. "Note sur la traduction arabe de la *Politique*, derrchef, qu'elle n'existe pas," 423–34.

BERTI, E. "*Phronésis* et science politique," 435–60.

VOLPI, F. "Réhabilitation de la philosophie pratique et néo-aristotélisme," 461–84.

In addition, *Arethusa* 8.2 (1975) is devoted to *Population Policy in Plato and Aristotle*.

POLITICAL THEORY

AMBLER, W. "Aristotle's Understanding of the Naturalness of the City." *Review of Politics* 47 (1985): 163–85.

ANNAS, J. "Aristotle on Human Nature and Political Virtue." *The Review Of Metaphysics* XLIX (1996): 731–53.

BARNES, J. "Partial Wholes." *Social Philosophy and Policy* 8 (1990): 1–23.

BERNS, L. "Spiritedness in Ethics and Politics: A Study in Aristotelian Psychology." *Interpretation* 12 (1984): 335–48.

BLUHM, W. T. "The Place of the 'Polity' in Aristotle's Theory of the Ideal State." *Journal of Politics* 24 (1962): 743–53.

BULLEN, P. "Lawmakers and Ordinary People in Aristotle." In Leslie G. Rubin, ed., *Justice v. Law in Greek Political Thought* (Lanham: Rowman and Littlefield, 1997): 229–41.

CASHDOLLAR, S. "Aristotle's Politics of Morals." *Journal of the History of Philosophy* 2 (1973): 146–60.

CHAN, J. "Does Aristotle's Political Theory Rest on a 'Blunder'?" *History of Political Thought* 13 (1992): 189–202.

COOPER, J. M. "Justice and Rights in Aristotle's *Politics*." *The Review Of Metaphysics* XLIX (1996): 859–72.

DEPEW, D. J. "Humans and Other Political Animals in Aristotle's *History of Animals*." *Phronesis* 40 (1995): 156–81.

DEVLIN, R. "The Good Man and the Good Citizen in Aristotle's *Politics*." *Phronesis* 18 (1973): 71–79.

EVERSON, S. "Aristotle on the Foundations of the State." *Political Studies* 36 (1988): 89–101.

FERGUSON, J. "Teleology in Aristotle's *Politics*." A. Gotthelf, ed., *Aristotle on Nature and Living Things* (Mathesis Publications: Pittsburgh, 1985): 259–73.

HALLIWELL, S. "The Challenge of Rhetoric to Ethical and Political Theory in Aristotle." A. O. Rorty, ed., *Essays on Aristotle's Rhetoric* (Berkeley: University of California Press, 1996): 175–90.

JOHNSON, C. "Who is Aristotle's Citizen?" *Phronesis* 29 (1984): 73–90.

———. "Aristotle's Polity: Mixed or Middle Constitution?" *History of Political Thought* 9 (1988): 143–54.

KEYT, D. "Aristotle and the Ancient Roots of Anarchism." TOPOI 15 (1996): 129–42.

KRAUT, R. "Are There Natural Rights in Aristotle." *The Review Of Metaphysics* XLIX (1996): 755–74.

KULLMANN, W. "Equality in Aristotle's Political Thought." I. Kajanto, *Commenatationes Humanorum Litterarum* 75 (1984): 31–44.

LINTOTT, A. "Aristotle and Democracy." *Classical Quarterly* 42 (1992): 114–28.

LORD, C. "Politics and Philosophy in Aristotle's *Politics.*" *Hermes* 106 (1978): 336–59.

MAYHEW, R. "Aristotle on Property." *Review of Metaphysics* 46 (1993): 803–31.

MILLER JR., F. D. "Aristotle and the Origins of Natural Rights." *The Review Of Metaphysics* XLIX (1996): 873–907.

MILLER, R. W. "Marx and Aristotle: A Kind of Consequentialism." *Canadian Journal of Philosophy* VII (1981): 323–52.

MULGAN, R. G. "Aristotle's Sovereign." *Political Studies* 18 (1970): 518–22.

———. "Aristotle's Doctrine that Man is a Political Animal." *Hermes* 102 (1974): 438–45.

———. "Aristotle and the Value of Political Participation." *Political Theory* 18 (1990): 195–215.

NUSSBAUM, M. "Human Functioning and Social Justice: In Defense of Aristotelian Essentialism." *Political Theory* 20 (1990): 202–46.

———. "Aristotelian Social Democracy." B. Douglass, G. Mara, and H. Richardson (eds.), *Liberalism and the Good* (New York, 1990): 203–52.

POLANSKY, R. "The Dominance of Polis for Aristotle." *Dialogos* 33 (1979): 43–56.

POPPER, K. R. *The Open Society and Its Enemies*. Princeton: Princeton University Press, 1971.

REEVE, C. D. C. "Philosophy, Politics, and Rhetoric in Aristotle." A. O. Rorty, ed., *Essays on Aristotle's Rhetoric* (Berkeley: University of California Press, 1996): 191–205.

ROBERTS, J. "Political Animals in the *Nicomachean Ethics.*" *Phronesis* 34 (1989): 185–205.

ROWE, C. J. "Reality and Utopia." *Elenchos* 10 (1989): 317–36.

SALKEVER, S. G. "Aristotle's Social Science." *Political Theory* 9 (1981): 479–508.

SCHOFIELD, M. "Sharing in the Constitution." *The Review Of Metaphysics* XLIX (1996): 831–58.

SPELMAN, E. V. "Aristotle and the Politicization of the Soul." S. Harding & M. B. Hintikka, eds., *Discovering Reality: Feminist Perspectives on Epistemology, Metaphysics, Methodology, and Philosophy of Science* (Dordrecht: Reidel, 1983): 17–30.

SPRINGBORG, P. "Aristotle and the Problem of Needs." *History of Political Thought* 5 (1984): 393–424.

SWANSON, J. A. *The Public and the Private in Aristotle's Political Philosophy.* Ithaca: Cornell University Press, 1992.

TAYLOR, C. C. W. "Politics." J. Barnes, ed. *The Cambridge Companion to Aristotle*, 233–58.

VANDER WAERDT, P. A. "Kingship and Philosophy in Aristotle's Best Régime." *Phronesis* 30 (1985): 249–73.

WINTHROP, D. "Aristotle on Participatory Democracy." *Polity* 11 (1978): 151–71.

ZUCKERT, C. H. "Aristotle on the Limits and Satisfactions of Political Life." *Interpretation* 11 (1983): 185–206.

ECONOMICS

LEWIS, T. J. "Acquisition and Anxiety: Aristotle's Case Against the Market." *Canadian Journal of Economics* 11 (1978): 69–90.

MCNEILL, D. "Alternative Interpretations of Aristotle on Exchange and Reciprocity." *Public Affairs Quarterly* 4 (1990): 55–68.

MEIKLE, S. *Aristotle's Economic Thought.* Oxford: Clarendon Press, 1995.

POLANYI, K. "Aristotle Discovers the Economy." K. Polanyi, C. M. Arensberg, & H. W. Pearson, eds., *Trade and Market in the Early Empires* (Glencoe, 1957), 64–94.

SOUDEK, J. "Aristotle's Theory of Exchange: An Enquiry into the Origin of Economic Analysis." *Proceedings of the American Philosophical Society* 96 (1952): 45–75.

LAW

BRUNSCHWIG, J. "Rule and Exception: On the Aristotelian Theory of Equity." M. Frede and G. Striker (eds.), *Rationality in Greek Thought* (Oxford: Clarendon Press, 1996): 115–56.

HAMBURGER, M. *Morals and Law: The Growth of Aristotle's Legal Theory.* New York, 1971.

MacDowell, D. M. *The Law in Classical Athens*. Ithaca: Cornell University Press, 1978.

———. *Spartan Law*. Edinburgh: Scottish Academic Press, 1986.

Schroeder, D. N. "Aristotle on Law." *Polis* 4 (1981): 17–31.

FAMILY

Booth, W. J. "Politics and the Household: A Commentary on Aristotle's *Politics* Book One." *History of Political Thought* 2 (1981): 203–26.

Clark, S. R. L. "Aristotle's Woman." *History of Political Thought* 3 (1982): 177–91.

Golden, M. *Children and Childhood in Classical Athens*. Baltimore: The Johns Hopkins University Press, 1990.

Horowitz, M. C. "Aristotle and Woman." *Journal of the History of Biology* 9 (1976): 183–213.

Lange, L. "Woman Is Not a Rational Animal: On Aristotle's Biology of Reproduction." S. Harding & M. B. Hintikka, eds., *Discovering Reality: Feminist Perspectives on Epistemology, Metaphysics, Methodology, and Philosophy of Science* (Dordrecht: Reidel, 1983): 1–15.

Modrak, D. "Aristotle: Women, Deliberation and Nature." Bat-Ami Bar On, ed., *Critical Feminist Essays in the History of Western Philosophy* (New York: SUNY Press, forthcoming).

Morsink, J. "Was Aristotle's Biology Sexist?" *Journal of the History of Biology* 12 (1979): 83–112.

Mulgan, R. G. "Aristotle and the Political Role of Women." *History of Political Thought* 15 (1994): 179–202.

Okin, S. M. *Women in Western Political Thought*. Princeton: Princeton University Press, 1979.

Salkever, S. G. "Women, Soldiers, Citizens: Plato and Aristotle on the Politics of Virility." *Polity* 19 (1986): 232–53.

Saxonhouse, A. W. "Family, Polity, Unity: Aristotle on Socrates' Community of Wives." *Polity* 15 (1982): 202–19.

Schott, R. "Aristotle on Women." *Kinesis* 11 (1982): 69–84.

Smith, N. D. "Plato and Aristotle on the Nature of Women." *Journal of the History of Philosophy* 21 (1983): 467–78.

Sparshott, F. "Aristotle on Women." *Philosophical Inquiry* 7 (1985): 177–200.

SLAVERY

AMBLER, W. "Aristotle on Nature and Politics: The Case of Slavery." *Political Theory* 15 (1987): 390–411.

GARLAN, Y. *Slavery in Ancient Greece.* Ithaca: Cornell University Press, 1988.

WIEDEMANN, T. *Greek and Roman Slavery.* Baltimore: The Johns Hopkins University Press, 1981.

EDUCATION, ART, MUSIC, AND LEISURE

LEAR, J. "Katharsis." A. O. Rorty, ed., *Essays on Aristotle's Poetics* (Princeton: Princeton University Press, 1992), 315–40.

LORD, C. *Education and Culture in the Political Thought of Aristotle.* Ithaca: Cornell University Press, 1982.

REEVE, C. D. C. "Aristotelian Education." A. O. Rorty, ed., *Philosophy as Education.* London: Routledge and Kegan Paul, forthcoming.

SOLMSEN, F. "Leisure and Play in Aristotle's Ideal State." *Rheinisches Museum* 107 (1964): 193–220.

STOCKS, J. L. "Scholē." *Classical Quarterly* 30 (1936): 177–87.

WEST, M. L. *Ancient Greek Music.* Oxford: Clarendon Press, 1992.

CRITIQUE OF PLATO'S REPUBLIC AND LAWS

MAYHEW, R. "Aristotle on the Extent of Communism in Plato's *Republic*." *Ancient Philosophy* 13 (1993): 313–21.

MORROW, G. R. "Aristotle's Comments on Plato's *Laws*." I. Düring & G. E. L. Owen (eds.), *Plato and Aristotle in the Mid-Fourth Century* (Göteborg, 1960), 145–62.

NUSSBAUM, M. "Shame, Separateness, and Political Unity: Aristotle's Criticisms of Plato." A. O. Rorty, ed. *Essays on Aristotle's Ethics.* Berkeley: University of California Press, 1980.

MORROW, G. R. *Plato's Cretan City.* Princeton: Princeton University Press, 1993.

REEVE, C. D. C. *Philosopher-Kings: The Argument of Plato's Republic.* Princeton: Princeton University Press, 1988.

SAUNDERS, T. J. *Plato, the Laws.* Harmondsworth: Penguin, 1970.

STALLEY, R. F. *An Introduction to Plato's Laws.* Indianapolis: Hackett, 1983.

HISTORY AND HISTORIOGRAPHY

ARISTOTLE. *The Constitution of Athens*. In J. M. Moore, *Aristotle and Xenophon on Democracy and Oligarchy*. Berkeley: University Of California Press, 1975.

ASHERI, D. "Laws of Inheritance, Distribution of Land and Political Constitutions in Ancient Greece." *Historia* 12 (1963): 1–21.

BURNS, A. "Hippodamus and the Planned City." *Historia* 25 (1976): 414–28.

CARTLEDGE, P. "Spartan Wives: Liberation or License?" *Classical Quarterly* 31 (1981): 84–105.

———. "The Politics of Spartan Pederasty." *Proceedings of the Cambridge Philological Society* 207 (1981): 17–36.

DE LAIX, R. A. "Aristotle's Conception of the Spartan Constitution." *Journal of the History of Philosophy* 12 (1974): 21–30.

FINLEY, M. I. "Athenian Demagogues." *Past and Present* 21 (1962): 1–23.

FORREST, W. G. *A History of Sparta 950–192 B.C.* New York: Norton, 1968.

HODKINSON, S. "Land and Inheritance in Classical Sparta." *Classical Quarterly* 36 (1976): 378–406.

HUXLEY, G. "Crete in Aristotle's *Politics*." *Greek, Roman and Byzantine Studies* 12 (1971): 505–15.

———. "On Aristotle's Historical Methods." *Greek, Roman and Byzantine Studies* 13 (1972): 157–69.

RHODES, P. J. *A Commentary on the Aristotelian Athenaion Politeia*. Oxford: Clarendon Press, 1981.

SCHÜTRUMPF, E. "Aristotle on Sparta." A. Powell & S. Hodgkinson, eds., *The Shadow of Sparta*. London and New York, 323–45.

STOCKTON, D. *The Classical Athenian Democracy*. Oxford: Clarendon Press, 1991.

VON FRITZ, K. "Aristotle's Contribution to the Practice and Theory of Historiography." *University of California Publications in Philosophy* 28 (1958): 113–37.

LITERARY REFERENCES

ALCAEUS
(Diehl I.427, fr. 87) 85^{a}39–^{b}1

ANTISTHENES
84^{a}15–17

ARCHILOCUS
(Diehl I.230, fr. 67b) 28^{a}5

EURIPIDES
Aeolus (Nauck 367, fr. 16 lns. 2–3)
77^{a}19–20
Bacchae 381 39^{a}18
Iphigenia in Aulis 1266, 1400 52^{b}8
(Nauck 646, fr. 891) 10^{a}33
(Nauck 672, fr. 975) 28^{a}15

HERACLITUS
(Diels–Kranz B85) 15^{a}30–31

HESIOD
Works and Days
25 12^{b}4–5
405 52^{b}11–12

HOMER
Iliad
I.544 59^{b}13–14
II.204 92^{a}13
II.372 87^{b}14–15
II.391–3 85^{a}13–14
IX.319 67^{a}1–2

IX.649 78^{a}37
X.114–15 52^{b}22–23
X.224 87^{b}14
XVI. 59 78^{a}37
XVIII.376 53^{b}36–37
Odyssey
IX.7–8 38^{b}29–30
XVII. 382–85 38^{b}25–26

PHILEMON
(Kock II.492, fr. 54) 55^{b}28

PHOCYLIDES
(Diehl I.50, fr.10) 95^{b}34

PLATO
Republic
500d 29^{a}21

SOLON
(Diehl I.21, fr. 1.71) 56^{b}33–34

SOPHOCLES
Ajax 293 60^{a}30

THEODECTES
Helen (Nauck 802, fr. 3) 55^{a}36–38

TYRTAEUS
(Diehl I.7–9, fr. 2–5) 06^{b}39

UNKNOWN
(Nauck 854, fr. 78) 28^{a}16

INDEX OF NAMES

276

GENERAL INDEX

81[a]12, 83[a]17, 83[a]31, 83[a]41, 88[a]15, 89[b]30,
90[a]10, 90[a]38, 90[b]2, 91[a]34, 91[b]8, 91[b]33,
93[a]8, 93[b]38, 94[a]16, 95[b]2, 96[a]12, 96[a]28,
96[b]22, 96[b]31, 97[a]9, 99[b]26, 00[a]2, 02[a]2,
02[a]28, 03[a]12, 04[b]1, 05[a]23, 05[b]2, 07[a]19,
08[b]28, 08[b]30, 09[a]6, 09[a]26, 09[b]39, 10[a]5,
13[b]18, 15[a]33, 16[b]7, 16[b]7, 16[b]13, 17[b]9,
18[a]7, 18[a]31, 18[b]20, 20[a]25, 20[a]35, 21[a]13,
21[a]20; *see also* wealth
rule 77[b]7, 78[b]30, 88[a]11, 25[a]27, 28[a]7, 33[a]3,
33[b]28; autocratic, 85[a]8, 95[a]12; of a master, 54[b]5, 55[b]16, 77[a]33, 85[a]22, 85[a]24,
95[b]21, 10[b]19, 24[a]36, 33[a]5; political, 54[b]3;
see also office

sacred ambassadors 10[b]22
sacred recorders 21[b]39
sacrifice, religious 80[b]37, 85[b]10, 85[b]16,
21[a]35, 22[b]26, 24[b]39; supervisor of, 22[b]24
science 'marital', 53[b]9; 'procreative',
53[b]10; *see also* master, politician
sea 56[a]37, 58[a]24, 91[b]20, 27[a]4–[b]17, 30[a]35,
31[b]3
self-sufficiency, self-sufficient 52[b]27–53[a]1,
53[a]26–29, 56[b]4, 56[b]32, 57[a]30, 61[b]11–15,
75[b]21, 80[b]34, 91[a]10, 91[a]14, 21[b]17, 26[b]3,
28[b]17, 28[b]18
senate 70[b]24, 72[b]37
slave, slavery, slavish 52[a]31–[b]9, I.5–7,
58[b]38, 59[b]21–60[b]7, 73[b]37, 78[a]7,
78[b]32–37, 80[b]30–34, 83[a]19, 85[a]20, 91[a]8,
91[a]10, 95[b]20, 97[a]2, 10[a]35, 10[b]37, 11[a]20,
13[b]9, 13[b]35, 15[a]37, 17[b]13, 19[b]28, 27[b]28,
29[a]26, 30[a]26–33, 33[b]41, 34[a]2, 34[a]21,
37[b]21; freed, 78[a]2; and justice, I.6; lack
of, 23[a]6
soul 54[b]4–9, 60[a]4–7, 77[a]6–7, 86[a]18–20,
33[a]16–30, 34[b]17–28, 42[a]4–7, 42[a]22–23
statesman 52[a]7–16, 54[b]5, 55[b]16–20, 56[b]37,
58[a]20, 59[a]33, 59[b]1, 59[b]4, 66[a]32, 74[b]36,
76[a]34, 77[b]4, 78[b]3, 87[b]38, 88[a]12, 88[b]2,
88[b]27, 91[b]1, 08[a]34, 09[b]35, 24[a]37, 24[b]24,
25[a]19, 26[a]4, 33[a]35, 33[b]35
statesmanship 53[b]19, 58[a]22, 68[b]37, 82[b]16,
24[b]32, 38[b]34
steward 55[b]36, 14[b]38, 15[b]2
subject peoples 69[b]3, 71[b]30, 72[a]1, 03[a]8,
27[b]11, 29[a]26

superiority 82[b]24, 84[b]16, 84[b]27, 88[a]23,
88[a]27, 89[b]1, 90[a]12, 91[b]11, 93[a]4, 93[b]41,
95[b]14, 96[a]31, 96[b]19, 96[b]27, 96[b]34, 97[b]18,
02[a]27, 02[b]2, 04[a]37, 07[a]19, 10[b]11, 14[a]8,
26[a]21, 32[b]21
supervision 99[a]20, 99[a]39, 99[b]7, 00[a]5, 21[b]12,
22[a]29, 22[b]6, 22[b]18, 22[b]30, 23[a]1, 28[b]12,
31[b]7, 34[b]25, 34[b]31, 37[a]5, 37[a]23
supervisor 99[a]15, 21[b]39
suspension of the order-keepership 72[b]8

task 52[b]4, 53[a]23, 53[b]26, 53[b]35, 54[a]27,
54[b]18, 55[b]28, 57[a]20, 57[b]6, 57[b]31, 57[b]39,
58[a]35, 60[a]17, 60[a]18, 60[a]36, 60[a]39, 60[b]5,
63[a]40, 63[b]8–14, 73[b]10, 76[a]26, 76[b]29,
76[b]39, 77[a]37, 77[b]3, 77[b]25, 82[a]9, 82[a]10,
83[b]11, 88[a]16, 89[a]3, 91[a]28, 99[a]36, 99[a]39,
09[a]35, 14[a]1, 19[b]35, 23[b]39, 24[a]20, 24[a]22,
24[a]24, 24[b]30, 26[a]13, 26[a]32, 24[b]14, 28[b]5,
28[b]15, 28[b]19, 28[b]27, 29[b]8, 31[b]21, 32[a]32,
32[a]10, 33[a]6, 33[a]8, 34[a]17, 37[a]20, 37[a]36,
37[b]6, 37[b]8, 38[b]8, 38[b]34, 39[a]37
taxes, taxation 13[b]26, 14[b]14, 20[a]20
temperance 59[a]24, 59[a]28–60[a]4, 60[a]21,
63[b]9, 65[a]29–37, 67[a]10, 77[b]16–25, 19[b]32,
23[a]28, 23[b]29, 26[b]31, 34[a]19, 34[a]24, 35[a]22,
40[a]20
temple 04[a]3, 20[a]9, 31[a]24–30, 31[b]6,
31[b]17–18; guardian, 22[b]25; robber, 04[a]3
Thirty, Athens 05[b]25
tool 53[b]27–54[a]8, 56[b]35, 41[a]17
town 03[b]12, 11[a]14, 19[a]9, 19[a]29, 21[b]19,
21[b]29, 27[a]34; manager, 21[b]23, 22[a]13,
31[b]10
trade, trader, trading 58[b]22, 91[a]5, 91[b]24,
20[a]39, 27[a]17
tradesman, trading class 89[b]31, 91[a]4,
91[b]19, 19[a]28, 21[a]6
train, training 71[b]6, 36[a]21, 37[a]27, 37[b]3,
41[a]8
treasurer 21[b]33
treaty 75[a]10, 76[a]10, 80[a]37, 80[a]39, 83[a]33; *see
also* contract
tyranny, tyrant 67[a]14, 77[a]24, 79[b]5, 84[a]34,
85[a]32, 85[b]26, 85[b]26, 86[b]16, 86[b]39, 87[b]39,
89[a]28, 92[a]22, 93[b]28, IV.10, 96[a]2, 05[a]8,
06[a]23, 08[a]21, 10[b]2–11[a]22, 12[b]20, 13[a]2,
13[a]13, 13[a]36, 13[b]10, 13[b]36, 13[b]41, 14[a]6,

C.D.C. REEVE is Professor of Philosophy and Humanities at Reed College. He is author of *Philosopher-Kings* (Princeton, 1988), *Socrates in the Apology* (Hackett, 1989), and *Practices of Reason* (Oxford, 1992). Hackett published his highly acclaimed revision of the Grube translation of Plato's *Republic* in 1993.